DIRECTIONS IN SAFETY

DIRECTIONS IN SAFETY

A Selection of Safety Readings
for the
Student and the Practitioner
and for the
Teacher and the Safety Professional

Edited with Commentary by

TED S. FERRY, Ed.D., CSP

*Institute of Safety and Systems Management
University of Southern California
Los Angeles, California*

and

D. A. WEAVER, CSP, CPCU

*Policyholder Education Director
Employers Insurance of Wausau
Wausau, Wisconsin*

CHARLES C THOMAS · PUBLISHER
Springfield · Illinois · U.S.A.

Published and Distributed Throughout the World by

CHARLES C THOMAS · PUBLISHER

Bannerstone House

301-327 East Lawrence Avenue, Springfield, Illinois, U.S.A.

© 1976, by CHARLES C THOMAS · PUBLISHER

ISBN 0-398-03365-X

Library of Congress Catalog Card Number: 74-23873

Printed in the United States of America

N-8

Library of Congress Cataloging in Publication Data

Ferry, Ted S   comp.
    Directions in safety.
    1. Safety education—Addresses, essays, lectures.
2. Accidents—Prevention—Addresses, essays, lectures.
I. Weaver, Dennis A., joint comp. II. Title.
HV675.F47   363.3   74-23873
ISBN 0-398-03365-X

INTRODUCTION

N O ONE BOOK gives a comprehensive picture of the safety profession, not even a few books. Even when the best of the safety books are shelved together, the concepts, functions, and scope of the safety profession are not readily discernible. Many of the finer writings are not even in safety books, journals and magazines. Many are in books, professional journals and publications which bear no safety label, thus making it impractical for the lay reader, or even the safety professional, to gain a full appreciation of the profession.

This book permits a fuller appreciation of the safety profession. While much excellent safety literature exists, much of it is focused at some specific narrow target. The felt need was for a book of safety background material, something that could not readily be garnered even from a number of publications. The project began as a search for ideal materials, and quickly turned into a difficult process of choosing from the great volume of material available. As the selection process expanded, it became apparent that every continent, every business, every industry, and every profession were possible contributors. The international flavor of the readings proved to be inevitable. The whole world has contributed to safety literature and the prevalence of American articles merely reflects the availability of American materials, and the prolific writing and publishing activities of Americans. It does not reflect a monopoly on safety.

In a sense these readings may be considered a safety sampler. The reader may sample what suits his fancy. Each sample may well represent a sizable body of safety literature, or even a number of excellent books directed to that specific aspect of safety. Of necessity, such a book would be relatively narrow in its scope. This volume, in contrast, is meant to be general in nature and to avoid any detailed examination of any one aspect of safety. Hence, the idea of a sampler whose primary intent is to furnish a general background in safety.

As the work proceeded, another objective came into view. The book can serve to indicate some of the directions of safety thought. Though the book seeks to indicate the scope of safety, it cannot cover the whole, even if there were agreed definitions as to just what is included in the scope of safety. For instance, the subject of fire has no sample in the selections, as is true of some other aspects of safety. Though the book could not encompass the whole scope of safety, it could seek to indicate what direction modern safety thought is taking. The items selected discuss the problems of safety as a profession, and emphasize safety as an emerging discipline. In some measure the book counters the simplistic formulas of some safety thinking; in some measure it reveals the complexity of the subject and offers an appreciation of its multi-disciplinary aspects.

Both as a profession and as a body of concept and knowledge, safety is in ferment as never before. The ferment originates in social change which is challenging the whole nature and structure of our society. Those challenges have immense implications in safety. The new ideas in safety are not a brand of philosophy; they are pragmatic attempts to deal with practical problems in a rapidly changing world.

As the process of winnowing a vast amount of material proceeded, three potential audiences for this book were kept in mind.

1. The people interested in safety or on the fringes of the safety movement who want to know more about it.
2. The safety newcomer who needs an appreciation of the depth and scope of safety.
3. The safety professional who values the thoughts of others in his field and wants to enlarge his own vision.

The chores involved in reading, selecting, compiling and editing this book were rewarding chores even as the project progressed. Most notably, rewarding friendships developed with many people by mail, by telephone and by personal contact. Authors and publishers gave freely and willingly of their time often at the expense of considerable personal involvement. The willingness to contribute to the advancement of safety is characteristic of the profession. Some authors generously wrote or rewrote articles. The stringent selection process, sadly, made it necessary to leave out hundreds of fine articles. Special thanks are extended to those who willingly contributed but whose fine articles were simply too long or too similar to other articles.

Two giant repositories of safety expertise—The National Safety Council and The American Society of Safety Engineers—were outstanding in their support. Finally, the editors were encouraged and supported by Employers Insurance of Wausau and by the Institute of Safety and Systems Management at the University of Southern California, Los Angeles.

Ted S. Ferry
D. A. Weaver

CONTENTS

Part I. CONCEPTS AND PHILOSOPHIES

Part II. SAFETY TODAY

CONTRIBUTORS

Contributors have been merely listed in lieu of extensive biographies which their attainments deserve. Consistent with the purposes of this volume, every use of CSP (Certified Safety Professional) has been verified. Certain designations such as PE (Professional Engineer) and CPCU (Chartered Property and Casualty Underwriter) and other attainments have been indicated only when sure facts were at hand.

ROBERT A. ALKOV, Ph.D.
  Naval Safety Center

WILLIAM W. ALLISON, CSP
  Sandia Corporation, Albuquerque, New Mexico

DORIS BALDWIN
  Editor
  Job Safety and Health, Occupational Safety and Health Administration, Washington, D. C.

CHARLES I. BARRON, M.D.
  Medical Director, Lockheed California Company

ROBERT C. BEHAN, M.D.
  Wayne State University, Detroit, Michigan

MICHAEL F. BIANCARDI, PE, CSP
  Assistant Vice President, Employers Insurance of Wausau

L. B. BLANK, Ed.D.
  Douglas Aircraft Company, McDonnell Douglas Corporation

MURPHY W. BRADHURST

DAVID B. BROWN, Ph.D.
  Industrial Engineering, Auburn University, Alabama

VIRGIL R. CARLSON
  National Institute of Mental Health, Bethesda, Maryland

T. J. CRESSWELL
  Director
  FAA Center, Oklahoma City

PHIL DYKSTRA
  National Safety Council

LEROY FAULKNER, PE, CSP
  Liberty Mutual Insurance Company

TED S. FERRY, Ed.D., CSP
  The Safety Center, University of Southern California

LEO GREENBERG, Ph.D., CSP
  University of Michigan

D. J. GRIEP
Institute for Road Safety Research
(S.W.O.V.), Voorburg, The Nether-
lands

VERNON L. GROSE
Vice President
Tustin Institute of Technology

A. H. HANDS, M.D.
British Leyland Motor Corporation,
Ltd.

WILLIAM HADDON, JR., M.D.
President, Insurance Institute for
Highway Safety

R. O. HELBERG
Vice President
Employers Insurance of Wausau

ALEXANDER H. HIRSCHFELD,
M.D.
Wayne State University, Detroit,
Michigan

W. G. JOHNSON
Former General Manager, National
Safety Council

R. E. McCLAY
Naval Ordinance Station

MRS. JOYCE A. McDEVITT
Naval Ordinance Station

FRANCIS G. McGLADE, Ph.D.
Department of the Army

DAVID V. MacCOLLUM, PE, CSP
U. S. Army Electronic Proving
Grounds

E. DUNCAN MACKENZIE
Formerly, Boeing Company

CHAYTOR D. MASON
University of Southern California

DAVID MEISTER, Ph.D.
U. S. Army Research Institute

CHARLES O. MILLER
Director
Bureau of Aviation Safety

COLONEL DAVID L. NICHOLS
U. S. Air Force

E. R. NICOLAI
Office of the Secretary of the Interior

GEORGE A. PETERS, J.D., CSP
Attorney at Law

DAN C. PETERSEN, CSP
Management Consultant

W. C. POPE, PE, CSP
President, Safety Management Information Systems, Inc., Washington, D. C.

ROY REIDER, CSP
Los Alamos Scientific Laboratory

LYNETTE SHAW
Managing Director, Industrial
Testing Services, Ltd., Bramley,
Transvaal, South Africa

THOMAS L. SHIPMAN, M.D.
Los Alamos Scientific Laboratory

HERBERT S. SICHEL
Co-author, *Accident Proneness*
(1971), Pergamon Press, Ltd.

D. A. WEAVER, CSP, CPCU
Employers Insurance of Wausau

E. C. WIGGLESWORTH, B. Sc.,
Dep. Ed., M. Sc.
Defense Standards Laboratories;
Australian Defense Scientific
Service

HAROLD R. WILLIS
The Martin Company

ARCHARD F. ZELLAR, Ph.D.
United States Air Force

DIRECTIONS IN SAFETY

PART I
CONCEPTS AND PHILOSOPHIES

It is, of course, impossible to incorporate all safety concepts and philosophies in one part of this book, or to exclude them from other parts.

By highlighting concepts and philosophies, the editors merely hope to create awareness of the nature of the assumptions and assertions which underlie safety thinking.

1

ACCIDENT PRONENESS– FACT AND FICTION

LYNETTE SHAW AND HERBERT S. SICHEL

Common sense observation supports the idea that some people are accident prone. It can be explained in ordinary words by most any articulate neophyte in safety. And therein lies the reason for a whole book on accident proneness, a whole book after more than fifty years of research, argument and acrimony on the subject, a whole book of which this excerpt is the opening chapter.

With its opposite poles of simple clarity and profound obscurity, the concept of accident proneness illustrates two ever present problems in safety thought. The first is the problem of common sense and the second is the problem of terminology. Safety thought seeks to usurp a phenomena which, until recent times, has been the domain of the gods—"an accident." Safety thought asserts that accidents have causes and can be controlled by man's will. The effort to impose man's will on the phenomena, and to explain how to do it and why we fail, strains our capacity to communicate. Terminological problems run the gamut from the naive to the unscrupulous. The authors of this excerpt, surveying world safety literature from their South African homeland, call specific attention to the problem.

In the process, they incidentally illustrate the problem of common sense. Common sense in safety often has more authority than expertness. Common sense induces facile solutions and offers facile explanations when things don't work out. The disciplined study of accident proneness offered in this excerpt can hone the mind to perceive some of the requisites of disciplined safety thought, and to perceive their more frequent absence.

Aside from that, the concept of proneness has practical relevance. No other publication has delved so deeply into both the theoretical

° Reprinted with permission from Mrs. Lynette Shaw, *Accident Proneness* (Pergamon Press, Ltd., 1971).

and the practical aspects of the subject. The reading of this excerpt, the first chapter of the book, can be rewarding at several levels of perception and application.

THE STUDY OF accident proneness has been aptly described as an attempt to give scientific backing to a common-sense notion that most people accept almost without thinking.

The man in the street definitely subscribes to the idea that certain people are far more likely to have accidents than others—and he is quite emphatic on the subject of road accidents. He will laugh at you if you suggest that accidents (except perhaps his own) are a matter of chance, and that there is no great disparity between one driver and the next. He thinks there is all the world of difference, and at the drop of a hat he will tell you just what sort of people are the ones who are the bad accident risks. And although he will probably be far too specific, and far too inclined to air his own pet theories, nevertheless his views, compared with the views of the man in the next street, and the man in the street after that, will have one major factor in common, namely the belief that certain people are indeed more likely to have accidents than others; and that these people will continue to have accidents —unless they get killed or incapacitated in the process, or some change within themselves brings about an equally radical change in their usual driving behaviour.

And who is to say that the man in the street is wrong? Apparently not the officials who handle the traffic offenders among the driving public—or the insurance companies for that matter. They seem to argue on exactly the same lines; and the idea that some people are much more susceptible to accidents, and that this susceptibility can continue for long periods, seems to play a very prominent part in their thinking.

The insurance companies seem to think that a man's past accident record is an indication of the shape of things to come— hence their reluctance to go on insuring certain people. And the traffic officials seem to consider that there are indeed people who drive so badly, or so dangerously, that they are actual or potential accident cases, and therefore a danger to the community—hence

points systems designed to pick up the people with repeated traffic violations or accidents and prevent them from driving.

Yet, strangely enough, the concept of an unequal propensity
for accidents, or of accident proneness, does not receive anything
like the same unanimous backing from the scientists. In fact it is
a subject on which, even after fifty years of research, there is still
a great deal of argument, controversy and disbelief. Every aspect
of the concept is still being debated and argued: so much so that
it would probably be difficult to find any other subject on which
so many words have been written to so little effect.

What is more, there is no sign of this controversy dying down
—on the contrary, there is every sign that opinions are getting
more divided and the arguments growing more acrimonious.

However, when my coauthor and I were first invited to contribute this present volume on the subject of accident proneness,
I, for one, was unaware of just how divided the scientific thinking
was really becoming. Having always regarded the concepts of
certain people being unduly prone to accidents as a most rational
one, and having had these views confirmed by every aspect of
our own very practical research in South Africa, I found it very
difficult to believe that anyone could seriously doubt the accident
proneness concept. Argue about the finer points? Yes. But deny
that people differ in their susceptibility to accidents, and maintain that accidents are largely random occurrences? No, that I
did not really believe. I felt that any doubts there were about the
concept were only what one might call technical ones—a sort of
scientific pedantry which demanded that all the t's be crossed
and all the i's be dotted before the concept could be given official
scientific approval. I, therefore, welcomed the opportunity to join
once more in the discussion, and even entertained optimistic
hopes that by putting up some new evidence in support of the
concept I could speed up its scientific acceptance and approval.

However, in the meantime, several things have happened
which have opened my eyes somewhat. During the last year or
two there has been a decided swing of the pendulum of scientific
opinion on the subject of accident proneness, and the accident
literature, particularly in the United States and to a lesser but
still noticeable extent in Britain and other countries like Ger-

many, has developed a marked anti-proneness bias. Apart from
the appearance of a number of very critical articles and statements in various journals, two full-scale books have been published, both of which have repeatedly and emphatically condemned the validity of the proneness concept. The first one,
published in England, Cresswell and Froggatt's *The Causation
of Bus Driver Accidents* (1963) was primarily a description of
a particular research project carried out in Northern Ireland. Its
appearance therefore was not so very significant. But the second
volume, published in the United States, was something different
altogether. This book, *Accident Research*, by Haddon, Suchman
and Klein (1964) was a major publication of some 750 pages
dealing with every aspect of the human element in accidents,
and intended apparently as a textbook for accident researchers
in all fields. The enthusiastic reception which was given to this
book, with its strong anti-proneness bias, by bodies such as the
American National Safety Council, is a definite indication of the
growing tendency to absolve the driver from any great degree of
responsibility and to maintain instead that accidents are largely
unfortunate occurrences which can happen to anyone at any
time.

Difficult as it is to believe that such an attitude can have developed, nevertheless I have found, from personal experience,
that this is very much the case. Having spent five months travel-
ling through Europe and the United States talking to accident
researchers, I have discovered by first-hand experience just how
deeply entrenched, in some quarters, is the opposition to the
proneness concept.

I did not find this attitude to be prevalent in Europe—in fact
in most of the continental countries the proneness concept is accepted without question. It is accepted, on the basis of logic,
backed by observation, that certain people just do have worse
accident records than others, and the research tendency is to
examine these people, as individuals, in order to establish just
why they are having these accidents and to see what can be done
about it. In other words, the research approach is largely a clinical one and therefore is not bedevilled by the problem of statistical reliability or validity.

It is particularly in the United States that opposition to the concept is so deep-rooted. Here the whole research approach has such a strong statistical bias that every contention must be tested by statistical procedures before it can be accepted. This means the group approach as against the individual one, and the acceptance of the concept only if group data can produce evidence to support it. The stated basis of the opposition to the accident-proneness concept is the contention that this evidence has not been forthcoming. In fact the opponents of the concept maintain that not only does the group statistical evidence lend very little support to the concept, but that in many instances the evidence actually refutes it.

However, even in the United States, which is certainly the stronghold of the group statistical approach, opinions are still rather divided. In fact they range all the way from acceptance of the concept, to a very limited and guarded acceptance, to outright denial. At the one end of the scale of opinion are the psychiatrists, and those psychologists whose approach is orientated more toward clinical or "generalist" psychology. These researchers still seem to subscribe to the proneness idea. Certainly they do not think that accidents happen indiscriminately to just anybody—and some of them go so far as to say that there are a great number of people who are such inherently bad risks that they should not be driving.

At the other end of the scale are a number of statisticians, supported by those psychologists whose orientation is toward the earlier forms of behaviorism and the strictly experimental approach—and particularly toward a peculiar American psychological doctrine (which seems to have no name, unless one could call it "specifism") which denies both the consistency and individuality of behavior. These researchers are, in turn, strongly opposed to the concept, and speak of "a folklore of accident proneness" and "the universal discredit into which the subject has fallen among scientists."

In between the two groups, though still rather inclined to the "anti" side, are a number of researchers whose attitude seems to be that there is no definite proof one way or the other, but that by and large there seems very little actual evidence (by which

they mean statistical evidence) to commend the proneness concept. The following sort of statement is very representative of
the thinking of this group: "It has not been convincingly demonstrated that an appreciable number of people tend to have more
accidents than others under conditions of equal exposure"
(McFarland, 1962). And in a leading article which appeared in
the *New York Times* on 20 December 1964, on the occasion of
the publication of Haddon's *Accident Research,* Robert Darnton
quotes the opinions of leading accident research workers in the
United States as follows:

> The favorite concept of psychologists in the field during the
> nineteen-twenties was accident-proneness, an attempt to explain why
> some individuals have more accidents than others. Psychologists
> have almost abandoned the concept now, because they have been
> unable to find enduring psychological traits that differentiate these
> unfortunate persons from others. They tend to believe that most
> "accident-prone" individuals are victims of the laws of probability.

The trend is therefore very much toward denying the proneness concept.

However, strangely enough, even the strongest opponents of
the "proneness" concept do still sometimes seem to find it necessary to give it limited recognition. Haddon's book is an example
of this. The main trend is definitely critical, and he and his co-
authors maintain that offering accident proneness as the *explanation* why some individuals have more accidents than others "is a
point that has aroused first minor and now major protest." And in
discussing the Cresswell and Froggatt book on bus accidents,
the authors say: "This is but the latest evidence that the burden
of proof that there are 'accident-prone' individuals must rest
with those who defend the concept, since this most definitive
study fails to provide evidence that such individuals exist." However, elsewhere in the same chapter, they say: "For one cannot
claim that no cases of accident proneness exist. At the present
state of knowledge we must best conclude that accident proneness as an explanation for any major proportion of repeated accidents is unwarranted but that, as a clinical phenomenon limited
to some individuals, it may have some validity."

This dual thinking, which is always somewhat reminiscent of

the sort of legal plea which states: "The defendant maintains that he did not do it—but if he did, it was unintentional," seems to appear quite often in the American accident research literature. It seems part and parcel of a rather strange anomaly where, although the proneness concept is widely condemned, and there is constant repetition of the belief that accident-prone repeaters (if they exist at all) are responsible for only a fraction of the accidents, nevertheless a considerable (though lessening) amount of research time and research money is still being spent on trying to develop psychological tests which will distinguish between the people who have many accidents and the people who are accident-free—to say nothing of the almost nationwide operation of points systems, the main purpose of which is to pinpoint the bad accident risks.

To an outsider these contradictions between theory and practice, let alone theory and logic, are, to say the least of it, a little odd. In fact one cannot help feeling that the amount of attention which the practical traffic officials in the United States give to accident repeaters and to traffic violators (who are presumably regarded as potential accident offenders, else why prosecute them) should sow a few doubts in *somebody's* mind—for according to widely accepted scientific theory these people are virtually nonexistent, and certainly do not represent any appreciable danger to the community.

In fact one cannot help feeling that the wide discrepancy which exists between the basic thinking underlying, on the one hand, some rather untried theories, and, on the other hand, some very well-tried practices, indicates that the fault may possibly lie with the theories—and with the statistical data on which they are based.

Is it not perhaps more than likely that the traffic officials are quite right in their thinking? That accidents are very often anything but random events and that there are indeed such beings as accident-prone drivers, but that they are not a class all of their own, distinct in their abnormality—in fact that there is a whole spectrum of accident proneness ranging from the accident-free right up to the chronic accident repeater? That it is the *principle* underlying proneness which matters, namely the principle not only of unequal involvement in accidents but of unequal accident *potential?* That it is not just the tip of the iceberg, the multiple serious-accident offenders, whom the traffic officials are worrying about, but a much larger section of the community who, for all sorts of reasons, such as lack of driving skill, or physical defects, or personality defects, or wrong attitudes, have a *dangerous amount of accident potential;* potential which, under conditions of strict supervision is likely to manifest itself only in occasional bad driving or the occasional accident, but which would show itself far more clearly if the supervision were less strict—as is indeed demonstrated in countries other than the United States, where the driving is not nearly so disciplined and the accident rates far higher?

Nor does it seem very likely that the traffic officials are worrying about people whose weaknesses or faults are merely transitory, or about a problem which is of minor significance. They appear to consider the problem to be a serious one, and the reasoning underlying their policy of enforcement is that people do indeed differ fundamentally in their potential for accidents, just as they differ in their potential for crime, and that there are a number of basic similarities between the prevention of one and the prevention of the other.

But if, as the traffic officials seem to think, there are indeed fundamental differences between people's accident potential, how is it that the statistical evidence (derived from figures on reported accident occurrence) on which so much of the theoretical research thinking is based, does not show this up? Is it not possible that the fault may lie with the statistical evidence? That the figures which are always quoted as evidence against the concept are so incomplete, or so selective, that they do not give a true representation of the picture? That the figures on big intra-state studies, for instance, represent only the accidents involving injuries or fatalities or major property damage, and not all of those either—again just the tip of the iceberg? Or that the figures on professional drivers relate only to the more successful drivers, the men with long and continuous service, and exclude all the unsuccessful ones among whom one would expect to find the worst accident records?

And is it not also possible that there are significant shortcomings in much of the evidence (let alone theory) on which the psychological opposition to the proneness concept is based; such as the many failures to find, by means of psychological tests, enduring traits which distinguish the accident repeater from the relatively accident-free? Is it not possible, to quote Eysenck (1965), that "many of the investigations which have failed to produce positive results have been characterized by a poor choice of tests, a poor choice of problems, a poor choice of statistical methods of investigation, and a poor control over relevant variables?"

Moreover it would appear that some of these doubts as to the validity of the evidence against the proneness concept are also present in the minds of even its most severe critics. Otherwise why should they bother to mention that it is easier to find evidence of "proneness" in situations where accidents are more frequent or where accident recording is more complete? Or that there is some justification for believing that there is a relationship between accidents and social maladjustment? One has the feeling that underneath the condemnation of the proneness concept, on the basis of insufficient scientific "evidence," lies a certain amount of bewilderment as to why, for instance, so many of the studies involving the personality of the accident offender come up with such similar trends. One feels that, to say the least of it, there is still a vague suspicion in the minds of even some of the critics of accident proneness that there are indeed such beings as accident-prone drivers, displaying a whole range of proneness and influencing accident rates to all sorts of degrees, but that they are so well camouflaged by the statistical and psychological "evidence" that they do not show up.

If this is indeed the case it seems to place many accident researchers rather in the position of the leopard in Kipling's *Just So Stories* whose plaint was: "I can *smell* giraffe, I can *hear* giraffe, but I can't *see* giraffe." (Although it also seems more than likely that there are a number of researchers whose credo is: "For purely ideological reasons I would prefer *not* to see giraffe.")

However, be this as it may, it is still very important to establish in some detail how all this contradictory thinking has come about.

Just why is it that there is so much controversy? Why is it that the accident-proneness concept is accepted by scientists on one side of the world and rejected by scientists on the other? Why is it that if the concept is eminently acceptable to some scientists, there is still so little statistical evidence to support it?

It seems to me that unless we can examine the point of view of both sides of the argument, sort out the contradictions, and provide some detailed answers to these questions, then further discussion on the subject is futile, and that the contribution which theoretical, psychological and statistical research can make to the pressing problem of road accidents will continue to be depressingly negligible. In fact it is eminently possible that an actual retrogression will take place—if it has not already started. For it seems as though the constant belittlement by so many important and influential writers on accident research of even the basic principle underlying the proneness concept, namely that certain people are inherently worse accident risks than others, is already beginning to play a part in influencing the trend of accident-prevention policy in a country like the United States. Here the emphasis on accident prevention is swinging very noticeably away from the driver and towards the vehicle. Whereas the driver used to be regarded as Scapegoat Number 1, he is gradually being allotted the role of the innocent victim of circumstance, while the vehicle is now being groomed for the role of the villain of the piece.

For the moment this may be all very well, for there is undoubtedly much room for improvement in the safety aspects of vehicle design. But the real danger would come if the pendulum were made to swing too far; if the weight of the counsel of the accident researchers resulted in any discrediting of enforcement or even withdrawal of financial support from measures designed to discipline drivers and clamp down on traffic offenders.

An outcome like this may not be as far-fetched as it sounds. Already there is a good deal of talk in American research writings about the very doubtful value of punitive measures. There is also a good deal of talk about the doubtful relationship between accidents and traffic violations—which have even been described in a recent statistical paper (Haight, 1964) as a "schedule of actions

harmless in themselves, which are supposed to 'cause' accidents!"
And in the same article in the *New York Times* quoted earlier,
one of the leading members of the Accident Prevention Section
of the United States Health Department is quoted as saying that
"law enforcement is a doubtful technique for reducing road accidents."

If this development does indeed take place it may well prove
to be a most costly and retrogressive step. For in the United
States, where big cities and high traffic density should, by rights,
have resulted in one of the highest accident rates in the world,
it is largely the work, not only of the highway engineers and the
traffic controllers, but of the practical officials who discipline
and control the drivers, that appears to have brought down the
country's accident rate and held it at a figure which is the lowest
in the world per mileage driven.

No one disputes the fact that the accident problem is a complex
one, but this has not stopped the practical men from making a
very good job of tackling it. And in all fairness to them one must
admit they have achieved what they have achieved with very
little assistance from the theoretical driver researchers. It would
be a most unfortunate state of affairs if theoretical thinking, based
on evidence much of which is still open to dispute, should be allowed to curtail in any way the activities of the practical officials
—activities which appear to have brought about a most far-
reaching and beneficial change in the whole atttiude of the
American driving public. It would be even more unfortunate if
this sort of reaction were to spread to other countries where the
need for controlling the driver is much greater.

This is why I feel that someone ought to make a determined
effort to sort out the confusion in scientific thinking. I have my
doubts as to whether yet another book on the subject of accident
proneness will have any marked effect on entrenched opinion.
Yet I feel all the more that one should be written, particularly one
which is specifically aimed at reconciling theory with practice.
Hence this dual volume in which I have covered the general and
psychological aspects while my coauthor has covered the statistical aspect.

As we feel that we would like the book to be of some use to the

practical traffic officials, as well as to the research workers, I
have given my section a more practical orientation than is usually
given in a publication of this kind. I have also tried to write it in
less technical language than is usual in a scientific work. The
personal studies on which many of my coauthor's and my conten-
tions are based have been carried out on a large scale, over a long
period of time, and with strict scientific "methodology"; and our
findings have scientific authenticity. These findings, and those of
many other researchers, are presented with scientific exactitude
in certain chapters of the book; but in others which deal with the
general aspects of the concept of accident proneness the presentation is less formal. It is my hope that what these chapters may
lose in the way of scientific "elegance" will be compensated for
by practical usefulness.

I have no intention of making this book yet another review of
the accident research literature as there are a number of very
comprehensive ones already available. In dealing with the literature my sole aim will be to endeavour to trace the trends of thinking on accident proneness and the developments which have influenced present attitudes, to see whether it is possible to discover
the underlying reasons for the disagreements and the contradictions.

But in addition I would also like to do something more constructive, namely to put forward, with ample supporting evidence, a more moderate and flexible version of the proneness concept than is usually presented—a version which, to my mind,
could account for a lot of the anomalies and bridge a number of
the gaps.

However, I must reiterate that this concept is intended to refer
specifically to the question of road accidents—not industrial accidents, or home accidents, or childhood accidents. In the first
place I do not claim to have any specialized knowledge in these
fields. And secondly I do not for one moment believe that it is
justifiable to generalize from accidents in one sphere to accidents
in another, and it has always struck me as most illogical that anyone should have even contemplated doing so. Because, surely,
there is no justification for generalizing from one set of data to
another when the circumstances are so diverse that there is even

a fundamental difference in what constitutes an *accident?* Nor can one compare *situations* which make different demands on people's capabilities, or which call into play such different psychological forces, or serve such different psychological needs.

Unfortunately, however, when it comes to tracing the development of the thinking on accident proneness it is quite impossible to separate the road accident research from the research on other types of accidents. It is all too hopelessly interwoven. Not only has the thinking in one sphere influenced the thinking in the other, but figures relating to one type of accident have constantly been used to support or repudiate arguments about a completely different type of accident. In fact anyone wishing to study the road-accident proneness literature will find references to figures pertaining to everything from industrial accidents among British munition workers, to shunting accidents among South African railwaymen, to poisoning accidents among four-year-old children, to horse kicks among Prussian cavalrymen—which no doubt accounts for at least some of the confusion!

2

MISHAP ANALYSIS

David L. Nichols

Anyone who thinks about safety sooner or later quotes H. W. Heinrich. The author of "Mishap Analysis" does so in this article which he bills as an improved approach to aircraft accident prevention.

The safety practitioner as well as the student may choose to read this article with something in mind other than aircraft. He may choose to think about "near misses." He may choose to compare and contrast "near misses" with "mishaps" as defined by the author. He may choose to look up the ingredients (and the definitions of the ingredients) that went into Heinrich's original statement of the 300–29–1 ratio, which the author refers to as Heinrich's theory. He may note the congruence of the two sets of data despite the fact that the ingredients are quite different. He may recall a dozen similar sets of data, all with different ingredients, but all remarkably congruent with Heinrich's 300–29–1 ratio.

And he may ask himself what it means or what it proves and whether it means or proves anything. In any case, if he is practical, he can see practical applications. If he enjoys theory he can go on pondering about cause and effect, about the nature and the measurement of the safety problem, and about what needs to be measured to assert control and to assess results.

> Commanders are responsible for using all Air Force resources effectively and judiciously to successfully complete assigned missions, and so contribute to the progressive achievement of overall Air Force objectives.
>
> —USAF Management Process *

O NE OF THE BEST manifestations of effective and judicious use of Air Force resources is reflected through the Safety Program. The goal of this program is ". . . to conserve the combat

Air University Review, July–August, 1973, Vol. XXIV, No. 5
* *USAF Management Process*, Air Force Manual 25-1, Department of the Air Force, 15 October 1964, p. 1.

capability of the United States Air Force through the preservation of its personnel and materiel resources." † Each commander is directed to take action within means available (1) to prevent accidents, (2) to eliminate or minimize the effects of design deficiencies, and (3) to eliminate unsafe acts and errors that represent accident potential.‡

To date, the Air Force has been most successful in aircraft accident prevention, as a brief look at history clearly illustrates. In 1947 the major aircraft accident rate was forty-four accidents per 100,000 flying hours. By 1953 to 1954 the rate had been halved, and by 1959 the rate was below ten. The improvement gradually continued over the next twelve years to a low rate of 2.5 achieved in 1971.§

The Air Force is justifiably proud of this record, but an inevitable question arises: Can the accident rate be further reduced? How far can we go? An answer to this question is unknown, but it is obvious that the Air Force has reached a point where continued improvement is increasingly difficult. Major General John D. Stevenson addressed this problem in 1960 when he stated, ". . . the accidents ahead of us are going to be the most difficult to prevent in our history, for the things that are easy to do have already been done by our predecessors" (Stevenson, 1960).

What he said has proven to be true, and the challenge will be even more difficult in the next decade. The Air Force cannot relax but must continue to explore and develop improved methods of preventing accidents. Old methods need not be discarded, but new methods must be innovated to meet the increased challenge effectively. This article reports on such an innovation: Mishap Analysis.

Mishap analysis is basically a trend analysis program that looks in detail at potential sources of accidents. Many flying units already have some form of trend analysis program, but in most

† *Responsibilities for the USAF Aerospace Safety Program,* Air Force Regulation 127–1, Department of the Air Force, 11 June 1971, p. 1.

‡ *Ibid.,* pp. 1–2.

§ *USAF Aircraft Accident Summary* 1971, Directorate of Aerospace Safety, Norton AF Base, California, 1972, p. 2.

cases they lack depth, timeliness, and credibility. The inadequacies of such programs will not meet future requirements. To be effective, a safety trend analysis program must incorporate three essential characteristics: (1) it must provide a realistic data base for analysis; (2) it must provide timely identification of accident potential; and (3) it must highlight problems arising from the materiel/maintenance complex—the primary source of today's accidents.|| This article shows how these essential characteristics relate to mishap analysis.

Realistic Data Base

Several years ago a waterfront community was threatened by an epidemic from unknown causes. More than a thousand residents became ill within a week, and one person died. An autopsy was performed and revealed that death resulted from uremia, probably aggravated by impure food. The circumstances indicated that shellfish were the cause. Armed with this information, the local authorities acted promptly to correct the shellfish problem. But unfortunately, several other persons became seriously ill before it was discovered that the first fatality was not indicative of the real cause of the epidemic. The basic cause was not the shellfish but was, in fact, water pollution (Heinrich, 1941).

This story brings to light several fallacies highlighting the importance of learning the following lessons. The first lesson is that isolated and/or spectacular cases do not provide the best guide for corrective actions. A second lesson is that a wrong diagnosis of cause factors usually results in the wrong remedial actions. And finally, the true source of a majority of ills is the best foundation upon which to base analysis (Heinrich, 1941). Thus, while attacking the shellfish, one should not overlook the possibility of water pollution.

Today's Air Force is subject to three fallacies, too, and they impose limitations on the safety program.

FALLACY I. Today, relatively few problem areas are identified through accident investigation. One reason for this is that most causes do not reach the "accident" stage, because someone—usually the pilot—saves the aircraft. Airborne emergencies that are safely recovered belong in this category; they are events that could have been accidents. In reality, they should be considered as accidents, accidents that did not result in injury or damage. And it is here that a fallacy becomes apparent; these "accidents" will not be analyzed for accident potential because there was no injury or damage. They are ignored in much the same way as the polluted water.

The seriousness of this shortcoming was identified by H. W. Heinrich, a noted pioneer in the scientific approach to accident prevention, when he observed that ". . . for every mishap resulting in an injury (or damage) there are many other similar accidents that cause no injuries (or damage) whatever" (Heinrich, 1941). He reached the conclusion that, in a group of similar mishaps, 300 will produce no injury whatever, twenty-nine will result in minor injury, and one will result in major injury. He emphasizes that the importance of an individual mishap lies in its potential for creating injury and not in the fact that it actually does or does not. Therefore, any analysis as to cause and remedial action is limited and misleading if based on one major accident out of a total of 330 similar accidents, all of which are capable of causing injuries or damage. In other words, those who limit their study to isolated, spectacular cases—major aircraft accidents— are looking only at the tip of an ominous iceberg.

FALLACY II. Another reason many "causes" go undetected is that accidents are extremely difficult to investigate and analyze *accurately*. Often investigation boards have little more than a "smoking hole" for evidence; consequently, it is easy to arrive at erroneous conclusions in spite of the most commendable efforts. A more critical observer reports that ". . . accident boards, forced by expediency, sometimes find it easier to assume pilot error than to prove materiel deficiency or maintenance error" (Fair, 1968). He supported his case with the following logic:

> Over a nine-month period a fighter wing's mishap experience included 204 reportable and nonreportable incidents. In the same period the wing had six accidents. Analysis of the incidents revealed 9 percent were caused by pilot error, while 90 percent resulted from materiel failure and/or maintenance malpractice. However, pilot error was assessed as the primary cause in 83 percent of the accidents. Materiel failure was *proven* in only one case (Fair, 1968).

A more recent twenty-month study in a different wing revealed 975 mishaps (accidents, reportable incidents, and nonreportable incidents). Pilot error was the cause of approximately 5 percent of the total.¶ This should indicate that pilots cause less than 10 percent of the accidents. Yet during this same general period, Air Force-wide statistics reflect that pilots cause over 40 percent of the accidents.*

Do accident investigation boards fail to uncover true cause factors? If so, numerous problems have been neglected and hence will contribute to other accidents.

FALLACY III. Accidents do not occur frequently enough to establish trends, particularly at lower echelons of command. Unless a trend is established, commanders may be forced to treat the effect rather than the cause of accidents.

Air Force directives require reports on those incidents that are "almost accidents," and this is particularly useful information because the aircrew and equipment are intact for a logical and thorough investigation. Thus reportable incidents provide more accurate cause factors and a better data base for analysis and remedial actions than actual accidents.

So those who analyze reportable incidents as well as accidents are on somewhat firmer ground, but this also is only looking at the tip of a large iceberg. The tip, in this instance, allows study of both accidents and "almost accidents," but it ignores data from "could have been accidents." Moreover, this tip is still too small for trend analysis at wing level.

The most reliable source of information is that which includes all problems that could result in an accident. These problems will

¶ Analysis revealed cause factors assessed to materiel factor, 599 (61%); maintenance factor, 173 (18%); pilot factor, 14 (1.5%); and 189 (19.5%) were undetermined. A further analysis of the undetermined causes revealed at least 119 of these could not have involved pilot factor, whereas the other 70 could have derived from pilot, materiel, or maintenance factors. Assuming that all 70 of these were caused by pilot factor, the percentage for pilot factor increases to about 8.5 percent. Therefore, the actual pilot factor mishaps in this study fell somewhere between 1.5 and 8.5 percent of the total.—Extracted from XX Tactical Fighter Wing's Safety System Analysis data (a PACAF subordinate unit), September 1970—April 1971. Hereafter cited as *Safety Analysis*, XX TFW.

* *US Air Force Accident Bulletin* 1967–1970, Directorate of Aerospace Safety, Norton AF Base, California, 1969–1971, p. 1.

be found by studying the *mishap rate,* which measures accidents, "almost accidents," and "could have been accidents." A truer definition of the mishap rate might be *the recording of all unexpected events, occurring in flight, that did result or could have resulted in an airborne emergency.*

Timeliness

For many years, . . . safety organizations have been doing a thorough job of investigating, analyzing, reporting, and taking corrective action after an accident, and in analyzing trends from records that are weeks, months, or years old. Important as this is to a safety program it is "after-the-fact"—too late to provide effective controls to prevent these accidents. It is apparent that we need the facts on our safety situation as of the moment. Therefore, we need a method to pinpoint the accident-producing, unsafe acts *before* the accident happens (Bailey, 1966).

What could be more useless to a commander than a thorough in-depth analysis of how to prevent an accident after it has already occurred? Any hint of increased accident exposure before-the-fact is without doubt more useful.

The central objective of mishap analysis is to get *early* identification of potential problems so that prompt corrective actions can resolve same *before an accident occurs.* To accomplish this, a properly managed accident-prevention program will have documentation that is accurate, timely, and up-to-date. When analyzed, it will provide trends or spotlight areas requiring attention. The program must not degenerate into history. It must be an active day-to-day program which points out problems that exist now.

This day-to-day program is therefore based at wing level. The mishap data are collected and reviewed daily, and a formal analysis is completed monthly. However, the daily reviews will bring to light potential problem areas; therefore, supplementary analyses are frequently required during interim periods to insure timeliness.

Also the program uses manual inputs and analysis rather than computer techniques. For a program of this scale, manual techniques are more desirable for many reasons: the inputs/outputs are more timely; the manager develops complete familiarity with the data; they are more responsive to the unprogrammed needs of accident prevention; they tend to be simpler and provide outputs that are not burdened by irrelevant data; they are less expensive; and they are available to all. This sounds like heresy in today's computer-oriented world, but this program is more productive when given the personal attention that is associated with manual operation. Possibly some future evolution of mishap analysis will fruitfully incorporate computers.

Man Versus Machines

Mishap analysis concentrates more on the machine than the pilot because aircrews are the strongest element in preventing accidents (Stevenson, 1960). Therefore, emphasis is placed on increasing aircraft reliability.

The safety philosophy has too often leaned upon the pilot by giving him the responsibility to cope with malfunctions rather than providing better equipment. Aircrews have done an exceptional job in accepting this challenge. A survey completed in 1960 illustrates this point. It showed that during a six-month period Air Defense Command had 681 in-flight emergencies due to maintenance or materiel deficiencies. Extraordinary aircrew performance overcame 659 of these. In the same period, ten accidents were attributed to pilot error. This means that pilots saved 66 aircraft for every accident they caused (Stevenson, 1960).

Recently, a more detailed study was completed in a large tactical fighter wing equipped with several different types of aircraft. During a twenty-month period, 299 in-flight emergencies occurred due to maintenance or materiel factors. Four of these led to aircraft accidents, one of them attributed to pilot error. In this case study, pilots saved 299 aircraft compared with their one failure.†

Thus pilots do an exceptional job of coping with emergencies. But the fact remains that if aircrews did not have to cope with serious malfunctions, or at least such a large number of them, the accident rate would be greatly reduced. Therefore, a most fruit-

† *Safety Analysis,* **XX TFW.**

ful area for increased attention relates to the machine—the product of the materiel/maintenance effort.

Some General Guidelines

The first step in a mishap analysis program is to establish priorities. Ideally, a commander would give each type of aircraft equal attention to prevent accidents; however, since resources are limited, priorities must be established. In other words, if one type of aircraft is well protected by the existing procedures, then additional effort should not be wasted. But if accident exposure is high, then normal procedures should be augmented with mishap analysis.

Next, the data base must be established for the type(s) of aircraft to be influenced by mishap analysis. The amount and type of information collected are critical; therefore, the first step is the collection of complete, factual data, without regard to severity or cause. This concept permits investigation of the entire iceberg rather than just the tip.

The data collection process could begin in many ways; however, for ease of control and to insure complete coverage, the best starting point is the aircrew/maintenance debriefing that follows each sortie. At debriefing, a "description of occurrence" is completed on a mishap report work sheet whenever an unexpected event occurred that did result or could have resulted in an airborne emergency. If an emergency actually occurred, the work sheet description should be augmented by personal contact between the safety officer and the aircrew to be sure that all details are clear.

One copy of the work sheet is turned over to safety personnel during a daily pickup, and another is sent to Maintenance Quality Control for investigation. Quality control determines what system component failed and, if possible, how it failed. The completed report is then forwarded to the safety office, where it is evaluated against criteria in Air Force Regulation 127–4 for a reportable or nonreportable incident. Reportable incidents receive further investigation and are submitted to higher headquarters in accordance with directives. For nonreportable incidents, a cause factor is assessed based on the investigation by quality control. The wing then has available for analysis the causes of all accidents, "almost accidents," and "could have been accidents."

The next step is to record the data by methods that will provide early detection of problems. The information is shredded out by subsystems and cause factors. The subsystems are those in which a malfunction could lead to an accident: landing gear, engine, drag chute, flight controls, hydraulics, autopilot, fuel system, instruments, electrical, weapons, etc. The cause factors include aircrew, maintenance, material, and undetermined sources. When tabulated, this information provides the basis for trends in numbers and types of subsystem failures and causes of failures. The use of these data is limited only by the imagination of the safety officer. The information can be set forth in various types of graphs, tables, and charts to identify trends not only by subsystem but also by type of aircraft, by individual aircraft tail number, by squadrons, by maintenance sections, etc.

Detailed discussion of various graphs, tables, and charts is not within the scope of this article. Most methods in common use are quite simple. However, one technique that merits comment, because seldom used by the safety officer, is the control limit chart. It has unique value in that it gives a quick and simple summary of the mishap data. The chart can be constructed for many things, such as failure rates of subsystems, mishap rates for each type of aircraft, or an overall mishap rate of all aircraft influenced by the program. The accompanying control limit chart, an actual chart used by one wing, represents the overall rate (Fig. 2–1).

The chart shows when mishap rates are normal (the grey area) and when rates deviate from normal. Normal experience is defined by the area within the "control limits." This area is derived by setting limits that are one standard deviation eihter side of the mean rate. Thus 68 percent of all mishap rates will fall within the control limits. Mishap rates that exceed one standard deviation are out of the control limits and require special attention. When mishap rates exceed the upper limit, accident exposure is excessive. The problem(s) should be ferreted out by analysis of mishap data presented in other graphs, charts, and tables. Conversely, when mishap rates fall below the lower limit, this must also be analyzed to determine *what is right*. With this approach,

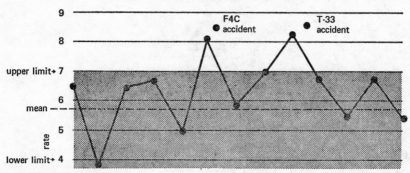

Figure 2–1. A Control Limit Chart Derived From One Tactical Fighter Wing's Mishap Experience, The Rate Based On The Number of Mishaps per 100 Sorties.

commanders can exploit those assets that are good and enhance safe operations. Therefore, mishap analysis capitalizes on positive as well as negative experiences to provide before-the-fact accident prevention clues.

Is It Valid?

Has mishap analysis been tested? Is it worth the extra effort? The program has been used in two large fighter wings, but it is difficult to measure the degree of success. One seldom knows how many accidents were prevented in any situation. But the author, having managed both programs, feels that the degree of success was significant. The programs were also inspected and studied by many safety experts in all echelons of command from the Directorate of Aerospace Safety down through air divisions. In each instance, the program was praised as a strong deterrent to aircraft accidents.

There is another, less subjective way to evaluate mishap analysis through the use of Heinrich's theory. The theory states that investigation of any random sampling of 330 mishaps shows that the same set of circumstances will usually result. In this group, there will be twenty-nine which produce only minor injury/damage and one which will produce major injury/damage. Heinrich's theory can be summarized in a pyramid, or as an iceberg structure. (Fig. 2–2)

The top blocks of the pyramid—the tip of the iceberg—directly

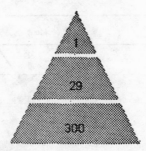

Figure 2–2. Heinrich's Theory.

relate to the Air Force reporting system of accidents and incidents. For example, in 1970 Pacific Air Forces Command suffered
sixty major accidents and 1739 minor accidents and reportable
incidents. Thus for every major accident there were 28.9 accidents
of lesser damage. Heinrich says there should be 29 (United
Safety Officers Guide, 1971). Also in 1970, the Air Force experienced 200 major accidents and 5800 minor accidents and
reportable incidents.‡ This represents exactly twenty-nine accidents of lesser degree for every major accident. In other words,
the findings of Heinrich and the Air Force are compatible as far
as the top blocks of the pyramid are concerned. But the Air Force
presently has nothing that relates to the base of Heinrich's pyramid; therefore, we overlook the most promising source for trend
analysis.

In contrast, the mishap analysis program appears to relate to
all segments of the pyramid. The twenty months of data collected
in one wing revealed three major accidents, 87 reportable incidents, and 885 nonreportable.§ This is a relationship of 295
accidents with no damage or injury and 29 accidents with little
damage for each major accident. (Fig. 2–3)

Admittedly, the sample is small, but the correlation is so close
as to indicate that mishap analysis does fill in the gap and provide
the needed data base for analysis. If this is true, the proposal is
valid and worth the extra effort.

MISHAP analysis does not by any pretext establish the ulti-

‡ US *Air Force Accident Bulletin* 1970, Directorate of Aerospace Safety, Norton
AF Base, California, 1971, p. 1.
§ *Safety Analysis*, XX TFW.

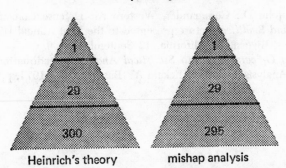

Heinrich's theory   mishap analysis

Figure 2–3. A Comparison of Heinrich's Theory With Mishap Experience.

mate, but it does open a new avenue to accident prevention. It is an underdeveloped approach that is begging for additional attention.‖

Such a program takes on increased importance during periods of austere funding and personnel cuts. Equipment is getting older and will be more prone to materiel failure; also manpower cuts increase the possibility of rising personnel factors in accidents. These must be countered with improved supervision, increased surveillance, and improved management tools. Mishap analysis is offered with these factors in mind, but it does impose an additional workload. However, when the cost of this effort is compared against the multimillion-dollar cost of most accidents, the expense is insignificant. It certainly represents an effective and judicious use of Air Force resources.

REFERENCES

Bailey, Jack E.: *Safety Sampling Program.* Professional Studies Paper, Institute of Aerospace Safety and Management, University of Southern California, Los Angeles, California, December 1966.

Fair, John C.: *Calculating the Risk.* Professional Studies Paper, Institute of Aerospace Safety and Management, University of Southern California, Los Angeles, 16 December 1968, p. 4.

Heinrich, H. W.: *Industrial Accident Prevention, A Scientific Approach.* New York and London, McGraw-Hill, 1941, p. 29.

‖ Within the past two years, Air Training Command has expanded its aircraft safety trend analysis program; however, that program is fundamentally different from the concepts set forth in this article. The author feels the most important differences are related to concepts of (1) appropriate data base, (2) timeliness, and (3) level of management.

Stevenson, John D.: Commander, Western Air Defense Command, ADC, *Ideals and Realities,* lecture presented to the First Annual USAF Safety Congress, Riverside, California, 12 September 1960.

Unit Safety Officers Guide to Statistical Analysis, Headquarters PACAF, Safety Analysis Division, Hickam AF Base, Hawaii, 1971, pp. 5–6.

3

HIGH POTENTIAL
ACCIDENT ANALYSIS

William W. Allison

The title of this article suggests that the author will arrive at the significant by dealing with the insignificant, a familiar pattern in safety thinking.

In this case, severe personal injury is the significant event. In the mass of minor accidents resulting in minor injury, only a few have the potential to cause severe injury. These few can be identified by the method of high-potential-accident analysis. Corrective action can then be directed to forestall those particular accidents in which severity has been foreseen.

The words used to convey safety ideas are often used in a special context and they often conflict with words used in another context. In one context, severity is regarded as fortuitous. Both student and practitioner might check their thinking on that point in the light of this article.

THE KEY TO ACCIDENT PREVENTION is accident analysis—once the cause is found, it can be remedied. Such analysis and corrective action are usually focused on accidents that cause serious injuries. But this approach is incomplete; it does not cover the minor accident that, give or take an inch or step, could have been fatal.

When an accident occurs, supervisors must use their imagination and judgment. Suppose two men report minor injuries. One man has a bad bruise from pinching his fingers in a car door. The other has been barely nicked by the chain drive of an industrial truck. Because accidents that lead to time off the job are reported

31

as a big loss, the tendency too often would be to focus investigation on the more serious injury.

But a supervisor should always consider the potential of each accident situation. In this case, he would pay less attention to the accident that caused the serious bruise and more attention to analyzing the accident that barely nicked an employee. He would recognize the high potential of the power-drive chain for serious injury, convince higher management of the potential, and help initiate corrective engineering action *before* a disabling injury occurred. This is the basic approach of high-potential-accident analysis.

High-potential accidents are those that could, under similar or slightly different circumstances, result in serious injury or damage. Here are two examples, plus corrective measures taken after they occurred.

1. A pipefitter was working under a sink when a particle hit his unprotected eye. Although the injury was slight, the supervisor ruled that eye protection must always be used when work is above the face or head and wherever chemicals are used.

2. A worker was moving a load of glass on a small four-wheeled cart when the wheels hit a joint in the pavement. The glass slid out and broke, cutting him on the thigh and ankle while he was trying to support and protect the glass load. Although no arteries were severed, the potential was there, and the supervisor requisitioned special material-handling equipment.

Recognizing Danger Signals

A study has indicated that out of every 330 accidents, 300 are near-misses or no-injury accidents, twenty-nine result in minor injuries, and only one is a major injury. In other words, after two major injuries to subordinates, a supervisor has had about 600 danger signals in the form of no-injury accidents and about fifty-eight danger signals in the form of minor-injury accidents (including those not reported). If only about 10 percent of these 658 danger signals had been recognized as high-potential accidents and corrective action had been taken, the two serious injuries might not have occurred.

Under many injury-record systems, a serious injury is followed by a strong drive on minor injuries—which generally inhibits workers from reporting such injuries. Nobody wants to spoil the record. Danger signals decrease and serious injuries continue to occur.

Getting Reports of Near-Misses

To get employees to report their high-potential near-misses, supervisors must change the terminology and emphasis in their reporting systems. The terms *accident* and *injury* should not be used interchangeably. An accident may, or may not, result in injury, damage, or loss; an injury is the result of an accident that physically harms a worker.

The investigation must include not only *what* happened, but *why* it happened. The reason may lie in an employee's carelessness or in inadequate design of layout, equipment, or facilities.

Because most safety programs put a penalty on reporting near misses, employees often conceal their knowledge of any close calls. If supervisors would convince their subordinates that they really want high-potential no-injury reports, it would be relatively easy to get their cooperation.

An alert supervisor can soon learn to recognize the actual causes of accidents and concentrate his efforts on those that have high potential for causing serious injury or damage. By conscientiously completing a report for the high-potential accidents —which represent only about 10 percent of all no-injury, no-damage, minor-injury, and near-miss accidents—a supervisor can identify and correct conditions that cause serious, disabling injuries. His experience can also be used to alert other supervisors and prevent similar accidents throughout the corporation.

A simple approach? Yes—most good procedures are fairly simple (or seem to be) once they have been worked out. But it depends on the exercise of good judgment.

4

A TEACHING MODEL OF INJURY CAUSATION AND A GUIDE FOR SELECTING COUNTERMEASURES

E. C. WIGGLESWORTH

The author offers a model of the injury process. The casual reader may be astonished to discover what this entails, and he may catch a glimpse of the conceptual difficulties of understanding an event that can be dismissed as an accident.

To the student, this tightly reasoned article is a lesson in disciplined safety thinking. The author's adherence to careful definitions keeps the thought process on the track. Along the way he puts into perspective many of the major concepts and philosophies of safety, at least in a capsule form. Each capsule is a world of knowledge in itself, and yet the reader can find a path beginning in traditional safety engineering and tracing through epidemiology into ergonomics and touching on systems safety.

The title suggests two practical purposes in the author's mind. To the student and to the teacher he offers a methodology of teaching injury prevention. To the practitioner, he offers a guide in selecting countermeasures. It can safely be said that in one too brief article he goes a long way to accomplish these two notable purposes.

EFFORTS TO IMPROVE our understanding of accidents have been rare; accidental injury is now probably the only source of large-scale morbidity without benefit of continuing research into its causation. Attempts to evolve a comprehensive theory of injury causation have been hampered by lack of adequate data

From *Occupational Psychology*, 46:69–78 (1972).

and by the almost total lack of precision in the relevant terminology.

Perhaps the greatest handicap to the evolution of a systematic approach has been the folk-lore that permitted intelligent and rational men and women, including those trained to adopt precise analytical techniques in their own disciplines, to accept accidents as Acts of God or the inflictions of a malevolent Providence, and to believe that their causal sequences involved chance or luck and were incapable of any form of examination beyond mere tabulation.

However, there has recently been an extensive and authoritative advocacy of the epidemiological approach to the accident problem (Haddon, 1967) which has brought our understanding into a more rational framework. There has also been a gradual advance in our understanding of the importance of human factors in the causal sequence. These two trends taken together permit the construction of a model of mechanisms that lead to injury and offer a theory of how to select countermeasures.

HISTORICAL DEVELOPMENT OF SAFETY ENGINEERING

The techniques for preventing occupational injury have been developed from the work of the original four British factory inspectors who were appointed in 1833. As part of that development, a coherent methodology, with four essential components, has gradually emerged.

The four components are:

> Recognition that a problem exists
> Acceptance of responsibility
> Motivation for injury control
> Application of relevant knowledge.

The attack on occupational injuries has been most successful in those establishments where all four of these components were present. However, they are as important on the macro-scale as on the micro-scale and the absence of one or more of them on the macro-scale is a major cause of the general lack of success in preventing domestic, road and recreational injuries. This lack of success is evidenced by Table 4–I which shows the increase in

TABLE 4–I
ROAD INJURIES AND INJURY RATES
VICTORIA 1960–1969

Year ending December	Persons killed	Persons injured ('000)	Rate per 100,000 of mean population	
			Deaths	Injuries
1960	760	16.7	26.6	583
1961	794	16.1	27.1	551
1962	808	16.8	27.1	562
1963	780	17.6	25.7	578
1964	904	19.8	29.1	639
1965	929	20.4	29.4	646
1966	955	20.2	29.7	626
1967	887	20.6	27.1	630
1968	949	22.1	28.5	664
1969	1,011	23.8	29.8	703

road injuries and deaths in Victoria for the period 1960 to 1969.

This paper will concentrate on examining those aspects of safety engineering that are known to contribute to the selection of countermeasures.

The preferential sequence of safety engineering countermeasures has long been incorporated, under Topic 01 of the Syllabus, in the industrial safety training courses conducted twice a year by the Royal Society for the Prevention of Accidents, London. This sequence can be considered under the headings:

Hazard removal

Hazard control

Personal protection

Education and training

For convenience, the first two items will be considered together.

Hazard Removal and Control

The most effective actions are those that remove the hazard from the environment, or, where this is impracticable, those that introduce engineering modifications to reduce or control the injury potential of the hazard.

Total abolition of the hazard is rare; but the removal of one hazardous process and the substitution of another with less potential for injury is often possible, and this technique is frequently employed. The substitution of bromochlorodifluoromethane for carbon tetrachloride is one such example. In consequence of this substitution, the toxicity hazard from vaporizing fire extinguishants has largely been eliminated. Another example is the introduction in industry of individual motors in place of transmission systems using overhead shafting and belting. This has substantially reduced the mechanical hazard in machine shops, and has thereby reduced the incidence of those fatal and disabling injuries for which the earlier type of transmission machinery was—and is—notorious.

Where hazard removal is not practicable, engineering modifications to control the hazard are widely practised. These permit the retention of the potentially damaging energy, but either circumscribe its area of operation or interpose a barrier or an attenuator between it and the inhabited environment. The engineering techniques of machine guarding, of fume control, and of the prevention of falls all have this aim. In general, the value of this type of countermeasure has been commensurate with its ability to limit energy release in the physical environment. Where containment has been only partial, the success of the countermeasure has usually also been only partial. There is increasing realization of the practical importance of guards that protect areas other than the expected points of danger, i.e. at the rear of presses and guillotines. Moreover, the requirement that guards should incorporate maintenance and lubrication access to obviate the need for their removal is now well established.

Personal Protection

Personal protection differs from these countermeasures as it permits the continuing release of the hazardous energy and operates by reducing the local or whole-body exposure to injury. In practice, the continuing presence of the hazard permits injury if the operator is not making use of the recommended protection, which is often cumbersome, restrictive or unsightly. More importantly, the continuing presence of unmodified hazardous energy permits injury to any unprotected person who enters the area.

Education and Training

Safety training has, in general, attempted either to change operator attitudes or to improve operator techniques. It developed logically from early work suggesting that 88 percent of industrial accidents were attributable to human failings, 10 percent to mechanical failures and the remaining 2 percent to Acts of God (Heinrich, 1931). Other investigators offered generally similar values, and although we now distinguish sharply between human failings and nonculpable error, there is still general acceptance of the importance of human factors in the accident process. Many attempts have been made to produce practical injury prevention techniques that would overcome human failings. These attempts have been built into a variety of training programs. In many cases, the objectives, in terms of the behavior changes that the training was intended to induce, have not been clearly defined, and such programs usually foundered on discussions of "carelessness," "inattention" or "proneness." None of these terms has provided information that was helpful or meaningful for injury prevention and the absence of precise behavioural objectives has placed a serious limitation on the utility and areas of applicability of safety training programmes.

A noteworthy contribution of safety specialists is the separation of causation and culpability. Safety engineering has long rejected the view that allocation of culpability is synonymous with identification of causation. Instead, safety specialists adopt an epidemiological approach by trying to identify the items in the causal chain of events that precede injury, so that one or more appropriate countermeasures can be incorporated in a revised sequence.

Achievements of Safety Engineering

Modern techniques based on this knowledge have achieved considerable success. The occupational accident rate for the State of Victoria for the years 1960 to 1969 is presented in Table 4-II and shows an improvement of over 30 percent. The information relates to compensation injuries that led to absence of one week or more (the only statistics available), and this limitation

TABLE 4–II

OCCUPATIONAL INJURIES AND INJURY RATES
MALES—VICTORIA 1960–1969

Year ending June	Number of accidents ('000)	Males employed ('000)	Accidents per 1,000 employees
1960	32.7	622	52
1961	32.9	644	51
1962	31.5	644	49
1963	30.0	654	46
1964	32.2	675	48
1965	30.3	703	43
1966	31.0	723	43
1967	32.1	734	44
1968	28.2	745	38
1969	26.6	763	35

of the data precludes interstate or overseas comparisons (Wigglesworth, 1970a).

This is unfortunate, for the improvement shown in Table 4–II, though creditable, tends to distract attention from the fact that the actual number of injuries is high. The only comparisons that can be made are internal ones, comparing the effects of occupational injury with other causes of absence from work. For example, Table 4–III shows that in Victoria, for the same period as in Tables 4–I and 4–II, absence from work through industrial injuries was three times as frequent as absence from work through industrial disputes.

TABLE 4–III

ABSENCE FROM WORK
MALES—VICTORIA 1960–1969

Year ending June	Cause of absence	
	Industrial disputes	Industrial injuries
1960	103	708
1961	72	657
1962	101	697
1963	173	657
1964	360	696
1965	214	652
1966	220	665
1967	107	746
1968	244	669
1969	717	636
Total	2,311	6,783

FUTURE DEVELOPMENT OF SAFETY ENGINEERING

There can be little doubt that the successful trend of Table 4–II may be ascribed to the engineering techniques of hazard removal and control, for it is axiomatic that the presence of a hazard is a necessary condition for injury to occur. It is not, however, a sufficient explanation, for a recent analysis of accidents in Australia (Wigglesworth 1970b) showed that age, sex and experience influenced injury incidence to a greater extent than differences in exposure to hazard. This was held to imply the existence of at least one other systematic causal factor.

The present paper suggests that that factor is the behavioural one of nonculpable error. The definition of this phrase requires particular emphasis. *An error is defined as a missing or inappropriate response,* and the term is used as a factual description of a particular type of human behaviour. It carries no connotation of blame nor implication of delinquent malpractice. This distinction requires the strongest possible emphasis, for it is crucial to the development of rational countermeasures.

This approach stems logically from the work of McFarland who, after showing that the rate of improvement in America had slowed up considerably in the years since 1956, said:

> This (slower rate) suggests that methods previously used may be reaching the limits of their effectiveness and newer approaches may be needed to effect reductions. Now there are indications that an engineering approach may again be of prime importance in achieving control over accidents; an approach, however, in which there has been a reorientation, so that engineering is tied in with the findings of human factors research developed in the last decade (McFarland, 1967).

The Role of Nonculpable Error

Treatments of the relationship between errors, accidents and injuries have been published (McFarland, 1967; Altman, 1970). They have, in general, agreed that "accidents and near-accidents arise from an error in the performance of the task." Error, it is suggested, is induced by some aspect or component of the environment; by identifying and modifying these environmental aspects, the likelihood of error, and hence of injury, can be reduced.

With this shift in emphasis to identify nonculpable error as an initiating factor in the injury sequence, and with an increasing flow of human factors research findings, a second point for the application of appropriate countermeasures is now feasible. This uses a human engineering approach, directed at the removal or reduction of the causes of human error. It replaces the older concept of safety training and, by identifying the required behavioural objective, gives purpose to it.

MODEL OF INJURY MECHANISM

This new human engineering approach, designed to remove or reduce the likelihood of error, can be combined with the traditional engineering approach, designed to remove or reduce potentially damaging energy. The resultant combination, applied in the conceptual framework of Haddon (1967), permits the construction of a model of injury mechanism, shown schematically at Figure 4–1. In this model, some terms that are in common usage are given the more precise definitions listed below.

An accident is an unplanned event that interrupts normal activity. It may or may not result in personal injury or property damage.

An injury is a unit of bodily damage caused either by the delivery to the body of amounts of energy in excess of the corresponding local or whole-body injury threshold (as by impact or electric shock) or by interference with the normal whole-body or local energy exchange (as in suffocation).

A hazard is a potential source of bodily damage. Hazards may be classified in terms of the type of energy that they deliver, i.e. mechanical, thermal, electrical, chemical, or ionizing radiation, or in terms of the energy exchange which they interrupt, i.e. thermal balance or oxygen utilisation.

An error is a missing or inappropriate response.

The definition of accident is one frequently used by safety engineers, and the definitions of hazard and injury are based on the work of Haddon (1967).

The injury causal sequence always contains a hazard and an error. In most cases, an error will lead to an unplanned event, i.e. an accident. If no hazard is present, the sequence will end at that

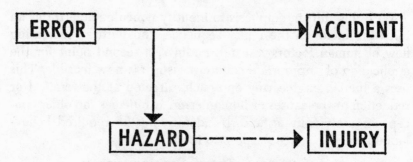

Figure 4–1. Injury Causation Model.

point, but if the error-accident transition takes place in the presence of a hazard, or if the transition itself introduces a hazard, then, depending on a variety of factors, an injury may ensue.

The model shows that the hazard may be introduced in two ways. It may occur through an error on the part of the subsequent victim, for example, the inadvertent ingestion of a toxin. Alternatively, it may be introduced by an error on the part of another person, remote in time or space, for example, when a design fault causes a weakness in a structure that remains as an unsuspected hazard for a substantial period before eventual collapse. In both cases the causal sequence remains unchanged.

The model also demonstrates the role of probability in the sequence. The presence of a hazard does not automatically lead to an injury but depends upon some nonrelated factor. For example, when a brick is dropped from a height, the likelihood of injury is a function of the population density at lower levels and the height fallen.

Utility of the Model

The model has three principal advantages. The first is that it accords precisely with the traditional techniques of industrial safety engineering and extends those techniques into the areas of ergonomics and systems engineering, i.e. the areas that are in the forefront of contemporary work in injury prevention.

Secondly, the model has been found useful in teaching the

methodology of injury prevention. It identifies the two main areas for applying countermeasures and permits the development of detailed expositions of appropriate measures in a thoroughly practical manner.

A Teaching Model of Injury Causation

Finally, it identifies the role of nonculpable error and, by defining this as a missing or inappropriate response, prompts the question "Response to what?" This immediately changes the emphasis from an emotive discussion of patterns of behavior to a meaningful search for the stimuli that produce them.

Application of the Model

The model can be applied to any system where there is a man-machine dependency and it is particularly appropriate for studies of the man-traffic and man-occupation situation.

The customary ergonomics representation of a man-machine system is schematically illustrated at Figure 4–2. The ergonomist's

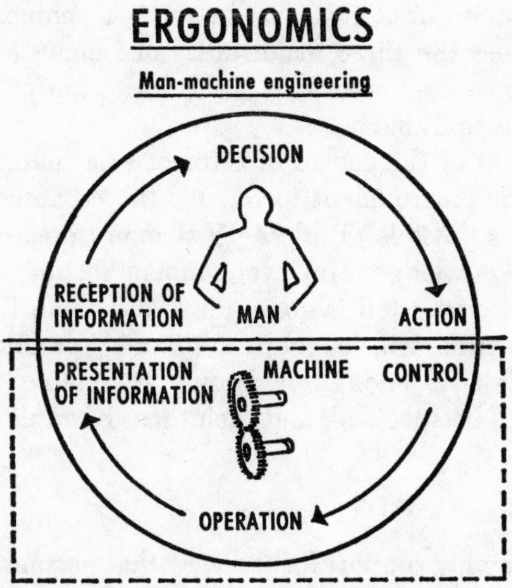

The figure shows the three areas in which non-culpable error can occur.

Figure 4–2. Components of Man-Machine System.

interest in injury prevention is primarily directed at identifying and removing the sources of nonculpable human error. His work is located in the "man" segment in the upper portion of the diagram but also includes the important interface between the upper and lower segments.

In contrast the earlier "hazard" approach was directed at identifying and removing or controlling sources of potentially damaging energy. This forms the basis of conventional safety engineering in which interest is confined to the lower half of the diagram in the area enclosed by the dotted line. It includes neither interface.

THE PREVENTION OF ERROR

The human engineering approach to injury prevention has two principal areas of application. The first concerns the mechanics of error causation, and the second concerns those factors that are thought to increase error incidents.

Error Causation

An error can occur at any point in a man-machine system. Figure 4–2 enables the three major areas of human activity to be considered separately and types and causes of error in each area to be listed, as in Table 4–IV.

Identification of the causes of error can be followed by modification of the environment to remove those causes. But this is not yet always possible; Table 4–IV demonstrates limitations of our existing knowledge. However, human factors research into many of the items listed is continuing, and there is little doubt that the findings will suggest additional practical countermeasures. Already, enough is known to enable some causal mechanisms to be specified, and their areas of application identified.

Error Incidence

There is growing support for the view that persons under stress have increased vulnerability to injury. In this context, stress is considered as a disharmony in some part of the man-machine system. This system has five components, *viz.* (i) the operator;

TABLE 4–IV

TYPICAL HUMAN ERRORS AND THEIR CAUSES

Reception of information
1. Failure of detection
   a. input overload   b. input underload   c. poor contrast
2. Incorrect identification
   a. as 1 above   b. conflicting cues

Decision
1. Failure to reach decision
   a. lack of information
2. Incorrect decision
   a. lack of information   b. incorrect priorities
   c. correct action inhibited

Action
1. Failure to act
   a. underlearned sequence   b. inability to reach
2. Incorrect control selection
   a. lack of uniform layout   b. inadequate separation or coding
   c. unintentional activation
3. Incorrect control adjustment
   a. presence of noncontrolling position   b. nonconformity with
                                                  stereotype

(ii) the machine; (iii) the process or operation; (iv) the physical environment; and (v) the behavioural environment. Stress can be induced by any of these components or by relationships between them.

Using this approach, some factors previously seen as separate issues can now be considered as discrete manifestations of a common problem. Thus, such factors as sleep deprivation, worry in the operator, inadequately sized or badly located controls in the machine, temperature extremes from the process, noise or poor illumination in the physical environment, and monotony or punitive supervision in the behavioral environment can all be considered as stress inducers.

Some items on this list have been investigated and the results have suggested that, at levels below the threshold of direct physical damage, susceptibility to injury increases.

This approach, outlining the effects of system components upon the individual, leads to the concept of increased vulnerability to injury when under stress, and several writers have so postulated. Kerr (1957) suggested that certain factors contributing to the occurrence of injury could be considered as variants of adjustment stress. Rogg (1961) commented on the role of emotions; Schulzinger (1956), on the evidence of 35,000 consecutive patients, suggested that accidents were more likely to arise when the individual was under stress.

The concept seems reasonable but is not easy to verify, for it requires measurement of total stress loading on the individual and this is most difficult to obtain. The British Medical Research Council (1968) commented that some stresses may combine to increase the total stress loading while others may have opposing effects, so that the total stress loading is less than the sum of the individual components. Moreover, certain stresses may combine synergistically at one level and antagonistically at another, as in the case of sleep deprivation and alcohol.

A solution to the practical problem of assessing the effects of stress was proposed by McGlade (1968); he pointed out the consequences of stress that were both measurable and significant for preventing injury were human performance decrement and inappropriate human response. Measurement of these, he suggested, would help to establish the influence of stress on injury incidence.

Limitations of the Model

There are two apparent objections to the model. First, it seems drastically to oversimplify the chain of events that culminate in injury, and therefore to discount the multifactorial causality that is present in most injury sequences. This is not so, however, for the model is directed at an evaluation of all the behavioral, mechanical and environmental factors in terms of their significance and their consequences on error commission and intensification of hazard. In short, the model is concerned, not with causal factors themselves, but with the mechanism through which they operate; thus it relates the effects of those factors to injury as a possible consequence.

The other apparent objection to the model is that, by emphasizing the role of human error, it may appear concerned with blame, since the term "error" commonly carries a connotation of fault. For this reason, the phrase "nonculpable error" has been used as a necessary, though rather clumsy, means of emphasizing that the concept of fault cannot arise from the definitions of the terms used. Descriptions of missing or inappropriate responses are statements of fact and are not emotive attributions of faulty behavior. They are intended to permit the identification of causal factors and, hence, the selection of effective countermeasures. This emphasis is wholly intentional, for it is suggested that the community acceptance of culpability as a sufficient description of causes of injury has been a major obstacle to work aimed at its prevention.

Summary

In this paper a model of the injury process is presented in a form suitable for use in teaching techniques of countermeasure evaluation. The model postulates that the conditions necessary for injury to occur are hazard and error. Both terms are defined and the paper stresses the need to regard error, not as a blameworthy act, but as a response governed by some aspect or aspects of the environment. Consequently, by identifying and modifying these aspects, the likelihood of error, and hence of injury, can be reduced.

REFERENCES

Altman, J. W.: Behaviour and accidents. *Journal of Safety Research,* 2:109–122, 1970.

Haddon, W.: The prevention of accidents. In D. W. Clark, and B. McMahon (Eds): *Textbook of Preventive Medicine.* Boston, Little, Brown & Co., 1967.

Heinrich, H. W.: *Industrial Accident Prevention.* New York, McGraw-Hill, 1931.

Kerr, W.: Complementary theories of safety psychology. *Soc Psychol,* 45:3–9, 1957.

McFarland, R. A.: Application of human factors engineering to safety engineering problems. *Transactions of the National Congress, National Safety Council, Chicago, Illinois,* 12:49–62, 1967.

McGlade, F.: Psychology in safety management. *Safety Standards,* May–June, 11–17, 1968.

Medical Research Council Applied Psychology Unit: Comment in *Safety and Health: Register of Research,* Addendum No. 1, Para. 1. 2(a) (iii). London, Department of Employment and Productivity, 1968.

Rogg, S. G.: The role of emotions in industrial accidents. *AMA Archives of Environmental Health,* 3:519, 1961.

Schulzinger, J. S.: *The Accident Syndrome.* Springfield, Thomas, 1956.

Wigglesworth, E. C.: Incidence and distribution of occupational injuries in the states of Australia 1965–66. *Journal of Industrial Relations,* 12:20–38, 1970a.

Wigglesworth, E. C.: Accidents in Australia. *Med J Aust,* 1:1113, 1970b.

FOOTNOTE TO REFERENCES

Since completing this paper, the author has read with great interest the recently published result of research carried out in England. Had these references been available to him when writing his paper, he would undoubtedly have wished to cite:

Powell, P. I., Hale, M., Martin, J., and Simon, M.: *2000 Accidents: a shop floor study of their causes.* NIIP Report 21. London, National Institute of Industrial Psychology, 1971.

Hale, A., and Hale, M.: Accidents in perspective. *Occupational Psychology,* 44:115–121, 1970.

5

ON STAGE FOR
SYSTEM SAFETY

E. Duncan Mackenzie

The reader should view this article as an introduction to system safety with the difference that it is worth reading even if one has long since been introduced to system safety.

Part of the difference lies in the author's sketch of the role of the individual in system safety as contrasted with the role of the individual in typical industrial safety. The uses and limitations of system safety on the industrial scene are clarified in that contrast. His brief catalog of methods of analysis gives this article some special uses to the student of safety. Finally, his exposition of fault tree analysis, and the symbols used in the logic diagram, are fundamental and remain as good today as when the article was written.

SYSTEM SAFETY has evolved as a discipline in aerospace engineering because it was found necessary in the industry to insure product function and consequent personnel safety. It is a new and relatively unknown discipline to the industrial safety engineer, by whom it is misunderstood and often felt to be an intrusion on his normal function.

Industrial safety and system safety have a common base in saving lives, yet there is considerable difference in their philosophy and approach. Stripped to the naked bones, system safety is oriented to "hardware systems" while industrial safety is more in the direction of a people-directed activity.

There are good reasons for this—some are historical and others are the result of circumstance. The industrial safety engineer usually finds himself in a fixed manufacturing situation that neither legislation nor heaven can change. The very history of

From *Journal of American Society of Safety Engineers*, October, 1968.

industrial safety is that of Topsy; it "just grew," and with its engineering requirements, it developed over the years to become a recognized engineering discipline.

Well-rounded industrial safety is a function of the larger industry. Without activity of governmental agencies and the insurance industry there would be very little done in the small shop. However, small shops prosper and grow larger, and once a serious loss occurs, there is an overnight awakening and a desperate need for a safety engineer.

When this happens, the industrial safety engineer is pushed "on stage" in an industry which is running with equipment and methods that cannot be altered radically. He finds himself in the midst of hazards, all of which have been accepted as part of the industry. His only approach is one of either isolating the people from the hazards or the hazards from the people. The hazards themselves may often be beyond redemption, although the safety engineer who is worth his desk space will ingeniously continue to dull their fangs.

The system safety engineer is interested primarily in the function of a system. In the areas in which systems are analyzed, lives may be lost if the systems do not work, regardless of the actions of the individual. The first concern thus is that the system work as intended. If it does, then it is impossible for an injury to occur. For example, in an airplane engine, if the ignition fails, instead of coasting to a stop and tying a handkerchief to the door handle as one would do when riding in an automobile, a person may have to swim many miles to the nearest restaurant or be unwrapped from a stubborn tree. Thus, aircraft engines have dual ignition systems. In a spacecraft, if the retro rockets fail to fire when it is time for reentry, sailing through space for the next month or two with only one week's supply of oxygen can be fatally depressing.

System-safety techniques were thus the result of a need to investigate and eliminate hardware malfunctions or discrepancies in design that could have disastrous results. In these examples, you will note that the individual has no control over the hazards to which he is subjected. The hazard is the system and it must be guarded as one does a hazardous machine. The only means of guarding is to analyze it so that perfection can be anticipated. Obviously an individual, in the use of a perfect system, can make errors which will cause accidents. Regardless of what precautions are taken, people will forever be the unknown quantity in accident events.

The primary difference between the approach to safety problems, system versus industrial, is the control over the accidental event which is exercised by the individual. In most industrial situations the worker can exercise unusual care, use safety equipment, be well supervised, and avoid injury. In a system safety area there is nothing that the individual can do to prevent an accident if the system fails. It is the system itself which must be made fail-proof.

There are situations in industry where systems may fail and cause accidents which the individual cannot control. For example, a crane may fail and drop a load, yet the individual has partial control in that he can keep himself from under the load. Many of the unusual expensive accidents that occur in industry are the result of system failure either in procedure or equipment. Proper procedure may not have been followed because it was not studied and written, or equipment has failed because it was not adequately examined in a system-safety manner.

Aerospace systems are very complicated and are so interdependent that they are not analyzed as easily. Many analysis methods, such as the following, are now in use:

Gross-Hazard Analysis

Performed early in design; considers over-all system as well as individual components; it is called "gross" because it is the initial safety study undertaken.

Classification Of Hazards

Identifies types of hazards disclosed in Step 1, and classifies them according to potential severity (would defect or failure be catastrophic?); indicates actions and/or precautions necessary to reduce hazards. May involve preparation of manuals and training procedures.

Failure Modes And Effects

Considers kinds of failures that might occur and their effect on the over-all product or system. Example: Effect on system that will result from failure of a single component (a resistor or hydraulic valve, for example.)

Hazard-Criticality Ranking

Determines statistical, or quantitative, probability of hazard occurrence: Ranking of hazards in the order of "most critical" to "least critical."

Fault-Tree Analysis

Traces probable hazard progression. Example: If failure occurs in one component or part of the system, will fire result? Will it cause a failure in some other component?

Energy-Transfer Analysis

Determines interchange of energy that occurs during a catastrophic accident or failure. Analysis is based on the various energy inputs to the product or system, and how these inputs will react in event of failure or catastrophic accident.

Catastrophe Analysis

Identifies failure modes that would create a catastrophic accident.

System/Subsystem Integration

Involves detailed analysis of interfaces, primarily between systems.

Maintenance-Hazard Analysis

Evaluates performance of the system from a maintenance standpoint. Will it be hazardous to service and maintain? Will maintenance procedures be apt to create new hazards in the system?

Human-Error Analysis

Defines skills required for operation and maintenance. Considers failure modes initiated by human error and how they would affect the system. The question of whether special training is necessary should be a major consideration in each step.

Transportation-Hazard Analysis

Determines hazards to shippers, handlers, and bystanders. Also considers what hazards may be "created" in the system during shipping and handling.

Of these techniques, one of the most revealing is the fault tree, a relatively new method originated at the Bell Telephone Laboratories and further developed by Boeing for safety analysis. In addition to finding human errors, and hardware failure results, fault trees find critical errors which may be committed in assembly, maintenance, checkout or installation. Starting with the worst cases, the fault tree is an excellent tool for determining the criticality of the errors it considers.

To illustrate the use of the fault tree and the philosophical difference between system and industrial safety in a very simple way, the punch-press problem may be used. The fault tree is shown in Figure 5–1, and explanation of the symbols in Figure 5–2.

First, an undesired event must be selected. In the case of the punch press it could be "injury to operator" (Fig. 5–1). The fault tree is made by listing events which may occur, all dependent on one another and connected by either AND (.) gates or OR (+) gates. The difference between the gates is that flow through an AND (.) gate is possible only when every event listed is occurring. Thus, A, B, and C all must be occurring before F can occur. The flow through an OR (+) gate happens when any of the listed events occurs; thus D or E together or separately can cause A to occur.

From examination of the fault tree, it immediately becomes apparent that for an accident to happen, three things must occur and they must occur together.

1. The press must be operating (C)
2. The ram must be in the descent mode (A)
3. The employe's hand must be under the die (B)

Obviously, if any of these three conditions can be eliminated,

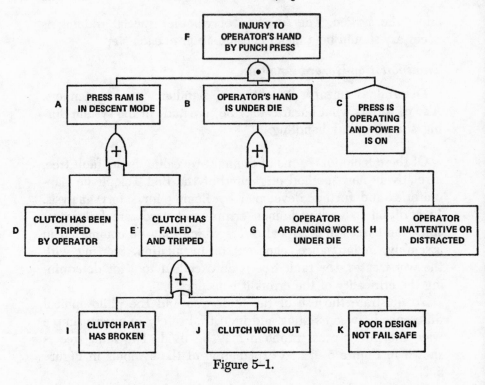

Figure 5–1.

an accident on the press is an impossibility. Knowing this, the industrial safety engineer recognizes that the easiest and most practical means is the elimination of B, that is, keeping the employee's hand from under the die. The means of doing this are many and are known to every industrial safety engineer.

By the very nature of his aerospace experience, however, the system engineer looks to the equipment or system for a solution to the problem. He thus is forced to find means of making the hardware (punch press) foolproof or fail-safe. This would mean a continuing examination of the hardware until some means could be found to eliminate the chances of a system failure that could cause an accident such as:

1. Clutch has been tripped
2. Clutch has failed
3. Part has broken
4. Design is poor (not fail-safe)
5. Maintenance is poor (clutch worn out)

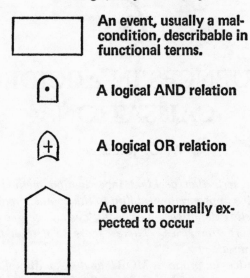

An event, usually a malcondition, describable in functional terms.

A logical AND relation

A logical OR relation

An event normally expected to occur

Figure 5–2. Explanation Of Symbols Used In Figure 1.

You will note in the above list that human failures (4 and 5) have been included in the analysis. Possibly a solution would not be found that was in the range of reason operationally and cost-wise. In these instances the hazard must be assessed and proper trade-offs made.

The fault-tree example used in this article is most simple and uncomplicated. Visualize a complicated system with interfacing and equally complicated systems and it becomes apparent that the tree can become unusually complex. Before the tree can be used properly it must be reduced to its simplest terms. Since it is a logic diagram this is done by means of Boolean algebra. For a complicated tree the only efficient means is the computer.

In this discussion the differences between system and industrial safety have been pointed out. System safety is a very specialized area and technique, some of which can be used to advantage in industrial safety. It would be particularly useful in analyzing products and systems for safety and performance, and in the study of power networks to eliminate the Eastern seaboard blackout of a few years back. Once thoroughly understood, it should become another tool in the ever-growing safety arsenal.

6

SEQUENCES IN ACCIDENT CAUSATION

W. G. Johnson

The author asserts that accident investigation methods and summaries must "give appropriate visibility to the complex realities, rather than the simplistic categorization of conditions and acts so often found in accident report summaries." There's more to it than mere unsafe conditions and unsafe acts.

As an alternative, he proposes MORT analysis, a disciplined method for determining the causes and the contributing factors of serious accidents. The method is rigorous but its application in a few cases gives "more useful information than less rigorous study of a large number of accidents." It offers a glimpse of the inner mystery of the accident phenomenon and, more pragmatically, "focuses heavily on a rational assessment of management control systems."

ACCIDENTS ARE USUALLY multi-factoral and develop through relatively lengthy sequences of changes and errors. Even in a relatively well controlled work environment, the most serious events involve numerous error and change sequences, in series and parallel. Review of individual reports in organizations with good safety programs shows surprisingly frequent multi-person or inter-department involvements leading to serious accidents. The high frequency of more complex accident causations may arise from the fact that good organizations have successfully handled the simpler potentials. In any event, the very complexity of events leading up to an accident implies that there are many *opportunities* to intervene or interrupt the sequences. It seems essential, therefore, that accident investigation methods and sum-

Reprinted with permission from the *Journal of Safety Research*, a National Safety Council Publication, Volume 5, Number 2, June, 1973.

maries give appropriate visibility to the complex realities, rather than the simplistic categorization of conditions and acts so often found in accident report summaries.

Schulzinger (1956) after a twenty-year study of 35,000 accidents offered two provocative descriptions of sequences:

1. "a dynamic, variable constellation of signs, symptoms and circumstances which together determine or influence the occurrence of an accident."

2. "a synthesis of environmental, psychological, physiological, characterological, and temporal factors."

One of the most useful attempts to show the multi-factoral background of an accident was the "Dynamics of Home Accidents" developed by NSC's Home Safety Conference in the mid-50's (Fig. 6–1). Unfortunately, no parallel occupational diagram has been developed. The model would be appropriate for a self-employed person, except that it fails to recognize the role of purpose, goal, or performance, that must be stressed in models of the occupational safety system. The typical industrial situation also stresses supervisory control and intervention.

Examination of occupational accident case histories suggests that antecedents often develop in a number of sequences involving physical, procedural, and personal elements. Because the occupational setting is more highly structured and controlled, we can look for the sequences of events that affected or changed the separate elements in every aspect of the industrial process, including:

Management
Planning and design
Work environment (including arrangement and signals)
Machine (including tools and equipment and signals)
Material
Supervision
Task procedure
Worker
Fellow worker (or other third party)

Frequently, we find that a number of sequences were developing over a period of time before the interaction that produced an accident. Events in retrospect were on a "collision course."

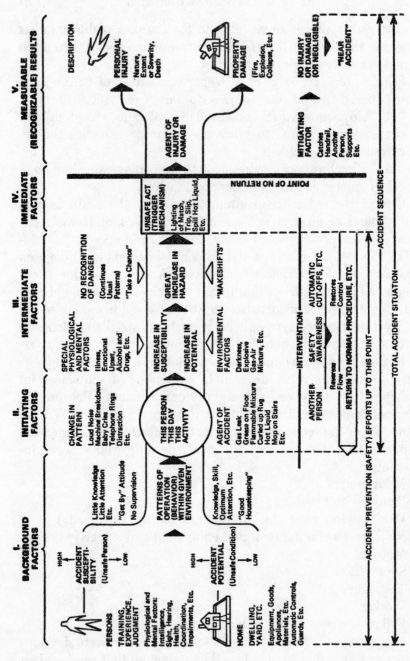

Figure 6-1. The Dynamics Of Home Accidents.

Thus, if we superimpose the home accident model on the above factors, we begin to have a truer picture of accident complexity. We have seen cases where the personal background factors of the designer and planner, the supervisor, and his supervisor all contributed. For example, in discussing a serious incident generated in part by an anomaly in hardware (a failure to match up), a division manager of the plant in which it occurred said, "The plan was written by my worst project engineer and the job was being done on the graveyard shift by my worst maintenance foreman with my weakest building supervisor. In all, four other persons were involved, and three of them made mistakes."

Among the apparent sources of complexity revealed in accidents is the nonroutine operating mode. Trials and tests, maintenance and inspection, change-over or repair, starting or stopping, special jobs, trouble-shooting, and incipient problems (rather than normal routine operations), appear with startling frequency in thorough investigations. From the preventive view, this suggests that the Hazard Analysis Process (HAP) should consider nonroutine operations and specify needed controls. Failure to see or heed signs of impending trouble and failure to pause or stop for diagnosis/correction are frequent. Thus, HAP should give careful thought to signals and appropriate action.

The use of conditional probabilities (a measurement technique finding value in medicine) has been suggested by Edwards (NSC Symposium, 1970) as a method of hazard analysis for lengthy sequences.

The major investigation reports prepared under Atomic Energy Commission procedures commonly show lengthy sequences of causal factors, an average of sixteen per case for one sample. Similarly, the reports of major investigations of the National Transportation Safety Board (NTSB) contain a substantial number of recommendations for interrupting sequences leading to accidents.

A recent pipeline accident report (1972) by the NTSB provides the basis for sequential analysis (See Fig. 6–2). An error at inception (faulty weld) was undetected (which could be shown as another error). Corrosion (a change over time) combined with a failure to detect resulted in a weakened condition. In a separate

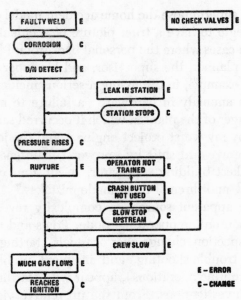

Figure 6–2. Gas Pipeline Accident Sequence.

sequence, a station leak and automatic stop of pumps caused pressure rise and rupture. After rupture, three sequences increased the severity: (1) An untrained operator (a management error) erred in not using a crash button; (2) omission of check valves was a very early error or assumed risk; and (3) a field crew was slow in isolating the rupture. Thus, much gas flowed, filled a rural valley, and reached a source of ignition. Even this lengthy sequence understates the management failures in design, installation, operating, and monitoring.

To more fully reflect the complexity of real world accident events in the industrial field, I have developed the Management Oversight and Risk Tree (MORT). MORT is a complex analytic procedure that provides a disciplined method for determining the causes and contributing factors of serious accidents. Significantly, it is also a format for evaluating the quality of safety programs intended to control accidents in general. MORT is sufficiently searching and revealing that full scale analysis of only a few serious accidents or incidents can point to many needed program improvements. A few MORT analyses give more useful information than less rigorous study of large numbers of accidents. Structurally, MORT is a logic tree in the form of eight pages of interrelated diagrams. While similar in some respects to fault tree analysis, it is more generalized and has several innovative characteristics. In its current form, MORT identifies 222 specific problem areas that are explored through concise, relevant questions. Applied in sequence, these questions probe factors that constitute three major areas: Specific oversights and omissions, assumed risks, and management system failures.

MORT systematically incorporates such concepts as hazard review, life cycle, energy exchange and barrier analysis, human factors engineering, and job safety analysis. Unlike most other accident investigation and safety program appraisal techniques, MORT focuses heavily on a rational assessment of management control systems. Management program elements are specified in extensive detail and judged to be adequate or less than adequate (or excellent or poor). The standards used for judgment are high and include the best organization practices known as well as system safety principles.

Investigators have said that MORT not only provides a check list of potential factors but also provides an authorization to examine and report management oversights.

Once completed, the MORT procedure provides an all important *visibility* to the accident analysis process than enables an investigator to review the findings, present them meaningfully to others, alter the analysis as additional facts warrant, and record the total effort for later use. MORT provides a comprehensive and practical guide as to *what facts to seek* in completing an accident investigation.

MORT analysis of serious accidents typically shows on the order of twenty-five specific factors and fifteen systemic failures, many of them linked in causal or temporal sequences.

One accident report showed cross-linked sequences of errors and changes that could be diagrammed as shown in Figure 6–3. A man was distracted (change), slipped on wet sealer (error), and fell from sloping roof (accident). He had not tied off to a safety harness (error) because he was hurrying to finish after delay by a safety meeting on falls (change). The supervisor was

FIGURE 3
SEQUENCES OF ERRORS AND CHANGES

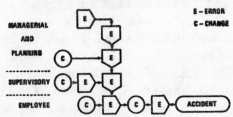

Figure 6–3. Sequences of Errors and Changes.

new (change), he had no written procedure for job (error), and he conducted no pre-job review or briefing (error).

When the building, previously slated to be torn down, was continued in service (change), the engineer ordered a roofing job but failed to comply with a previous accident recommendation to provide a cable for tie-off (error). Intermediate supervision failed to assist new supervisor or audit work order preparation methods. Management failed to specify audit, monitoring, assistance to supervisor, and written procedures.

Having spoken of lengthy sequences, a word of caution may be in order. In either analysis or prevention we are wise to order our thinking in terms of "closeness" to the point of accident, that is, to begin with the accident and work back. Although background situations, if improved, may affect hosts of accidents, there are grave dangers in working on "problems in general." Particularly in trying to deal with the exasperating human factor, we must begin with actual behavior rather than with the often vague antecedent concepts of attitude, responsibility, education, or motivation.

REFERENCES

National Transportation Safety Board: *Pipeline accident report.* Washington, Author, 1972.

Schulzinger, M. S. M. D.: *The accident syndrome.* Springfield, Thomas, 1956.

Surry, J.: *Industrial accident research—A human engineering appraisal.* Toronto, Toronto University, 1968.

7

WHY "SYSTEM SAFETY"?

CHARLES O. MILLER

The author, himself a notable contributor to the emergence of the discipline of system safety, offers more in this article than a historical review. He tells us rather how we came to be where we are.

Caesar's legions are reputed to have had a safety officer, though one wonders why. We sense the "why" of early factory laws even though life was still as cheap as in the days of Rome. Suddenly, in a short decade men thought the thoughts that turned into system safety. Why? What impelled the mighty labors that developed a rigorous discipline from a mere gleam of inspiration? This is what the author seeks to explain. Along the way he suggests much about the modern world and why the safety profession is in ferment.

ONE OF THE impressive-sounding terms you are likely to hear bandied about these days is *system safety*. Does it mean no more than the safety of a system? Or is it a new sort of safety, different in kind from the classical safety of, say, the sword of Damocles?

In fact, the latter is rather nearer the truth, for *system safety* denotes a relatively new way of thinking and working, which emerged formally about seven or eight years ago in the aerospace industry and is now beginning to filter through into civilian life. There are two possible approaches to talking about it: one can try to improve on Webster's, or one can tell the story of how the new philosophy arose. I shall try to do both, in that order.

It can be argued that there is no such thing as "safety." Webster talks about freedom from harm or freedom from hazard. Now, who ever heard of that? Safety, as literally defined, is just an abstraction. But in the working world, safety usually has either

From *Technology Review*, edited at the Massachusetts Institute of Technology, February, 1971. Copyright 1971 by the Alumni Association of the M.I.T.

a "condition" definition or an "activity" definition. It is either a certain state of existence, or it is something we do, intending to prevent harm to somebody (or some thing). In any case, we usually acquire a reasonable feeling for what safety means in our daily lives.

But for the word *system,* you can find many different interpretations. Some people understand the term only as in, say, physical weapons systems—the system comprises, perhaps, an airplane, facilities, personnel, and so forth to accomplish a mission. But it is a mistake to think that the concept of system safety applies only to concatenations of this kind. A much more generalized and, I think, practical approach can be arrived at by thinking as follows. Consider, say, the C-5 airplane. You can view this as an entire weapons system. But just as reasonably, you can isolate a certain part of the C-5—the flight-controls equipment—and call that a system. To one of the subcontractors to the flight-controls manufacturer, a power control unit is a complete system. And so on down to the last nut-and-bolt of the humblest production line worker. The point is that you begin by defining the limits of the system. You view it as something that has inputs and outputs. Knowing of a variety of safety measures, you then begin to see how some of them can be applied in this particular case.

To me, system safety is the integration of skills and resources *specifically organized so as to achieve safety over the entire life cycle of a system.* Albeit this implies some specialists working in safety, all personnel are part of the system-safety effort, and therein rests the power of a system-safety approach. This may all seem somewhat tautologous, but consider what happens when this philosophy is not followed. Suppose a serious catastrophe occurs in operational flight, and it is discovered that, years before, some designer thought this particular failure might conceivably happen, but he considered it was of low priority; later, a flier had worried a little about it in the test phase; but the people who might between them have made an informed judgment never talked to one another. It is not as simple as handing over a product from the man who builds it to the man who operates it. Safety thinking must be organized-for at management level, bringing in all parties.

What does this require that management should know? A generalized professional safety task has been outlined by the American Society of Safety Engineers (in 1966) which, in general terms, is outstanding. But one must be more specific. The table on the next page is a list of fourteen different specific safety tasks that one can present to management as requirement for work assignment. Failing such specificity (and the details of each item are a story unto themselves) the necessary resources will rarely be made available.

When all is said and done, what can really be said to be new or different or unique about system safety? The answer is not simple. However, within the frame of reference of the people operating in system safety today, there are three things which are relatively new ("relatively" meaning the last five years or so).

The first thing is adopting an interconnected (or "systems" approach, rather than just treating each component *in vacuo*. The second is looking at matters on a life-cycle basis, rather than attending only to a thing's ideal, initial performance. Every element of a structure has its own life cycle. And third, people are paying money specifically for our work, because customers are beginning to demand it.

Now how did we arrive at this point? A history of aerospace safety might begin with the 1926 Air Commerce Act, or with the laws that were passed in eighteenth-century France concerning ballon flights over the English Channel, or for that matter with Daedalus's instructions to his son concerning the temperature-dependent behavior of adhesives. But it is really not until World War II—or rather, the years immediately following—that we find anything resembling modern concepts in aerospace safety.

Stateside Losses of World War II

Statistics show that far more aircraft, and indeed far more pilots, were lost in stateside operations during that war than ever were in combat. In 1943, for example, something like 5,000 aircraft were destroyed stateside, against 3,800 in the war proper. Similar ratios held for crewmen. Some statisticians tried to point out that these data really were not significant because, after all, more flying was done stateside than in combat. But the top generals, looking at the war in retrospect, saw that their ability to do a job (in this case combat) was being severely degraded by losses that were just pure accidents. Thus, people came to realize that safety means more than just concern for people—it also concerns the overall mission of an organization.

Then, shortly after World War II, in the period 1946 to 1948, people in military aviation were astonished by a new accident peak. They had thought that when the number of operations decreased things would calm down. On the contrary, the effects of minimal training of new personnel and the demobilization of experienced people produced a fantastic rise in the accident rate. Thus the war experience, plus this immediate postwar experience, resulted in a call to the technical community for help.

In 1948, William Stieglitz, who is still quite active in automotive as well as aviation safety, gave the landmark paper in what today has become known as system-safety engineering. "Safety," he said, "must be designed and built into airplanes just as are performance, stability, and structural integrity . . . a safety group must be just as important a part of a manufacturer's organization as stress, aerodynamics, weights, and so forth . . . safety (too) is a specialized subject." He made one interesting prediction: that accident prevention would have to be improved at a much accelerated rate if a rapid increase in the total number of accidents and fatalities was to be prevented. In other words, more than twenty years ago he described what is facing the civil aviation community today. The accident *rates* are low—very low—but projected ten or twenty years into the future they combine with the rising numbers of aircraft to produce a totally unacceptable situation.

The same period saw the development of atomic energy and atomic weapons. This was a rather interesting event in safety because by edict, the numerical requirement was that we should have no accidents. As a result, certain "system-safety" techniques were developed.

The decade of the 1950's will go down in the safety business as reflecting the influence of the military. I am primarily speaking of the aviation, missiles, and space field; I leave it to the reader's judgment as to whether my remarks are more generally applicable. In the early 1950's, the Directorate of Flight Safety Research was formed at Norton Air Force Base; it was formed by General Victor E. Bertrandias, who had a unique philosophy of life: if a contractor would like to do business with the Air Force, then he should get some people involved in safety work at Norton. The theory that accidents can be prevented, though simple enough, was nevertheless revolutionary in those days. Shortly thereafter, joint Air Force-industry meetings began to be held. There have been nearly sixty of them over the years, where the lessons of experience have been exchanged on a highly informal basis.

The same General Bertrandias, together with the late Dean Carl Hancey, started the University of Southern California's safety activities. Since 1953 U.S.C. has graduated somewhere between 5,000 and 6,000 safety officers, civilian and military, from a course that gives them the equivalent of a year of college specifically in accident prevention.

The early 1950's also saw the formation of other military safety centers in aviation: by the Navy, a couple of years after the Air Force, and the Army, a couple of years after the Navy. Plots of accident rates of the Air Force, Navy, and Army, in that sequence, show similar time intervals between marked decreases in slope.

The Complexity Barrier

As far as I know, the first paper that had the term *system safety* in its title was written about this time. The term came into use when the "complexity barrier" raised its ugly head among the weapon systems. I vividly recall trying to understand a fully powered aircraft flight-control system and then trying to explain to some ingenuous pilot that he was connected from his stick to the airplane's elevators by a little slider valve which could move his elevator to its full throw by moving something like a quarter of an inch—an idea that the pilot didn't buy too easily, and perhaps with good reason.

When failures occurred in this kind of equipment, the hazards broke across us like a tidal wave. We were soon concerned not only with trying to develop weapons systems from a standpoint of schedule and cost, but also with how to keep them in the air without killing people faster than they were being trained. And, except for the benevolence of some managements, not too much of our thinking was finding its way into the actual programs at the early engineering phases.

The Navy then got into the act, in what I think is one of the key developments in this whole business. The Navy formed what they called the BuWeps Industry Material Reliability Board—the industry and customer getting together to try to solve common problems that showed up in bad accident records. In this case, the emphasis was on reliability and maintenance. This particular group in 1957 was significant, too, I think, because they recognized that you cannot deal only with the mainstream fields. They established working groups which eventually, over the years, recognized the so-called "ility" disciplines (maintainability, and so on, with safety included) that supplement the basic line management of a project.

There were a few other significant events late in the 1950's. There was an Air Force B-50 that inadvertently dropped a special weapon over South Carolina. Although nothing detonated except a few pounds of conventional explosive and the event was cloaked in security for a long while, the case caused something of a stir in U.S.A.F. Command circles. Many years earlier, a "no-accidents" requirement had been written, but when the Air Force took a look at the systems aspect of this incident (how well the crews were trained, what combination of circumstances initiated the dropping of this store, and so on) what they found was pretty shocking. History will show, I think, that this incident set off quite a bit of systems analysis thinking to try to preclude a special weapon from detonating inadvertently.

Then, of course, there was Sputnik. If the 1950's showed the influence of the military, the 1960's were mainly influenced by the space race. I recall a conversation at Boeing in Seattle, in the very early design stages of the DynaSoar project. We were trying to decide what kind of an escape system this boost-glide vehicle should have. Amid all the pontificating, one of the experts suggested that "we get back to the fundamentals . . . that what we really need is a lifeboat approach . . . if you get in trouble just put a lifeboat over the side." But then came a very fundamental question. "If you put a lifeboat over the side, you escape; but where are you escaping to?"

This, to my mind, symbolized the change that took place in aerospace safety as we entered the space age. We encountered much more complex hazards. This was true of the environment (radiation or meteorite penetration), of the energy that might be stored in the new booster engine, and of the unprecedented degree of complexity over what had seemed already too complex a few years earlier in aviation. We all had to become accustomed to another order of magnitude of hazards, not only in manned vehicles, but also, perhaps even more so, in missiles.

Arms Without the Man

Indeed, it was in the missile field that the first real breakthrough by way of a well defined system-safety program actually occurred. It began there not only because the customer demanded it, but also because, in a missile, no human operator was on the spot to correct misbehavior, so it had to be designed safer than when he was present. We often look upon man as the cause of accidents, but in my humble opinion he is really the most powerful means of preventing an accident. The proof was the emergence of system-safety engineering into legitimacy in unmanned programs like Atlas and Minuteman.

The influence that emanated from the missile program can be traced to a Navy specification, MIL-S-23069, dated October 31, 1961, which specifically dictated "system life cycle" programs for accident prevention. Most people in the aerospace field today, though, rightfully give the U.S.A.F. Ballistic Systems Division (B.S.D.) the lion's share of the credit for requiring, in some formalized sense, a system-safety engineering program. This effort was outlined in B.S.D. Exhibits 62–41 in 1962.

From then on, other specifications came into being. The first one applied to all U.S.A.F. aerospace systems (MIL-S-38130); the Air Force instituted this one in the fall of 1963. Certain parts of the Navy had been pushing for this approach as hard as they possibly could, but while they were attempting to get the basis of this specification "through channels," a very active gentleman in the Air Force pushed it through their administrative mill and got it out. It appears that some of the Navy people then decided they didn't need such a measure, if the Air Force was taking care of it. It wasn't until three years later that MIL-S-38130, with an addendum, became a Department of Defense safety-engineering specification. The current version of what the Department of Defense feels should be the elements on the system-safety program is known as MIL-STD-882. Significantly, MIL-STD-882 goes beyond the engineering approach per se and includes principles of a total system safety program.

All this activity in the military and space fields began to infect other areas. For example, in 1965, the supersonic transport program was in the final competition phase between Lockheed and Boeing. During this time, the Federal Aviation Agency established a system-safety office and told the contractors to come up with a system-safety program. In addition, Mission Safety 70 was created at the federal level, affecting all government agencies. Although this was basically ground-safety initiated and oriented, it had the effect of making people look around to see how many different safety branches—real or potential—they might have in a given organization. This was especially true in the Air Force, certainly true in other government agencies, and possibly true in many manufacturing organizations.

Next came the Apollo fire that killed three astronauts at Cape Kennedy. Until this time, N.A.S.A.'s safety program was fragmented at best. When the world spotlight focused on astronauts being killed by the simple ignition of some oxygen with some burnable materials, the event forced N.A.S.A. to consider the system aspects of safety, in a way that was probably unmatched by any single impact in any organization on our time.

Airliners, Railroads

In the last year or two, there is reason to believe that the Air Transport Association (which is concerned with air carrier aviation) has been giving serious consideration to a self-regulating system-safety specification applicable to commercial manufacturers. In the same recent period the Navy, through its ships divisions, has taken a much more than casual interest in the system approach to safety. In 1968, Joseph J. O'Connell, first Chairman

of the National Transportation Safety Board, asked the railroads
why they were not taking some kind of a system-safety approach
on their high-speed trains. Bob Currie and Jack Recht have introduced system thinking at the National Safety Council. Carl Clark
has done the same for the products safety field.

So the major influences have been of various kinds. First of all,
there is the effect of many, many agencies, government and non-
government. There is the effect of a number of individuals. There
is what I like to call the critical event syndrome (the Apollo 204
fire, the midair commercial aviation collision over New York, fires
in New York's garment district, and the like). Too often, we need
a catastrophe to get corrective action under way.

In the last few years, safety engineering and safety thinking
throughout the entire life cycle has acquired a recognizable philosophy. We have come to regard accident prevention as our *real*
objective (although injury prevention is never far from the surface). We certainly have come to see accident investigation as
just one (feedback) part of the whole prevention process, and
not as an end to itself. And most important, all safety fields (industrial, nuclear, missile, flight, transportation, or whatever) are
now a lot closer together—a lot more like a single discipline—
than, say, five or ten years ago.

8

PROPAGANDA AND ALTERNATE COUNTER-MEASURES FOR ROAD SAFETY

D. J. GRIEP

The author sees two problems with road safety propaganda, namely that it is usually negative in thrust and that it is aimed toward the difficult task of influencing attitudes. Mr. Griep examines the effect of safety propaganda in some detail. In the full length original article he also examined personalities, legal aspects, and suggested some priorities for research. Space does not permit inclusion of all of this material. The reader will find the examination and review of the findings of others most interesting, particularly the safety campaigns that have taken place in the United States. There is much to learn of American campaigns from the frank evaluation by a European.

THE GENERAL PROBLEM OF ROAD SAFETY PROPAGANDA

The first problem which confronts most road safety propaganda campaigns is the fact that, through coupling the desirable way of behaving with "safe" or "correct" behaviour, they approach the road-user in a negative way. They do this firstly because the road-user is being faced with the possibility of being involved in an accident, and secondly because it is being put to him that his behavior is open to improvement, even though he may have been involved in very few traffic accidents or none.

The probability, per mile travelled, of being involved in an accident is, after all, very low and consequently so is the personal experience of driving danger. This detracts from the credibility of the propaganda.

From *Accident Analysis and Prevention*, Vol. 2, Pergamon Press 1970, England.

Most drivers, moreover, rate themselves as having more than average ability where (safe)driving is concerned, so that the only occasion on which they actually did have an accident will sooner be blamed on the stupidity of other road-users than on wrong driving behavior on their own part.

The result will be that road safety propaganda may be looked upon as quite right and proper, but then as applying to all the other drivers. The second problem with safety propaganda is that it is generally aimed at influencing the "attitude" towards a certain way of behavior or possibilities of behavior. Attitudes and behaviour cannot, however, be regarded as one and the same thing; a person can agree entirely with statements about the undesirability of a certain line of behavior (e.g. because this incurs risks) and yet still act in this very way himself. Faverge (1967) gives striking examples of this in the observance of safety rules by industrial workers.

The reverse, too, can happen—the desired behaviour is practised without it necessarily stemming from a positive attitude. Enquiry as a rule then seems to reveal a positive attitude, but this may have sprung from the practising of the required behavior and will thus have played no part in the proper behavior coming about.

Before coming to any conclusion as to the value of propaganda as a means of influencing driving behavior (and, consequently, road safety) we shall first examine the empirical findings from research on the effects of road safety propaganda paying special attention to accident data.

THE EFFECT OF ROAD SAFETY PROPAGANDA

Propaganda as a means of influencing driving behaviour has a number of aspects, involving both the themes stressed and the method of approach. The approach may be "mass" (i.e. using a mass media of communication) or more individual (by means of a letter, a lecture or a group discussion).

Themes can be general or more specific; a general theme, for example, would be "Drive carefully, don't take risks," while a specific theme would be "Don't drink and drive."

Apart from being general or specific, themes can also differ by relating to a manner of behavior or a possibility for behavior. A manner of behavior is, for example, "keep over to the right"; a possibility for behaviour would, where the vehicle is concerned, be ensuring that the steering works properly, for road conditions it would cover good road markings and for the driver it would include good physical condition (not driving when tired or non-sober). Leaving aside the proper manner of behavior, the aspects of possibilities for behaviour which have been specially stressed in propaganda up to now have been those concerning the driver (and his car), while those concerned with the road have been covered very little if at all. These possibilities of behaviour lie outside the responsibility of the driver, but they are no less important for road safety—quite the contrary. We shall come back later to this topic of "alternative means of influencing driving behaviour." Data, in the form of campaigns already carried out and the results achieved, are not available for all types of propaganda. Details of two variants of the mass approaches, varying in the specificity of their theme are known; aside from these, there is also information in the literature on individual methods of approach.

Mass Approach with a General Theme

On December 1st, 1955, a "Safe Driving Campaign" was opened throughout the United States on the initiative of the then President, Mr. Eisenhower, and his special committee on traffic safety (see also Blumenthal, 1964). This campaign appealed to the moral and social duty of road-users to ensure safe driving behaviour. The idea was obviously that many, if not all, road accidents arise from human errors which could be avoided by adopting a better attitude towards one's fellow man.

For a month before Safety Driving Day and during the month that followed, no expense of effort was spared to bring the message of "a day with no accidents" home to every road-user through the media of press, radio, T.V., posters, stickers, match boxes, buttons, bracelets and even "Safety Day" balloons.

The results all over the country were rather disappointing. On Safety Day itself there was one road death more than on the corresponding day in the previous year; and over the whole campaign period (November and December) the number of deaths was 10 to 12 percent up on the same months of the preceding year, not lower as expected. The difficulty with this campaign was that the theme in fact told the driver nothing. The message that was being put over did not remove uncertainty in his mind in the sense that the person hearing it ended up not knowing whether he was acting "for" or "against" safety on the road.

Even if this were so, the message—which was appealing solely to the motivation—gave no information on what the desirable line of behavior was.

Mass Approach with a Specific Theme (Alcohol)

When we see the meagre—if indeed any—results of the 1955 Safety Day campaign in the United States, we may wonder whether this lack of any clear effect was due to concentrating too much on a general way of behavior, formulated in abstract terms, and not on a specific way or possibility of behaviour described in concrete terms.

The results of campaigns with specific themes have however, so far as we know, not been much better.

An example of this is the "Drinking and Driving" campaign run in Britain at Christmas 1964. No positive results from this could be seen in the shape of any reduction in the number of (alcohol) accidents over the period in question compared to the number of such accidents forecast on the basis of comparable periods in the preceding year (R.R.L., 1965).

The absence of any demonstrable beneficial effects on road safety from this campaign cannot be blamed on any lack of illustrations of the horrifying consequences of accidents. One might even suggest that these illustrations were too emotionally loaded; we shall consider this point in a moment.

The most realistic line of reasoning seems to be this: for most drivers who have been involved in an accident while intoxicated, the experience is enough to dissuade them from drunken driving in the future—so the propaganda will produce no extra effect. On the other hand the drivers who do occasionally drive when they are not sober, and yet have not so far been involved in an "alcohol accident," rate the chances of such a thing happening as very low.

Any further information, such as publicity based on the possible results of an accident, will not then be felt to be relevant.

Emotional, Humorous and "Realistic" Approaches

In 1961 a warning was given of the negative effects of emotional ("scare") techniques (Malfetti, 1961):

> Scare techniques intended to raise a high degree of fear to improve driving are common. They are practiced primarily by officials and citizen groups sincerely devoted to reducing highway tragedies. Informed opinion of traffic safety specialists and the findings of experimental psychological studies in related fields suggest that while these techniques are sometimes effective in creating public interest in safety, they are, as presently conceived, ineffective in improving the behavior of individual drivers. In fact, they may do more harm than good.

The same author concludes his article with the following words:

> My research for this paper convinces me that specialists in the human sciences have devoted extraordinarily little attention to the motivational aspects of pleasant emotions, and no attention at all to the relation of these to driving.

We may wonder in this correlation whether an approach which drew attention to the pleasures of driving on the one hand and the pleasures of drinking on the other, at the same time pointing out the incompatibility of the two, might not have more effect than an approach which stresses the miseries and dangers of both activities.

One must however comment, as an aside, that this approach in fact provides no other information than advice to abstain from one or other of these activities. It is not made clear how the driver is to be compensated for following this advice.

In the Netherlands we have the humorous slogan "Glaasje op? Laat je rijden" (Had a couple? Let someone else drive), in which the pleasure of having a drink is linked with a pleasant alternative for driving oneself. Whether it is a possible or inviting proposition to "let someone else drive" is unclear so long as adequate facilities for this are not created, e.g. in the form of public transport during the night hours, and especially at weekends when the number of nonsober drivers is at its highest.

This furthermore shows how the claim that less horrifying campaigns of this kind do have an effect can be disputed so long as these do not put forward any concrete alternative and desirable ways of behavior, and most of all so long as adequate and inviting facilities to help bring this better behavior about are not available. These facilities will be inviting when the alternative means of transport are cheaper, quicker and more comfortable or when there are cheaper and more pleasurable (but less dangerous) luxuries. These two conditions were not met at the time of the campaigns carried out to date.

There then remains the "realistic" approach—pointing out the adverse consequences of the undesirable behavior, in the form of fines, imprisonment, disqualification from driving and paying compensation for damages caused; in other words, bringing home the threat of punishment.

Two points have to be borne in mind here:

1. Up to now there is evidence that moderate punishments do not have a lesser effect than heavy ones;

2. We do not know whether the tendency among gamblers to place greater faith in a small chance of a big win than in a greater chance of a small win also applies if "loss" is substituted for "win" and in particular when the "loss" is that suffered from legal prosecution and the "chance" is that of being caught in the act.

Individual Approach

IMPROVING MORAL STANDARDS. In some countries, notably the United States, an attempt has been made to persuade drivers who have, within a short period of time, been involved in a relatively large number of traffic accidents or offences to improve their behavior by means of a "driver improvement programme."

This program usually has a number of components: an official letter in which the driver is warned, or advised to attend an improvement course; the improvement course itself, consisting of an interview with the police and/or group discussion with other "traffic offenders"; and, as a last resort, suspension of the driving license.

The idea is that a personal interview and/or group discussion can achieve an improvement in moral standards and consequently also in behavior and traffic safety.

Kaestner (1968) gives a survey of the main studies so far carried out in this field, and their results. This shows that an effect can be seen in a number of the studies, in that the treated group when compared to a control group (who were not given this treatment but were otherwise comparable) were involved in fewer offences, although they were just as involved in accidents. Furthermore, where traffic offences were concerned it was found that a reduction could also be brought about by merely sending a letter telling the driver that, because of his past history of accidents and/or offences, he was being considered for a driver improvement program!

This kind of result is perhaps explicable when we consider that the drivers who are written to or given an improvement course may subsequently drive so as to attract less attention (from the police) but that this need not mean that their behavior reduces the likelihood of their having an accident. At best the attitude, but not the driving ability, will be affected, bearing in mind the aims and methods of the driver improvement program (Kaestner, 1968).

With courses of this kind it is made clear—in a favorable case —at verbal level that certain ways of behaving are more desirable and others less so; but the actual danger of a certain pattern of action is not personally experienced, nor are other patterns as an alternative to the undesirable one taught.

SUSPENSION OF DRIVING LICENSE. As for the last element in the driver improvement program, suspension of the driving license, it must be said that the effect this has in reducing the number of accidents is still not clear. For if this measure is to succeed, then the drivers whose license is taken away will need to be afflicted with an extra likelihood of having another accident in the future.

This is, in general, not the case since most (90% or more) accidents are "first" accidents compared to the preceding year. On the other hand it is found that, of the small group of "accident

TABLE 8–I

ACCIDENT CONTRIBUTION BY PREVIOUS DRIVING RECORD

	Total number of drivers *	Drivers involved in accidents in 1963		Drivers not involved in accidents in 1963		Total accidents in 1963	
		number	percent of total drivers	number	percent of total drivers	number	mean per 100 drivers
Drivers involved in accidents in 1961 and 1962	1,100	145 † 105 †	13	995	87	161	14–6
Drivers not involved in accidents in 1961 and 1962	129,524	6,931	5	122,593	95	7,340	5–7

* Totals exclude 17,382 subjects who had accidents in only one of the 2 years.

† In the original paper the number 145 is printed. This must be an error, since the total number of drivers then would be 1,140 instead of 1,100. The figure of 105 probably is the right number since then horizontal and vertical totals are correct (From Coppin, et al., 1965).

repeaters," not all drivers will be involved in a fresh accident in the future. Table 8–I gives an illustration.

These figures are based on a representative sampling of drivers in California for the years 1961 to 1963 (Coppin, et al., 1965). They illustrate that eliminating the 1100 accident repeaters would give only a slight improvement in the accident rate, from

$$\frac{7036}{130,624} = 5.39\% \text{ to } \frac{6931}{129,524} = 5.35\%.$$

The reduction of 0.04 percent less accidents per road-user per year can then be achieved only at the expense of a large number of false negatives (87% were accident-free in 1963, but not in 1961–62) and 5 percent false positives (accident-free in 1961–62 but not in 1963). The fact is that the number of repeated accidents rises as the period of observation extends further into the past. However, because the driving experience also increases with the years, so the liability to accident lessens. Additionally, the drivers who cover a very large mileage each year should, in particular, be eliminated.

It is of course possible that the picture will improve when we examine specific kinds of accident, e.g. accidents due to drinking. The exclusion of alcoholics and/or recidivists from driving would be indicated for safety reasons only if two conditions are satisfied:

1. Involvement in road accidents attributable to alcohol must be a stable phenomenon, i.e. it must be largely the same persons (recidivists) who are involved in this sort of accident.

2. Reliable prediction of the alcohol-accident rate must be possible on the basis of medical, psychological etc. characteristics of persons (alcoholics).

Data on these two conditions have been insufficient up till now. A reasonable assumption is: as stability of the criterion (a) (individual frequency of "alcohol accidents" within a given period of time) increases, the smaller the number of persons involved, and also the less small the possible effect in terms of a reduction of alcohol accidents that can be reached by elimination of these persons (Griep, 1969 and S.W.O.V., 1969).

ATTITUDE AND ACCIDENT LIABILITY

In the matter of propaganda and road safety it has up to now not been possible to show any clearly positive relationships, taking into account the findings of scientific research on the subject. It can be postulated that these meagre results can be blamed on the quality of the campaigns carried out, which have produced insufficient change in the driver's attitude; we do not know whether this is in fact so. One can, however, examine the relationship between existing attitudes and the accident liability. If such a relationship does exist, then propaganda directed towards altering these attitudes for the better can still be significant for road safety. If it does not exist, or applies to only a slight extent, then recommending propaganda campaigns as a means of promoting road safety cannot continue to be justified by pointing to an effect via driver's attitude.

There is a good deal of doubt whether a positive correlation between a favorable attitude and a reduced accident liability does actually exist, and this is true not only with traffic but in industry as well. A survey in this latter field is mentioned by Faverge (1967), showing the relatively minor importance of a favorable or unfavorable attitude compared to actual behavior and the (unintentional) consequences of this behavior in the form of accidents.

The study of Goldstein and Mosel (1958) is often mentioned as showing positive results where the importance of a favorable attitude for reducing the number of accidents is concerned (see, for example, the literature surveys by Goldstein (1961) and Schubert (1965)). The report of the investigation by Goldstein and Mosel shows that out of 24 correlations between 8 attitudes and 3 criteria (accidents, accidents responsible and violations) 3 proved to be greater than zero, with a 95 percent level of confidence.

Two of the correlations being negative, i.e. competitiveness-aggression x violations and competitiveness-aggression x accidents responsible. One correlation was positive, i.e. attitude towards causes of accidents x accidents responsible. That is so to say as the pointed causes of accidents are socially more desirable ("blaming the driver") the higher the accident rate. These findings apply for male drivers. For female drivers 3 out of 24 correlations proved to be greater than zero. All of them being negative, i.e. attitude towards speed x violations; attitude towards cops x accidents; attitude towards cops x accidents responsible.

Difficulties in the interpretation applies also for negative correlations. Goldstein and Mosel show a good deal of reserve: "It would appear that women's experience with cops by way of violations and accidents may promote undesirable attitudes towards cops." In other words, if we are to talk in terms of a possible causative correlation, the (poor) attitudes must be seen as the results rather than as the causes.

We can conclude that the findings in Goldstein and Mosel's study give insufficient support to the assumption that attitudes have a great deal of relevance for whether accidents happen or not. These findings may perhaps rather support the opposite view, that these attitudes are determined by the fact of being or not being involved in accidents. Even this interpretation, however, can be considered as premature, since—with a level of confidence of 95 percent—the probability of getting out of 24 at least 3 correlations greater than zero, amounts to 0.12. That is to say that the odds are 1 to 8 that the results of the study (3 out of 24 correlations significant) are coincidental.

Another study which is frequently cited is that of Tillman and Hobbs (1949) on "antisociability and traffic accidents." Major consequences have been ascribed to the findings, even in the field of psychological selection of drivers. In this study by Tillman and Hobbs it was said to have been found that "antisocial drivers" have a higher liability to accidents. This would however be relevant only if the control group were comparable to the test group in all respects other than this antisociability. If this is not the case, then the difference found could also be explained by more trivial circumstances, such as a higher mileage covered by the test group. From this viewpoint the Tillman and Hobbs study was unfortunate in its design.

A recent study on attitude and accident rate is that by Schuster (1968). This shows that accidents can—better than by chance—be predicted on the basis of the history of accidents and offences, as well as on the basis of an attitude scale. This, however, still tells us nothing about the number of persons who wrongly are, or wrongly are not, alleged to have a heightened accident-liability in the future.

The problem of road safety would, indeed, still remain in practically its entirety were the accident-prone individuals eliminated, unless virtually every road-user were to be prevented from using the road. Most traffic accidents are, after all, "first" accidents. Drivers who are repeatedly involved in accidents make up a very small group relatively speaking, even where the total number of accidents is concerned (see Table 8–1).

A special problem in predicting accidents on the basis of whether traffic offences have or have not been committeed is that, among recorded accidents, there are few which cannot result in a charge being brought, with a flattered correlation as a result. Schuster made allowance for this fact by taking different periods for the collecting of data on offences and data on accidents. In fact this procedure does not offer a satisfactory answer; even in the period during which the accident data are gathered the accidents will still as a rule only be recorded when charges for an offence can be brought (at least in the Netherlands, where official accident data are based on police records).

On the other hand most of the offences will go unnoticed by the police and if noticed will be recorded at places where and times when accidents happen to occur. In that case data gathered on the predictor variable (offences) are (implicitly) selected on the criterion variable (accidents) with a flattered correlation as a result.

Another recent study (Gumper and Smith, 1968) on the correlation between "risk-taking tendency" and accident liability provided no evidence for the hypothesis that car drivers with a high accident-liability can be identified in a reliable way through questionnaires designed to measure the tendency to take risks in various situations.

This is not to say that attitudes have no bearing at all. One can indeed assume that, as for accident-liability (Kerr, 1964) and driving behavior (Michaels and Stephens, 1963; Gordon and Mast, 1968), it is also true for attitudes that the influence of driving conditions on these can be greater than that of the individual differences between drivers.

REFERENCES

Ben-David, G., et al.: A research proposal for the correlation between traffic offences and road accidents and the possibility of changing driving behaviour by means of communication methods. Bar-Ilan University, 1968.

Blumenthal, M. (ed.): The Denver Symposium on Mass Communication Research for Safety. Chicago, National Safety Council, 1964.

Coppin, R. C., et al.: The 1964 California driver record study. State of California. Department of Motor Vehicles, Division of Administration, Research and Statistics Section. 1964.

Faverge, J. M.: *Psychosociologie des accidents du travail* Paris, P.U.F., 1967.

Goldstein, L. G.: Research on human variables in safe motor vehicle operation; A correlation summary of predictor variables and criterion measures. Washington University, 1961.

Goldstein, L. G., and Mosel, J. N.: A factor study of driver's attitudes, with further study on driver aggression. In Driver characteristics and behavior studies. Highway Research Board Bull. No. 1972. National Academy of Sciences, National Research Council, 1958.

Gordon, D. A., and Mast, T. M.: Drivers decisions in overtaking and passing. *Public Roads*, 35 (4):97–101, 1968.

Griep, D. J.: Traffic accidents, visual performance and driving behaviour. In Henkes, H. E. (ed).: *Perspectives in Ophthalmology.* Report of the

1967 Postgraduate Courses held under the auspices of the Netherlands Ophthalmological Society and the Medical Faculty of Rotterdam. Excerpta Medica Foundation, Amsterdam, 1967.

Griep, D. J.: The effectiveness of statutory countermeasures. Paper presented at the Working Party on "Efficacy of general deterrents and individual sanctions," 5th International Conference on Alcohol and Traffic Safety, Freiburg im Breisgau, 1969.

Gumpper, D. C., and Smith, K. R.: The prediction of individual accident liability with an inventory measuring risk-taking tendency. *Traff Saf Res Rev 12* (2):50–56, 1968.

Kaestner, N.: Research in driver improvement. The state of the art. *Traff Q, 22* (4):497–521, 1968.

Kerr, W.: Complementary theories of safety psychology. In Haddon, W. (ed): *Accident Research, Methods and Approaches.* New York, Harper & Row, 1964.

Levonian, E.: Prediction of accidents and convictions. *Traff Q, 15* (2):318–331, 1967.

Michaels, R. M., and Stephens, B. W.: Time sharing between compensatory tracking and search and recognition tasks. Highway Research Record No. 55. National Academy of Sciences. Highway Research Board, Washington, 1963.

Norman, L. G.: Professional drivers and road safety. *Proc 2nd Int Congress Association for Accident & Traffic Medicine,* Stockholm, 1966.

Ouweleen, H. W.: Opleiding en opdoen van rijervaring in verband met de leeftijd. *Nederlands Tijdschrift voor de Psychologie, 14* (1), 1964.

Parry, M. H.: Aggression on the road. A pilot-study of behaviour in the driving situation. London, Tavistock, 1968.

Road Research Laboratory: Road accidents in December 1964 and January 1965. Road Research Technical Paper No. 79. London, H.M.S.O., 1965.

Schubert, G.: Die Auswirkung von Konstitution und Personlichkeit auf die Unfallgefahrdung im Verkehr. Forschungsgemeinschaft "Der Mensch im Verkehr," Koln, 1965.

Schuster, D. H.: Prediction of follow-up driving accidents and violations. *Traff Saf Res Rev, 12* (1):17–22, 1968.

S.W.O.V.: Bijdragen voor de Nota Verkeersveiligheid. Staatsuitgeverij, 's-Gravenhage, 1965, 1967.

S.W.O.V. (Carlquist, J. C. A.): A study of the influence of age and driving experience on accident involvement rates. *Proc Int Road Safety Congress,* Barcelona. Theme V: The problem of the young driver, 1966.

S.W.O.V. (Griep. D. J.): Alcohol and road safety. Counter-measures and research. *A critical survey of the literature,* 2nd ed. Voorburg, Institute for Road Safety Research S.W.O.V., 1969.

Tillmann, W. A., and Hobbs, G. E.: The accident-prone automobile driver. In Haddon, W. (ed.): *Accident Research, Methods and Approaches.* New York, Harper & Row, 1964.

PART II

SAFETY TODAY

Much of the practice of safety today goes hand-in-hand with advancing concepts and philosophies. Thought almost instantly overlaps with someone's practice, even though the overlap may be on a very narrow front. As a result, the contributions selected for this part might readily have been put in other parts, and for that very reason justifies a part devoted to safety today.

9

ON THE ESCAPE OF TIGERS—
AN ECOLOGICAL NOTE

William Haddon, Jr.

The author has combined ideas and techniques on accidental losses into a fascinating, viable concept to reduce injury and damage by preventing unwanted energy transfer.

Ten definite strategies to prevent unwanted energy transfer have been developed. Each strategy counters an opposite that would increase damage. Practical applications can be detected in the work of the Insurance Institute for Highway Safety of which Dr. Haddon is president. The concept of energy transfer has also served in products safety to help a manufacturer foresee how his product might contribute to an accident in some unimaginable circumstance in which it might be used.

In all cases, the safety task is to prevent "the transfer of energy in such ways and amounts, and at such rapid rates, that inanimate and animate structures are damaged." That definition encompasses any task from mopping a slippery spot to inspecting a nuclear warhead to earthquake research. Is the perception of energy transfer a superior path to hazard recognition? Should the safety practitioner become attuned to perceive "energy" instead of "hazards."

Is the concept of energy transfer a gross simplification of the obvious; or has Dr. Haddon distilled a gem-like truth which puts a rock bottom foundation under the safety discipline?

A MAJOR CLASS of ecologic phenomena involves the transfer of energy in such ways and amounts, and at such rapid rates, that inanimate or animate structures are damaged. The harmful interactions with people and property of hurricanes, earthquakes, projectiles, moving vehicles, ionizing radiation, lightning, con-

From *Technology Review*, edited at the Massachusetts Institute of Technology, May 1970. Copyright 1970 by the Alumni Association of the M.I.T.

flagrations, and the cuts and bruises of daily life illustrate this class.

Ten Strategies for Reducing These Losses

Several strategies, in one mix or another, are available for reducing the human and economic losses that make this class of phenomena of social concern. In their logical sequence, they are as follows:

The *first* strategy is to prevent the marshalling of the form of energy in the first place: preventing the generation of thermal, kinetic, or electrical energy, or ionizing radiation; the manufacture of gunpowder; the concentration of U-235; the build-up of hurricanes, tornadoes, or tectonic stresses; the accumulation of snow where avalanches are possible; the elevating of skiers; the raising of babies above the floor, as to cribs and chairs from which they may fall; the starting and movement of vehicles; and so on, in the richness and variety of ecologic circumstances.

The *second* strategy is to reduce the amount of energy marshalled: reducing the amounts and concentrations of high school chemistry reagents, the size of bombs or firecrackers, the height of divers above swimming pools, or the speed of vehicles.

The *third* strategy is to prevent the release of the energy: preventing the discharge of nuclear devices, armed crossbows, gunpowder, or electricity; the descent of skiers; the fall of elevators; the jumping of would-be suicides; the undermining of cliffs; or the escape of tigers. An Old Testament writer illustrated this strategy in the context both of the architecture of his area and of the moral imperatives of this entire field: "When you build a new house, you shall make a parapet for your roof, that you may not bring the guilt of blood upon your house, if any one fall from it" (Deut. 22:8). This biblical position, incidentally, is fundamentally at variance with that of those who, by conditioned reflex, regard harmful interactions between man and his environment as problems requiring reforming imperfect man rather than suitably modifying his environment.

The *fourth* strategy is to modify the rate or spatial distribution of release of the energy from its source: slowing the burning rate of explosives, reducing the slope of ski trails for beginners, and choosing the reentry speed and trajectory of space capsules. The third strategy is the limiting case of such release reduction, but is identified separately because in the real world it commonly involves substantially different circumstances and tactics.

The *fifth* strategy is to separate, in space or time, the energy being released from the susceptible structure, whether living or inanimate: the evacuation of the Bikini islanders and test personnel, the use of sidewalks and the phasing of pedestrian and vehicular traffic, the elimination of vehicles and their pathways from community areas commonly used by children and adults, the use of lightning rods, and the placing of electric power lines out of reach. This strategy, in a sense also concerned with rate-of-release modification, has as its hallmark the elimination of *intersections* of energy and susceptible structure—a common and important approach.

The very important *sixth* strategy uses not separation in time and space but separation by interposition of a material "barrier": the use of electrical and thermal insulation, shoes, safety glasses, shin guards, helmets, shields, armor plate, torpedo nets, antiballistic missiles, lead aprons, buzz-saw guards, and boxing gloves. Note that some "barriers" such as fire nets and other "impact barriers" and ionizing radiation shields, attenuate or lessen but do not totally block the energy from reaching the structure to be protected. This strategy, although also a variety of rate-of-release modification, is separately identified because the tactics involved comprise a large, and usually clearly discrete, category.

The *seventh* strategy, into which the sixth blends, is also very important—to modify appropriately the contact surface, subsurface, or basic structure, as in eliminating, rounding and softening corners, edges, and points with which people can, and therefore sooner or later do, come in contact. This strategy is widely overlooked in architecture with many minor and serious injuries the result. It is, however, increasingly reflected in automobile design and in such everyday measures as making lollipop sticks of cardboard and making some toys less harmful for children in impact. Despite the still only spotty application of such principles, the two basic requisites, large radius of curvature and softness, have been known since at least about 400 B.C., when the author of the treatise on head injury attributed to Hippocrates wrote: "Of those who are wounded in the parts about the bone, or in the bone itself, by a fall, he who falls from a very high place upon a very hard and blunt object is in most danger of sustaining a fracture and contusion of the bone, and of having it depressed from its natural position; whereas he that falls upon more level ground, and upon a softer object, is likely to suffer less injury in the bone, or it may not be injured at all . . ." (Adams, 1939).

The *eighth* strategy in reducing losses in people and property is to strengthen the structure, living or nonliving, that might otherwise be damaged by the energy transfer. Common tactics, often expensively underapplied, include tougher codes for earthquake, fire, and hurricane resistance, and for ship and motor vehicle impact resistance. The training of athletes and soldiers has a similar purpose, among others, as does the treatment of hemophiliacs to reduce the results of subsequent mechanical insults. A successful therapeutic approach to reduce the osteoporosis of many post-menopausal woman would also illustrate this strategy, as would a drug to increase resistance to ionizing radiation in civilian or military experience. (Vaccines, such as those for polio, yellow fever, and smallpox, are analogous strategies in the closely parallel set to reduce losses from infectious agents.)

The *ninth* strategy in loss reduction applies to the damage not prevented by measures under the eight preceding—to move rapidly in detection and evaluation of damage that has occurred or is occurring, and to counter its continuation and extension. The generation of a signal that response is required; the signal's transfer, receipt, and evaluation; the decision and follow-through, are all elements here—whether the issue be an urban fire or wounds on the battlefield or highway. Sprinkler and other suppressor responses, firedoors, MAYDAY and SOS calls, fire alarms, emergency medical care, emergency transport, and related tactics all illustrate this countermeasure strategy. (Such tactics have close parallels in many earlier stages of the sequence discussed here, as, for example, storm and tsunami warnings.)

The *tenth* strategy encompasses all the measures between the emergency period following the damaging energy exchange and the final stabilization of the process after appropriate intermediate and long-term reparative and rehabilitative measures. These may involve return to the pre-event status or stabilization in structurally or functionally altered states.

Separation of Loss Reduction and Causation

There are, of course, many real-world variations on the main theme. These include those unique to each particular form of energy and those determined by the geometry and other characteristics of the energy's path and the point or area and characteristics of the structure on which it impinges—whether a BB hits the forehead or the center of the cornea.

One point, however, is of overriding importance: subject to qualifications as noted subsequently, there is no logical reason why the rank order (or priority) of loss-reduction countermeasures generally considered must parallel the sequence, or rank order, of causes contributing to the result of damaged people or property. One can eliminate losses in broken teacups by packaging them properly (the sixth strategy), even though they be placed in motion in the hands of the postal service, vibrated, dropped, piled on, or otherwise abused. Similarly, a vehicle crash, per se, need necessitate no injury, nor a hurricane housing damage.

Failure to understand this point in the context of measures to reduce highway losses underlies the common statement: "If it's the driver, why talk about the vehicle." This confuses the rank or sequence of causes, on the one hand, with that of loss-reduction countermeasures—in this case "crash packaging"—on the other.

There are, nonetheless, practical limits in physics, biology, and strategy potentials. One final limit is operative at the boundary between the objectives of the eighth and ninth strategies. Once appreciable injury to man or to other living structure occurs, *complete* elimination of undesirable end results is often impossible, though appreciable reduction is commonly achievable. (This is often also true for inanimate structures, for example, teacups.) When lethal damage has occurred, the subsequent strategies, except as far as the strictly secondary salvage of parts is concerned, have no application.

There is another fundamental constraint. Generally speaking, the larger the amounts of energy involved in relation to the resistance to damage of the structures at risk, the earlier in the countermeasure sequence must the strategy lie. In the ultimate case, that of a potential energy release of proportions that could not be countered to any satisfactory extent by any known means, the prevention of marshalling or of release, or both, becomes the only approach available. Furthermore, in such an ultimate case, if there is a finite probability of release, prevention of marshalling (and dismantling of stockpiles of energy already marshalled) becomes the only, and essential, strategy to assure that the undesirable end result cannot occur.

For Each Strategy an Analogous Opposite

Although the concern here is the reduction of damage produced by energy transfer, it is noteworthy that to each strategy there is an opposite focused on increasing damage. The latter are most commonly seen in collective and individual violence—as in war, homicide, and arson. Various of them are also seen in manufacturing, mining, machining, hunting, and some medical and other activities in which structural damage often of a very specific nature is sought. (A medical illustration would be the destruction of the anterior pituitary with a beam of ionizing radiation as a measure to eliminate pathologic hyperactivity.) For example, a maker of motor vehicles or of aircraft landing-gear struts—a product predictably subject to energy insults—could make his product more delicate, both to increase labor and sales of parts and materials, and to shorten its average useful life by decreasing the age at which commonplace amounts of damage increasingly exceed in cost the depreciating value of the product in use. The manufacturer might also design for difficulty of repair by using complex exterior sheet metal surfaces, making components difficult to get at, and other means.

The type of categorization outlined here is similar to those useful for dealing systematically with other environmental problems and their ecology. In brief illustration, various species of toxic and environment-damaging atoms (such as lead), molecules (e.g. DDT), and mixtures (garbage and some air pollutants, among others) are marshalled, go through series of physical states and situations, interact with structures and systems of various characteristics, and produce damage in sequences leading to the final, stable results.

Similar comments can be made concerning the ecology of some of the viral, unicellular, and metazoan organisms that attack animate and inanimate structures; their hosts; and the types and stages of damage they produce.*

Sufficient differences among systems often exist, however—for example, the ecology of the agents of many arthropod-borne diseases is quite complex, and the life cycles of organisms such as schistosomes require two or more different host species in sequence—to preclude at this time many generalizations useful across the breadth of all environmental hazards and their damaging interactions with other organisms and structures.

A Systematic Analysis of Options

It has not generally been customary for individuals and organizations that influence, or are influenced by, damage due to harmful transfers of energy to analyze systematically their options for loss reduction, the mix of strategies and tactics they might employ, and their cost. Yet, it is entirely feasible and not especially difficult to do so, although specific supporting data are still often lacking. In fact, unless such systematic analysis is done

---

* Actual and potential birth control and related strategies and tactics can be somewhat similarly categorized. Thus, in brief, beginning on the male line: preventing the marshalling of viable sperm (by castration or certain pharmacological agents); reducing the amount of sperm produced; preventing the release of semen (or of one of its necessary components, e.g. by vasectomy); modifying the rate or spatial distribution of release of semen (as in hypospadias, a usually developmental or traumatic condition in which the urethra opens on the underside of the penis, sometimes near its base); separating semen release in space or time from the susceptible ovum (e.g. continence, limiting intercourse to presumably nonfertile periods, coitus interruptus, and preventing a fertile ovum from being present when sperm arrive); separation by interposition of a material barrier (e.g. condoms, spermicidal creams, foams, jellies); increasing resistance of the ovum to penetration; making the ovum infertile, even if penetrated; prevention of implantation of the fertilized egg; abortion; and infanticide.

routinely and well, it is generally impossible to maximize the pay-offs both of loss-reduction planning and of resource allocations.

Such analysis is also needed to consider properly the problems inherent in the use of given strategies in specific situations. Different strategies to accomplish the same end commonly have different requirements; in kinds and numbers of people, in material resources, in capital investments, and in public and professional education, among others. In the case of some damage-reduction problems, particular strategies may require political and legislative action more than others. And, where the potential and actual hazard exists across national boundaries, correspondingly international action is commonly essential.

The types of concepts outlined in this note are basic to dealing with important aspects of the quality of life, and all of the professions concerned with the environment and with the public health need to understand and apply the principles involved— and not in the haphazard, spotty, and poorly conceptualized fashion now virtually universal. It is the purpose of this brief note to introduce the pathway along which this can be achieved.

SUGGESTED READINGS

Haddon, W., Jr.: Why the Issue is Loss Reduction Rather Than Only Crash Prevention. Presented at the Automotive Engineering Congress, S.A.E., Detroit, January 12, 1970, S.A.E. Preprint 700196.

Haddon, W., Jr.: The changing approach to the epidemiology, prevention, and amelioration of trauma: the transition to approaches etiologically rather than descriptively based. *Am J Pub Health*, 58:1431–1438, 1968.

Haddon, W., Jr.: The prevention of accidents. In Clark, D. W., and Mac-Mahon, B. (Ed.): *Textbook of Preventive Medicine*. Boston, Little, Brown, and Company, pp. 591–621.

Haddon, W., Jr., Suchman, E. A., and Klein, D.: *Accident Research, Methods and Approaches*. Harper and Row, 1964. (See especially Chapters 9 and 10.)

REFERENCES

Adams, F. (Trans.): *The Genuine Works of Hippocrates*. Baltimore, Williams and Wilkins, 1939.

A. Dismantling nuclear bombs and preventing production. A. I

B. Limiting nuclear bomb size and manufacture. B. II

C. Total nuclear use-ban treaty. C. III

D. Plastic surgery. D. X

E. Making polo goal posts to yield on impact. E. VII

F. Old tires on sides of tugs. F. VI

G. Snuggling auto bumpers in sheet metal. G. Opposite of V

H. Causing earthquakes by damming streams. (See "The Modification of the Planet Earth by Man," by Gordon J. F. MacDonald, Technology Review for October–November, 1969) H. Opposite of I

I. Skin tanning in relation to subsequent sun exposure I. A naturally occurring illustration of VIII

J. Railroad under- and overpasses. J. V

K. Parachutes. K. IV

L. Fire alarms. L. IX

M. Storm cellars in tornado areas. M. V and VI

N. Seeding an established hurricane. N. IV

O. Built-in automobile crash padding. O. VII

P. Fallout shelters. P. VI

Q. Sanding icy sidewalks. Q. III

R. Aircraft carrier arresting gear. R. IV

S. Keeping people out of dry woods. S. III

T. Fire doors. T. VI

U. Boiler safety valves. U. IV

V. Opening volcanoes to achieve controlled release. V. IV

W. Lubricating San Andreas Fault to cause a succession of small slippages. (See MacDonald, noted in question H) W. IV

X. Aircraft landing and takeoff priorities. X. V

Y. Spacesuits. Y. A variety of VI

Z. Underground disposal of radioactive wastes. Z. V and VI

AA. Skin grafts for burns. AA. X

BB. Diver's decompression routine. BB. IV

CC. Hanging padding in horse stalls CC. VI

DD. VI

EE. III
FF. IV
GG. VI
HH. III

II. Opposite of III
JJ. III

KK. IX
LL. Opposite of VII
MM. V

NN. VIII
OO. A variety of III, preventing *further* energy release.

PP. IX

QQ. X

RR. III

SS. VI to achieve V

TT. A variety of VI
UU. II

VV. A variety of III. It could be argued that the disconnection is usually achieved by V or VI (barrier, air), but whatever the physical means, the primary strategy is to prevent (further) release of energy.
WW. Opposite of III

XX. VI
YY. VI
ZZ. V
AAA. V (to allow the lighter to avoid injury)
BBB. VII

CCC. II

DDD. X

EEE. I

DD. Wrapping padding on goalpost supports.
EE. Window washers' belts.
FF. Fire retardant clothing.
GG. Sunburn lotion that blocks U.V.
HH. Chaining tigers.

II. Smoking in bed.
JJ. Not moving flowerpots over onto windowsills.
KK. Stopping hemorrhage.
LL. Pointing a spear; edging a sword.
MM. Banning explosives in tunnels or under "air rights" buildings.
NN. Skiers' "pre-season conditioning."
OO. Release bindings on skis.

PP. Mouth-to-mouth resuscitation.
QQ. Teaching Braille to a blinded soldier.
RR. Use of retaining walls to prevent California mud slides.
SS. Fences around transformer stations.
TT. Earmuffs.
UU. Reducing amount of explosive in each shipment.
VV. The electrical fuse.

WW. Playing with matches in pine woods.

XX. Welders' goggles and helmets.
YY. Fire fighters' suits.
ZZ. Fire escapes.
AAA. Lengthening fuses on explosives.

BBB. Roadside ("breakaway") poles that yield gently when hit.
CCC. Lowering crib heights to reduce brain and other injuries when infants fall out.
DDD. Developing less expensive fender repair methods.
EEE. Preventing the conception of tigers to prevent subsequent human injury.

10

WHY SAFETY?

Leo Greenberg

The author balances the cost of achieving safety against the cost of "unsafety." Accidents, property damage, injuries and suffering are the cost of "unsafety." On both sides of the scale, the cost is borne in differing proportions by the victim, by society in general and by the employer. The scales can be tipped more favorably to the side of safety by the safety professional who can shed more light on existing facts and by the acts of government which can create new facts.

Restricting himself to the activities of government, the author illustrates how government can shift the balance. Unfortunately, no act of government, even with the sacrosanct aim of safety, will be perceived as unalloyed good by all segments of society. The prevailing values of a society restrict or augment the arts and science of the safety practitioner and are as much in the arena of the safety professional as the shop floor.

Hazard Prevention, the Journal of the System Safety Society, January–February, 1973.

IN ANY DISCUSSION on the pursuit of occupational safety,* there is an implicit assumption that such an activity is to the advantage of the employees and employers and hence, one need concern himself only with the question of choosing the best available safety techniques. Toward this end, many articles and books have been written on the subject. Unfortunately, safety has become such a sacred cow that one hardly dares question whether and to what extent this basic assumption is, in fact, true. Since this matter is quite important, we shall risk professional and social opprobium by examining this specific point.

Those who speak for safety are thoroughly convinced of the

---

* In the following discussion, the terms "occupational safety," "employee safety" are used interchangeably to refer to the overall subject of occupational safety and health.

beneficial effects of engaging in it, to those so engaged. If the intended beneficiaries were equally convinced of this, there would be very little left for the safety practitioners to do, other than distributing instructions for how to best provide for safety. Under such circumstances, all existing safety knowledge would be applied, and more demanded. We know, however, that such is not the case in reality, for much available knowledge is not being put to use, for which reason there is much repetition, year after year, of the same types of accidents. One is therefore forced to the conclusion that what is basically lacking is not the desire to know how to provide for safety, but whether to do so, in the first place. The above may seem to clash with the fact that one rarely, if ever, hears a voice of protest against or disagreement with the basic principles upon which safety rests. In fact, many managers and union leaders voluntarily express their personal concern for and interest in this subject, and agree to participate in various propagandizing activities aimed at improving employee safety. Need one ask better proof that the above conclusion is erroneous?

In answer, we must distinguish between safety as an isolated and theoretical entity, and safety as a consideration in the overall decision-making process. There is no doubt that with but few exceptions everyone wishes to remain well and not be harmed anywhere, especially at work. Similarly very few, if any, employers would want their employees to come home any less well physically and mentally than when they left it. Hence from this point of view, there is full agreement that safety is a very important and worthwhile effort to pursue.

The problem arises when we attempt to put this conviction to practice, whereupon conflicts arise. Like most things desired in life, there is a price to be paid for obtaining safe conditions, a price which may take on monetary, social, political, egotistical, psychological and other forms. If safety glasses would not cost money, impose no discomfort, and not involve derision of their wearer by one's colleagues, there would be but little objection to their use. But in reality, these and other disadvantages do exist. One must therefore choose between a number of desirable alternatives, all accompanied to some extent by undesirable results. Normally, one tries to select that alternative which yields maximum desirable effects ("good"), at the price of the least possible undesirable results ("bad"). It is at such times that safety is often thrown by the wayside, when it yields less "good" than its cost. Hence, in the real situation, safety appears as one of a number of considerations, some of them mutually conflicting; from among these, the decision-maker must make his choice. Safety does not stand alone as a consideration, as would appear from the propaganda—you are either for or against it. Actually, everyone is for it, but . . .

All too often, the decision-maker will reach the conclusion that his interest in safety notwithstanding, it is more profitable to ignore than pursue it. The worker, while interested in preserving his well-being, must also provide for a family. If using the safety guard will slow his production rate, and thereby reduce his take-home pay, he will likely forgo the safety and seek to earn extra cash which he needs urgently.

From this we see that the problem with which the safety practitioner and government are confronted is how to increase the weight of safety considerations during the decision-making process so that the scales will tip more favorably to its side. Put differently, one wishes to make the pursuit of safety yield more "good," while its neglect more "bad." In this, the safety practitioner can only attempt to shed more light on existing facts, whereas the government is able to create them.

Restricting ourselves to the activities of the government, we shall examine the various means available to it for achieving this objective, and their characteristics. In other words, we should like to review the methods available in attempting to shape the behaviour of a group of persons in a certain direction, and dissuading it from behaving otherwise.

One possibility which immediately comes to mind is for the government to pass a law requiring all employers to provide certain stipulated safety conditions, upon pain of fine. Thereby, it would seem, the problem is resolved. This, in fact, is done, as we shall see. However, we must remember that laws do not enforce themselves; some enforcement mechanism must be provided to give them meaning. Barring that, they become dead letters.

Furthermore, even if enforced, the employer may reach the conclusion that it is cheaper to circumvent the law, and even be fined, than honor it. In such an instance, the law becomes impotent and worthless. Hence, unless the government is willing to provide an effective enforcement organization, it must rely on other, additional means for achieving its ends. This may be obtained by passing legislation which creates a climate conducive to those following the desired path, and vice versa. That is, the lawmaker creates conditions under which those individuals behaving in the desired manner will enjoy certain benefits. Hence, they will seek to take advantage of the law, using the courts for this purpose, if necessary. Upon pain of repetition, it must be stated clearly that the employer will take safety matters seriously only if he is convinced that this is to the overall advantage of the firm, and not otherwise, safety propaganda notwithstanding. The government must therefore ask itself whether it has provided the conditions which are conducive to the encouragement of safety activities.

The Enforcement of Safety Laws

Almost every country has safety laws, which incorporate penalties to be imposed upon infractors by the Courts. The maximum fines stipulated are sometimes quite high, leading one to the belief that the employer can be forced into providing a safe work environment, despite himself.

Reality seems to indicate otherwise. Two studies (Reference 1 and 2) of the deterrent value of safety legislation have failed to support this hypothesis. The reasons for this can be quite readily understood. Under normal circumstances, quite a few unsafe conditions are created in a work place during the course of a year, but the safety inspector is rarely in the premises to detect them. Many of these can be wilfully hidden from him by spreading the alarm through the plant when he arrives, and putting things temporarily in order, while he is being stalled in the office. If he encounters a hazardous condition, he will write the employer a letter to that effect, demanding remedy. He will then revisit after several months' time, and if no change for the better has taken place, the employer will be warned of impending legal action, and another visit carried out. If an improvement has still not been brought about, a criminal suit will be instituted which, by itself, will take several months to prepare. Note that probably more than a year, if not two or three, have passed since the original discovery of the violation. The employer can institute delaying tactics, if he so wishes and finally, at the last moment, plead guilty and get off with a very reasonable fine. If one considers the worth of the money saved in not investing in safety over this whole period, it is readily seen why the fine is much the easier way out.

The shortcomings in the enforcement of safety legislation are two-fold: (1) the shortage of inspectors, which is responsible for infrequent inspections, and (2) the low expected magnitude of the fine, if one considers the combined probabilities of being "caught," taken to court and fined, and the average value of the fine.

For safety enforcement to serve as a deterrent, both of the above shortcomings must be overcome by: (1) providing substantially more inspectors, and (2) raising the mandatory minimum fine to a much higher level. Realistically speaking, no government is presently disposed to either action.

Even so, it is doubtful that safety enforcement by the government, in the conventional sense, can force the employer to provide safe working conditions, if he wishes otherwise. This is due to the very dynamic nature of the work place, and the possible changes in conditions as a result of this. Hence, only internal full-time enforcement by management can be successful. We shall therefore consider here the various methods available to motivate management to such an effort.

Civil Damage Suits

If one person causes damage or loss, of whatever kind, to another, this can serve as a basis for a suit for damages. For this reason, an injured worker may file suit against his employer, basing it on the damage caused to his person. Of course, the employer has certain legal defenses in such an action. Nevertheless, the threat of such suits, whose awards are often quite substantial, should serve to encourage the employer to reduce to the least possible the chance of employee injury.

There is a catch to this, however. Employers are aware of this potential danger and for this reason purchase liability insurance. They then feel themselves quite immune to damage from such suits, and free to run their business as they wish.

Liability Insurance as a Separate Bookkeeping Entity

From that stated above, one may wonder why insurance companies should be willing to assume such losses; one would expect them to reject applications for insurance from those firms with a bad safety record and unsafe working conditions. This, in fact, is done in some countries. The insurance carriers are sometimes more demanding and less relenting than government inspectors, in requiring that premises be constructed and maintained properly. Furthermore, periodic inspections of the plant are made, and corrections demanded. On the other hand, there are those insurance companies who have no hesitation in underwriting all liability insurance. When claims are filed, their attorneys do their utmost to refuse payment, and draw out the proceedings for as long as possible, so as to soften the plaintiff's demands and thereby have him settle for little.

What enables such firms to assume the risk of losses is the fact that they cover themselves well with profits from other types of insurance. They normally offer such branches of insurance as fire, theft, calamity, liability and other. Should losses be suffered in one of these areas, profits from the others will cover it. The customer, knowing this, maintains a bargaining position by threatening to withdraw all insurance with the firm, if liability coverage is to be refused him. The insurer may thereupon be quite willing to forgo his previous demands for improved safety, hoping to cover his potential loss from profits in the other types of coverage.

This strategy may be overcome by requiring (on the part of the government) that liability insurance exist as a separate self-supporting entity. Losses in this area may not be covered by profits from other sources. Should the balance sheet be unbalanced, the threat of bankruptcy would hang over the head of the firm. In order to protect the insured against bankruptcy, a common fund would be created by law with contributions from all such carriers to cover this contingency.

Flexible Linkage Between Workmen's Compensation Premium and Worker Claims

There is workmen's compensation legislation in almost every country, whether the insurance itself be provided by a governmental agency or private carrier. The employer pays a monthly premium on his payroll to the insurer. In exchange, the workers are entitled to free medical care if injured at work, are provided with an income while absent from work because of the injury, and are given rehabilitation training, if necessary. The premium in initially set according to the claims experience of the insurer with that industrial branch. So as to encourage the employer to provide safe work conditions, and thereby reduce the workers' claims for workmen's compensation, a discount from the official premium rate is offered to those firms with fewer-than-average claims. The converse is also true.

The premium is of the order of two or three percent of the payroll. Hence, a discount even of 20 percent of this premium is not very meaningful to the firm for, in real terms, it represents a reduction of the order of ½ percent of the overall payroll. Considering the fact that improving safety conditions also requires money, this type of discount does not mean very much.

While the idea, in itself, has much merit, for it to obtain meaning, the premium, and the discount, must become more substantial. It would appear that the premium paid by the employer does not fully pay for the cost of the injury to society. This is especially true of the permanent disabilities, wherein the disabled will likely earn less than he was accustomed to. As a result, his family will suffer financially by this, and become a welfare case. Why should not this, too, be paid for by the workmen's compensation insurance? Why should society, at large, have to make good what was spoiled by the work place?

Whatever answer one wishes to give to the above, there is little room for arguing against the notion that increase or decrease in workmen's compensation premium should be directly related to the actual expenditures of the insurer, and not on an arbitrarily specified rate. Let the employer enjoy fully the fruits of his safety program, or be penalized accordingly.

The Disallowing of Safety-Related Fines as Business Expense

So as to make the expenditures resulting from "unsafety" more expensive to the employer, they should be made nondeductible as business-related expenditures.

Presently, any fine imposed by the Court for a safety violation, surcharge demanded by the workmen's compensation agency, compensatory payment of any sort made by the employer to the injured or his heirs, and liability insurance premiums, are considered legitimate business expenses. Inasmuch as in many countries the corporate income tax is approximately 50 percent, this means that the government subsidizes half of these outlays. In other words, the taxpayer is made responsible for half the cost of these expenses, though the act of employment created them. This should not be so; they should be made nondeductible for tax purposes. The employer can then be expected to be somewhat more anxious to reduce these expenditures.

A Personal, Criminal Responsibility of the Employer for Work-Related Injuries

If the law were to stipulate that the employer is to be held personally responsible for injuries sustained by his employees, any such incident arising from his negligence could be considered a criminal act, with all that this implies. Fear of the consequences of such events will hopefully motivate the employer to greater concern for the safety of his workers.

It is not unusual that, despite the warnings of a safety inspector, a hazardous condition is not corrected. Various excuses for this are put forward, but the fact remains that the hazard is allowed to remain. Should an accident occur and a person be injured, rarely will the police charge the employer with a crime. Only in the case of a fatality may this occur, and even so, rarely.

It is difficult to grasp why society looks upon the negligent employer as any less culpable for a crime, than it does a person who is deliberately misusing a dangerous object. Whether the motive for this act is the desire to save money, or just "kicks" is irrelevant. It surely does not make the occupationally injured any less injured.

This lack of personal sense of responsibility is especially highlighted by the fact that when a firm is charged with a safety violation, the person sent to Court to represent it is some third-rate employee or attorney. At no time is there a personal charge against the employer, nor is he required to attend Court and face the charges.

The funds available in any given country for investment comprise the resources of that country. Every government wishes to make maximum use of its resources so as to produce many goods and export them. Hence, those investments are especially sought out which will yield maximum return. In this respect, investment in safety does not necessarily qualify for funds, especially if quick results are desired. Thus, the government itself tends to discourage what it considers excessive outlays in this area. This phenomenon is especially prevalent in the cash-short developing countries. Their leaders seem to say, "development now, safety later." This is one of the reasons why these countries make such poor use of existent safety knowledge.

Inasmuch as safety costs money, the product manufactured may be more costly than one produced under less safe circumstances. This then impairs the competitive position of the country's industry in international markets. For this reason, the government is deterred from pressing safety strongly.

No less important is the fact that if the government will make strong safety demands, the same will be demanded of it. This means that it will have to enlarge and improve its safety enforcement apparatus, and upgrade the level of safety in its own factories. All this will cost much money. It thus prefers to let sleeping dogs lie.

We have seen, then, that providing for safe work conditions involves very often discomfort or expenditure, or both, making this highly desired objective less desirable. The government, in wishing to enhance work safety conditions, will be well advised to counteract this fact, over a broad legal front, so as to give greater weight to the pursuit of safety.

REFERENCES

Greenberg, L.: The deterrent value of the safety-legislative system in Israel (in Hebrew). *Avodah Uvituach Leumi,* 23:No. 1, 20–22, 1971.

Greenberg, L.: The Relevance of Governmental Enforcement Activity in Industrial Safety. Mimeographed report. 1971.

Munkman, J.: *Damages for Personal Injuries and Death.* London, Butterworths, 1970.

11

SAFETY AIDS
DECISION MAKING

W. C. POPE, T. J. CRESSWELL AND E. R. NICOLAI

To those who have long cried "the system is all wrong," have hope. The three authors base their ideas on the system and what's wrong with it instead of what is wrong with the worker. Though not a new idea, it is seldom voiced in safety circles as strongly as you will find it here.

The authors advance a basic philosophy, a concept of operation for the new breed of safety professional: "Once the safety program administrator has made it clear that his role in the organization is that of safety evaluator, talented in identifying mistakes in the management routine because of accidental incidents, he becomes a full partner on the management team—not a social worker operating in an organizational vacuum."

The "old time" safety man may well be shocked to see what the authors think about some time honored safety functions such as first aid, filling out claims forms, and training. The modern safety man will be interested in how the safety manager functions on the management team.

All-in-all, those who are open to safety as largely a management function will find this chapter gourmet food for thought.

MANY, including St. Augustine, are credited with coining the saying: "To err is human." But St. Augustine added a fillip, if not specifically for management people, at least applicable to them. He said: "It is devilish to remain wilfully in error."

Today's management is working slowly, but surely away from perdition by viewing accidental incidents as errors; by concluding

From *Loss Control Publication No. 1*, National Safety Management Society, Post Office Box 14092, Benjamin Franklin Station, Washington, D. C., 20044 that the thing to search for in the forest of accident statistics is the management tree—in other words, to find out what is wrong with the "system" rather than what is wrong with the workers.

Administrators of safety programs have evolved and flourished in industrial organizations primarily because mistakes by management generated accidental incidents. Compensation insurance, union pressures, community relations, lost time, and other factors forced top management to take action to prevent mishaps. So entered the safety engineer.

Why engineer? In the early days of industry, management found that large numbers of injuries were due to poorly guarded machinery and equipment. A natural reaction was to look to the engineering staff to correct the problem, and usually a qualified engineer was assigned to the task. The result was the creation of the "Safety Engineer."

Because of the humane aspects of their jobs, many of these men became dedicated to their work of curbing hazards, applying enthusiasm and technical skills to correct undesirable conditions.

Most of them used variations of the "scientific" nature developed by Heinrich (1931) in the early 1930's. While progress has been made in accident prevention since those days, few major changes have been made in his original approach to the safety problem.

Total solution to the safety problem—if such ever becomes a possibility—must ultimately be based on integrating safety philosophies and techniques into the national education system at all levels. While we strive toward this distant and somewhat utopian goal, we can make great progress in preventing tragedy by simply adjusting our present-day thinking to put safety programs in proper perspective within the management hierarchy.

The key to this, of course, is full appreciation and understanding that any accidental incident is an indicator . . . a warning . . . to the management team that something has gone wrong with the system.

Once the safety programs administrator has made it clear that his role in the organization is that of a systems evaluator, talented in identifying mistakes in the management routine because of accidental incidents, he becomes a full partner on the management team—not a social worker operating in an organizational vacuum.

To achieve this stature is not easy. It requires a complete re-orientation of most safety specialists along with most other members of the management echelon.

To assist in such reorientation, this presentation offers five major areas for consideration: (1) the social phenomenon of safety; (2) the flexibility of safety programs; (3) the understanding of the word "management" (4) capitalizing on mutual functional interests of the entire group; and (5) use of electronic data processing to provide necessary, and somewhat awesome, finger-pointing statistics.

AREA I—THE SOCIAL PHENOMENON OF SAFETY

Are safety administrators being deluded into a false sense of security by thinking that safety programming is fully understood and accepted as a necessary component of good management? This question may at first seem ridiculous to those who feel it is unthinkable for any sane management group not to understand the importance of safety programming. But if management *does* understand the importance of safety, then why do safety administrators put so much emphasis on "selling" the program whenever they convene to discuss mutual problems; pleading with top management for its support at every turn of the road; and arguing among themselves as to where safety should be established in the organization? The answer seems generally that fellow members of the management team do not fully understand and appreciate the safety function.

Roethlisberger (1959) asserts that "industry is a social as well as an economic phenomenon." (His thinking on this matter might well be required reading for safety administrators.) Transferring his ideas of the safety function, we find that skill in working with other managers and obtaining their interest and support depend on the nature of their social sentiments concerning safety and what it will do for them. In short, they must understand how the safety function relates to *their* function if they are to support it. A wide sea of misunderstanding seems to lie between safety managers and other management officials with whom they must work. Safety managers often do not appreciate all the rules of the management "game," while other managers frequently fail to visualize how safety can possibly be intergrated into many of their operations. This lack of understanding and appreciation of common functional interests is a serious and fundamental safety program weakness.

The word "safety" is ambiguous, emotional, and loaded with sentiment. Such words usually are not connected with a corporate entity that "has no heart." Sir Edward Coke, noted barrister, wrote in 1683: "A corporation, aggregate of many, is invisible, immortal, and rests only in intendment and consideration of law. They cannot commit treason, nor be outlawed, nor be excommunicated *for they have no souls*. Neither can they appear in person, but by attorney . . ."

If the concept of a "soulless" organization is accepted, it is not difficult to recognize that those in it play shifting roles. So it is that the warm, personable department head who shares a coffee break or plays golf with the safety manager becomes the "hard-headed" administrator when approached on official business. He thinks officially of safety as related to the business activity and ponders the question of "worthwhile," rather than a "good thing" to do.

How then, does management generally react to the word "safety"? Since management is essentially "persons managing persons," it probably reacts much as an individual might react. In trying to analyze the average person's response to the word "safety," one finds a mish-mash of feelings. People tend to identify "safety" with emotional words such as "love," "hate," "fear." It receives a wide range of interpretation, depending upon the context in which it is used. For example: safety to the young mother is probably closely related to the activities of her children; to the community-minded individual, it may signify "law and order;" to those who may be approaching retirement, the word could embrace freedom from want; to a banker, it might signify the security he demands on loans; to the building manager, it sometimes is the symbol of a "busybody" inspector who insists on checking his fire extinguishers. What then, does it mean to management? An experienced safety manager might easily conclude that it comes close to meaning a do-good program, something like a social betterment campaign, a program that no self-respecting organization would reasonably say it does not have, but certainly not one to be taken seriously in connection with the science of administrative controls.

To promote a better management understanding of the safety function, some safety managers have experimented with the term "accident prevention" as a substitute for the word "safety." Here, too, we find a wide area of misunderstanding. Many responsible officials do not recognize an accident unless blood flows. The term "accident" is used all too often synonymously with "injury." If the top officials of an organization feel this way toward "accidents," it is not surprising that so few property-damage accidents ever are reported by operating supervisors, in government and elsewhere.

Heinrich (1959), in explaining his theory of the foundation of a major injury, estimated that "on the average, in a unit group of 330 similar accidents occurring to the same person, 300 will result in no injury. . . ." The writers have not succeeded either in proving or disproving his theory, since neither has completed the campaign to transfer the eyes of the management team from injuries to accidents.

We also should point out that many safety administrators still do not recognize the difference. For example, many industries still proudly post their low "accident rates," when actually they are referring to their "disabling work-injury frequency rate."

Some leading insurance carriers favor the term "loss prevention" to describe their safety program. They probably find this approach useful to increase understanding of their services to the policyholders, but it has drawbacks when applied internally, since it can create overlapping of functional objectives. A business suffers "loss" in other ways than by accidents.

The word "safety" might well be dropped and replaced by a title more easily understood by administrators—and more definitive. However, tradition cannot be changed overnight, so the immediate effort should be devoted to creating in the minds of the management team the image of "mistakes" when referring to accidents. Management must be educated to the fact that the function of safety is to locate and define operational errors involving incomplete decision-making, faulty judgments, administrative miscalculations, and just plain stupidity. These expressions are well understood up and down the ranks. Success with this approach is possible, but it will require considerable study, discussion, and change of viewpoint before being accepted. In the words of one top administrator: "I have not thought of safety in this light and I am not sure I can support the idea of a program purposely designed to pinpoint my deficiencies, but the concept certainly is progressive and might prove fruitful—if it can be made to work."

AREA II—THE FLEXIBILITY OF SAFETY PROGRAMS

In a widely used textbook, Drucker (1954) says: "To find out what activities are needed to attain the objectives of the business is such an obvious thing to do that it would hardly seem to deserve special mention. But analyzing the activities is as good as unknown to traditional theory. Most traditional authorities assume that business has a set of 'typical' functions which can be applied everywhere and to everything without prior analysis." Drucker, an authority on management principles, feels that activities of any function to be managed deserve extremely careful review and analysis. Only through such examination can we identify those activities that appropriately belong to the safety function.

To illustrate the type of analytical review to which the safety function should be subjected, the following two generalizations are presented:

1. management comprehension of the scope of safety activities will increase in direct proportion to the program emphasis placed upon each activity, and
2. by avoiding those activities that are not appropriately a part of the safety function, prestige will be gained with the management team and, at the same time, energy will not be dissipated on peripheral activities.

As previously mentioned, management is oriented to the narrow concept of the safety function as simply an injury-prevention activity. It is not difficult to rationalize the administrative views on safety "programming." In reality, the safety function consists of several programs, the magnitude of each depending upon the scope of operations. Management must be educated to think not in terms of *the* "safety program," but of each of the following separate programs comprising the safety function: 1. the work-injury prevention program; 2. the motor vehicle accident-prevention program; 3. the fire-loss prevention program; 4. the property damage prevention program; and 5. the public safety program.

Most safety managers have been content to refer collectively to these programs as *the* "safety program." This is unacceptable to the remainder of a management team that has oriented itself to think of the safety program only as a work-injury prevention activity. By referring to each *separate* program of the safety function at every opportunity, safety managers ultimately will educate administrators by underscoring the specific areas where they should be cooperating on matters of common interest.

This is a wholly realistic and practical approach commonly practiced by the other segments of the management team in dealing with other problems. Take the function of personnel management as an example. It has delineated programs on compensation, labor (group) relations, employee (individual) relations, employment and placement, program review, training, and so on. These are "personnel" programs within a personnel system. This does not convey the suggestion that the safety function requires a large staff. On the contrary, methods of doing a better job of safety programming with a relatively small staff is entirely possible.

In selling the safety function as a parcel containing several separate and distinct endeavors, it is important that program capacity not be overextended. In other words, it is not necessary to attempt empire-building to gain status on the management team. Management, being human, tends to make the safety function a sort of catch-all for fringe or marginal activities that do not seem to fit into any other slot. This is because managers do not fully understand the functional objectives of the safety programs and mistakenly load the safety experts with a wide range of extraneous duties that weaken the effectiveness of the entire effort.

As any safety authority can attest, the nonsafety activities often assigned to the safety staff can be quite lengthy. The most common peripheral assignment is the employee health program. It could well function as a separate unit, but where management has not given it individual organizational status, the passing out of aspirin and salt pills, and the bandaging of wounds, becomes a "safety" activity. Safety and health programs can and should operate in a complementary manner, since one group can help the other in many instances. Generally, however, the effectiveness of employee health programs is not directly related to accident prevention, but is more appropriately the responsibility of personnel people. This concept, of course, can be the subject of extensive discourse, but the trend toward health programs as a personnel function is definitely well advanced; so we will not interfere with what has become a reasonable and successful fact. Occupational disease is technically considered a work injury by state labor laws on compensation and by the Federal Employees' Compensation Act of September 1916. Occupational disease prevention is, therefore, a legitimate part of the safety function. This is a classic example of how health programs and safety programs can complement one another.

Traditionally, also, safety managers have become responsible for first-aid instruction. Here is another activity difficult to associate with the safety expert's job of locating and defining management deficiencies. First-aid is nothing more than emergency medical treatment administered by a trained layman. The almost universal concept of accidents, blood, and first-aid again brings to the foreground management's philosophy that anything remotely related to employee injuries and must automatically be a part of the safety function. First-aid actually is a postlude to a management function that did not function.

The administration of workmen's compensation systems seems inevitably to fall into the lap of the safety managers. Reports processed in connection with workmen's compensation are personnel items, since they are primarily *claims* forms, not accident reports of value in safety programming. Management may be justifiably confused on this point since personnel officers normally do not handle accident reports, and there is a widespread misconception that these *claims* are accident reports.

Training seems interwoven with every part of the safety function—so much so that it is often erroneously stated that "safety" is just another training activity. So many misunderstand the principles, objectives, and methods of the safety function that safety managers are constantly required to conduct educational campaigns to clear the atmosphere. Training is not a function of safety. In the absence of a qualified training officer, it may be necessary for the safety staff to direct the training of employees, but even this is not desirable. Training should be a separate activity, managed by those particularly qualified in training others. Safety's basic responsibility is to provide the training staff with essential material for a regularly established training program, and to assist in other ways, as requested.

AREA III—UNDERSTANDING "MANAGEMENT"

Despite its critical importance, management often is the least understood of our basic institutions. Definitions for it are many and varied. "Getting results through people" (Drucker, 1954) seems the most appropriate for our use since "people" are of the first order of importance in the safety function. One expert asserts that management is an organ which can be described and defined only through its *functions*. Since support by top management appears to be a critical issue with most safety people, it is necessary to examine these functions as they relate to safety. "We can't operate without top management support," is an expression frequently used by safety managers, but the term "top management" must be defined to determine specifically from whence the support should come. There is an understandable tendency to consider management in a singular form. Many feel that if a certain administrator will give his unqualified support and interest to safety, program problems would be solved. But functional management (Taylor, 1911) does not center on any one man. True, the signature of one top official is required to set policy in motion, but the creation of policy usually starts within a management "team." This team consists of administrators in staff and line positions representing different functions in the entire organization. Safety, as a basic staff function within the organization, must be represented on all such management teams.

Here is Russell Robb's explanation of the development of the management team:

> As an industry or business begins to involve large size, great numbers, and complexity, organization becomes necessary for direction, control, and handling of affairs, quite aside from any question of direct economy. It becomes necessary to set off groups of workers, divide responsibilities, duties and processes, so that affairs may be kept within the scope and ability of those who are directing the undertaking. A virtue has, however, been made of this necessity for division, because it becomes possible, by dividing duties and functions to conserve skill, ability, and use, and to direct all efforts into definite paths, to which it becomes accustomed and thus gains in efficiency (Robb, 1948).

The concept of the management team starts with, but is not limited to the top management level. The management hierarchy may be considered as having three levels: the planning level, the controlling level, and the operating level. Representatives at each level form lines of communication from top to bottom or bottom to top. Thus, at whatever level safety is being considered, program matters can be coordinated. This layering of management prevails in the headquarters office, at regional offices, and at plants or installations. It is among these team members that safety managers must gain proper recognition, become identified as working partners and prove their worth to the particular interests of all team members.

By focusing attention on the management "team," the safety expert has a closeup view of activities where his work should be concentrated. First, areas of mutually complementary relationships should be found. Since people and property are primary considerations in any accident situation, the functions of personnel and property management have logical points of common interest. Next, because accidents generate economic loss, financial managers must be reasonably involved with safety. Many accidents involve tort claims which form a common bond between safety people and attorneys. Similar relationships with other functions can be cited, but these four illustrate the point. Regardless of how they may be labeled, these particular four functions should be at the top of every safety administrator's list for making friends and influencing people and policies.

Consider for a moment where these program "interests" might be joined. The late Dale Carnegie, in his famous book on winning friends and influencing people, paid particular attention to the subject of gaining objectives by consolidating common interests. This principle applies as well to members of the management team. If the safety function is to have the interest and support of other functions, then it must be programmed to capture information and present it in a manner that stimulates mutual interest— to tie a management deficiency, when found, into the management area that should be most interested in its removal.

No matter what the level of management, members of the "team" have their functional problems. If information, located through accident analysis, can be presented in a manner that will help solve, or at least highlight these problems, the safety function will quickly be identified as an important contributor in the constant search for management improvements. To accomplish this, however, safety administrators will do well to adopt the slogan: "IT'S NOT WHAT IS WRONG WITH PEOPLE, BUT WHAT IS WRONG WITH THE (MANAGEMENT) SYSTEM!" Labor-management antagonism should not be bolstered by pitting supervisors against employees in attempting to explain why accidents occur.

To illustrate: Note the natural cycle when the lights in a home suddenly go out. Usually the appropriate fuse is replaced. If the new fuse blows, it too can be replaced. This process can be repeated endlessly, but it does not solve the basic electrical problem. Something is wrong with the electrical system when fuses fail repeatedly. The defect must be traced to the source of trouble and corrected. Of course, there are those who would put a penny behind a fuse, relax, and let the house burn down.

If a finger is lost because of an unguarded machine, the obvious thing to do is have the machine guarded. But a guard (or fuse) promptly installed at the scene of an accident does not solve the "systematic" trouble. Why was the machine not guarded when purchased? Or, what is wrong with the day-to-day inspection plan that permits this unguarded condition to go unnoticed? Or, where did job orientation fail, since the employee did not report the deficiency? These and other questions stem from management deficiency and cannot be attributed directly to the safety function.

Note that each question relates back to a particular management function embracing a directive, policy, or organizational practice over which the immediate supervisor or the employee may have had no direct control. In a more practical sense, then, the accident situation becomes the focal point for a study of the management problems that permit undesirable conditions to develop. This leads to discussion of mutually functional interests prevailing between safety and other management areas.

AREA IV—CAPITALIZING ON MUTUAL FUNCTIONAL INTERESTS

To integrate completely the safety programs in many management activities requires identification of areas of mutual interest and concern. In this exercise, by definition, the examination includes the *whole* management system to locate basic accident situations, the causes and subcauses of which can be traced to other functions. Under this concept, accident prevention can establish itself as a specialized management improvement activity intimately associated with all other functions. Each management area has two responsibilities: First, it executes its own programs, and second, it should support others in performing theirs. The task of the safety expert should not be limited to "trouble finding" but should include support for other functions by calling attention to potential weaknesses in their policies, directives, program objectives, and long-standing practices.

Figure 11-1 illustrates an example of the way some safety administrators are presenting statistical analyses of accidents (as problem areas) to management today.

An effort to determine the relationship between the accident causes, listed on the left, to the functional interest listed on the right should make it fairly obvious that some basic changes must be made in the present system of cause analysis to establish func-

Directions in Safety

Cause Classification	% of cases involved *		Areas of functional interest
		Personel Function	Compensation Labor relations Employment Program review Training
Electricity	.2	Supply or Logistics Function	Procurement & Contracting Transportation Service Space Service Records Service Utilization and Disposal Administrative Services (housekeeping)
Flash burns	.2		
Dusts, gases, chem. ...	1.7		
Handling material or equipment	28.2		
Falling objects	3.0	Engineering Function	Design Construction Standards Repair
Falls of persons	17.2		
Jumping to or from places	.4		
Striking against material	11.8	Finance Function	Internal auditing policy Accounting policy and financial procedures Financial reporting Accounting systems Budget review Budget formulation Budget execution
All other	37.3		
Total 100.00			
* Percent of cases totaled for all Federal agencies in 1960.			
			Contractual agreements
			Claims & Contract Appeals

Figure 11–1. Typical Accident Analysis.

tional interest in safety. The accident causes are not expressed in management's language. Human errors and condition defects must be translated into broader areas of responsibility involving communications, policies, directives, and the like. Safety managers should stop thinking in terms of the individual, step back, and see the problem from the whole management point of view.

When analysis reveals problems involving physical examinations, training, seasonal employment, aging employees, labor-

Figure 11–2 illustrates a sample accident cause analysis clearly establishing management deficiencies. The relationship between causes and functional objectives is expressed in the ordinary language of management and is easily understood by administrators.

Cause Classification	Percent of management problems involved
Task performed not related to the job classification or qualifications standards	23.5
Task should be identified as hazardous and requiring a periodic fitness-for-duty physical exam	21.7
Cause due in part to a wage differential problem	0.1
Purchasing contract involved did not have appropriate safety provisions	24.5
Safety regulations not adequately covered in the current operating and maintenance instructions	43.7
Uniform testing and licensing program needed to maintain operating proficiency	10.3
Budget request did not include estimate for safety funds to cover this situation	11.2
No stated policy, or policy not clear	10.1
Question of employee-supervisor relations a basic issue in the accident	33.0
Standard storage, handling, and transportation instructions not adequate to cover the accident situation	28.3

Figure 11–2. Sample Accident Cause Analysis—Progressive Approach

management difficulties, and so on, those responsible for the personnel function will certainly be interested in the findings. Likewise, if the analysis turns up problems dealing with space service, utilization and disposal, procurement, contracting, and the like, those administering the supply function should be interested. Thus, safety as a staff function must work across divisional lines and embrace all opportunities to do this are directly proportional to the management deficiencies found in each accident situation. Each accident cause is an opportunity to make a management improvement. Safety managers, then, must take full advantage of their staff role as the catalyst in improving management effectiveness.

AREA V—ELECTRONIC DATA PROCESSING IN SYSTEMS SAFETY MANAGEMENT

The Department of the Interior's "systems safety concept" is designed to isolate—to pinpoint—deficiencies in the mainstream and tributaries of management. A textbook definite of "systems" is presented this way:

> The systems concept is primarily a way of thinking about the job of managing. It provides a framework for visualizing internal and external environmental factors as an integrated whole. It allows recognition of the function of subsystems as well as the complex supersystems within which businessmen must operate.

Systems safety embraces the concept that good management constantly seeks ways to promote error-free performance, but admits that this goal, like perpetual motion, may be approached, but never reached.

Regardless, the whole system of management must be headed toward a given and realistic goal or set of goals and it must do so with a minimum of side trips and explorations. The whole is considered more important than its parts . . . and the interaction of the systems of management is far more important than management itself.

As stated earlier, the key to systems safety management is the full appreciation—the admission, if you wish—that any accidental incident conceivably could have been a full-blown injurious accident, complete with ambulance, doctor, hospital, nurse, and forms and more forms to be filled out in a familiar cadence.

It is the responsibility of the safety manager to make it clear that his job is to detect these warning incidents, minor as they may appear. He takes a positive role in the organization as a systems evaluator and exercises his talents in isolating mistakes in policy, practices, and attitudes. He is a searcher of facts, and, hopefully, always a friend, but never a Pollyanna.

The Interior safety function looks to automation as a newfound device in aiding the systems concept of safety management. This layout of wires, cables, printers, switches, and various other gadgets, is eliminating the need for manual handling of the massive pile of accident data. In a completely impersonal manner it has a fantastic memory and spews out its findings at speeds never dreamed possible.

Computers are the new weapons of the safety specialists, but they are not secret devices. Safety authorities are fully willing to share their mysteries with anyone who will listen.

Interior's automated safety management information system (SMIS), capable of linking one management area with another, can isolate in moments the basic managerial problems related to manpower and economic loss and then relate these problems to a system whose prime function is to eliminate drains on brains, budgets, and manpower.

Electronic data processing installations have their limitations: They are no more helpful than the accuracy and completeness of information fed them. Given chaff, they will turn out inedible cereal.

But if the game is played "fair and square," the printouts will point unerringly to the problem area.

Conclusion

Only a few of many evolving concepts have been advanced here in advocating a progressive new approach to safety programs management. Much more work is necessary in developing these and other ideas before they can be completely acceptable. The proposals, if put into use, could lead to some radical changes in administering safety programs.

At the risk of oversimplifying, the concepts presented may be summarized as follows:

1. The word "safety" is sentimental in nature and without a common meaning to most persons. Persons managing persons tend to depreciate the basic objectives of a safety function because they do not understand them. Management tends to shy away from an abstraction couched in unfamiliar terms.
2. Safety administrators must understand organization and processes of management to bring about the quality of interest and support required by the safety function from other functional members of the management "team."
3. Interfunctional interest begins with the identification of common program concerns. Interfunction support is fostered by a cooperative effort to fulfill common program objectives.

Use new concepts of safety management based on theory and management of systems and utilize principles of behavioral science.

4. Causal analysis of accidents will be recognized as an important tool of administration when it is based on identification of management deficiencies and not on faults of individuals.

5. Computer methods for accession, storage and retrieval of accident cause, cost and related data combined with concepts of "systems safety" provide the safety manager a valuable and versatile tool for research, development and control of accident loss prevention programs.

REFERENCES

Drucker, P. F.: *The Practice of Management.* New York, Harper and Bros. 1954, p. 195.

Heinrich, H. W.: *Industrial Accident Prevention.* New York, McGraw-Hill, 1931.

Heinrich, H. W.: *Industrial Accident Prevention.* New York, McGraw-Hill, 1959, pp. 26–34.

Johnson, R. A., Kast, F. E., and Rosenzweig, J. E.: *The Theory and Management of Systems.* New York, McGraw-Hill, 1967, p. 3.

Roethlisberger, F. J.: *Management and Morale.* Cambridge, Harvard University Press, 1959, pp. 27–45.

Robb, Russell: *Lectures on Organization,* reprinted in *Processes of Organization and Management.* Washington, Public Affairs Press, 1948, p. 112.

Taylor, F. W.: *Principles of Scientific Management.* New York, Harper and Bros., 1911, p. 99.

Urwick, L. F. *Notes on a Theory of Organization.* New York, New York Management Association, 1952, p. 7.

12

TOR ANALYSIS: A DIAGNOSTIC TRAINING TOOL

D. A. Weaver

The concept of operational errors which could lead to accidents has been approached by many safety professionals. Because operational errors are symptomatic of supervisory-management deficiencies, the practitioner is faced with finding an appropriate technique to reveal these deficiencies in a manner which involves rather than agitates.

Technic of Operations Review (TOR) as developed by Mr. Weaver is a deceptively simple method of letting supervisors and managers find out for themselves their role in operational errors. He introduces a technique of locating and defining operational errors which underlie the daily load of headaches, errors, rework, waste, and eventually accidents and injuries. Through a diagnostic procedure he has created a learning situation that has practical application for the safety manager, training staff, line managers and supervisors.

TOR is not just a proposal; it is an active tool that has been presented and used hundreds of times over the past several years. The technique appears to work equally well in any situation involving operational errors.

ABSTRACT: The author introduces a method of locating and defining the operational errors which underlie the daily load of headaches —snafus, ball-ups, errors, rejects, rework, waste—and accidents and injuries. The diagnostic results and the learning situation created by the process make the method of interest to the safety professional, to the training staff, and to line managers and supervisors.

TOR ANALYSIS is a quite simple process. The technique may be demonstrated in moments, though its exposition on paper may take a bit longer. It is essentially a group process, but it can be applied in silent cogitation by a sole person.

From *Journal of American Society of Safety Engineers*, June, 1973.

A Sort of Instant Case Study

In any case, its effect is to create a sort of instant case study. Unlike the typical case study, however, it does not deal with hypothetical events in a hypothetical organization with hypothetical people leading to hypothetical insights. Rather, a TOR group deals with real events in their own organization. TOR Analysis is triggered by those real events, creating a learning situation of intense involvement, and leading to real insights into their own organization.

TOR must first be perceived as a process, a thing to do in step-by-step sequence. That sequence will be herein explained. The explanation should enable anyone who wishes to conduct his first TOR sessions. But TOR must also be perceived on two other levels. It must be perceived as a training tool which creates a learning situation as the group pursues the step-by-step process. And it must finally be perceived as a tool to assist in the diagnosis of the causes of an untoward event.

Technic of Operations Review

TOR stems from the designation, "Technic of Operations Review." * Hence, the process is called TOR Analysis; and we have TOR sessions, and TOR groups, and TOR leaders. Technic of Operations Review was originally conceived as a tool for smaller business operations, as a tool to be used by line managers and supervisors in the absence of staff help. Larger organizations, blessed with staff help, have used it for the very reason that it can be used by line personnel.

Before considering how to conduct TOR Analysis, the nature of Technic of Operations Review might be explained. This is best done by studying the TOR Analysis form, popularly called TOR Yellow Sheets. As a TOR session begins, each person has one before him. It is the only item essential to conduct a TOR session.

A glance at the TOR Analysis form quickly reveals that TOR Analysis deals with the supervisory-management factors which underlie the events of the work day. In the language of safety

* *How to Conduct TOR Analysis,* by Employers Insurance of Wausau, Wausau, Wisconsin 54401.

management, it is a page of "operational errors" set forth under eight headings.

These operational errors (and many more whose inclusion would have made TOR Analysis unworkable)—these operational errors exist, or happen, or are committed in every organization. The more they exist the more sloppy the organization. The more they exist, the more they combine in unexpected and often improbable ways to produce the daily load of headaches—snafus, ball-ups, errors, rejects, rework, waste—and accidents and injuries.

"Operational error has occurred whenever unplanned and undesired results stem from the acts and decisions of supervisory management, or the failure to act or decide" (Weaver, 1971). TOR is triggered by one of those unplanned and undesired results. Examples are endless—the truck dispatched to the wrong city, "$9,000 worth of scrap," an accident, an injury—all are unplanned and undesired events behind which lie operational errors. TOR probes into the supervisory-management deficiencies which caused them or failed to prevent them. Accident investigation seldom dwells on this aspect of accident causation, yet deficiency in supervisory-management (usually more rather than less so) is a causative factor in any accident.

At this point the not-too-hasty reader has questions which may be dealt with in a forthcoming question-and-answer section. A final section will deal with the simple but crucial role of the TOR leader. For now the necessary task is to describe the steps of TOR Analysis.

HOW TO CONDUCT TOR ANALYSIS

Figure 12–1 sets forth the steps of TOR Analysis. The explanation can be demonstrated in ten minutes. In ten minutes, a group that never heard of TOR will have their heads bent over the TOR Yellow Sheets in earnest discussion. In this exposition, the explanation of the steps has been intermixed with certain lessons of experience ("list vertically!"), and an attempt has been made to describe the group interaction and the nature of the learning situation. Forewarned, this should not distract from the main purpose.

STEPS OF TOR ANALYSIS

Minutes
5 to 10   Get FACTS on the table.
5 to 10   STATE proximate cause.
20 to 30 TRACE underlying contributing causes.
──────
30 to 50

         ELIMINATE: reconsider; isolate important
factors.

         SEEK feasible corrective action.

The steps of TOR Analysis will usually fit into a one-hour
supervisor's meeting, with time available for the final two
steps.

Figure 12–1. Steps Of TOR Analysis.

In a typical TOR group, all supervisors in the same organization, the steps of TOR Analysis need not be explained at all. The
TOR leader simply directs the group through the process. The
steps need to be explained only in a classroom situation whose
purpose is to demonstrate TOR. In that case, the explanation
need go no further than the TRACE step, leaving the final two
steps to be explained when they get there in the demonstration.

If a demonstration is thought to be necessary before applying
TOR to a real life situation, a one-page incident has been used
successfully.* Far more effective has been TOR Analysis of an
incident portrayed by a film. The movie displays facts far more
effectively than many pages of reading. Turn the projector off at
that moment when the scenario undertakes to resolve the questions raised by the film. At that moment, let the TOR leader take
over. Two films, "Fatal Accident Report" † and "The Unplanned," ‡ have been used in this manner, but any film which
centers on an incident might be used.

As the group assembles, they must have in mind some incident,
some unplanned and undesired result, some snafu, ball-up, or accident which triggered the calling of the TOR session. The first

* *Mankator Co., Inc.*, one-page incident to demonstrate TOR Analysis, Employers Insurance of Wausau, Wausau, Wisconsin 54401.

† *The Fatal Accident Report*, 25 minutes, color, 1962. Sponsor—Employers
Insurance of Wausau, Wausau, Wisconsin 54401.

‡ *The Unplanned*, 20 minutes, color, 1971. Sponsor—Labour Canada, 3155
Cote de Liesse Road, Montreal 379, Quebec, Canada. Producer—National Film
Board of Canada.

step is to get FACTS on the table. The incident is described. All question each other to bring out the facts. One can picture the submission of reports of prior investigation, and if such information exists, it should be brought in. In point of fact, this first step is seldom that elaborate. Usually in five or ten minutes all anyone knows has been drawn out. As discussion becomes redundant or begins to fragment into problem-solving, the TOR leader quells the incipient bull session by demanding an answer to the next step.

Step two requires the group to STATE the proximate cause. They select this from the TOR Yellow Sheet. From the whole page, what one number best states the cause? In a few moments first one and then another proposes a number. Three, four, five numbers may be advanced. They must reach consensus on just one. They debate and discuss. They ask what the terms mean and define them to each other. They are learning. The TOR leader presses for decision, presses to limit the field. In 5 or 10 minutes, since they are told they must, the group settles for one number as the beginning point of TOR Analysis. Holdouts are placated with the assurance that their favorite number will be reconsidered in the trace step next. Above all, they are learning. They are applying the words and concepts to their own organization and their own ways of doing things.

To STATE the proximate cause of an accident or injury, start in Section 7. This block deals with personal traits and is used only with accidents and injuries. If nothing fits as a proximate cause in Section 7, determine a proximate cause anywhere from the page.

Having stated the proximate cause, each person writes that number at the top of a sheet of paper. Next they TRACE contributing factors. To the right of each cause factor there are one or more trace numbers. List these vertically under the beginning number. Each is now brought up in turn and discussed *briefly* (perhaps two minutes each). Brevity is impelled by the point of the discussion: "Did this factor contribute to cause the incident? Is it in or out, yes or no?"

If it's "in," the trace numbers that go with it are added to the list. If it's "out," just cross it out and go to the next number. Figure 12–2 illustrates the TRACE step.

THE TRACE STEP

TRACE starts with one number, producing a growing list of contributing factors, each of which is considered in turn, and comes to a natural close by a series of small "in" or "out" decisions.

35 Orders
~~40 Morale~~
~~46 Team~~
13 Correction
15 Tell Why

Brief discussion rejects #40 and #46, but #13 and #15 seem to apply, producing cross reference to six additional items.

~~42 Acts~~
20 Duties
~~30 By Passing~~
~~44 Initiative~~
~~24 Pressure~~
83 Span

Brief discussion rejects four items, but #20 and #83 produce cross reference to another six items, one of which (#44) you've already considered and rejected.

44
~~34 Decision~~
14 Instruction
~~53 Prop. Loss~~
~~12 Training~~
~~86 Staffing~~

Discussion rejects all but #14, which cross references to three additional items.

~~15~~
16 ~~Listen~~
~~42~~

You've already rejected two of these, and brief discussion rejects #16. The trace step is complete.

Figure 12–2. The Trace Step.

Every "in" number adds to the vertical list of trace numbers, and each is considered in turn as the group proceeds down the list. At first the list seems to grow rapidly, but the process soon reverses itself and tracing comes to a natural end, usually in twenty or thirty minutes.

The TRACE step is a quick overview. The group quickly learns that this is not the moment for indepth discussion. Sometimes a number is quickly struck out because it clearly did not contribute to the incident. Others are obviously "in." When discussion threatens to turn into a bull session, the TOR leader presses for decision: "Is it 'in' or is it 'out'?"

Thus, by a series of small decisions, the group is led along in a review of its own organization. They will question and disagree. In the process, they will perceive supervision not as words but as facts in their daily work.

When tracing comes to its natural close, the group has a score or more of numbers in a vertical list, many of which have crossed out. It is a good idea at this point to make a neat list of the "in" numbers, the factors which the group, in hasty overview, believes contributed to the incident. The incident, by TOR Analysis, has become a sort of instant case study, producing a list of perhaps a dozen factors which need further consideration. Since, however, the case concerns real, not hypothetical, events the situation calls for a practical turn. That is the purpose of the final two steps in TOR Analysis.

These steps seek to ELIMINATE some of the contributing factors, to isolate the important factors, and finally to SEEK feasible corrective action. A dozen things cannot be corrected at once. We must ELIMINATE in order to focus on the important factors. The list of contributing factors is now discussed in more depth. Some items can be eliminated for whatever reason seems appropriate to the group—because exposure and discussion was itself sufficiently corrective, because it is relatively unimportant, for whatever reason.

The ELIMINATE step merges insensibly into "SEEK feasible corrective action." Both steps tend to be simultaneous, a process of focusing the lesson to be learned, of defining the problem, and discussing what can be done about it. The SEEK step is problem solving. TOR leads to problem solving, but it does not produce a slide-rule solution.

What happens depends on many things. Often plans can be proposed and implemented within the powers of the group. Sometimes the problems extend beyond them. Sometimes the SEEK step loses its way and turns into a bull session. Action is not the sole purpose of TOR Analysis, and not all sessions end in definitive action. However, action not knowledge is the purpose of education. TOR Analysis seeks action in its final step.

What then has been gained? As a result of insights gained, individual supervisors can improve their performance even though group or company action may not be achieved. The causes for the trigger incident remain as a valid diagnosis even if corrective action does not immediately follow. The cumulative record of a series of TOR sessions creates a deeper diagnosis, revealing recurring operational errors which appear again and again. The record of these recurring operational errors, drawn from diverse incidents, serves to pinpoint frequent deficiencies, to define training needs, and to give direction to the thrust for improvement.

Questions and Answers

Q. Supervisory-management improvement is sought by many means. What advantage is there in the TOR method?

A. Perhaps the advantage that TOR gives words to real life situations, gives words to facts observed in the shop. Learning moves from the abstract to the concrete. Perhaps, also, advantage lies in the fact that the smaller firm, or the line supervisor, can conduct successful TOR sessions without necessarily possessing skill as a conference leader or teacher.

Q. Is TOR Analysis problem solving?

A. It is offered as a tool to diagnose and define rather than to solve. In part, it's a question of semantics. The key fact is that TOR is triggered by an incident not a problem.*

Q. Is TOR Analysis a process of accident investigation?

A. TOR produces no facts other than those already known by some member of the group. Therefore, it is not investigation. Rather, the results of accident investigation should be presented at the TOR session.

Q. What is gained by presenting the facts of accident investigation at a TOR session?

A. The hasty investigation typical of the majority of accidents, and the paucity of facts, will be observed. It may expose facts which have been overlooked, and expose conclusions "proven" with a neat array of selected facts. Above all, it scrutinizes the supervisory-management aspects of accident causation, an area insufficiently probed by many investigations.

Q. In cases of accident or injury, TOR begins in Section 7 on personal traits. Why?

A. We accept personal traits as a factor in accident causation, often expressed in the form of blame. TOR begins there but

---

* The difference between an incident and a problem is pursued further in Daniel C. Petersen, *Techniques of Safety Management* (McGraw-Hill, 1971).

then traces into supervisory-management factors over which supervisors may have more control.

Q. Suppose nothing in Section 7 fits?

A. The items in Section 7 merely hint at the rich jungle of physical and psychological factors in accident causation. If nothing fits, simply start a trace sequence in another block; that is, STATE the proximate cause in another block.

Q. Suppose we begin in Section 7 but all the trace numbers cross out?

A. That can happen. It means that some personal trait contributed to the accident, but the TOR group denies that it could have been controlled by supervisory action. Simply start another trace sequence in another block to see what else contributed.

Q. Who should be in a TOR group?

A. Normally, a manager and his subordinate supervisors, or a supervisor and his subordinate foremen. Interdepartmental incidents would require the presence of selected people from other units, or alternatively, the incident would be submitted to TOR Analysis at a higher echelon.

Q. Who is the TOR leader?

A. In smaller operations, the "boss" is TOR leader in the absence of staff help. In larger operations, staff may introduce TOR and teach the method, but its regular use would seem to depend on line supervision.

Q. What about #45 "honest error?"

A. People do goof, and if that is all there is to an incident, TOR Analysis starts and stops at #45. Frequently, however, a long trace sequence stems from the decision to blame George, which is done tactfully by calling it an honest error.

The Role of the TOR Leader

The TOR leader is pictured as a line supervisor or manager not necessarily possessing skills as a conference leader or a teacher. With perhaps limited talent as a discussion leader, he directs the course of discussion and controls the aimless bull session by insisting on a series of small decisions.

He begins by telling why the TOR session was called and gives

TECHNIC OF

1 COACHING

10 Unusual situation, failure to coach (new man, tool, equipment, process, material, etc.) 44, 24, 62

11 No instruction. No instruction available for particular situation 44, 22, 24, 80

12 Training not formulated or need not foreseen 24, 34, 86

13 Correction. Failure to correct or failure to see need to correct 42, 20, 30

14 Instruction inadequate. Instruction was attempted but result shows it didn't take 15, 16, 42

15 Supervisor failed to tell why 44, 24, 83

16 Supervisor failed to listen 11, 81

17

18

19

3 AUTHORITY (Power to decide)

30 Bypassing, conflicting orders, too many bosses 44, 13

31 Decision too far above the problem 36, 83, 85

32 Authority inadequate to cope with the situation 81, 83

33 Decision exceeded authority 20, 26, 14

34 Decision evaded, problem dumped on the boss 36, 14, 81

35 Orders failed to produce desired result. Not clear, not understood, or not followed 40, 46, 13, 15

36 Subordinates fail to exercise their power to decide 26, 12, 83, 85

37

38

39

2 RESPONSIBILITY

20 Duties and tasks not clear 44, 34, 14, 53

21 Conflicting goals 80, 33

22 Responsibility, not clear or failure to accept 26, 14, 54, 82

23 Dual responsibility 47, 34, 13

24 Pressure of immediate tasks obscures full scope of responsibilities 36, 12, 51

25 Buck passing, responsibility not tied down 44, 26, 55, 60

26 Job descriptions inadequate 80, 86

27

28

29

4 SUPERVISION

40 Morale. Tension, insecurity, lack of faith in the supervisor and the future of the job 15, 56, 64, 80

41 Conduct. Supervisor sets poor example 13, 84

42 Unsafe Acts. Failure to observe and correct 24, 11, 52

43 Rules. Failure to make necessary rules, or to publicize them. Inadequate follow-up and enforcement. Unfair enforcement or weak discipline 25, 36, 12, 52

44 Initiative. Failure to see problems and exert an influence on them 22, 34, 30

45 Honest error. Failure to act, or action turned out to be wrong 10, 12, 15, 81

46 Team spirit. Men are not pulling with the supervisor 40, 21, 56

47 Co-operation. Poor co-operation. Failure to plan for co-ordination 23, 25, 15, 66

48

49

©EMPLOYERS INSURANCE OF WAUSAU

Figure 12–3. TOR Technic Of Operations Review.

)PERATIONS REVIEW

DISORDER

51 Work Flow. Inefficient or hazardous layout, scheduling, arrangement, stacking, piling, routing, storing, etc. 41, 24, 31, 80

52 Conditions. Inefficient or unsafe due to faulty inspection, supervisory action, or maintenance 21, 32, 14, 86

53 Property loss. Accidental breakage or damage due to faulty procedure, inspection, supervision, or maintenance 43, 20, 80

54 Clutter. Anything unnecessary in the work area. (Excess materials, defective tools and equipment, excess due to faulty work flow, etc.) 44, 36, 80

55 Lack. Absence of anything needed. (Proper tools, protective equipment, guards, fire equipment, bins, scrap barrels, janitorial service, etc.) 44, 36, 80

56 Voluntary compliance. Work group sees no advantage to themselves 40, 15, 41

57

58

59

OPERATIONAL

60 Job procedure. Awkward, unsafe, inefficient, poorly planned 44, 32

61 Work load. Pace too fast, too slow, or erratic 44, 51, 63

62 New procedure. New or unusual tasks or hazards not yet understood 43, 44

63 Short handed. High turnover or absenteeism 80, 40, 61

64 Unattractive jobs. Job conditions or rewards are not competitive 81, 46

65 Job placement. Hasty or improper job selection and placement 80, 86

66 Co-ordination. Departments inadvertently create problems for each other (production, maintenance, purchasing, personnel, sales, etc.) 45, 35, 13

67

68

69

7 PERSONAL TRAITS (When accident occurs)

70 Physical condition — strength, agility, poor reaction, clumsy, etc. 44, 26, 65

71 Health — sick, tired, taking medicine 44, 24, 65

72 Impairment — amputee, vision, hearing, heart, diabetic, epileptic, hernia, etc. 44, 24, 65

73 Alcohol — (If definite facts are known) 80

74 Personality — excitable, lazy, goof-off, unhappy, easily distracted, impulsive, anxious, irritable, complacent, etc. .. 44, 13

75 Adjustment — aggressive, show off, stubborn, insolent, scorns advice and instruction, defies authority, antisocial, argues, timid, etc. 44, 13

76 Work habits — sloppy. Confusion and disorder in work area. Careless of tools, equipment and procedure 44, 13

77 Work assignment — unsuited for this particular individual . 42, 65

78

79

8 MANAGEMENT

80 Policy. Failure to assert a management will prior to the situation at hand 24, 81, 83

81 Goals. Not clear, or not projected as an "action image" .. 83, 86

82 Accountability. Failure to measure or appraise results ... 36

83 Span of attention. Too many irons in the fire. Inadequate delegation. Inadequate development of subordinates 12, 86

84 Performance appraisals. Inadequate or dwell excessively on short range performance 20, 65

85 Mistakes. Failure to support and encourage subordinates to exercise their power to decide 36, 33

86 Staffing. Assign full or part-time responsibility for related functions 66

87

88

89

Each section contains blank numbers. In your operation, TOR ANALYSIS may reveal factors in addition to those listed, TOR factors special to your organization. Insert these additional cause items under their proper heading, with a cross reference number (or numbers) leading to TOR factors controlling this special aspect.

such facts as he knows. He calls on others for facts, and joins in questioning. In such a discussion, people tend to jump ahead. They often propose solutions and argue alternative proposals and tend toward an aimless bull session. The TOR leader controls this by pointing to the TOR form and asking the group to STATE the immediate cause. He calls for a decision.

As the group tries to STATE the immediate cause, the TOR leader insists that consensus must be reached on just one number. Disagreement and debate are desirable, for therein lies learning; but the aimless bull session must be controlled. Many skills can be brought to this task, but in their absence it is sufficient for the TOR leader to insist on decision.

The urge to decide also impels the TRACE step on its way. The TOR leader keeps the vertical list of trace numbers, and he directs attention to each number in turn so that all members of the group are considering the same point at the same time. And he asks for a decision: "Is it in or is it out?" The TOR leader must be sufficiently dominant to keep the group on the same point and insist on decisions. Talent as a conference leader will help, but learning takes place even if the TOR leader merely keeps the TOR process on its tracks.

As the TRACE step ends, the discussion trends toward problem solving by eliminating minor factors and seeking corrective action. Skill as a conference leader becomes increasingly important as these steps proceed. The group at this point tries to agree on a procedure, or a recommendation, regarding their daily work. Sometimes this evolves with ease since the group has a common viewpoint as a result of TOR Analysis. Sometimes the TOR session has exposed issues not readily resolved and no conclusion can be reached. In that case the TOR leader defines issues and viewpoints and summarizes as best he can and brings the TOR session to a conclusion.

One quick demonstration would enable anyone to try TOR Analysis in his own organization. It is hoped that the same result has been achieved by the more tedious process of reading. That has been the purpose: to enable the reader to try TOR, to gather the experience of several TOR sessions, to evaluate its possible uses in his own organization. Complimentary supplies of the TOR form (TOR Yellow Sheets) are available from the author.

REFERENCES

Weaver, D. A.: Symptoms of operational error. *Journal of American Society of Safety Engineers,* October, 1971.

13

IMPROVING EXPLOSIVES SAFETY

R. E. McClay and Joyce A. McDevitt

This selection, dealing with the relatively narrow field of explosives safety, was included as an example of specific accident prevention techniques applied in a particular situation which also have a general application to the safety profession.

The article deals with one of the most hazardous of situations where, typically, tradition and old methods combine with new techniques and procedures. There is little opportunity for experimentation and no room for mistakes in this situation.

There is a limit, however, even in this hazardous occupational field, on the amount of resources that can be expended in the name of accident prevention. The authors explain how this problem has been tackled with an analytical approach requiring the use of computer programming. While not the ultimate in hazard analysis, it is an excellent example of a modern safety application of computerized management information systems.

WHEN an installation performs over 2500 different industrial operations involving dozens of types of final and intermediate ordnance products comprised of many hazardous chemical ingredients, it is difficult for management to know if, where, and how the safety of these operations should be upgraded. At the Naval Ordnance Station, Indian Head, some of these operations have evolved over an 80-year period.

New processes coexist with the old like the production of single-base naval gunpowder which has remained virtually unchanged since World War I. While the NAVORDSTA has pioneered in remote, automatic processing of hazardous materials,

From *Lifeline*, November–December, 1972.

most processes still call for operating personnel to come in close contact with the materials at one point or another.

The nature and quantity of materials handled is also a variable with time. An empirical knowledge of hazards common to standard double-base formulations has been gained over the years, and this forms the basis for many existing operating procedures. As these formulations are made more energetic, accepted practice often becomes an unknown risk.

Propellant types ranging from highly loaded solids to exotic liquid monopropellants diffuse the familiarity of operating personnel and strain both the hazard evaluation capability and the judgment of firstline supervision. In addition, the transfer of hazard data to process design and operating techniques occurs strictly within the realm of engineering judgment. Thus, in this setting, risk management is not a sometime thing but an everyday fact of life.

Given the above variability of operations and their associated risks and hazards, how does management achieve a goal of improving explosives safety within finite economic constraints? At the NAVORDSTA, a first step has been taken.

Using the evolving tools of system safety analysis, a computerized assessment of explosive hazards has been made resulting in a ranking of operations by their level of short-term risk. This study, called a PHRA (Preliminary Hazards Ranking Analysis), has been performed to accomplish the following:

- Identify the most hazardous feature of each operation for possible remedial action.
- Generate a systematic review of all operations by operating personnel.
- Establish a system safety data bank on NAVORDSTA explosive operations.
- Construct a priority list for further analysis.

Analytical Approach

The system was defined for purposes of this study as several sets of operations involving propellants, explosives, pyrotechnics, flammable solids/solvents, and other hazardous materials in the process of physical or chemical conversion, measurement or testing, assembly or disassembly, transportation, packaging, storage, etc.

Each individual operation is completely defined by a Special Job Procedure. The SJP is a document detailing each step of the operation. It provides personnel and explosive limits, designates facilities, specifies emergency procedures, and describes all personnel protective systems.

Operations are segregated into sets by their highest degree of hazard potential. The sets are constructed as hazard categories, defined as follows:

Category I—Those operations potentially capable of producing only equipment damage.

Category II—Those operations potentially capable of producing a minor facility loss.

Category III—Those operations potentially capable of producing a major facility loss.

Category IV—Those operations potentially capable of producing personnel injury.

Category V—Those operations potentially capable of producing a fatality.

The immediate objective established for the PHRA was to identify all operations within Category V and to provide some ranking of these by their inherent hazard potential.

Only fire and explosive hazards have been considered in this analysis. This stems from the premise that to combine industrial and explosive safety objectives in one program serves only to weaken both.

To examine only inherent hazards, it was necessary to further simplify the analysis by eliminating human error and equipment failure as possible contributing conditions. It is not that these vital factors can ever be disregarded: strong justification can be made for conducting a separate detailed analysis to determine the impact of human error and equipment failure upon inherent hazards. This would identify specific areas for increased inspection, training, and more sophisticated personnel protection systems. The preliminary hazards ranking thus provides a means to pinpoint operations where this detailed analysis (referred to here as an Operating Hazards Analysis) is most urgently needed.

Recognizing that every explosive operation has some potential for producing a fatality, it was necessary to specify some threshold or cutoff probability below which such an event can be considered exceedingly improbable. For several rather arbitrary reasons, this benchmark probability was established as 1×10^{-6}.

The fault-logic diagram in Figure 13–1 shows the Category V

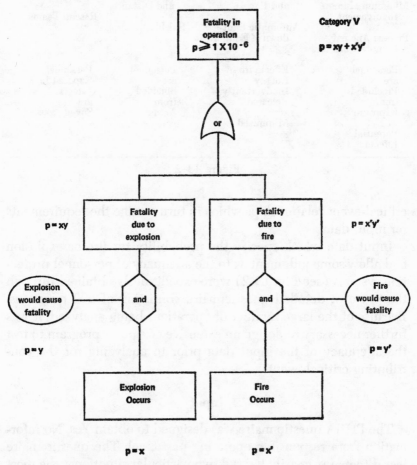

Figure 13–1. Fault Logic Diagram NOTE: The above algebraic relationships presume all events are independent and that all associated probabilities are very small.

A GENERALIZED PERSONNEL PROTECTION SYSTEM

Isolation Subsystems	Mollification Subsystems	Shelter Subsystems	Preservation Subsystems
Remote Automatic Controls	Pressure Reliefs	Protective Walls	Protective Clothing Against Heat and Fragments
	Blast Diverters		
nterlocks		Barriers	
	Deluge and Sprinklers		Quick Egress and Escape
Warning Lights, Signs, etc.		Barricades	
	Blow Out Walls and Panels	Dead Spaces and Distances	Medical Aid
Minimum Human Involvement			Rescue Teams
	Automatic Shutdown of Equipment	Shields	
Process Anomaly Remote Detectors			
Personnel are Precluded from Exposure to Potential Effects	Effects from Energy Inadvertently Released are Minimized	Personnel are Shielded from Actual Effects	Personnel Exposed to Effects are Saved

Figure 13-2

critical-event relationships which in turn outline the requirements for input data.

Input data which specify the probability for fire or explosion and allow some judgment as to the adequacy of personnel protection systems (see Fig. 13-2) were expeditiously obtained through the use of a detailed questionnaire consisting of 200 questions. Because of the large number of operations being analyzed, it was further necessary to design an extensive computer program to test the adequacy of the input data prior to analyzing for the contributing critical events.

Input

The PHRA questionnaire was designed to obtain Yes/No information from responsible operating personnel. The questionnaire was directed primarily toward two particular situations: the most hazardous step of the operation (defined as that step where an inadvertent initiation is most probable) and the step where the operator(s) is/are closest to the hazardous material (presumably where protection systems may be least effective).

Questions were included to provide three basic types of data:

a. Probability values for critical events such as accidental initiation of hazardous material, explosion, fire, and sympathetic reaction.

b. Factual data concerning the type, quantity, and sensitivity of hazardous material: the number of operators, supervisors, and observers present: and the protection afforded them during various phases of the operation.

c. Reliability of protective equipment such as interlocks, sprinkler/deluge systems or automatic shutdown equipment.

Program

A computer program was prepared to analyze the input data from the questionnaire. Yes/No answer combinations (test strings) were developed to serve various functions in the analysis.

- Category C test strings indicated that input data are improper or contradictory.
- Category V test strings indicated that the probability for a fatality in an operation exceeds 1×10^{-6}.
- Category N test strings indicated a high rate of personnel exposure among Category V operations.

Category C strings check for inconsistencies within a question, when more than one Yes answer is incorrectly given, or between questions: e.g. one answer indicated that the operator is shielded by a concrete wall when other answers indicate that no shield is present.

The fault-logic diagram shown in Figure 13–1 indicates how the fatality probability is developed for the Category V test strings.

Answer combinations have thus been formed represented by the probability products for explosion or fire (X or X′) and fatality in the event of an explosion or fire (Y or Y′). Probabilities for fire and explosion are direct inputs from the answer sheet.

For personnel protection, the assumption was made that the probability for having a fatality could still be 1×10^{-6} if only the minimum required protection exists. Criteria for construction and shielding to provide adequate personnel protection are stated in the NAVORDSTA safety manual.

If little or no protection exists, the probability of a fatality approached 1.0 for every fire or explosion. When the protection is significant but below that required, then intermediate fatality probabilities were assigned.

As an example, a test string was developed to describe the following (XY) situation which would result in a Category V operation, i.e.

$$P_{xy} < 1 \times 10^{-6}$$

Probability for explosion is .01 $<X<1$ during the most hazardous step of the operation as stated by the responder on the answer sheet. No automatic sprinkler, deluge, or shutdown system was indicated, which would interrupt the transition from initiation to full explosion, the probability would be in the upper portion of the range, approaching 1.

Probability for fatality in the event of an explosion is $Y>1 \times 10^{-6}$. The responder indicated that material is Class A, 1–10 pounds are within the work space, operator is in an adjoining bay during the most hazardous step, and protected by one 12-inch reinforced concrete wall. This is the minimum requirement specified in the NAVORDSTA safety manual.

Category N operations are those which meet Category V criteria and involve a high rate of hazard exposure—over 50,000 times in the next year. The Category N string were formulated as follows:

$N = N_p X\ N_e X\ N_o$
where:
N_p = number of personnel exposed per operation.
N_e = number of hazard exposures per person.
N_o = number of operations forecast for the next 12 months.

The probability for a fatality occurring each time a Category N operation is performed is not necessarily greater than other Category V operations. However, the probability of having a fatality within the next year is likely to be greater. This allows a ranking of Category V operations with Category N operations having the higher hazard priority.

Findings

A great deal of the first input data received was screened by the computer and found to be inconsistent or deficient in some respect. However, with the aid of operating personnel, the input was modified until a complete categorization was obtained on all current, explosive operations.

A substantial number of the NAVORDSTA current, explosive operations was found to meet Category V criteria though only 25 percent of these involved high-hazard exposure (Category N).

The number of answer combinations programmed as Category V strings found in each set of input was printed as program output. Since each of these represents a discrete critical-event probability combined with a corresponding personnel protection scheme, every such combination found in the input adds to the relative confidence that the operation is within Category V. This is not to say that each string is a different explosion or fire event possibility, but rather a logic string leading to the conclusion that a fire or explosion can occur.

Thirty-eight operations, placed in Category V with a high-hazard exposure rate, were found to have input corresponding to twenty-five or more Category V strings. These operations then were deemed most likely to cause a fatality in the next year.

The Preliminary Hazard Ranking Analysis has, in the manner described, identified a small number of industrial operations for further analysis to determine what specific steps can be taken to reduce hazard potential. In addition, an Operating Hazards Analysis can be performed on all Category V operations in order to learn how this potential is increased by human error or equipment failure. Future operations can hereafter be examined with the PHRA to provide a meaningful comparison of their hazard potential with that of existing operations.

Management now has a system analysis tool to show the measure of risk associated with each operation, which implies corrective measures needed and, most importantly, points out where remedial action should first be taken.

14

WHEN YOU'RE SPEAKING
OF SAFETY, IS ANYBODY
LISTENING?

Employers Insurance of Wausau

This little booklet, reprinted here in its entirety, is a report of a research project. It deals with safety communications and seeks to answer the question posed in the title: Is anybody listening?

Can a poster prevent an accident? Can a film, a speech or a safety meeting? Posed baldly, the judgmatic answer would appear to be, "It depends!" This research report gives some objective evidence about what it depends on. The evidence has credence partially because the research was done by a nationally known firm of research specialists in communications media. It also has credence—and practical application—because it is not a theoretical question to an insurance firm which invests major sums in safety media and education.

PEOPLE HAVE BEEN talk-talk-talking safety for years—from the early factory safety meeting days to modern day color motion picture showings. Is anybody listening?

What does "Safety" mean to employees?

How do employees feel about their company's safety activities?

Do safety posters, literature and films really influence attitudes and behavior?

We asked a prominent motivational research firm to find answers for these and other important questions. Here is a summary of their significant findings.

WHY A SAFETY MEDIA STUDY?

As a major producer of safety educational material, we realize that our subject is no natural spell-binder. We are also keenly

146

aware that there is much potential humor, drama and human interest in accident prevention—appeals that are too often buried under statistics, uninspired wordage, and anemic cliches.

In the many and varied safety materials we produce for policy-holder use, we have always tried to remain aware of—and fully utilize—the potentialities of our subject. Until recently, however, we never tried to measure the effectiveness of our efforts. In fact, we know of no extensive study which has tried to measure the effectiveness of safety media.

To try and obtain some insights into this relatively unknown field, and to see if some types of safety media are more effective than others, we engaged Social Research, Inc., of Chicago, nationally known research specialists in communications media, to conduct a special study for us. Their psychologists interviewed a large and representative cross section of industrial employees who have been well exposed to a balanced variety of safety educational materials.

All employees were interviewed at length, in their homes, where skillful attempts were made to measure the effect that safety media have had upon their attitudes and behavior, both on and off the job.

The major findings of this special study are summarized on the following pages. We are certain that some of these conclusions will impress you as they did us. They are a valuable guide for the future development of safety materials and activities, and for the effective use of safety media.

WHAT "SAFETY" MEANS TO EMPLOYEES

In trying to discover what employees think about safety media, the interviewers first probed their attitudes toward safety in general. Most workers are well aware of the hazard-ridden aspects of modern life. As one put it:

> Practically everything is unsafe—walking down the basement stairs, driving your car, working, lifting materials. I keep thinking about dropping something on my toes and ruining them, or lifting something heavy and putting myself out of commission.

Employees feel the need to integrate safety with their daily routine; to take proper precautions without conscious effort. Once a new safety procedure or new protective equipment is well established, they take it in their stride; but when it is first introduced, they tend to resist. Helping people to accept new precautions and deal with them comfortably is one of the challenges of safety communications.

Safety Means Conformity

Absolute safety is not an attractive goal. A bit of risk seems to be a necessary ingredient for dealing with tensions and anxieties.

Safety means conformity, and conformity seldom appears interesting or rewarding. However, most workers realize that being safe in conforming ways is necessary to hold a job, support a family and get ahead.

Safety is a Mutual Affair

Employees who rush, who like to take risks, who "horse around" or let off steam are generally seen as somewhat alien and threatening to the group. The over-all group pressure is for conformity; this pressure is strong, and helps keep people in line. A foundry worker said: "Most of the men are safety-minded, because it's for your own interest. Of course you'll always find some guy who'll be a little lax on safety; that's the kind we have to keep in line." The newcomer or minority group member is usually suspect, and considered outside of the group.

Safety is a Status Symbol

Being involved in a company's safety effort is regarded as a reward for good behavior; it is a status symbol which sets a man a bit above and apart from the group.

Productivity is More Rewarded than Safety

Many workers fail to see that productivity depends upon safety, as well as upon efficiency and other factors. Those on piece work, especially, feel that if they want to earn and get ahead, they must get things done fast—even at the cost of a little unnecessary risk. A welder expressed it this way: "It's just go—go! Everyone is climbing all over you to get the job done. It's dangerous when we work so fast. You try to be careful, but sometimes you have to take a chance."

Very cautious workers are regarded as timid, slow, even soft. Such accusations can lead to deliberate risk-taking. Older men, especially, tend to make fun of younger ones who try to be careful. They feel that skill and know-how are the important things, and that being overly cautious gets you nowhere.

Recklessness is "Blowing Off Steam"

Taking a chance, endangering oneself and others, violating safety rules—these are common reactions against pressures and tension. Some workers occasionally feel the need to kick up excitement, because they feel hemmed in by rules and warnings.

Monotonous, repetitive jobs make some employees feel occasionally that they have to take unnecessary risks to gain some emotional gratification. Recklessness is often an unconscious way of hitting out at life.

Fear also contributes—fear of certain equipment and hazards. This adds to the tension which might sometimes lead to accidents. Occasionally, an accident might be "allowed" to happen, to ease the strain. Some people seem more compelled than others to by-pass the rules and safeguards, and to neglect wearing protective equipment. One man observed: "Lots of men take accidents as a joke. Something happens and they feel they have to laugh it off. I think this is sort of protection against being scared."

Overconfidence, Fatigue, Monotony

Some workers feel so protected on the job that personal efforts at safety seem unimportant. In addition to complacency, such overconfidence sometimes results in reckless showing off.

At the other extreme, fatigue and boredom often make the simplest precautions loom as impossible efforts. This tends to encourage a fatalistic attitude about job injuries.

A Real Challenge for Safety Media!

Safety posters, literature and films have a complex job to perform. They should teach employees, not only the technicalities of working with tools and skills, but also:

How to maintain control.

How to "blow off steam" safely.

How to find it worthwhile to pursue company goals and rules.

How to make life on and off the job safer and more tolerable.

What does all this mean? That there are many avenues for communicating to employees about safety. Chances are that in many companies, not enough use is being made of some of these avenues.

HOW COMPANIES INFLUENCE EMPLOYEE ATTITUDES TOWARD SAFETY ACTIVITIES AND MATERIALS

Employees generally appreciate the dollar value of safety media, equipment and activities.

In companies where morale is high, employees are much more aware that there is genuine concern for their well being; but in all companies, the general feeling is that employees benefit greatly from safety media, equipment and activity.

How Workers Visualize their Companies' Safety Efforts

Employees have clear-cut ideas about their companies' safety activities—the methods, goals, and the amount of vigor and sincerity put into it.

This is an important point, because the way a worker conceives of his company's safety efforts strongly influences his behavior on the job, and his ability to learn from and respond to safety media.

The following variety of company "types" was consistently observed by workers who were interviewed:

The Lively Company

There are companies that succeed in creating and sustaining a spirited interest in safety performance through various means, and they dramatize the value of safety through attractive bulletin boards and special displays. They persuade workers to take personal interest in and identify themselves with company goals concerning the prevention of injuries.

This fosters pride in the company, and in its record of efficient, accident-free productivity. There is a sense of pace and teamwork in such a plant which makes safety a lively and challenging thing, and makes employees feel they are a solid part of the effort. They show keen interest in safety media and activity. The following expresses the typical feeling of the worker in the lively company . . .

> They have a system of lights; red means someone's injured and green means nobody missed a day. The company checks equipment daily and if someone gets hurt, they make a poster about it for all the guys to see. Once in a while they have a movie and pass out leaflets afterwards. I think all of this is good, and the men like it.

Some companies stress incentives—prizes for top safety performance, or for winning various types of safety contests. There is a sense of lively competition for the rewards, and real enjoyment is gained by the prizewinners, as the following remark discloses . . . "It's a good place to work; not much friction; everybody seems to work together. Right now we got a safety slogan contest going on. They give dinners to a guy and his wife if he answers the slogan right."

Such rewards may not tap the deeper loyalties, but there is worthwhile benefit—particularly when these rewarding activities are not overstressed, but merely supplement basic safety efforts. Employees then seem to appreciate the importance of safety, and they feel rather secure and well protected.

The Overzealous Company

There is a happy median, of course, insofar as safety activity is concerned; if a company overdoes it in this respect, workers tend to feel snowed under. They complain about endless meetings, films, literature, and preach-preach-preaching about safety. They regard their company as a heavy-handed parent. They feel overguarded, that too much is expected of them, and they are fearful of punishment.

In such a company, response to safety media is not enthusiastic; employees say they are overexposed to it, that it's "just one more thing." Accidents can be retaliatory—a way of getting even.

There is a strong tendency to forget safety procedures, or to defy them.

The Negligent Company

On rare occasions, a company may seem to get busy about safety only after a major accident occurs. There is a brief flurry of effort, which gradually dies out . . . until another serious injury temporarily stirs things up again.

Employees, under such circumstances, feel that the company has no sincere interest in their safety or personal welfare. They feel neglected and resentful. There is a sense of barrier and distance between employee and company. Employees are apt to scorn safety media and activity, and take little interest in them. One employee declared in an interview: "Pamphlets and posters are a waste of money when the company doesn't follow through. They only seem to have safety meetings after a serious accident, and then it's only for the supervisors."

Who Do Workers Blame for Injuries?

Employees are not quick to blame the company, or supervision, for accidents. They feel it is usually the injured person's action— or lack of action—that is at fault. Skilled workers take more pride in their efforts, and are generally more careful than less skilled workers.

Accident causes that workers most commonly feel are management's responsibility are poor housekeeping, old or defective machinery or plant, overcrowding, piece work pressure, or improperly trained new employees.

Attitudes of Women Workers

Women are more serious than men about safety. They generally believe that they are well protected, but they feel somewhat left out of main safety activities.

The greatest worries of female employees are about protecting their fingers, hair and toes, and about the dangers of flammables, crowding, and lifting. Restrictions that they find the most annoying are those against smoking, and prohibiting the wearing of open-toed shoes.

THE INFLUENCE OF SAFETY COMMUNICATIONS

Employees Show High Tolerance for Safety Media

Generally, workers feel that posters, leaflets and films on safety are useful, interesting, and valuable for their private and working lives. They feel their jobs are safer, as a result, and that safety tips they have learned have probably saved them from minor or serious injuries.

A Valuable Type of Company Communication

The interviews revealed that safety media are an important company communication. They help build ego and foster pride in work and productivity. They also help make a company seem less distant and impersonal.

Safety media help maintain desirable employee relationships. They provide points of joint interest and a common basis for conversation.

Most workers read more safety material than they will openly admit. They refer to safety media spontaneously at meetings, when accidents occur, and during talks with superiors to back up their opinions. Most employees can recall posters and leaflets so vividly that they apparently read them thoroughly, and learn from them.

It is customary for many working men to carry home safety leaflets, where they are often a matter for family discussion. Safety literature provides a way for a man to show authority and dignity in his home, and employees feel they get many useful tips from it.

Following are a few revealing comments resulting from the interviews . . .

> I think safety materials are wonderful—most helpful. They put everyone on guard, and I picture myself in the dangerous situation, and make sure I'm not the next one.
> They are pretty good. You stop to think the company is actually worried about you.
> I always bring them home and talk to the family about them. I've actually seen the two older boys discussing them. Subconsciously they absorb the information.

Effectiveness of Different Types of Safety Media

All types of media—posters, literature, films—appear to contribute something important, and to produce worthwhile results. All types have obviously helped bring employees to the high level of safety concern generally evidenced by the interviews, and play a necessary part in sustaining this high interest level.

Posters

Employees generally prefer posters over leaflets—especially if the posters are clever, colorful or comic. They say that they look at posters several times daily, and the impact appears to be quick, precise and factual. Workers see posters as valuable job reminders about relatively simple things that one needs to remain alert to.

Posters stimulate more free interchange of conversation than do leaflets. There is usually interaction and talk among men as they look at safety posters. When a new poster appears, there are many lively conversations about it for a few days afterwards.

Posters are especially important because they are the primary means of reaching the men who are not particularly safety conscious (generally the older, less skilled worker). These men cannot stay outside of the general awareness at bulletin boards, since safety is then part of the common language of the moment. If they laugh or scoff, they are involved in safety discussion, and the pressures of the group and the more commonly accepted attitudes are pressed upon them.

Clever or humorous posters are preferred because they give a man a chance to study them without appearing naive. They also allow him to laugh about things he may feel tense or anxious about. Humor also greatly increases tolerance for repetition.

More serious posters bear less repetition, and are less openly responded to, but they also seem to make an impression and convey a message.

Following are some significant remarks about posters, by those interviewed . . .

> I talk about a poster when I see someone violating a safety rule, like a guy working without safety glasses.

I've seen fellows point posters out when someone uses a rope that's tore, or a broken chain.

The gory ones you want to keep out of your mind. They are impressive, but then you try to forget them. The comic ones have a punch line that you want to remember for a long time.

The plant bulletin board provides a point where men can meet a few times daily, where safety posters inform along with other important or interesting communications. Cheerful and informative communications at such a point are for many workers a consistently pleasant and rewarding experience.

Safety Literature

Safety literature is a more personally rewarding kind of communication. It is held, read more thoroughly, and it explains in detail the "how?" and "why?" It makes people knowledgeable about many things—on the job, in the home, on the go—and this is satisfying for most persons.

Many companies keep leaflets readily available in reading racks or at other established distribution points. This is an effective way to reach many, but some employees are naturally reluctant to reach for leaflets because of shyness, or fear of being thought unmanly or naive. Getting literature into employees' hands through mailings to homes, having foremen pass it out, or through other methods, is less frequently done and perhaps should be more widely practiced.

Workers today are becoming more sophisticated about safety. They show more interest in complex subjects than in common and elementary dangers. They are interested in specifics such as life-saving techniques, visual habits in driving, safe lifting techniques. Information that is more elaborate and sophisticated is a source of pride and superiority, especially when it enlarges their skill and knowledge. They resent information so simply presented that it seems to "talk down" to them.

Literature that is associated with a man's work, with his personal life, and with the wonder of his physical being—his legs, hands, eyes, senses—has great appeal. The magic of seeing, hearing, doing, achieving, is very stimulating to most people.

Workers tend to avoid leaflets which are introspective, which deal mainly with attitudes, and which seem to be "preachy." They prefer information that deals with things in straightforward ways. They are attracted to the dramatic and the gory if it appears relevant to their jobs and lives.

Safety subjects can be related over and over again, and when the telling is done with enough liveliness and a sense of pertinence to a person's job and personal life, he will pay attention. A sophisticated worker who has worked with tools most of his life can respond attentively to a leaflet on hand tools if it is skillfully designed and written.

Following are some revealing comments concerning safety literature . . .

> There is more information in leaflets than in posters. Some have a good story—are well illustrated, have lots of safety information, and enough humor to take the dryness out. Just the right mixture, I think.
> This leaflet is right to the point. People get so damn lazy they don't keep clean, and they just invite skin diseases.
> This leaflet is real interesting, about keeping medicine out of the reach of children. I was a medic in the navy, and anyone with children would be interested in this.

Safety Films

The only serious problem concerning safety films seems to be that employees don't get enough of them. Most workers are almost childlike in their response to educational films, which is somewhat of a surprise in this television age. There is a sense of excitement about getting to see safety films. While we know of some companies that have tried lunch-hour showings with little or moderate success, workers interviewed in this study revealed much enthusiasm for showings during this period. In companies where films are mainly reserved for supervisors and others up the line, employees feel resentful and left out.

Most workers feel they have seen relatively few safety films, but that they have benefited very much from the showings; they remember them over a long period of time, feel very affirmative about them, and through the information recalled, they have obviously learned a great deal from them. The impact seems much greater than from any other type of safety media.

Films offer a great many handles for teaching in vivid and personal ways, where they are effectively animated and specific, and where showings are well planned and conducted. The capacity and willingness of people to absorb safety and job information through this medium seems very extensive . . . and relatively untapped.

WHAT WE'VE CONCLUDED FROM THIS STUDY

The findings of this media study by Social Research, Inc., convince us that safety educational materials have greatly influenced industrial employees—to the point where they are a solid part of the working man's way of life, and of his outlook upon himself, his company and his job.

All the various types of safety media—posters, literature, films —perform different and important functions; all have been instrumental in bringing workers to their present high level of safety awareness, and all are necessary in sustaining this awareness.

The young people coming into industry today have learned in their schools, in their homes, and on television, that safety is a way of life. They look upon those who think otherwise as being somewhat odd and foolhardy.

To be active and knowledgeable about safety, today, is regarded as more masculine and more rewarding than it used to be. To "horse around" and flaunt the rules is less acceptable than formerly, with many pressures by the employee group being brought to bear upon those who do not conform.

How Safety Media Can be Improved

The study revealed a number of things that can be done to heighten the effectiveness of safety media:

Need for Realism

There is increasing need for safety media to be realistic. It must give a true sense of the activity, the tension, the pressures of the job and working conditions. It needs to be more personal. There is need to reduce the sense of distance and barrier between the communications and those who work in industry.

Need for Diversification

There is increasing need to teach varied and specific things about safety. There is more and more diversification in industry, and in off-the-job activities; all of this has created many different kinds of safety problems and goals. Safety media must be less generalized if it is to seem pertinent to the lives of individuals, both on and off the job.

Need for Sophistication

People are attracted to posters and literature that communicate quickly, easily, and with an economy of language. However, they do not want to be "spoken down to." They strongly desire to know complex and technical things, as they are anxious to enlarge their knowledge and skill.

Coordination with Company Activities

Safety educational media are most useful when they are tied into company activities—meetings, demonstrations, film showings, other safety activity. Using educational materials as a point of departure for these interactions, and as something concrete to take away from such activities, is quite valuable.

Safety Media and the Female Employee

Most safety media is male oriented and dominated, and the role of the woman worker is largely minimized or overlooked. Thus she is much less responsive to safety educational materials than is the male worker. Women need to be more directly involved in both safety media and safety activity.

As industry—and life, itself—grows ever more complex and fast-moving, the challenge for safety educational materials intensifies. But if safety communications keep pace with progress, change with the ever-changing times, and speak directly, personally, appealingly to people, there is no doubt that they will find a large and responsive audience . . . or that they will beneficially influence employee attitudes and behavior.

15

IDENTIFYING SAFETY
TRAINING NEEDS

Dan C. Petersen

The focus of this article is best stated by the author himself: "It seems particularly true in the safety profession that training is often used as a panacea—as the solution selected regardless of the problem defined (or without any definition of the problem). The purpose of this paper is to look at the identification of training needs, or rather, the definition of the problem for the purpose of determining whether or not it is a training problem in fact, or some other type of problem."

Safety creates its own body of professional knowledge often by borrowing from all disciplines and all fields of human endeavor, a fact illustrated in the author's generous tribute to the previous contributions of Peter Pipe and Robert Mager.

THE PROFESSIONAL SAFETY man spends a good deal of time in training activities. He more often utilizes training or suggests training as solutions to our safety problems than any other type of solution. It's true that training is a powerful influence over employee behavior. It's true that when you train you not only provide knowledge and skill, but also motivation (see Petersen, 1971).

Some Cautions To Be Observed

However, there are some cautions to be observed. One of the better texts on industrial training (McGehee and Thayer's) warns that: "Proper utilization of training in modern industry and business requires that it be put in its proper context. It is not an end in itself, but a means to an end."

They further state that: "To be effective, this management tool

From *Journal of the American Society of Safety Engineers*, March, 1973.

must be used when and where it is needed and not as window dressing to impress visiting firemen with the alleged personnel-mindedness of an organization. We suspect that the effectiveness of a training program may be an inverse function of the elaborateness of the lithography, and the multiplicity of forms and manuals which are shown visitors."

It seems particularly true in the safety profession that training

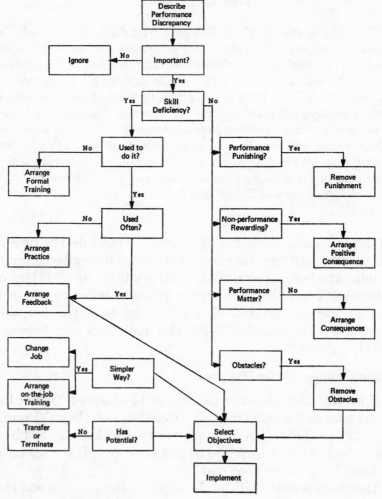

Figure 15–1. Mager's Basic Model.

is often used as a panacea—as the solution selected regardless of the problem defined (or without any definition of the problem).

The purpose of this paper is to look at the identification of training needs, or rather the definition of the problem for the purpose of determining whether or not it is a training problem in fact, or some other type of problem.

Peter Pipe and Robert Mager recently published one of the simplest and finest books available on problem definition entitled *Analyzing Performance Problems* (or "You Really Oughta Wanna").

The entire book is written around the flow chart shown in Figure 15–1. The original flow chart is included here for its value in organizational non-safety problem analysis, but our main purpose is to adapt this chart to the field of safety management and to use it as a tool to help us identify and analyze safety problems as a pre-step to objective setting.

We can look at a flow chart or model such as this from two standpoints: (1) from the standpoint of a safety director or middle manager analyzing the performance discrepancies of first-line foremen or (2) from the standpoint of a first-line foreman analyzing the performance problems of his workers.

Analyzing a Supervisor's Performance Discrepancies

Placing ourselves first in the position of the corporate safety specialist or middle manager with a job of assisting the first-line foreman, we find the original model slightly adapted as shown in Figure 15–2.

We start by a simple description of his performance discrepancy, such as "Joe is not adequately investigating accidents," or "George is not teaching his new employees the safety rules."

Our second step is to ask the question, "Is the discrepancy important?" The central idea here, of course, is whether or not the alleged problem is really a problem; whether or not the discrepancy is really worth spending our time on. For instance, we may have cited George's "attitude" as a problem. Every time we survey his department he gets highly abrasive and irritated with us for interfering with "his" safety program. Is this a problem? Maybe—maybe not. It could be a serious problem if George is

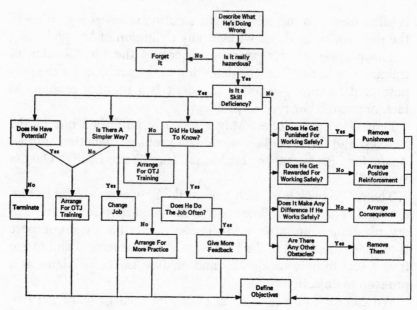

Figure 15–2. Supervisory Model.

also not doing a job (not performing) in safety; or it may well be no problem if he is performing, and in fact doesn't need any help from us.

Assuming however the discrepancy is important, we go to the next step which is the determination of whether or not the performance discrepancy is or is not due to a skill deficiency. This is the key branching point in the model, for it leads us to either a training solution or a non-training solution. How do we make this determination? Mager and Pipe suggest a simple question: "Could he do it if his life depended on it?" If the answer is no, there is a skill deficiency—it is a training problem. If the answer is yes, it is not a training problem.

Let's assume we answer this key question "yes" and branch left on Figure 15–2. We might then first ask whether or not he ever knew how to perform satisfactorily. If the answer is no we must provide some real initial training. If the answer is yes, he only needs practice—we should arrange situations where he can "brush-up" on his unused skill.

A second question might be to ask if there is a simpler or different strategy or approach he might use to get results. Would

5-minute safety talks to the group achieve his purpose instead of individual employee contacts? Would delegating the inspection task to a lead man serve the purpose? If the answer is yes, a simple change may suffice. If no, we are back to supervisory training to improve his performance in the needed strategy. We must, for instance, train him to properly investigate accidents.

A third question is "Can he once trained, perform satisfactorily?" If we answer this no, we have the wrong man. If we answer it yes, we again come back to supervisory training. After answering these three questions, we are now ready for the definition of our training (or non-training) objectives.

What We Are Going To Do

In other words we now at least are ready to sit down and specify what we are going to do. Actually, to properly define our training objectives, we have a somewhat more complex task than just specifying what we are going to do. We will briefly discuss this task later.

Let's now assume we answered our earlier question on skill deficiency with a no—he *could* perform if his life depended on it. We then branch right on the model.

There are four questions we ask on this branch of the model:

1. Is he punished for performing in safety? This may sound unreal, but actually it is quite real in safety. There are several ways a supervisor could be punished for performing in safety.

—By a management who rewards only for production, thus punishing a supervisor for spending time only on safety.

—By peers who ridicule safety performance.

—By subordinates who scoff at him for his efforts.

—By management who undermine his safety efforts.

If such punishment exists, it should be identified and attempts made at removal.

2. Is he rewarded for not performing in safety? Is he rewarded more for performance in other areas? He will spend time and effort where there is potential for reward.

3. Does safety performance matter at all? Or does nothing happen to a supervisor for either good or poor safety performance?

4. What other obstacles lie in the way for safety performance?

Either branch of the model ends up at a point where we are ready to define objectives. This supervisory model might be summarized by the following checklist of key issues and questions to ask:

I. The supervisor isn't doing what he should be doing in safety. I think I've got a training problem.

1. What is the performance discrepancy?	—Why do I think there is a training problem?
	—What is the difference between what is being done and what is supposed to be done?
	—What is the event that causes me to say that things aren't right?
	—Why am I dissatisfied with the situation?
2. Is it important?	—Why is the discrepancy important?
	—What would happen if I left the discrepancy alone?
	—Could doing something to resolve the discrepancy have any worthwhile result?
3. Is it a skill deficiency?	—Could he do it if he really had to?
	—Could he do it if his life depended on it?
	—Are his present skills adequate for the desired performance?

II. Yes. It is a skill deficiency. He couldn't do it if his life depended on it.

4. Could he do it in the past?	—Did he once know how to perform as desired?
	—Has he forgotten how to do what I want him to do?
5. Is the skill used often?	—How often is the skill or performance used?
	—Does he get regular feedback about how well he performs?

	—Exactly how does he find out how well he is doing?
6. Is there a simpler solution?	—Can I change the job by providing some kind of job aid?
	—Can I store the needed information some way (written instructions, checklists) other than in someone's head?
	—Can I show rather than train?
	—Would informal (i.e. on-the-job) training be sufficient?
7. Does he have what it takes?	—Could he learn the job?
	—Does he have the physical and mental potential to perform as desired?
	—Is he overqualified for the job?

III. It is not a skill deficiency. He could do it if he wanted to.

8. Is desired performance punishing?	—What is the consequence of performing as desired?
	—Is it punishing to perform as expected?
	—Does he perceive desired performance as being geared to penalties?
	—Would his world become a little dimmer (to him) if he performed as desired?
9. Is non-performance rewarding?	—What is the result of doing it his way instead of my way?
	—What does he get out of his present performance in the way of reward, prestige, status, jollies?
	—Does he get more attention for misbehaving than for behaving?
	—What event in the world supports (rewards) his present way of doing things? (Are you inadvertently rewarding irrelevant behavior while overlooking the crucial behaviors?)

	—Is he "mentally inadequate," so that the less he does the less he has to worry about?
	—Is he physically inadequate, so that he gets less tired if he does less?
10. Does performing really matter?	—Does performing as desired matter to the performer?
	—Is there a favorable outcome for performing?
	—Is there an undesirable outcome for not performing?
	—Is there a source of satisfaction for performing?
	—Is he able to take pride in his performance, as an individual or as a member of a group?
	—Does he get satisfaction of his needs from the job?
11. Are there obstacles to performing?	—What prevents him from performing?
	—Does he know what is expected of him?
	—Does he know when to do what is expected of him?
	—Are there conflicting demands on his time?
	—Does he lack the authority? . . . the time? . . . the tools?
	—Is he restricted by policies or by a "right way of doing it" or "way we've always done it" that ought to be changed?
	—Can I reduce "competition from the job"—phone calls, "brush fires," demands of less important but more immediate problems?

IV. What should I do now?

| 12. Which solution is best? | —Are any solutions inappropriate or impossible to implement? |

—Are any solutions plainly beyond our
resources?
—What would it "cost" to go ahead
with the solution?
—What would be the added "value" if
I did?
—Is it worth doing?
—Which remedy is likely to give us the
most result for the least effort?
—Which are we best equipped to try?
Which remedy interests us most?
(Or, on the other side of the coin,
which remedy is most visible to those
who must be pleased?)

Analyzing a Worker's Safety Problem

The same general approach can be used for diagnosing worker
safety performance problems. The model in Figure 15–3 has been
adapted for this. This model can be used by first-line supervisors
as a pre-step to setting objectives for worker improvement.

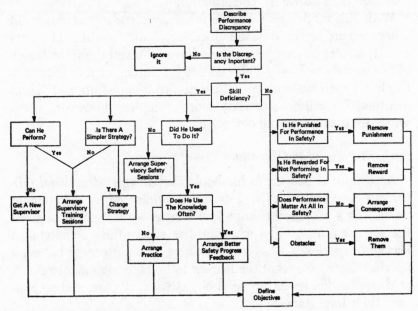

Figure 15–3. Employee Model.

In the employee model, we ask almost the same questions in the same order as before. We initially describe what he is doing wrong, determine if it is really hazardous and then determine whether or not it is a skill deficiency by our question: "Could he do it if his life depended on it?"

If we determine that it is a skill deficiency, we ask three similar questions as before; did he used to know, is there a simpler way, and does he have potential. The answers to these questions lead up to giving workers more feedback, more practice, more training, job changes, or transfers.

If we determine that we do not have a skill deficiency, we then ask the same four questions as before:

—Does he get punished for working safely (by his foreman due to less production and by his peers through ridicule)?
—Does he get rewarded for working safely (by anybody)?
—Does it make a difference to anybody if he works safely?
—Are there any other obstacles?

It is perhaps easier to see how these four questions can be very real factors in his safety performance.

With this model, as with the others, we end up at the point where we are ready to define objectives. This definition of objectives is a relatively easy task if we have followed the right hunch of our models and have a non-training situation, or if in following the left hunch we end up with a non-training solution. It is, as mentioned earlier, somewhat more complex, however, when we're discussing training objectives.

Preparing Training Objectives

According to Mager, in his book, *Preparing Instructional Objectives,* an objective is an intent communicated by a statement describing a proposed change in a learner—a statement of what the learner is to be like when he has successfully completed a learning experience. It is a description of a pattern of behavior (performance) we want the learner to be able to demonstrate.

Mager further spells out what objectives really are, and emphasizes their importance:

The statement of objectives of a training program must denote measurable attributes observable in the graduate of the program, or otherwise it is impossible to determine whether or not the program is meeting the objectives.

When clearly defined goals are lacking, it is impossible to evaluate a course or program efficiently, and there is no sound basis for selecting appropriate materials, content, or instructional methods. After all, the machinist does not select a tool until he knows what operation he intends to perform. Neither does a composer orchestrate a score until he knows what effect he wishes to achieve. Similarly, a builder does not select his materials or specify a schedule for construction until he has his blueprints (objectives) before him. Too often, however, one hears teachers arguing the relative merits of textbooks or other aids of the classroom versus the laboratory, without ever specifying just what goal the aid or method is to assist in achieving. I cannot emphasize too strongly the point that an instructor will function in a fog of his own making until he knows just what he wants his students to be able to do at the end of the instruction.

Finally Mager describes his method for writing objectives that describes the desired behavior of the learner:

First, identify the terminal behavior by name; you can specify the kind of behavior that will be accepted as evidence that the learner has achieved the objective.

Second, try to define the desired behavior further by describing the important conditions under which the behavior will be expected to occur.

Third, specify the criteria of acceptable performance by describing how well the learner must perform to be considered acceptable.

When you have completed this process you have adequately written your training objectives (set your terminal behavior). Having completed this, you are now ready to decide what you will do to the learner to get him from his present state of performance to your written statement of desired terminal performance. The difference between these two levels of performance is what must be taught.

While this process may sound like excessive work and very time consuming, most trainers who actually do this find it is less work than expected and an extremely valuable way to spend time. Many find that when they actually properly develop training objectives in this manner that the best instructional methods become obvious, and the training content is a long way toward completion.

Using the Models

These models and the questions listed earlier describe a way of analyzing human safety performance. Since the large majority of safety problems we face are human problems, this analysis process might be a handy way of analyzing many of our major problem areas in safety. The key questions are simple to remember; and if you find the process valuable, you will find yourself mentally going through them in analyzing your safety problems.

REFERENCES

Mager, R. F.: *Preparing Instructional Objectives.* Belmont, Fearon Publishers, 1962.

Mager, R., and Pipe, P.: *Analyzing Performance Problems.* Belmont, Fearon Publishers, 1970.

McGehee, W., and Thayer, P.: *Training in Business & Industry.* New York, John Wiley, 1961.

Petersen, D.: *Techniques of Safety Management.* New York, McGraw-Hill, 1971.

16

MANAGEMENT INVOLVEMENT FOR SAFETY ENGINEERS

R. O. Helberg

The safety climate has changed notably since this article first appeared. Nonetheless, the portrait of the safety professional functioning within an organization is still relevant today and equally instructive to the safety neophyte.

Since this article appeared much has been written to explicate the role of the safety professional operating as a manager and of necessity acquiring a knowledge of management and practicing the skills of a manager. The special quality of this item lies in the sense of opportunity the author conveys. Despite the pace of change, he still evokes the life and career of a safety professional.

THE SAFETY ENGINEER's involvement in management can be a many-faceted problem or opportunity, depending on how you look at it, and there are certain principles of management which need to be understood before his work can become more productive and effective. It seems desirable here to outline some of the relationship situations that exist among members of the safety engineering profession.

Insurance company safety engineer: He is in a line position within his own organization, responsible to a manager of the safety engineering department, or if he is the manager of the safety engineering department he has other safety engineers responsible to him. If he is a manager in a field operation, he probably is responsible to either a branch or regional vice president or to the home office department head.

In his relationship with his company's customers, he finds that he is on a consulting basis. He can only observe conditions and

From *Journal of American Society of Safety Engineers*, July, 1968.

recommended changes. He can also, through various communications and educational facilities, seek to improve the general level of safety intelligence among the management, supervisory, or worker personnel in his customer's organization. He has no authority to make change but must do it through logic, good communications, and real salesmanship.

Corporate safety director and safety engineer: Depending on the size of the company, this individual can be at many levels and in fact, can be a part of a department or division in a very large company. In this particular case, the position has been created under a variety of situations and there could be numerous reasons for it. In my experience, it is quite unusual for the safety engineer or even the safety director to be considered a part of the top management team of the organization. He is usually responsible to a vice president, in some cases the management member who has the insurance-buying responsibility.

At times, it may be the top management individual who is responsible for industrial relations. Most often, he is considered a staff man and not a line man. He would seldom have a large staff, clerical or otherwise, that is responsible to him. Many times, his duties would embrace other areas in addition to his safety responsibilities. Most often, his findings relative to physical conditions or personnel problems that might involve the need for change would require that he submit his recommendations to higher management or line management before they can be implemented.

There is a third category of safety engineer who may be found throughout industry. His basic function is something other than a safety engineer. However, because of the safety relationship of his product or his work, he is designated as such. This may range all the way from the salesman of safety products to the mechanical engineer who assists in the safety design of the company's products. He is strictly a specialist, and safety engineering is but a small part of his overall function.

These of course are only some of the situations under which we can find safety engineers working. The three examples are cited as an indication that there is variety and difference in duties and functions within our profession. It would be as impossible to say that we all have the same need for management relationships as it is to say that we do not all need to understand some basic principles involved in management relationships. It is as important for the person who is managed to understand these principles as it is for the person who does the managing.

I think it is also important to realize that regardless of the position or relationship to the organization, every safety engineer has the same ambitions and desire to move upward in an organization as do other people. While the title of the job may seem to narrow the natural path upward, I think that you will find that how a man applies his special knowledge and shows his attitudes to the overall goals and objectives of his company will really be the measure or criteria for upward movement.

Let us consider two reasons for the safety engineer needing a good knowledge of management concepts. Number one is, of course, the need to fulfill his own ambitions by choosing the right path to advancement and higher earnings. The second is just as important because it will establish the productivity and effectiveness of his work upon which he will be measured and from which he will derive work satisfaction.

What should the safety engineer know about management within his own company? First, he ought to know the table of organization. Surprising as it may seem, many people only think they know who runs the company and who is responsible for certain areas of its activity. Some companies have prepared elaborate organization charts which spell out quite carefully not only the job titles but the functions and relationships of each management position. If your company has done this, you should familiarize yourself with the formal (and I underline the word formal) company organization charts. Then, you should establish through your superiors the exact relationship of your position to the formal organization.

At this point, many people believe that they now understand the company's management organization. They think that they know how management decisions are made, how orders for activity are given and how the job gets done. This is an exceedingly naive assumption. In reality, in almost all organizations, the bulk of the work, most of the orders that are given, and many of the management decisions are made through what might be called the informal organization. This comes about for several reasons. One may be the weaknesses that are bound to crop up in the person filling a position in the organization. After all, in spite of a weak person, the job must get done. Or, at the other extreme, because of exceptional abilities of some people in areas outside of the scope of their job description, intelligent management may use their abilities to obtain additional effort or to get other worthwhile activities accomplished. Therefore, it is important that you also become familiar with the informal organization, the one that really gets things done in most organizations.

Once you have become familiar with these two management organizations in the company, or charts if you prefer to call them that, you are in a position to judge how your actions or activities can best accomplish the duties involved in your job description as well as your own personal goals. There is one word of warning here. If you become involved in controversial matters, you can be absolutely sure that someone within the management organization is going to take time to check the responsibility authority relationship on the formal organization chart to make sure that the fellow stepping on his toes has the authority to do so. If the formal chart has been bypassed and an informal line followed, someone ends up in a bad position even though his intention and the action involving a particular project is right.

In considering one's own objectives, it is well to consider that there is no more chance of those people in management positions above you being perfect in all aspects as there are of having those people subordinate to you perform in a perfect manner. It is just a fact of life that greater experience, either through work or education, will usually give a person who has risen to the management level a little better odds for making more right decisions than he makes wrong decisions.

Mistakes Will Occur

What I am trying to say is that your relationship with your management will be much better and your work more agreeable if you recognize that everyone who must make decisions or take action has the right to make a mistake. The people who never make mistakes through actions make the more serious mistakes of omission. This theory can also work in your favor if you will recognize that, if you have been granted authority for making decisions or taking action on your own, you also have been given the opportunity to err in your decisions or take action that might be considered not absolutely correct. If you make mistakes, if your decisions are wrong, you must then make a perfect decision —tell your superior that you made a mistake.

In the formal organization chart, there is very seldom any opportunity for even the president of a company to make a single decision that will result in a total collapse of the company. Responsibility of individual positions can never be disregarded even though action or decision authority has been delegated to individuals in lower management positions. It is quite likely that any decision or action taken directly by a safety engineer in an organization will also have a higher authority who is responsible for the decision or action. The individual who delegated authority to you may raise the devil over your decision or your action. But believe me, it won't be anything like the conversation that his superior carries on with him about the decision that he made to give you authority to make this mistake.

This may sound like a very frightening situation that might discourage people from making decisions and using initiative in taking action. In reality, modern and enlightened management realizes that many decisions have to be made and a lot of action has to take place in order to carry on a business. Mistakes sometimes costly, will occur. However, it is well to look at the overall results in relation to the rest of the industry before becoming too critical of the mistakes that were made through action or positive decisions. Most often, those companies who fail are the companies who have made all of their mistakes or at least most of them, through undecisiveness and inaction. Therefore, if your motives are proper and your enthusiasm for achieving your company's goals has caused you to make a mistake, take heart—it may be the best thing that happened to you. At least, you will be noticed.

Now for a look at the second need for understanding management principles. This involves the need for us to perform our duties effectively and to get optimum productivity from the energies that we expend. This is necessary in order for us to have a feeling of accomplishment and work satisfaction.

Perhaps the most frustrating aspect of the safety engineer's job is that so often, when he is in a relationship of consultant or staff man to line management, he just cannot get the things done that he knows should be done because he has no authority to order them done. This can be true of the safety engineer or consultant for the insurance carrier who is working with a customer or it can be true of the safety engineer within a company who has not been given a written line management-safety engineer responsibility-authority communication. There is only one answer to this safety engineer's problem. He must be a good salesman and he must be able to prepare and present his arguments in a logical and practical manner so clearly understandable that it will be accepted.

Over the years, I have many times wondered why it was so much easier for a salesman for our company to sell insurance to a risk than it was for me to sell the safety recommendations which could result in the real savings in insurance premium. Many times, my recommendations have involved very little or no cost. So, why, then, did he not take steps to implement what could only be a money savings program? The answer, of course, is simple. I didn't convince him that it would do that or that it was worthwhile for any other reason. As I look back now at our efforts to convince people I can see many reasons why we were not 100 percent successful.

Perhaps most important of all is that in the field of safety engineering, because we do feel that we are in a professional category, we very often try to adopt terminology that sets us apart, or that identifies us with our profession. We discuss results in terms of frequency and severity and loss ratios; and even though they are understood by the management people that we are talking to, the real impact of the word "dollars" is lost. If I were to do it over again, I would sell every recommendation that I made on the basis of how many dollars it would save the management man I am trying to convince. Management, whether at the line, staff, or the top level, talks in terms of dollars. Almost every other criteria used to measure the success of a business is expressed in terms of dollars.

Here is a simple test. If in giving a report to your superior, assuming you are the safety director of a business, you told him that you had reduced the loss ratio from 65 to 60 or the frequency from five to four, you would probably get a nice pat on the back and the complimentary "You're doing a good job, Joe." But if you expressed yourself in giving your report in terms of stating, "We reduced our accident cost by $10,000 last year," your superior would not only give you the slap on the back and the complimentary "Good job, Joe," but would send the report immediately on up to his superiors and perhaps to the president of the company calling attention to the excellent "money saving" job that has been done. And believe me, he would mention specifically the number of dollars that had been saved.

I have seen more unenthusiastic letters of commendation sent out to employees of companies by top officers because they were citing the employees for the great improvement in their accident frequency or severity. Frankly, I believe that this is a term to be used within our profession, for our own use and in our own attempts to measure our progress. If we are going to sell management on safety, if we are going to get company leaders to make investments that would make our job more effective, we are going to have to talk in terms of money. A principle of modern management—its most understood term—is dollars.

Another principle that can make our work more effective evolves around the fact that today's manager wants more than ever to feel the security of knowing what's going on. Years ago, it would appear that many managers cared only about their particular responsibility and only the details of their job function. Today, a manager realizes that he must know more about the total operation of the company. In your staff relationship, you are in a unique position to carry on good communications that will increase his confidences in his own knowledge of the total company picture as well as increase his confidence in your ability to be of help to him.

Needless to say, if he is confident about you, you will be able to secure the cooperation necessary to carry on your work. It should be a mandatory policy that the manager of a department or division be fully informed by you of any matter involving accidents or safety that occurs within his jurisdiction. We commonly assume that this information originates from him or his department and that he knows all about it. A good review of your own experience will soon dispel this idea. So many managers really don't know what's going on, safety-wise. You are the one man in the position to set up a communication link that will keep him well posted.

I haven't tried to put into any order of importance any of these thoughts for increasing your effectiveness through your management. Obviously, each situation is different, and not all of these principles will apply in every case. However, I believe that there is a need for you to know that you can deal more effectively with management if you think and act like a manager as well as understand management.

Although there are hundreds if not thousands of management training programs under way, it is a well-known fact that executive development is self development. I am sure that you will find within your job and duties many opportunities for practicing the art of management. You've often heard that one of the prime performance standards for managers involves the elements of planning. Managers never have time to do all of the things that they want to do. The managers who get the most done are those who plan well. Certainly, planning your own activities so that you can get more done will demonstrate your ability to be a manager. Whether your aspirations are for promotion or just to get the job done, your good demonstration of planning will probably accomplish both.

Another good measure of a manager's ability is how well he delegates work to his subordinates. Unfortunately, many of us as safety engineers have difficulty in finding a subordinate. Nevertheless, there are individuals within the organization who because of their own desire for knowledge and progress are willing to accept additional responsibilities in activities that fall within the scope of their department's function. If you have safety activities that can be delegated to such individuals, and through your guidance and training effective delegation takes place, you are again demonstrating your ability to manage.

Perhaps the most important ability for good management is the ability to see the "big picture." Perhaps the safety engineer has more of an opportunity to demonstrate that he can see the total operation than most other people in the organization, at least more staff people. He has an opportunity to observe firsthand all physical properties as well as operational procedures. He can understand the interrelationships that exist between departments and between production and safety. If he can discipline himself to conduct his activities and relate his arguments on the basis that recognizes a total concept, he should be able to make his work effective and his own stature increasingly important.

Perhaps one of the greatest opportunities for demonstrating leadership is in the area of safety training that is carried on by safety engineers. Recognizing that the human factors have become increasingly apparent as the greatest single obstacle to any further rapid progress and optimum results in the safety field, the educational or training area for supervision has become a prime activity for safety engineers.

It is little realized, but very obvious when carefully thought out, that there is hardly any management position that does not involve personal supervision. Regardless of what level of management we talk about, everyone supervises someone else. It is true that at some levels, not very much personal supervision takes place. It is also very obvious that not enough takes place at most levels. Of course, this implies trained and intelligent supervision. Demonstrating your knowledge of supervisory skills by training supervisors in these skills can only increase the awareness of your ability by management whom you hope to influence. I urge you to familiarize yourself with this activity.

So to the question "Should the safety engineer involve himself in management activities or should he consider himself a technician aloof from the problems of management" I believe I have given my answer here.

My experience indicates that you cannot get the safety engineering job done without becoming involved with management and management problems. In my opinion, the greatest single element necessary to efficient loss control is management interest. The second is skilled supervision, and the third is well-trained people working in a climate of confidence.

There are a number of other elements, to be sure—those that involve the safe workplace, safe equipment and protective devices. But in today's market, the greatest accomplishment will come in the organizational development areas of management and supervision. The safety engineer who fails to recognize the need for becoming well trained in management principles and supervisory skills will be left behind in the parade of those folks who first of all derive work satisfaction through getting things done. In addition, he will not be recognized as leadership material in the organization for which he works.

Get involved with your management and with the management of the customers you serve.

17

FIT THE JOB TO THE MAN

Doris Baldwin

In a few well chosen paragraphs, Ms. Baldwin has emphasized the need to mold man, machine and environment into an effective operation. She points out the involvement of many disciplines in the field and with clear examples, illustrates the need for a multidisciplinary approach to fitting the job to the man.

WHAT DIFFERENCE does it make to management if a worker's chair is comfortable, his job well lighted, and his tools designed with a thorough knowledge of human anatomy?

Plenty, say specialists in a relatively new field that is attracting a lot of attention in industrial safety circles. The new point of view is given various names: biomechanics, ergonomics, human factors engineering. By any name, however, it means one thing: a change from the old way—obliging workers to adapt to machines—to the new way of considering first the man and then the machinery.

Increasingly, large U. S. companies are employing experts and teams of experts from many disciplines—medicine, physiology, anatomy, psychology, industrial engineering. Their purpose? A reordering of the man/machine/environment system to remove whatever is conducive to human error on the job. The ultimate goal: complete loss control in terms of manpower, time, and materials.

For the most part, studies in biomechanics and ergonomics have been sponsored by industrial giants who can afford consultation with scientists in diverse fields. But smaller companies suffer from similar problems—worker dissatisfaction and inefficiency,

From *Job Safety and Health,* March 1973. Occupational Safety and Health Administration, U. S. Department of Labor.

absenteeism, job injuries—and the money drain these problems represent.

Now the smaller companies can learn what large companies have paid to find out: the profitability of fitting the job to the man.

How can management do this? By starting with evaluation of both job and man: scientific classification of jobs according to their physical and psychological demands; and preemployment and preplacement medical examinations of workers to determine capabilities and limitations. The result of such measuring and matching can be optimum work organization and work safety. In addition, plant production tends to increase as health hazards and human error decrease.

There is a school of thought that operator error is, in fact, design error. Evidence of this can be found in many, if not all, plant accidents ascribed to human failure.

Consider the case of a shipfitter killed on the job last year. While removing a twist drill from a spindle socket, the shipfitter unintentionally bumped the machine's operating control lever out of neutral and started the spindle revolving at 187 rpm. His arm was caught up and ripped off. He died soon afterwards.

Why should an operating control be situated where it can be activated by mistake? The study of placement of machine controls comes under close scrutiny of biomechanical research teams.

In another case, a worker operated a large machine whose drop gate guard was adequate only so long as the man stood up. One night he worked overtime, got tired of standing, and sat down. This changed the angle at which his hands entered the die area and rendered the guard useless. On the job that night, a tired man lost both of his hands to a machine.

Should a machine be hazard-free only when the operator assumes one specific stance before it? Ergonomists are working toward risk control for operators in any posture. Studies also aim at finding and eliminating all the complex fatigue factors of the workplace.

For example, the relation of body posture to energy expenditure and muscle fatigue is often overlooked. A standup worker should be permitted to stand erect at his job; physical effort is much greater when a man works stooped, crouched, or reaching over his head.

Biomechanically, heavy work and the onset of fatigue are gauged by changes in the working heart rate, respiratory volume, and oxygen consumption.

Foundry men were tested working in various positions: chipping a casting that was on the floor, stooping over the casting on a lowered hydraulic lift table, and finally working with the lift table at optimum height. The floor-level work took 25 percent more effort than work in the stooped position. Standing erect cut another 10 percent from the energy cost.

Some jobs involve the whole body. Most do not. Wherever possible, it seems best to let the worker sit down on the job. This spares him the exertion of muscles unrelated to his task.

What kind of seating should be provided? A vital question. Ergonomists report that inefficient seating decreases speed, attention, motor response, and accuracy of perception. This leads in turn to frequent human failure, damaged materials, and work injuries. The more intense the work, according to consensus, the more important seating comfort becomes.

What parts of the seated body need support? Only those uninvolved with the task. The abdomen, seat, and feet, for example, aren't needed in a hand-eye task and therefore ought to be supported. If a seated worker must bend from the waist to do his job, the back support of his chair must not be rigid; it must flex to accommodate his movements without causing abrasion, fatigue, or frustration.

Seating faults conducive to fatigue and human failure are: uncomfortable position of feet; pressure of the seat on thighs; pressure from the front edge of the seat; pressure of the thighs on abdominal area; disturbance of the blood supply; tension in back and neck; loading in shoulder zone because of weight of hands; and excessive pressure on contact surfaces of arm rests.

A study was done in a printing factory where workers complained of chest ache and arm ache. Results revealed that workers without adjustable chairs and keyboards compensated by moving either closer to the board or farther from it, with resulting muscle discomfort and eyestrain.

In a textile plant where sewing machine seats were of unsuit-
able height, knee and ankle pains, as well as backaches, were
common causes of absenteeism. An investigation informed management that people were using makeshift devices to adapt to
their machines—cushions and pads to adjust seating height and
protect knees from pressure against a metal stand. Worker ease,
endurance, and concentration were improved with a simple
change in seating equipment.

But seating is only one factor vital in the layout of a safe workplace. Another consideration is how much space workers of all
sizes, shapes, and strengths needs in order to function with maximum comfort, efficiency, safety. Extensive research has measured
the human operator and the workspace zones of importance to
him—the zones of the eyes, of work with the hands, of work with
the feet.

When a task is a vision task, it is the eyes which should move to
do the job—not the head or neck. All visual work, therefore,
should be within the 60 degree range the eyes can easily accommodate.

In doing hand work, wrists should be held unbent. (Designers
of hand tool grips and machine controls, take note!) The most
efficient tools, controls, and displays are not hostile to man's sense
organs and natural body movements but function as compatible
extensions of human arms, hands, eyes, and feet.

Arranging work within 16 inches of the shoulders improves endurance, efficiency, comfort, and safety. Correct layout also permits the worker to function with his elbows down, not raised.

If it is necessary for a worker to reach, arrange for a forward
reach. When a worker has to shift his weight and lean sideways,
the direction of forces acting on his vertebral column is changed,
and he tires more rapidly.

Many industrial accidents start with unexpected disturbance of
a worker's movement pattern. An accessory tool falls to the floor.
In moving to catch it, the worker may injure himself on the tool,
and possibly upset other materials in the process. Frequently, machines such as lathes have no space for an operator to safely put
down a tool—a shortcoming which increases the likelihood of the
"recovery accident."

Another common design shortcoming: knobs, buttons, or switches on an instrument control panel are likely to be identical, making discrimination by touch impossible. Yet, when moving a control, the worker ordinarily looks not at the knob but at the changing display. Bringing his sense of touch into play by giving him differently shaped controls—which studies show can be easily learned—might reduce costly errors and accidents.

The best of displays will be of little avail if a worker can't see what he is doing. What about the influence of lighting in the workplace? All studies agree that efficiency goes up when the level of light is improved. It is important, too, to eliminate sources of dazzle and glare, such as highly polished machine surfaces and bright window areas within workers' ranges of vision. Visual errors, as most plant managers know, can be both costly and dangerous.

Industrial noise is an environmental aspect receiving heightened attention. Work speed may not be affected in a noisy area (or so the studies indicate), but the quality of work deteriorates. The implication: by the time the industrial hygienist isolates a case of hearing damage, it probably has been preceded by years of work less efficient than they might have been!

Heat stress also greatly concerns biomechanical experts. Accident rates tend to be higher in extremes of temperature, with summer slow-downs and absenteeism evident in many plants. Man readily absorbs heat from hotter objects and radiates body heat to cooler areas, white and black skins being equally adept at this transfer. Because excessively hot or cold work environments make workers uncomfortable, multiply errors, and increase accidents, temperature regulation is a requisite of the ideal work environment.

Paradoxically, as increased job mechanization and automation release men and women from the burdens of physical work, their mental and psychological burdens increase. New problems are introduced. Faulty exchange of information and action between man and his more complex machine can result in delay and error ruinous to the point of shutting down entire plants or sections of plants.

There is significant risk where industrial computers are in nonstop operation to justify their cost. As a consequence, operators may be asked to work changing shifts. What effect does this have on performance and safety?

Physiological changes and social disturbances make nightshift work far more fatiguing than dayshift. Studies indicate that short shift changes of a few days at a time, however, or long shift periods of months or even years, are preferable to shift changes every week or two.

Worker fatigue must be fought relentlessly. It leads to exhausting tension even in muscles unrelated to the task—the clenching of teeth and tightening of neck muscles, for example—as well as to deterioration of efficiency and vigilance. Rest periods at scientifically scheduled intervals are most effective in preventing fatigue. (When authorized rests are not provided, workers somehow devise them!)

Long hours, poor lighting, frustrating workplace design—the human operator can adapt to all of these. But in so doing his work suffers and eventually his health will suffer, too.

Industrial management in pursuit of complete loss control will reexamine the man/machine/environment system in the plant. Is there incompatibility? Clearly, it is not man who can be redesigned.

18

SCHOOL BUS ACCIDENT
INVESTIGATION

SAFETY INFORMATION NEWS RELEASE
NATIONAL TRANSPORTATION SAFETY BOARD

As in any field the investigative teams of the National Transportation Safety Board (NTSB) have their detractors among other experts in the field. Never-the-less, the NTSB is the leading accident investigative body in the country.

A main role of accident investigators is assisting in the prevention of future similar accidents. The success of this role is largely determined by the ability of expert investigators to delve with complete freedom into accident causation and to make appropriate corrective recommendations without fear of recrimination and letting the chips fall where they may.

The NTSB may indeed go "'all the way" on its investigations and recommendations. Although a relatively small governmental body, the importance and influence of the Board may be judged by the fact that the board members are cabinet level officers and that the board reports directly to Congress.

The Board is responsible for investigating all types of transportation accidents, but is best known for large scale investigation of aircraft accidents. The complete and final report might go to hundreds of pages and photographs. Meanwhile, a summary is released to the public for accident prevention purposes. The item that follows is such a public information release, in this case, a school bus accident at a railroad crossing.

The school bus driver failed "to stop at the stop sign until the crossing was clear of railroad traffic." Simplistically, that explains everything except what to do about fallible human nature. For reasons known and unknown, people failure must be anticipated sooner or later in doing any task. Ignoring the reasons for the failure of the driver, which could not be determined, the Board nonetheless came up with specific recommendations probing deep into the nature of our society. These recommendations carry the weight of a major governmental department and get careful consideration by the agencies responsible for corrective action.

T HE NATIONAL TRANSPORTATION SAFETY BOARD today released its report on a fatal collision between a Penn Central freight train and a schoolbus which occurred near Congers, New York, about 7:55 A.M. on March 24, 1972. As a result of the accident, five students died; the remaining forty-four students, and the driver were injured and the schoolbus was destroyed.

The schoolbus was being driven across a grade crossing on Gilchrist Road near Congers when it was struck by the lead locomotive of a Penn Central freight. The Board noted that although there was a stop sign and a standard railroad-crossing advance warning sign at the accident site, the crossing was "not specially protected" by any active devices. After the impact, as the schoolbus was pushed 1,116 feet down the track by the train, the bus disintegrated.

The Safety Board determined that the cause of this tragic accident was

. . . the failure of the schoolbus driver to stop at the stop sign until the crossing was clear of railroad traffic. The reason for this failure could not be determined.

Contributing to the accident was the unnecessary routing of the schoolbus over a not specially protected railroad/highway grade crossing. Contributing to the number of fatalities and severity of injuries were: (1) the lack of structural integrity of the body of the schoolbus, (2) the absence of highback padded seats and an occupant-restraint system in the schoolbus, (3) the presence of standing students in the bus, and (4) the action of the coupler of the lead locomotive, which caused the crash forces to be concentrated on the bus.

On the morning of the accident the driver drove the schoolbus from the garage at 7:30 A.M., but before making his first pickup, he encountered an unexpected detour on Gilchrist Road which made it necessary to drive the route in reverse of the course normally followed. This resulted in the schoolbus approaching the railroad crossing 20 minutes later than usual and from the opposite direction—and with 49 passengers on board instead of six.

However, the visibility available to the driver "was unobstructed and more than adequate" and several bus occupants saw the train when the bus was as far as 600 feet from the crossing. In addition, several passengers and a witness near the crossing heard the locomotive horn throughout the train's approach to the crossing.

The Board said there was a "momentary deceleration" of the bus some distance before it reached the stop sign which was followed by an immediate resumption of speed. This decision might have been based on a misperception of the train's speed—estimated at 25 mph—and distance from the crossing.

Another factor affecting this decision could have been the bus driver's realization that he was already behind his normal schedule, due to the detour, and if he had to wait for the freight train to clear the crossing, he would be further delayed in reporting for work at his primary job, scheduled to begin at 9:00 A.M., with the New York City Fire Department.

In reviewing the bus driver's workday routine, the Board found that he usually returned the bus to the garage at 8:25 A.M. On the days he worked as a New York City fireman he then had to drive 30 miles in rush-hour traffic to reach the firehouse. A test run between the garage and firehouse, over the best route and complying with all traffic regulations, revealed a minimum travel time of 1 hour and 5 minutes—which meant that the driver would not have been able to arrive at the firehouse at 9:00 A.M. on any day that he drove the schoolbus.

"This driver's work schedule was not considered by either the contractor or school administrators," the Board said and noted further that there was no standard or regulation for New York employers "to examine the hours of primary employment of their schoolbus drivers to determine to what extent their schedule might cause them to hurry to complete their routes or affect their safety performance in any other way."

The schoolbus involved in the accident was a 66-passenger 1967 Carpenter body mounted on a 1968 General Motors Coach frame. The Board found that the crash forces produced on the schoolbus by the train locomotive moving at about 25 mph injured only those passengers in the area directly impacted—some of the fatal injuries resulted when the bus structure disintegrated. "At least two of the five fatalities were ejected as a result of floor separation—and the lack of availability and use of an occupant-restraint system in the bus," the Board said. The controversy over the feasibility of installing active occupant-restraint systems in schoolbuses indicates the need to obtain data which can be used to resolve this question, the Board concluded.

In commenting on the structural disintegration of the schoolbus, the Board said that several occupants experienced severe crash injuries from sharp metal edges which were exposed by the separation of structural parts of the bus body. The disintegration "displayed many examples of failures at joints assembled with relatively few fasteners," the Board said, and noted further that "such construction is typical of current schoolbus construction practices."

The Penn Central freight train was operating with three diesel-electric locomotive units, 83 freight cars and caboose, with a total gross weight of 4,230 tons. The coupler of the lead locomotive immediately penetrated the outer wall of the bus and contacted floor panels, which buckled and began to separate, and allowed the coupler to penetrate further inboard. The Board pointed out that this protruding coupler was not necessary for the operation of the locomotive on the mainline. There are practical means of covering the coupler so that it has greater deflective qualities. "Future locomotive designs could reduce one source of collision damage through recessing the front-end coupler, as provided on passenger train locomotives," the Board said.

Last September as a result of its investigation of this accident the Safety Board recommended that the National Highway Traffic Safety Administration "expeditiously adopt" a Federal Motor Vehicle Safety Standard to control the strength of structural joints of schoolbuses, including strengthening the window column of such buses. This is now under review by NHTSA.

In its report issued today as a further result of its investigation and findings the Safety Board made seven additional recommendations as follows:

1. *The Department of Transportation* seek legislation to extend the use of Federal funds now available for grade-crossing safety and improvement on the Federal Highway System "to include

those . . . crossings on non-Federal aid highways" such as c.
isted at Congers.

2. The *National Highway Traffic Safety Administration* in re-
vising the Federal Highway Standards continue the requirement
that schoolbus drivers be qualified under the Motor Carrier
Safety Regulations and extend this provision "to include all
drivers of schoolbuses regardless of whether they or their employer is subject to these regulations."

3. The *National Highway Traffic Safety Administration*, in re-
vising the Federal Highway Standards, include a provision to
require those persons responsible for hiring schoolbus drivers to
conduct pre-employment inquiries and continued surveillance
"to assure that other employment requirements of schoolbus
drivers do not adversely influence their schoolbus driving."

4. The *State of New York,* and *all other States* "adopt and implement" the present Highway Safety Program Standard No. 17
"Pupil Transportation Safety" with "special emphasis" on provisions relating to "the selection and training of personnel, the safe
routing of schoolbuses, and the elimination of standees in schoolbuses."

5. The *New York Department of Education* "expand" its pupil-
transportation safety activities to provide "liaison, management
consultation, and supervision" at the local level to assure compliance with its policies and procedures, including "active assistance in training pupil-transportation personnel."

6. The *National Highway Traffic Safety Administration* assess
the human factors involved in seat belt usage in schoolbuses
through a demonstration project, using a number of schoolbuses
equipped with seatbelts and highback, padded seats.

7. The *International Association of Chiefs of Police* use its
"influence and resources" to redirect the attention of law enforcement agencies to the need for "uniform enforcement of traffic
laws pertaining to railroad/highway grade crossings" and provide
special emphasis on those crossings protected solely with stop
signs.

19

HOW TO KEEP A SAFETY PROGRAM ALIVE

MURPHY W. BRADHURST

This short article finds a place in this book mainly as a specimen. It illustrates a type of safety literature typically directed at supervisors—"for he's the only one mainly responsible for safety."

The safety professional will see a listing of well-worn safety gimmicks, a term not necessarily derogatory. The neophyte currently charged with safety responsibility will find something to try. The student may be astonished at the simplicity of it all. It is a specimen, and like any specimen, its value at all three levels of perception lies in the questions it raises as much (or even more!) than in the answers it gives.

JOHN MacDOUGALL, the operator of a drill press, did not wear his safety goggles one day and got a steel splinter in his eye. The entire plant was galvanized into action. The word came down from on high, supervisors called meetings, sent memos, used strong language. Some of them posted penalties for infractions of safety rules. Others prowled their departments on inspection tours. All safety devices were in constant use—for about two weeks. But gradually the crisis faded, the employees and the supervisors became careless. And in about two months, there was another avoidable accident.

Most company safety programs are sound; it's in the follow-through that they fall down. This is where the supervisor comes in, for he's the only one who's mainly responsible for safety.

Reprinted by permission of the publisher from *Supervisory-Management*, February, 1966, copyright 1966 by the American Management Association, Inc.

The supervisor's job—and it's a tough one—is to make sure that safety is not a spasmodic, sometime thing. He has to keep the workers interested in safety. This isn't easy, because safety can become a pretty tired subject. But here are some suggestions on what supervisors can do to make employees safety-conscious. They are based on programs that have worked for other companies.

1. Get employees actively working on a safety program. Pick out a couple of workers to act as safety inspectors each month. Rotate the assignment, so that everybody gets a crack at it. Give them a checklist of what to watch for in the way of safety violations. At the end of the month, have them turn in a report on any unsafe practices and conditions they have noticed. Of course, serious problems should be reported at once. It helps if they have special badges indicating they are inspectors.

At one company that tried this kind of program, workers reported 306 unsafe conditions in a 12-month period. Almost all were important enough to require action.

2. Rate the safety performance of every worker in the department. And make sure that everyone knows that safety is an important category in the performance rating.

3. After an accident, capitalize on the natural curiosity that results. Explain in detail what happened.

4. Publicize cases where safety equipment has prevented an accident. Some companies maintain displays of cracked safety glasses, dented hard hats, etc., with the name of the worker who avoided having an accident because he was protected: "Joe Blank can still see because he was wearing these safety glasses."

5. Another gimmick is the "X marks the spot" technique—putting signs up wherever an accident occurred. A typical sign might read something like this: "Injury No. 12 occurred here. Joe Johnson slipped on a grease spot, sprained his ankle."

6. Try to sell employees on the need for reporting "near misses" as well as actual accidents. It may seem to an inexperienced person that the cause of a near accident is something that will never happen again. But if the incident is reported

and studied by a safety expert, it may reveal certain conditions that should be changed.

7. Have safety offenders prepare a written report stating what they should have done to avoid the accident. This may stop them from making the same mistake again. Also, don't forget that safety violators are choice candidates to serve on the safety committee.

8. At least one company is using a camera to take on-the-spot accident photos. The pictures make it possible to study the conditions that caused the accident, and can be posted on bulletin boards to dramatize the mishap.

9. As much as possible, try to get safety into the home. The truly safe worker has to make safety more or less a way of life. To develop interest in safety at home, one company publishes a safety quiz for employees' wives in the company magazine. At frequent intervals, a plant safety man picks one of the wives' names at random and phones her to see if she knows the answer to the safety question. If she does, she gets a $10 grocery order.

Supervisors can do a lot to reduce accident rates if they are aware of certain accident facts. For example, there are accident "seasons" and accident "hours." Generally, more accidents occur in late summer and early fall, and during the hours just before lunch and just before quitting time.

Supervisors should also remember that new workers are a definite safety liability. Research by one of the big automakers showed that nearly half of all its accidents were caused by workers who had been on the job less than a year.

The Danger of Monotony

There are also specific kinds of jobs that need close attention from the supervisor because they have built-in accident factors. Repetitive jobs are dangerous because they can become monotonous. The worker who is bored may be inattentive and, as a result, ripe for an accident. One solution to this problem is to try to break up the work by giving the employee other assignments or by having several workers take turns on the job.

20

THE STATE OF THE ART
OF THE HUMAN FACTORS
IN AVIATION SAFETY

CHARLES I. BARRON

The study of aviation safety has been pursued under highly controlled conditions with resources not generally available to other areas of safety. As a result, this article draws on an abundance of ideas and concepts which may be considered "advanced" even by some professional standards.

In aviation, the fallible human is extraordinarily crucial in the interrelationships of the man—machine—environment system. Doctor Barron centers this article on that fallible human. His insights have application, however, wherever human input is part of the system, increasingly so as human input becomes increasingly crucial in the system performance. While concentrating on the human aspect, the author illuminates the system concept of man, machine, environment interrelationships and exemplifies the power of the concept as a format to think with. Seldom are "state of the art" summaries so closely applicable to other spheres of safety.

Doctor Barron addresses the aviation accident rates of the U. S. Navy and Air Force, measured in accidents per 100,000 flying hours. As accident prevention becomes more and more successful, it becomes increasingly difficult to achieve further reduction in accident rates. More and more effort becomes necessary to achieve ever smaller reductions. The statistics, therefore, may be regarded as a measure of residual failures rather than a measure of the effectiveness or ineffectiveness of the accident prevention program.

Few experts dare to speak in public on the possibility of no acci-

Presented at the Aviation Contractors' Safety Representatives' Conference, Tuesday, 6 April, 1965, Norfolk, Virginia.

dents, a zero accident rate. The author addresses this subject briefly but in a manner worthy of note. For the sake of perspective, the date of the article might be noted; before "system safety" became a household word in safety, Doctor Barron formulated these thoughts under the powerful influence of the system concept.

W HEN FIRST INVITED to address this group, I was asked to speak on the Art of Human Factors in Aviation Safety. Lacking the courage of the other speakers, I requested a more restricted topic and was given a subject with which I was most familiar and one which required less preparation. Upon subsequent reflection, however, I have decided to revert to the broader theme of the conference and comment on the changing picture in aviation safety during the past fifteen years, as I interpret it in my capacity as a flight surgeon.

First, and of greatest significance, there can be little doubt that the concentrated drive for safety has been most rewarding in the preservation of aviators' lives and materiel, and that this accomplishment has enhanced the operational potential of Naval aviation. In my opinion, this objective has been achieved without compromising the quality of training or the combat potential of the individual aviator or his effectiveness as a member of a mission-orientated team. The progress made in the once stagnant and much maligned science of aviation safety demonstrates once again what can be accomplished by proper motivation, command support, education, communication, and self-discipline. It was but a few years ago that "aviation safety" were dirty words and the job of safety officer was frequently assigned to the misfit in the squadron—the pilot who did not fit into a logical slot. It is most gratifying, then, to see this important science prove itself and really come of age.

Today, we voice concern over a number of factors which have evolved during the past several years. Foremost is the declining rate of improvement in accident frequency. For example, the improvement in the accident rate from Fiscal 1961 to Fiscal 1962 in Navy aviation was 10 percent. This decreased to approximately 6.4 percent in Fiscal 1963 and improved slightly to 7 percent in Fiscal 1964. If the present trend continues for Fiscal 1965, however, the rate of improvement will have declined to an all-time low of 3 percent.

The significance of this declining rate of improvement has not been entirely defined. Certainly, we must take into consideration the type of flying, whether new aircraft have been introduced into the fleet, the age and experience range of aviators, the extent and quality of training, extra flying duties, and other factors. It is also obvious that as the overall rate becomes smaller, a few accidents will have a relatively greater statistical impact upon the improvement curve. Even a small reduction in the overall rate is most desirable and worthy of achievement. Based solely on statistics, each reduction of four accidents will save the life of a Naval aviator and one crewman or passenger and preserve approximately 2 and one-half million dollars worth of materiel. A reduction of only 1/10 of 1 percent would mean the saving of approximately eight Naval aviators. These are goals which justify continued vigorous effort in the pursuit of safety.

The second area of concern is the continuing high percentage of human errors in accident causation. This has increased steadily in the Navy during the past four years. The Air Force has been successful in reducing human errors to approximately 40 percent; however, the most recent figures in the Navy list human errors as primary accident causative factors in approximately 62 percent of all accidents, and 50 percent attributable to pilot errors. The significance of this trend is not well understood. We are aware that this area has been most thoroughly investigated in the Navy during the past several years, and the increase may reflect improved investigative techniques. Despite the increase, the total number of accidents attributable to human factors has remained fairly constant, since the overall accident rate has steadily decreased. A reasonable assumption is that while we are more adept in our investigation, we have not made real progress in applying the findings to the prevention of similar type accidents.

A third area of concern is the "cause undetermined" accident. In the Navy, this has averaged approximately 10 percent throughout the last ten years. While the percentage is not statistically great, the average number of fatalities contained within this 10 percent has been approximately 40 percent. The figures for Fiscal

1964 reveal 10 percent "cause undetermined" accident accounting for 40 percent of all fatalities. To phrase it another way, despite all our advanced and sophisticated investigation techniques,
we still do not know the cause of accidents which annually claim
40 percent of all lives lost. Little attention has been devoted to a
study and understanding of these accidents. An outstanding exception is a study conducted recently by the Safety Center at
Norton Air Force Base and reported by Colonel Lentz in the
March, 1965, issue of the *Journal of Aerospace Medicine.*

Colonel Lentz reports on an analysis of 182 Air Force accidents
which occurred over a four-year span. Difficulties in determining
the causes of the accidents relate to the fact that the majority are
fatal accidents, and the crewmen are not available for interroga-
tion. In addition, the majority of the accidents involved loss of
control with high impact forces, resulting in marked or total
destruction of materiel and personnel. Finally, a small number of
aircraft are either lost at sea or simply do not arrive at a destination and are never accounted for. Reviewing these accidents in
depth and identifying the most significant factors resulted in the
following conclusions:

> Very few accidents occurred during the "in-flight" stage; that is,
> from the end of climbout to the start of penetration. This would im-
> ply that the majority of accidents occurred during the most stressful
> phases of flight, the takeoff, and the accidents occurred on or im-
> mediately adjacent to the base during takeoff. With these exceptions,
> most of the accidents were known to have involved loss of control
> with high speed impact.
>
> In approximately 15 percent of the cases, materiel or system fail-
> ure or malfunction was suspected; however, the precise cause for
> these occurrences could not be determined with sufficient accuracy
> to list them as the single or major causative factors.
>
> Certain conditions of light were common to most of the accidents.
> Many were made on moonless nights, under adverse weather con-
> ditions, during operational phases of flight, or formation flight, or
> involved combinations of these factors. In view of this, it was de-
> cided that human factors were probably implicated in most cases and
> that additional investigation in this area would be most enlightening
> and rewarding.
>
> It was apparent in many cases that accidents were caused simply
> by overloading the pilot during a stressful phase of flight and exceed-

ing his capabilities to meet the extra demands. Using this assumption as a point of departure, it was decided to explore those conditions which might lead to incapacitation, unconsciousness, or death in flight. Following this, an attempt was then made to isolate and explore those conditions which might restrict, reduce, or degrade the normal capacity of the airman.

With respect to the former conditions, various pathological entities were considered, but in only a few cases appeared to be the most logical cause of the accidents. It is interesting to note at this time that the medical applications of investigation, and especially the use of forensic pathology and the autopsy were given their biggest impetus by the very excellent work performed by Italian and English pathologists in the two Comet accidents twelve years ago. With respect to degradation of normal performance capability, such conditions as anxiety-induced tensions generated by personal or domestic problems, those which might cause distraction, inattention, and interference with habit patterns, personal habits of pilots, especially with respect to fatigue, and the presence of disorientation and/or loss of control. Disorientation is defined here in its broadest sense; that is, lack of knowledge of the attitude, position, or movement of the aircraft in space.

A fourth major area of concern is the relative increase in maintenance error as a cause of accidents. In the past, this has constituted 1 percent to 3 percent of all accidents, but a few years ago, this figure increased to 8 percent in the Navy. When finally recognized as a major contributant to accidents, attention was focused upon this problem and the same professional techniques were used to contain the rate as had previously been applied to pilot errors, and the upward trend has been reversed.

One must appreciate the problems faced by maintenance and ground personnel to understand why the increase in errors could have resulted. The work environment of maintenance personnel has not improved with the development of turbine-powered aircraft. It is difficult to perform efficiently and at maximum capacity and effort while working in a high jet noise field. If properly motivated, psychological adaptation to noise can be accomplished; however, there is a normal tendency for people to avoid exposure to loud, sustained noises. In addition to working in an unpleasant environment, maintenance personnel must service, maintain, and repair increasingly complex materiel, demands which require more extensive training and skill. It has not been easy to obtain competent personnel to undergo this type of training, and perhaps even more difficult to retain them in the service once they have reached the desired skill level.

The fifth area of concern is one I call the "narcosis of complacency." While I recognize the fine effort in steadily reducing the accident rate, I do not imply that the ultimate goal has been achieved. There are some who claim the accident rate cannot be reduced to zero or even appreciably beyond that accomplished to date, for as long as man flies the plane, errors will be made. I do not agree with the concept that to err is human, or that errors must always be associated with human efforts. Human errors are invariably predictable, and what is predictable is also preventable. Once human limitations and capabilities are understood and accepted by designers and commanders and recognized by the pilots themselves, half the battle will have been won. With proper motivation by all to achieve perfection, the accident rate will approach zero.

A zero Defect program, predicated upon a positive approach to perfection and errorless work, has been started throughout the aerospace industry, and, I believe, recently introduced into the military services. The results in industry have been phenomenal. I believe the same positive attitude can be applied to aviation safety. In short, the motivational goal for all aviators should be perfection and zero accidents.

Most airplane accidents are caused by people, but in this highly specialized field of endeavor by a very special type of people working in an artificial time-space environment. It is doubtful whether any other persons are involved in a similar work activity which daily required them to bet their lives that they will accomplish their assigned tasks correctly.

The aviator is a most remarkable individual, and his job is one that requires a unique combination of courage, technical skill, knowledge, and motivation. As Captain Luehrs has stated, the two words most closely associated with pilots are "precision" and "aggressiveness." When an accident due to pilot error occurs, the fundamental cause is either an improper response or a failure to respond. We classify these as errors of commission or of omission; that is, the pilot has either initiated the wrong action or perhaps an incomplete action, or has failed to act at all. This, then, focuses attention upon the characteristics of the responses or actions expected of an individual operating in this unique man/machine environment.

The majority of responses are conscious ones and originate in the highest, most complex cells of the central nervous system located in the cortex of the brain, an area where judgments and decisions are made. If necessary, the organism may respond through purely reflex action and by so doing bypass the more complex and time-consuming decision centers in the brain. Nature thus assures a rapid response to save the organism from embarrassment when an acute, dangerous situation threatens its existence. If decisions or judgments are needed, and if these are made on new experiences or situations, the time factor becomes important and occasionally critical. Studies made on carrier accidents involving recognition of an emergency, decision to eject, and actual pulling of the face curtain handle, revealed that this complex perception, decision, and motor response loop could not be completed in less than three seconds. Studies of oxygen mask donning times in response to visual and auditory signals have also confirmed that even in the most skilled test pilots, mask application could not be accomplished in less than three to four seconds. Better understanding of the entire perception, decision, and motor response loop is indicated if we are to appreciate what happens to a pilot in a tense emergency situation and determine where and why he failed.

A person must first sense his environment; that is, he must become aware of his orientation or relationship to his surroundings. This is achieved by an influx of stimuli which bombard the sensory receptors of the body. Once the receptors are stimulated, the signals are routed by means of nerve fibers and tracts to specific areas of the brain, where they are integrated and judgments rendered. On the basis of such judgments, a decision will be made for action or no action.

If action is taken, signals are transmitted through the central nervous system to the muscles and limb or body movements are initiated, resulting in displacement of aircraft controls. If the environmental stimuli evoke fear, several choices or decisions are available to the receptor. These are based essentially upon the inherent tendency of the organism to survive.

Doctor Selye has best explained these reactions by his General Adaptation Syndrome. The initial reaction of the body is one of alarm, resulting in biochemical, psychological, and physiological changes alerting many body systems and organs. The type of threat or stressor is then identified, and a decision made either to run, fight, or, if possible, adapt. In any case, the organism responds in a more specific or channelized manner; that is, it selects the organs or organ systems most closely identified with the requisite response and mobilizes specific resources for survival.

If, for example, mild hypoxia is the stressor, adaptation will occur, and the body will eventually produce an excess of red blood cells through action of the spleen and the bone marrow and simultaneously assure a more efficient utilization of oxygen by accelerated adrenal hormone production. If infection is the stressor, the response will take the form of increased antibody production. If retreat or fight is indicated, blood sugar is mobilized immediately from reservoirs of glycogen in the muscles and liver, muscle tone is enhanced, circulatory changes occur, and the organism is ready for action.

Occasionally, a definitive decision cannot be made, and a compromise is reached at the subconscious level. Such a reaction occurs when a subject exposed to a great danger finds he can neither fight nor retreat and "freezes." We see another good example in retrograde amnesia, where the thoughts of unpleasant events become consciously unbearable and nature conveniently removes them from memory.

A study of a pilot's reaction to environment stimuli is incomplete unless considered in the proper perspective of man in a man/machine environment. Man and his machine must be considered as a single functioning unit. For example, the basic stimulation received by man is derived from the various displays within the cockpit of his aircraft. Having received this information, he may make a decision which results in a muscle response initiating changes in the attitude, speed, altitude, or power setting of the machine. This, in turn, is translated into a feedback of new information to the man which either may satisfy his desires or result in further commands and actions being relayed to the machine. Since both man and machine are responsive to stimulation within the ambient environment, we can logically delete neither the machine nor the total environment from a study of pilot behavior.

It has been stated that the two commonest causes of human factors accidents are the overloading of man's sensory channels and the simple "goof" caused by carelessness or inattention. Obviously, no pilot in his right mind will deliberately make a mistake which could result in his injury or death; consequently, it must be assumed that the majority of accidents are caused by the aforementioned factor. It becomes increasingly important for all people concerned with aviation—designers, operations and supervisory personnel—to better understand man's frailties and limitations to avoid exceeding his capacity to sense, integrate, make decisions, and act.

Even the most capable pilots may be guilty of so-called pilot error, but it must be remembered that we frequently assign the most difficult and exacting tasks to them—in short, the toughest jobs and the ones which require the most frequent and difficult types of decisions. What really happens, then, in the perception, decision and reaction interface in this complex physiological structure, biochemical laboratory, and emotional mass we call man? The answer is not a very simple one. We must know considerably more about the role of heredity, early training, ego needs, motivation, intellectual capabilities, predilection for success, and reliability under specific stress conditions. We must know how these influences affect man's actions in response to machine environment stimuli.

In other words, what I am really expressing is the need for a total systems study of the man-machine environment complex.

It has been stated that man has been studied for years and that we have a fairly good understanding of him, that he is really the known quantity in the system complex, that we are aware of his limitations, that basically man won't change, and that it does not appear he will be artificially altered to enhance his capabilities within the near future. I feel this is an oversimplification and not entirely correct. Although we know a great deal about man's general physiology, we have no such detailed knowledge about the intricate interactions of his systems, subsystems, and biochemical integrations.

We should certainly provide design engineers with as much positive knowledge as we have available today concerning man's capabilities and limitations and encourage them to design to known human criteria. Here, a basic decision must be made as to whether to design to more limited capabilities of the least able pilot, or whether to design for the pilot with average abilities. It is important, also, to indoctrinate the pilot with this knowledge, so that he recognizes and understands his limitations and avoids overconfidence and complacency. And, finally, I believe it desirable that this information be widely disseminated to supervisory, operational, and command personnel; for, if they are to effectively exercise their perogatives, they must have a basic understanding of the pilot's needs and capabilities.

I am certain that not all aviators fully appreciate the efforts made in their behalf. I know pilots who have sat through a full course in aviation psychology without acquiring any insight whatsoever into the possible application of this important subject in accident prevention and investigation. It requires no special knowledge or training or even an iota of common sense to elicit a statement from a pilot who had just made a wheels-up landing that he forgot to lower the gear, but that it won't happen again. Had the officers learned their lesson well, they would have used this explanation as a point of departure for the real investigation. Until it is determined why the pilot forgot to lower his gear at a critical time in his approach, and the answer applied to the prevention of future accidents, wheels-up landings will recur.

To study these problems in depth requires the use of specialized knowledge and techniques which are taught the safety officers in psychology and physiology courses. I am aware of cases where military pilots have experienced serious incidents in flight and have not communicated this information to their flight surgeons.

This, to me, indicates lack of proper rapport and communication between pilot and flight surgeon. Incidents are the precursors of accidents, and when properly explored, will identify potential sources of trouble in pilot or aircraft. Every attempt should be made to encourage mutual trust and confidence between pilot, flight surgeons, and safety officers, and the prompt reporting of incidents should be encouraged and studied in as much detail as accidents.

I also find that when safety officers are asked in the privacy of the classroom what they would like to have discussed in the human factors field, they most frequently request information on the combined effects of domestic stress, late hours, drinking, excessive smoking, and poor physical conditioning upon the performance capabilities of pilots. This indicates that pilots themselves are concerned about the subtle effects of these stressors, which, singly, may not result in serious degradation, but, when present in combination, may produce significant lowering of performance.

Another case of interest is that of a senior pilot, who, in speaking to a distinguished group of aeromedical experts, chided them for the lack of progress in the development of simple, reliable, protective equipment. Comfort, as well as safety, is important to pilots, and when they feel frustrated over what they believe to be the lack of interest and effort to make their life a somewhat easier and more pleasant one, a dangerous situation is created. This does little to produce the calm pilot we would like to see in the cockpit of a high-performance aircraft, when additional stresses, or an emergency, challenge his ability.

We are aware that aircraft accidents are seldom produced by a single, isolated event. Like most other accidents, they occur most frequently as the result of a chain of events with a final precipitating factor, usually induced by the person who makes the majority of decisions, the pilot.

I would like to reverse the sequence of analysis used by Colonel Lentz in his study on "cause undetermined" accidents, by placing primary emphasis on the conditions which degrade performance at the more subtle, non-awareness level. Certainly, single stresses can induce this state, but more often it is combinations of very subtle stresses which are responsible for the denigration of the pilot's ability. I would list as factors of secondary importance those conditions which cause incapacitation and death in flight. These latter are merely more obvious and detectable upon examination.

Basically, man perceives his environment by stimulation of the sensory receptors in the body. These sensory modalities are specialized appendages of the nervous system. As such, they are activated by specific stimuli which produce chemical changes within the receptor cells. These are translated into nervous impulses which ultimately impinge in select areas in the brain. All sensory receptors are limited in range and vary in sensitivity. Such factors as the intensity and duration of stimulation, the sequence in which they are received, and the latent or resting period between stimulations influence the response. Of the seven sensory modalities of vision, hearing, smell, touch, cold, warmth, and pain, hearing is the most responsive to simple reaction time, with the pain sense least responsive.

Under usual conditions, man uses his eyes most consistently to relate to his environment. These are his most reliable sensors, and he believes what he sees. Unfortunately, his interpretation of the visual image is affected by many factors. The eyes of a six-month-old baby perceives the same visual stimuli as those of a six-year-old boy, or a sixty-year-old man, but the interpretation of what is seen depends upon such variables as training, association, memory, and recent and past experiences. Vision is easily altered in aviation by hypoxia, acceleration, aeroembolism, glare, haze, heat, smoke, toxins, fumes, aircraft structure, personal equipment, disease, drugs, circulatory disturbances, fears, emotions, aging, and other stressors.

The hearing sense is used extensively in aviation to receive warning signals and to communicate. Yet, ears may receive, but not easily hear. There have been several cases where pilots on instrument approaches acknowledged radio messages that they were below the glide slope, yet continued on their original flight path until they crashed into the ground.

Touch and pressure, which are gravity-oriented sensors, are also useful; however, they are more often incriminated in disorientation in aviation than in orientation. The sense of smell, while important, is easily fatigued. It is possible to be exposed to highly noxious fumes, and after an initial exposure, to be totally unaware of continued contamination of the environment.

Once the stimuli are received in the brain, they are integrated, and a decision or judgment made. The decisions are made in the very highest and most differentiated centers of the brain, the centers of idea formation. This can be effected only if there is functional integration of the central nervous system. The information gained from the stimuli may be used immediately by being translated into a motor action, or, if insignificant or extraneous, may be completely discarded. If at all significant, the information is stored in the memory center of the brain. That which is received, but not properly mastered, will soon fade from memory. It is estimated that 50 percent of this type of information is lost within the first 24 hours.

Disease, drugs, environmental stresses, stresses induced by the aircraft, emotional factors, and other stressors, will alter this decision-making capability. It must be stressed that this unique capability to think and act depends upon the continued functional integrity of the brain and of the cardiovascular system. The brain does not store oxygen or nutritive material. Oxygen and essential chemicals must be supplied to the brain on a heart-beat by heart-beat action.

Finally, once a decision is made, action must be initiated through the muscular system of the body. Physical conditioning, training, and good habits will enhance muscle tone and assure a coordinated and effective neuromuscular response. Since we cannot basically change man, our goal is to optimize man's responses, define limitations, and, if possible, design to these criteria, or, if impossible, provide him with the mechanical or electrical side necessary to accomplish his mission in safety.

I have presented a rather confused picture of a complex situation. For years, we have been studying this problem. We have studied man, his systems, his subsystems, and sub-subsystems, his chemistry, his histology, his individual cells, and intracellular components. We have studied the aircraft in detail. We have considerable knowledge about the external environment. In fact,

we have been flirting around the edges of this total problem—
that of the man/machine environment complex. I believe that
considerable strides have been made in recent years in recognizing the need for an integrated study, and that efforts are now
being made to achieve this.

I feel that a better understanding of man can be accomplished
by a long-time longitudinal study, weighing the many variables
which affect his success or lack of success as a pilot. Longitudinal
studies, designed to investigate many variables involved in the
genesis of coronary heart disease, are now being conducted. Such
an effort is being started at the Naval Aviation Safety Center in
the Heraps Program, whereby pilots will ultimately be studied
as successful and unsuccessful pilots, with respect to accident
causation. Such variables as heredity, early training, early background, early experiences, presence or absence of disease, academic grades, avocational interest, flight training progress, fitness
reports, and many other factors, will be analyzed and evaluated
in the two groups to try to identify the factors of greatest significance in prediction for reliability and success.

There are a number of specific recommendations made by
Colonel Lentz with respect to the "cause undetermined" accidents which should be reemphasized. He suggests more effort in
personnel selection with the use of various psychomotor testing
under stress simultated situations and the elimination of those,
who, for example, show evidence of motion sickness or vertigo.
He further suggests continued psychological training and retrain-
ing and updating of individual skills and knowledge. And, finally,
he recommends that we make better use of machine technology
development in cockpit redesign and presentation. He suggests,
for example, that more emphasis be given to the development
of a "flight-path-in-the-sky" type of coordinated and integrated
visual display with intermittent presentation of certain critical
information should failure appear imminent and to give the pilot
the option of soliciting other specific information as he deems
advisable.

In closing, I again state that I believe a most outstanding job
has been accomplished by the Navy in the field of aviation
safety. I see no logical reason why further improvement should

not be anticipated; however I emphasize that the easy fixes have been made, and the task ahead will not be an easy one. The safety effort must be pursued with the same determination and vigor so characteristic of its drive in the past ten years and in the same professional vein.

Man must be even more exhaustively explored with respect to his role in the total man/machine environment complex. Continued improvement in the selection, training, and qualification and in proficiency flying for crewmen, top level command support of the safety effort, and reemphasis of professionalism and self-discipline among crewmen and maintenance personnel will be needed to achieve a zero accident rate. Channels of communication must be maintained, for this is vital to the perpetuation of any successful educational program. Aviators should be encouraged to discuss incidents with responsible personnel, for these are the most accurate weather vanes for prediction of future accidents. Above all, perfection should be the ultimate goal of the aviator's individual and daily performance. The philosophy of safety is implicit in such a disciplined program.

21

THE LIMITS OF MAN

Archard F. Zeller

Few safety programs have advanced so far and so fast in the last two decades as the program of the U.S. Air Force. Dr. A. F. Zeller has been in the forefront of that movement most of the time.

The demands of military flight often pushes man to the limit. Few readers are involved in occupations that push a man so close to the edge, nor are they generally involved in military flight programs. Never-the-less, they will find many of Dr. Zeller's observations directly applicable to their line of work.

Dr. Zeller speaks of man and his limitations as if man were a machine, a chemical laboratory, and a psychological being. Man is not automatically equipped with the knowledge to function to his limits in any of these capacities and thus must be given the knowledge. The author seldom mentions safety, but the application is direct since man's inclination to have accidents is directly related to knowledge of his tasks and the limitations of his performance.

ACCIDENTS DON'T HAPPEN; *they are caused!* The cause can be either failure of the materiel or failure of the human. Equipment changes. For this reason materiel failures are different from one piece of equipment to another. The human on the other hand does not change. During the period of recorded history there is little evidence to indicate that man has changed in any major respect. Because the man does not change, the kinds of errors he commits remain constant. The errors that he will make can be predicted from the errors he has made. A careful study of these can result in positive future accident prevention.

Errors can occur because of limitations within the man himself, because of his relationship with other men, and because of faulty instructions or other supervisory errors. Study of accidents shows

Courtesy Aerospace Safety, United States Air Force.

that very few human errors involve negligence. These studies also show few actual willful violations. Most human failure is the result of a situation. When the demands of the moment are greater than human capacity, adequate responses may not be forthcoming. The result is often an accident, loss of equipment and loss of life.

Let's look at man's limitations. Man is first a mechanical structure. He is a system of levers, weights, balances and counterbalances. He can only reach so far; he can only lift so much. He can only see so far.

Man operates in time. Every action follows a time sequence. At any point in this time sequence adequate functioning can break down. If the information supplied through the eyes or ears or by other means is inadequate, a proper decision and response cannot be initiated. If too much information is presented, too much time is taken in determining its meaning. If information is presented in an unsystematic way, a decision may be difficult or impossible in the time allotted. If the actions required exceed the individual's strength, failure can result. If the action required involves too complicated or too refined reactions, failure may also result.

Man is considerably more complicated than a test tube. When the blood is pumped through the body adequately and contains the proper chemicals, the body structures are nourished. This nourishment makes it possible for all of the previously discussed functions to operate properly. The sensory system remains acute. Decisions can be clearly reached and action can be accomplished efficiently. If the biochemical balance is upset, inefficiency results.

Another type of disruption occurs when the individual becomes tired. Biochemically this is the result of waste product in the bloodstream. These biochemical effects can be enhanced by boredom or other factors. When the body is tired, efficiency is also decreased and a man is more error prone and may even fail to notice that errors have been committed. The practical solution to this problem is to insure adequate rest and to insure that work policies are clearly defined and work periods well regulated.

It is well known that efficiency is reduced by illness. Subsequent medication may also be a factor in still further reducing an individual's effectiveness. When medication is administered by a physician, results can be monitored and predicted with a high degree of accuracy. Even minor illnesses should be treated by a physician. The dangers of self-medication should be stressed, since many medicines readily available to all have behavioral side effects.

Man is not only a chemical laboratory and a machine. He is more than this. He is a psychological being with aptitudes, desires, and feelings. These add further limiting or distracting conditions which may affect efficient operation.

Not all people can do everything equally well. When the position to be filled has very special requirements, critical selection becomes important. A missile equipped with a nuclear warhead is an awesome weapon. The inadvertent or intentional premature firing of such a weapon could be disastrous. It is important therefore that in the missile field selection not be left to chance. Each individual, particularly in the operating crews, must be carefully chosen.

Human beings do not come automatically equipped with knowledge. Most functions need to be learned. This implies that training programs need to be developed. At least three different kinds of training needs to be considered. First, there is original training in which the person learns the basic elements of the job to be done. Next, there is proficiency training in which the techniques learned are reviewed and procedures refreshed. Last, there is transition training in which an individual learns to do something new.

The learning period is consistently associated with a higher degree of error than any other. Experience has indicated that all learning follows approximately the same pattern. The curves of accomplishment, activity, production, etc., vs. time are usually called the "Learning Curves." The term is not often applied to error rate curves. There is probably a good correlation between error rate and rate of learning. In the initial learning period, which proceeds rapidly, there are probably more errors than later on when the rate of learning gradually declines. This applies whether it is an individual learning to do a certain task or a group producing a piece of equipment. In this curve each period of time is marked by a decreasing rate of errors. The curve descends rapidly and gradually smooths out at some level of efficiency, ordinarily less than perfection. Because of the great number of errors during initial learning, this period must be carefully controlled. A carefully prepared training program must be developed and adhered to. Every step of an individual's progress must be controlled to insure that the required learning is taking place with the least possible number of errors.

Once learning has reached an acceptable state it is necessary that an individual practice what he has learned.

Studies show that most information learned during a given lesson is lost during the first twenty-four hours. After this, lesser amounts are lost until complete forgetting takes place. When a person practices what he has learned, forgetting is retarded. If he practices enough, the function is improved rather than lost.

Missile crews are in a peculiar position. Some have learned to do something which they will never be called upon to actually perform. If performance is required, it follows so long after learning that much forgetting has taken place. It is important, therefore, that every effort be made to insure proficiency even though actual practice cannot be accomplished. The use of trainers, simulated exercises and relearning of the academic portions of the job are all useful means of keeping current in the job required.

The third type of training involves transition training or upgrade training. In this the individual must learn something new. Here again some of man's basic limitations make correct functioning difficult. When something is learned, some undefined change takes place in the nervous system. The result is that although learning is difficult, it is equally difficult to forget. In some situations the same act in a new situation will result in a different end result. For example, if identical switches are in precisely the same position in two different consoles but associated with different systems, the activation of the wrong system can sometimes result and be critical. In other instances, a switch in the same position associated with precisely the same system may have its direction reversed so that what is ON in one console is OFF in another. This is particularly hazardous although the new sequence may be learned quite easily. When a person is distracted, however, he tends to revert to the original pattern. Special checklists and resequencing of actions are aids in avoiding such problems.

Although people can perform mechanical type functions, unlike static pieces of equipment, they have emotions and feelings. If two people have the same basic talents and training, the one with the greater interest and motivation will consistently perform better. A person who is distracted by personal problems, worries, or tensions can consistently be expected to have these interfere in some way with the performance of his job. Emotional disruption in most instances leads only to inefficiency and relatively minor errors. In the critical missile field, however, it may lead to very serious and costly mistakes. This reemphasizes the need for careful selection of people in the first place and a continuous watch to insure that emotional difficulties do not develop.

It is seldom that an individual in a large society works alone. This brings into focus a major source of error. It stems from a lack of clear definition of what each individual's task is and from a lack of adequate communication between individuals regarding what they are to do. It is a fundamental of good working relationships that everyone knows precisely what he is to do and be reminded of this regardless of how many times it has been accomplished in the past.

The supervisor must understand the task to be accomplished. He must be acquainted with the capability of the people he has available. He must know the limitations of the equipment he is to use. The man and the equipment must then be integrated into a working unit to accomplish the assigned task.

In conclusion, we must realize that the operator of equipment is in a position to commit a great variety of errors which can lead to accidents. Inadequate familiarity, poor directions and long operating hours are a few of the conditions which can lead to difficulty. However, accidents can be prevented. Accidents are for the most part the result of human failure. Most human error is the result of people failing to accept what they know. Namely, human tolerance cannot be violated. Excessive workloads, poor environmental conditions or emotional tensions are all important considerations. If any task is to be successfully performed, full consideration must be given to the limitations of the human element. And, if a task is successfully performed, it is safely performed.

22

NO NEW CAUSES

Ted S. Ferry

*Although the author writes with tongue in cheek, he has no intent
to be flippant about the causes of accidents. He illustrates his points
from a lifetime of experience in aviation safety, but the lessons apply
in any circumstance.*

*The article may be read as a delightful experience with a hard core
of substance. Let the astronauts have an accident on the moon with
an exotic one-of-a-kind machine. No matter; cause factors in man,
machine, and environment remain the same, and Doctor Ferry takes
us on a tour of mythology, primitive science and the history of flight
to make his point.*

*Tomorrow's accident, which seems so unforeseeable today, will be
the result of the same old cause factors once it happens. There's comfort and some degree of clarification in that observation, and Doctor
Ferry makes points of practical relevance and wry wit along the way
as he arrives at it.*

THE PROBABLE CAUSES of modern aircraft accidents are not
likely to be new or unique. A session with the inner circle of
accident investigators will reveal many believe it difficult, if not
impossible, to find a new cause. Modern day causes have parallels
in mythology and history. While the incompleteness of early reports makes it necessary to speculate, it quickly becomes apparent
there is little new in the origins of aviation accidents. Then, as
now, the margin between success and failure was often narrow
and sometimes the risks involved were all for naught.

Consider the case of the first reported flight, that of a shepherd
named Etana who lived near Babylon. He was from a small vil-
lage where no children had been born for several years because
the wrath of the gods had been incurred. In his quest for a plan

From *U. S. Army Aviation Digest*, July, 1972.

that would restore the power of birth he found an eagle that had been hurt and nursed it back to health. For his kind action, the eagle flew him to the goddess of birth, Ishtar. Incensed at his audacity, the goddess had him hurled from her palace and he was killed in the fall. Although his flight was successful, the fact that his mission failed brings to mind one of the problems that exist today. Should the mission have been flown in the first place? Proper evaluation of the risks would have revealed his chances of success with Ishtar were so small that Etana's resources should not have been gambled on the flight.

An early recorded flight which ended in a hard landing involved Emperor Shun of China. While still a boy, he was imprisoned atop a tall granary which was then set afire. The young man survived by jumping and using two reed hats as parachutes. These were the same type of coolie hats still seen in the fields of Asia today and we can only conclude that he was either a very small boy, or the hats were exceptionally large. Since he escaped serious injury and the hats were apparently undamaged, Shun left it to others to write about his flight. This initial failure to write up a hard landing set in motion centuries of similar failures. Laced with pride, it is no doubt the origin of our troubles in getting proper write-ups today.

The flight of Daedalus and Icarus stands as an epic example of accident causes and was the first recognized fatal accident. As the story goes, Daedalus was a brilliant man, credited with many innovations and inventions, among them the saw and ax. His successes produced much jealousy and he and his son were imprisoned in a tower on the Isle of Crete. They fashioned wings of feathers and wax and succeeded in escaping from the tower. Their success was short-lived when they flew too near the sun. The hot rays melted the wax in Icarus's wings, the feathers came out and he fell to his death. Monday morning quarter-backing of this event brings out several items. Supervisory error was evident in that the senior man present did not plan the flight to avoid high temperatures, nor did he brief his wingman on the necessity to maintain formation and avoid the sun. Further review reveals quality control and design were involved, since ordinary candle wax with a low melting point was used.

Not too many years ago, an Englishman, no doubt a descendant of Icarus, demanded the case be reopened and subsequent investigation, involving a thorough review of witness statements and other testimony, revealed the accident may have resulted because the wax used to fasten the feathers together hardened at Icarus's higher altitude and cracked with the flexing of the wings. Thus, the true cause involved failure to use low-temperature wax. This was probably the basis for the current use of the term *probable cause*, which allows cases to be reopened, in view of subsequent events. The use of this term does not indicate final action and leaves the way open for changes of heart, mind and facts.

Bladud, the tenth King of England and father of King Lear, was one of the early tower-jumpers. While on a trip to Greece, he picked up some wild ideas about flying and, as was the fashion in those days, tried to prove his theory by jumping from a tower. He used a pair of homemade wings in his attempt to fly over London and crashed to his death. In the absence of a good accident report, we must conclude the cause was unknown, though speculation leads us to believe design error played a key role. Since he was the father of King Lear, there is also speculation that the pilot selection process was not what it should have been.

One of the early-day giants in flight was Simon Magus who was grievously hurt when he put on a show near the hippodrome in Constantinople. Lacking a public information officer, he loudly announced his intention to jump from a tower and fly. A large crowd gathered to watch him—"in a garment stiffened with willow reeds"—lean into the wind for an extended period before jumping into what should have been a slide. The maneuver was unsuccessful, but he gained everlasting fame, since the cause of his accident was well recorded: "The weight of his body having more power to drag him down than his wings had to sustain him, he broke his bones." Obviously, there is a case here for poor design, lack of quality control, crew error in flight technique and, possibly, a lack of self-discipline for being goaded into jumping by the impatient crowd. The latter is known today as an unusual sense of urgency about mission accomplishment.

Simon also gets a historical note by being one of the first anti-aircraft victims. His early success at flying around Rome enraged a certain gentleman of the city known as Peter. There are two versions of what happened. One claims that Peter, sick with jealousy, shot Simon down with an arrow. The assumption is that this happened before Peter became a saint. The other version indicates that Peter shot him down with a few well directed prayers, which may be one of the reasons he became a saint.

Next came a man of all trades, Oliver of Malmesbury, who fashioned some wings and, according to reports, flew more than a furlong before crashing and breaking his legs. While recuperating, he wrote up his accident report, claiming he crashed because he "forgot to fasten a tail to his hinder parts." Obviously, his failure to use a checklist played an important role in the crash. We cannot help but be impressed with his hindsight.

Another sportsman of the day was an Italian adventurer named John Damian. While in Scotland, he fashioned homemade wings and tried to glide from a high wall. While recovering from his injuries, he showed great insight into investigative techniques. He found the reason for his fall was the use of chicken feathers which had a greater affinity for the barnyard than for the sky. Once again, poor quality control and design error contributed heavily to an accident.

The era of tower-jumping ended about the middle of the 18th century and the balloon came into prominence. The first successful free flight by a man in a balloon is of interest because of hazardous events on the trip. A young Frenchman named Pilatre had made several captive balloon flights, but it was his first free flight in November of 1783 that marks the military entrance into aviation. As a passenger, Pilatre took an infantry major named d'Arlandes. Their journey was a great event, lasting twenty-five minutes and covering five miles across Paris. The balloon was of the hot air type which, in the style of those days, had a fire in an open grate and sparks were continually flying up and onto the varnished cloth used for the balloon covering. It was Major d'Arlandes's job to keep dipping a sponge into a bucket of water and apply it to the smoking cloth so it would not burst into flame. Today, his contribution would likely be recognized with a *Well Done* for saving the aircraft.

George Biggin is unknown in the Aviation Hall of Fame, except for a flight he made in 1785 with Mrs. Sage, a beauty of her day who weighed 200 pounds plus. It was the first flight of a woman in England and applies to our study because of the disaster which resulted when she accidentally planted her size ten shoe on the barometer. Certainly, there were cause factors present we recognize today: Poor design in that the instrument was placed where it could be stepped on by robust women; and the fragility of the barometer made it obvious it had not been tested to withstand prospective wear and tear. If fault tree analysis had been applied, the possibility of this event could have been forecast and avoided. Other more imaginative investigators might conclude there was an element of environmental design error in that the cramped quarters of a balloon basket was no place for amorous pursuits. There was absolutely no evidence to support this conclusion.

Earlier, the flight of Pilatre and d'Arlandes was mentioned. This same Pilatre decided he would be the first to fly the English Channel from east to west. He set out with the balloon's manufacturer, Romain, in June of 1785. Half an hour after takeoff, at 3,000 feet, something went wrong. Watchers on the coast below heard a muffled explosion and saw the passenger basket and balloon fall to the earth trailing fire and smoke. Their deaths were the beginning of the end for hot air balloons. In reviewing this accident, we find Pilatre used a combination of hot air and hydrogen. A more explosive mixture could hardly be found, particularly since there was a fire to generate the hot air. It was later learned that Pilatre did not think the flight could succeed, but goaded by the west to east channel crossings of others and handicapped by pride and jealousy, he talked himself into a flight from which he could not retreat. The cause factors for Pilatre's fatal accident have been repeated in many later accidents. There was design error in that the volatile mixture was known to be explosive. Elements of true pilot error were present in that Pilatre knew in his own mind that he should not attempt the flight under the circumstances.

Although there were other balloon accidents of interest, the accent in flying shifted to gliders and early attempts at powered flight. Between 1891 and 1896, near Berlin, Lilienthal made over

2,000 flights in gliders. While on his last flight, in blustery weather, a gust of wind pitched his glider sharply upward. It stalled and fell to earth. The great experimenter died the next day. The cause of his accident was lack of self-discipline. He flew when he knew the weather was blustery, with a gusty wind that was probably beyond his and his equipment's capabilities. The ugly head of complacency reared, as it so often does to those who gain great experience and fly what are considered proven machines.

Langley, the distinguished and respected secretary of the Smithsonian Institute, was well into his fifties when he decided that powered flight was for someone other than the birds. He invented a series of flying devices and built several successful flying models. Congress granted him $50,000 to build a flying machine and he ended up with a gasoline-powered monoplane to be launched from a houseboat on the Potomac River. A scale model worked very well. On October 7, 1903, his assistant, Manley, tried a take-off which ended with a plunge into the river. The machine was repaired and, on December 8, Manley tried again. This time the tail structure struck part of the launching platform and another plunge into the river resulted.

All agreed at the time that Langley's plane could probably fly. They were proven right when it was rebuilt years later and made a successful flight. Review of the two Langley accidents points to design error in the catapult mechanism on the first flight. On the second, ground support equipment appears to have been placed too close to the aircraft for takeoff. Some investigators will point out that Langley tried to use too short a runway and that the craft should have been placed on wheels for a more conventional takeoff. Later experiments brought out the truth of these observations.

While everyone realizes the Wright Brothers made their first powered flight in 1903, few realize their problems. They arrived at Kitty Hawk several weeks before the first successful flight. When the machine was assembled, the motor missed so badly that the resulting vibration twisted one of the propeller shafts and jerked the assembly apart. Both shafts were made over, then another mechanical problem arose. The magneto would not make a strong enough spark. Next, they had a problem with the sprockets to the propeller shafts. It seemed as if there were no end of mechanical failures. Finally, on December 14, Wilbur won the coin toss and took off. He went only a few feet into the air, then flew into the ground, breaking one of the skids and several other parts. By his own admission, an error in judgment was the cause.

Finally, came the great day of Thursday, December 17. The first successful powered flight was a mere 120 feet. The aircraft was slightly damaged on landing, but the cause was not recorded in the excitement. Three more flights were made, with the last being the longest. After flying about 800 feet, the aircraft began pitching. On one of its downward darts, it struck the ground. The cause was diagnosed as flying too close to the ground in gusty air. Pilot technique and weather are apparent factors. When the aircraft was carried back to the starting point, a sudden gust of wind struck it and turned it over several times, damaging it badly. It was never flown again. While not strictly an aviation accident, this ended powered flight for the year.

The accident rate for 1903 was fantastic! Considering the Wright Brothers' 4 minutes and 38 seconds of flying and their four accidents, the rate was around 5,200,000 accidents per 100,000 flying hours—a clear warning to those to follow. But the fatality rate was extremely good during those early years. Although flying activities mushroomed, there were no fatalities until 1908, when Orville Wright was flying with LT Thomas Selfridge of the Army Signal Corps as a passenger. During a demonstration at Fort Meyer, a propeller broke, severing a support wire and allowing the aircraft to plunge to earth. LT Selfridge was killed. This material failure gained an infamous place in history, since it involved the first fatality in powered flight.

This brings us to the realm of modern aviation and an era of accidents so numerous they are almost commonplace. Most of the causes of air accidents became known prior to this era. Current and future accidents will, for the most part, only point to probable causes established by prior accidents.

Before we close this saga of early accidents, one man should be mentioned. A hero of his time and champion motorcycle racer. Cal Rodgers tried to fly across the United States within 30 days to capture the Hearst price of $50,000. He didn't make it in 30 days. But, from an accident viewpoint, his 49-day flight from New York to Pasadena was epic. He made 69 stops, 23 in Texas alone. According to his flight the country was 19 crashes wide. Only the rudder and a single strut remained of the original aircraft when he arrived in Pasadena. A review of his flight and accidents revealed no new accident causes were involved. There were many—supervisory error; crew error; material failure; maintenance deficiencies; inadequate inspections; poor planning; weather; etc. At this early date, a new cause for an aircraft accident had become difficult to find. The probable causes of most aviation accidents were already written into history by 1911.

23

STATE OF THE ART
IN AIR SAFETY

C. O. MILLER

*Since writing this article, Mr. Miller has joined the National Trans-
portation Safety Board. Many of the ideas presented in this slightly
dated article have been solidified through actual usage by the Board.*

*The author sees aviation safety as a product of an evolutionary
period that began only a few decades ago. Mission accomplishment
and cost saving, according to Mr. Miller, have taken their place along-
side protection of life as objectives for modern approaches to accident
prevention. He describes precepts that are commonly accepted, some
that remain to be explored, and one that provides some consternation
at the law-saftey interface.*

*Mr. Miller has much of his expertise in the field of aviation, but the
reader will sense that the leadership exercised in safety by aviation
has direct application to nearly all fields.*

THERE HAS BEEN unprecedented attention focused on air safety
in recent years. Of that, there can be no doubt. Perhaps this
attention has been the result of socio-technological evolution . . .
a concern for fellow man's physical well-being amid astounding
mechanical marvels which often seem incomprehensible to the
point of being frightening. Perhaps it has simply resulted from
communications media being more effective in bringing tragedy
closer to the not-so-directly-involved personnel. Witness the reaction to the Apollo 204 accident. The philosophical reasons for
the *why* of a change notwithstanding, it behooves society in general, and professionals in particular, to periodically pause, and
ask, "Just where have we been, where are we, and what must we
appreciate about the future?" This paper attempts to do just that

From *Journal of Air Law and Commerce*, Volume 34, 1968.

for today's air safety art. Or call it air safety discipline if you will, depending on your standards of accreditation for a new field.

As part of the Symposium on Air Safety conducted by the School of Law at Southern Methodist University, this discussion extends somewhat beyond air safety per se. The purposes and practices of law and the purposes and practices of safety are not unrelated. Based on prior investigations by this author among others and a previous law-safety symposium, one might conclude that aviation law and safety are entwined much like separate vines in a dense forest, each striving for sunlight, but crawling all over each other enroute. When each truly recognizes the objectives of the other, and bends a bit to give a little more room, both prosper (Miller, 1962; 1963; 1964a; 1964b; 1966a).

Thus air safety will be discussed in terms of its state of development. But emphasis will also be placed on misunderstandings or unresolved problems in accident prevention that bear upon the law-safety interface.

Evolution of Safety

Within the span of two generations at best, aviation has transitioned from a "white scarf" barnstorming image to a rather integral part of our everyday life. Within this era, formalized safety efforts have evolved significantly, beginning with the licensing and regulatory procedures of the Bureau of Air Commerce in the late 1920's. A decade later saw the next major milestone in air safety. Modern day accident investigation procedures are traceable to the Civil Aeronautics Act of 1938 with the first major investigation involving, as aviation buffs might suspect, a DC-3! (Civil Aeronautics Board, 1940).

As World War II approached and was underway, however, safety was still something that impugned the ego of any red-blooded pilot. Persons suggesting that accidents were anything more that unfortuitous events were considered sissified. Certainly at that time, the moral motivation for protection of life in aviation was apparent; but luck was the name of the game. Only the most far-sighted individuals viewed accident prevention as a specific technique that could be applied in a rational sense. With few exceptions, like Jerome Lederer,* the names of these men have been lost in technology's cemetery of forgotten reports.

World War II had its effect on safety technology as it did in many fields. The accident scorekeepers were hard at work and a few safety education posters were utilized for good measure. When the bent aircraft and broken people were tallied, however, far more losses were found due to accidents than through combat (Stewart, 1965). The fatality and destroyed aircraft rates as a function of flying hours were not too bad when comparing stateside and overseas losses; but combat potential in terms of men and machines had been seriously compromised through sheer numbers of catastrophic accidents. As a result, a cry for professional flight safety work was noted early in 1946 (Wood, 1946). There was concurrent activity pertaining to civil aviation, as evidenced by the start of the Flight Safety Foundation near the close of the war.' Then a landmark paper by Steiglitz in 1948 clearly delineated the concept of a specialized approach to flight safety engineering (Stieglitz, 1948).

Thus, a major change in safety philosophy was born when comparing air safety to traditional modes of safety (e.g. industrial or traffic). Air safety was being cited as a means of enhancing mission accomplishment, whether that "mission" was delivering bombs or making a corporate profit while providing safe and sane air transportation. A suggested methodology breakthrough involved safety specialists, men whose specific job was accident prevention, as well as accident prevention being an inherent duty of each man in every organization.

The 1950's saw at least two more fundamental developments. First was the formation of the military safety centers at Norton AFB, California, Naval Air Station, Norfolk, Virginia, and the U. S. Army's Ft. Rucker. Concurrent in these actions was the assignment of safety officers at all levels of command through all

* Formerly Chief of the CAB Bureau of Safety in Pre World War II era, former Director of the Flight Safety Foundation, now Director of Manned Space Flight Safety, NASA.

† Flight Safety Foundation, Inc., Certificate of Incorporation, State of New York (filed 12 April 1945).

military services, i.e. the implementation of safety specialists in the operational world. The University of Southern California's safety education programs have provided over 5,000 graduates since 1953 of 10 to 12 week intensive study programs aimed at these positions. Attendees have also included representatives of 50 foreign nations, and occasionally, civilian personnel. In recent years, airlines, business aviation and other groups (including lawyers) have been provided similar education programs but on a reduced time scale. The evolutionary trend of prominence here was one of changing the emphasis from accident investigation to accident prevention.

The second major impact of the '50's was the realization of the economic motive for safety. Single seated aircraft were being delivered at more than $1,000,000 a copy; others came much higher. The military realized that while lives remained important and mission accomplishment their fundamental goal, economics was perhaps the greatest real world motivator for improved accident prevention. This trend has continued today when one realized the annual "book" dollar loss of air vehicle accidents by the U. S. military service approximates ¾ of a billion dollars! *

Safety specialist-oriented personnel were to be found in some airlines during the '50's, with Carl Christianson of UAL and Bill Littlewood of AAL being the most prominent. For the most part, however, the increasing complexity of the machines and the "system" had not fully arrived—or was not adequately recognized—by the airline community. There are many who feel the early losses of the first (and second) generation jets by airlines fall basically into this area of explanation.

The influence of the missile and space age then added still more dimensions to the safety art/discipline. Not only did a new order or hazards occur (propellants, space navigation, and the like), but the role of the flight crew was finally recognized for the tremendous contribution to safety that they really are. It was painfully recognized that without pilots aboard, air vehicles such

---

* A given accident's "book" dollar loss entails essentially the cost price of the air vehicle as represented by the total procurement contract divided by the number of air vehicles purchased. Values of human lives and indirect costs are rarely ever discussed.

as missiles had to be made right the first time; and the term "system safety" came into being.

Actually, there had been hints of the system safety concept in Stieglitz's 1948 paper and in early papers by this author in 1954 and 1957 (Miller, 1954; 1957). Also, an evolution in military weapon system procurement transpired in the late 50's and early 60's that further contributed to definition of the system safety concept. But all in all, system safety truly differs from previous accident prevention efforts in only three ways, albeit they are highly significant improvements.

1. The "System" could encompass much more than just the aircraft. It could include support equipment, facilities, the people involved, training programs, etc. Or, it could be applied to any identifiable segment of the whole.

2. The accident prevention scope involves planning and control on an entire life cycle basis, from conception of a system through its operational phase.

3. There are specific safety tasks contracted in the engineering phases to supplement those conceptually similar efforts going on during operations.

By the mid 1960's, the system safety concept was observable in the Supersonic Transport program (by direction of the Federal Aviation Administration). Within the past six months to a year, it has been observed to be applied by at least one major transport aircraft manufacturer of his own volition. Interest by the airlines in application of this concept has been minimal although it was suggested to them specifically in 1966 (Miller, 1966b).

The evolution of air safety can thus be summarized as follows:

1. The safety specialist has appeared at both the operational and engineering end of the system spectrum.

2. Economic and mission factors have joined moral justification as basic reasons for improved accident prevention.*

---

* A rather strong case can also be presented for the prestige factor as exemplified by the Apollo 204 loss. Cost, mission, or people are not considered to be the principal reasons why NASA has done so much towards modifying its safety programs in the past year. A similar situation arose recently following the USAF B52 accident near Thule AFB in Greenland. Cessation of airborne alerts was influenced by world opinion (prestige) as much as anything else.

3. The approach to safety today is *prevention,* not just after-the-fact accident investigation.

4. The system safety concept involving complex engineering, management, and operational relationships has become a part of aerospace life.

Although not germane to the air safety of the art, per se, it should be recognized that a major revolution is going on relating various forms of safety activity to one another. Heretofore, industrial safety, traffic safety, flight safety, missile safety, nuclear safety, etc., have tended to pursue their separate paths of technological development. As exemplified by major organizational changes in the military and industry, most of these areas are learning—at long last—that accident prevention as a discipline can best be achieved by a major amalgamation of these splinter areas. The system safety approach may well be the methodology that brings these various groups closer together since it has application in all fields.

Today's Precepts Concerning Accident Prevention

Traditionally, one can identify principal approaches to safety as practiced by particular organizations or groups of people. They are the identifiable philosophies and modi operandi, albeit not necessarily the only ones to be found in the total group. They are interrelated. They are changing, since nothing about safety is static.

Listed in Table 23–I are these principal safety images in the minds of the groups shown; images that one will encounter. They go well beyond aviation safety, just as law goes well beyond aviation law. They are shown in no particular order except perhaps the Public as the first one. The Public has had its thoughts shaped by a few million years or so trying to avoid danger. They deserve to be first!

Despite these oversimplifications for the sake of emphasis (and the parenthetical observations that just could not be resisted), the fact remains, P + NSC + DOD + USAF + USN + USA + NASA + FAA + NTSB + PHS + NHSB + AEC + ALPA + GA + FSF + USC + AI + ABA + many others equals one tremendous amount of accident prevention motivation, dedication,

TABLE 23-I

The Public (P) . . . Safety is restrictive; don't do this, don't do that. It is protection of person, not property. It is produced by a strange lucky combination of conscious and subconscious acts either *by* the individual or *for* him. (Ignorance is bliss!)

National Safety Council (NSC) . . . Copious statistics must be kept so that everybody can be told how bad things are. Education is the main tool of prevention. People are the only answer; they are the last ones on the responsibility chain. (They're the easiest to blame!)

Department of Defense (DOD) . . . Safety is a necessary part of mission effectiveness that involves both men and equipment. Put a number on it so that one may "scientifically" equate safety with other variables that affect decisions towards cost effectiveness. (When we try to find out what went wrong, the man who did the evaluations and made the decision has been transferred to a world bank, or somewhere!)

U. S. Air Force (USAF) . . . Regulations must be issued to cover all eventualities. Then there must be detailed inspections and reports to assure that people follow the orders. (By the numbers . . . 1, 2, 3, 4!)

U. S. Navy (USN) . . . Accountability is the middle name of the Captain of the ship. He is the Chief Safety Officer—and chief everything else. Accident prevention is his responsibility. Anyone else working therein is just a crutch for a less than 100% commander. (Hallowed are the banks of the Severn!)

U. S. Army (USA) . . . There's a group at the arsenal who have been building these things safe for a long time. Do the best with what's available. (Ya gotta expect losses!)

National Aeronautics and Space Administration (NASA) . . . Prior to Apollo 204: Make it reliable and it shall be safe. Instill constant awareness in highly selected and trained individuals and the good guys will prevail. After Apollo 204: All the above plus special attention to system safety engineering and management. (Just how much does Congress expect?)

Federal Aviation Administration (FAA) . . . Standards have been issued in accordance with authorities granted in the FAA Act of 1958. It is the FAA's duty to enforce those standards. All FAA work pertains to safety. (P.S. . . . Those are minimum standards.)

National Transportation Safety Board (NTSB) . . . Senator Magnuson called NTSB the "Supreme Court of Transportation Safety." An overview safety job is needed for all transportation modes. This includes what formerly were investigation functions of the Civil Aeronautics Board, Bureau of Safety. Objective, prevention-oriented studies are also to be accomplished. (But how can this be done with only 184 people? There were 125 for aviation alone when under the CAB.)

Public Health Service (PHS) . . . Accidental death is a leading cause of loss of life; ergo, a health problem. It is an epidemic and therefore is subject to the epidemiological approach. (First, however, someone will have to research all aspects of the situation!)

National Highway Safety Bureau (NHSB) . . . Until recently, accident prevention was a matter of "write an ordinance and enforce the law." (At least it produced revenue.) Today's program aims at the machine and environment as well as the man, both before and after the impact. (Thanks to Ralph Nader!)

Atomic Energy Commission (AEC) . . . It's obvious: there must not be any accidents. Accordingly, there can be no question that AEC regulations must be followed to the letter. (Besides, who knows enough about this business to ask—or answer—questions?)

Air Line Pilots Association (ALPA) . . . Pilot's opinion must be followed 'cause, after all, they're up there, too. They're also a rather professional group. (Look at their salaries.) Given better training and better facilities, they can "hack" anything. (If some of them don't trip on their white scarfs!)

TABLE 23-I

General Aviation (GA) . . . "Flying safety is when an airplane operates according to the pilot's will, totally," from "Quest for the Great God Safety," *Flying*, June '65. ("To be, or not to be . . . in the same sky as the airliners," from Shakespeare, 1603, and Miller, 1968.)

Flight Safety Foundation (FSF) . . . Everybody needs a conscience. Somebody needs to be a catalyst. (But when it comes to soliciting memberships, the question arises, "Why did you have to rock our boat?")

Institute of Aerospace Safety and Management (USC) . . . The name of the game is total system accident *prevention* through the interdisciplinary approach. Higher education plays a major role therein. (But how do you get a safety degree program through the curriculum committee without a hundred years of Ph.D. candidates?)

Aerospace Industry (AI) . . . Tell us what you want in accident prevention, and you'll get it. (For a price!)

American Bar Association (ABA) . . . Punishment or threats thereof represent deterrence to accidents. Within a main objective of social justice our ethical practices produce the greatest good for the greatest number of people. (Assuming the attorneys are equal in capability and there are capable judges and juries!)

and action, without which many of us would be lucky to be alive. The difference in approach, apparent in Table 23–I (and the shortcomings implied), simply reflect the different origin, evolution, and environment applicable to a given segment of the accident prevention world.

To suggest that any one approach is significantly superior to another, or that either can do the total job alone, would be quite foolhardy.

The previous discussion notwithstanding, there are certain accident prevention precepts that appear to enjoy near unanimous endorsement by safety personnel today.

1. Accident causation is a sequence of events describable in man, machine, media (environment), management, and other variables, depending upon the depth to which one wishes to take the analytical model. For optimum prevention activity, these variables are not describable by a single cause.

2. Accident causal factors are seen repeated over and over again. Indeed, with the possible exception of rare hazards brought about by highly advanced technology, one hardly ever sees a truly new safety problem.

3. Although accident prevention is far from being an exact science, its analysis methodology had made remarkable strides in recent years that entail highly advanced technical approaches (Miller, 1968).

4. Management responsibility cannot and should not be denied relative to accident prevention. Man is ultimately responsible for his own survival. But when groups are formed to better effect given missions, safety becomes more than protection effected through the individual; and group leaders must then assume responsibility for safety of the whole.

5. At some level of task complexity and size of the organization, specialized approaches to accident prevention in addition to safety being everybody's job produces more accident prevention per unit of resource expenditure than safety simply being everybody's job. This entails *additional* obligation/accountability through the specialist, not a substitution for that of others.

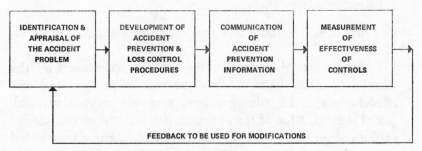

Figure 23–1. The Professional Safety Task.

Within this basic framework there have been efforts to clearly define the professional safety task. Figure 23–1 reveals a generalized view as developed by the American Society of Safety Engineers. On previous occasions, the author cited tasks in more detail as specifically applied in the aerospace field. These are shown in Table 23–II. These tasks have been exposed in their original form for over three years to numerous critical groups (including almost 200 Advanced Safety Program Management students). Modern aviation safety effort can be described by one or more of these functions. Competent management, through the division of work principle, will assign such tasks to their personnel, safety specialists or otherwise.

There remain several major challenges or unresolved problems that face the safety fraternity. While keeping the discussion

TABLE 23-II

SYSTEM SAFETY TASKS

1. Develop and coordinate implementation of safety plans including program accident prevention, system safety engineering, accident/incident investigation and disaster control plans.
2. Assist in establishment of specific accident prevention requirements.
3. Conduct or participate in hazard analyses, including the control process related thereto.
4. Determine and/or review emergency procedures.
5. Participate in design reviews and similar milestone events during product development and use.
6. Maintain an accident/safety information data center.
7. Effect liaison with other safety organizations.
8. Provide recommendations for and/or conduct safety research, study and testing.
9. Implement safety education, training, indoctrination and motivation programs.
10. Participate in group safety efforts such as councils, standardization boards, and surveys.
11. Direct or otherwise participate in accident/incident investigations.
12. Follow up all action resulting from accident/incident investigations.
13. Provide objective response to safety inquiry as a staff advisor; in the confidential sense when appropriate.

rather broad, and without any suggestion of priorities, these include:

1. Lack of total understanding and/or acceptance by the layman of safety being an integral part of mission and cost effectiveness, and involving more than merely personal survival.

2. Determination of the optimum level of system complexity or the nature of a given organization that merits a specialized approach to safety; e.g. an identifiable system safety organization containing specially qualified personnel.

3. An almost total lack of hard data bearing on the economics of safety. What really constitutes investments, losses, and returns associated with safety? Such information is needed by management to become more efficient in expenditure of funds towards accident prevention.

4. Limited ability to assess the reason for "action failure," i.e. the places between accident occurrence and similar accident recurrence where much of today's well meaning work falls down the proverbial crack.

5. The pitiful state of safety information storage and retrieval. There have been countless safety lessons learned but their identification and use within time constraints present on new programs is seriously compromised by inadequate storage and retrieval systems in existence today.

6. The need to provide a broad base safety education program to include professional development through the Ph.D. level.

7. Determination of a method of investigating accidents from the human factors viewpoint . . . psychological as well as physiological.

8. Better integration of the safety engineering and operational safety efforts, especially to ensure better test and indoctrination programs that minimize accidents during early parts of the learning curve on new vehicles.

9. Expansion of the systems concept into non-aerospace endeavors (with appropriate modifications), as a process that can more readily handle the multifactor basic nature of an accident than do current concepts.

10. Conflict between legal requirements to establish fault during investigations and the need for delineation of all causal factors in the interest of more fundamental approaches to accident prevention rather than just enforcement.

Item 10 cannot be emphasized too strongly as being the basic factor underlying misunderstandings between the legal profession and safety specialists. The lawyer, in seeking social justice through tort litigation, for example, must establish a proximate cause as a fundamental part of his case. In most situations, proximate cause becomes a single factor, or at least is identified in the minds of the layman as a single factor. The required proof of standard of care (duty) and failure to meet that standard of care (breach of the duty) entail a concept of negligence that carries with it a "fault" label. This, in turn, is interpreted by the layman as "who are they going to hang?" Suddenly the layman just does not want to become involved.

In accident investigation as a prevention task on the other hand, the purpose is not social justice, but rather it is protection of life, mission accomplishment or conservation of resources in general. It is a matter of trying to establish all factors as objectively as humanly possible. It is a matter of making recommendations and ultimately taking action on *any* factor that is determined to be potentially accident preventive in nature, consistent with resources and time available to take such action. There is no person

or organization as a target, or bastion to be defended. Any re-
semblance of these causal factors to the proximate cause as defined by law or determined by a judge or jury could be quite
coincidental.

It is fully recognized that the accident investigator must go
through the "cause" phase in his thinking, or more precisely, his
cognitive process. There is even experimental evidence to this
effect (Braunstein and Coleman, 1967). However, if professionally trained and motivated, he will not be satisfied to choose *the*
cause and build his report or recommendations only around that
finding.

Unfortunately, the charter provided the NTSB Bureau of Aviation Safety as carried over from FAA Act of '58 demands establishment of *the* most probable cause, as most military directives
insist on establishing *the* primary cause in their accidents. These
become accident board functions as compared to the functions of
an investigator in his fact-finding capacity. Hence, the conclusion
is reached that most accident boards have been directed to be
quasi-legal bodies regardless of their purported motives.

Despite the desire to think otherwise, this author believes that
any accident deliberative body that is directed to find the most
probable cause, the primary cause, or any similarly single factor
oriented conclusion is not optimally working in the accident prevention field. If fault or proximate cause is required, let that be
the function of a court of law or a military collateral investigation. If primary or probable causes are required for data classification purposes, let their determination be the prerogative of the
data processing group. If primary causes are required for management data chart presentation to show priorities in required safety
areas, let the chart preparers make the classification selection
(they'll probably distort them in any case to prove whatever they
are selling!).

If accident prevention boards cannot be established with
capability for attaining off the record evidence and developing
preventive recommendations without having to decide on *the*
cause, they had best be forgotten. Save the administrative expense
of two types of hearings; go to the complete adversary system; and
be satisfied with restricted data flow into and out of accident in-

vestigations. Be satisfied with deterrence being the principal mode of accident prevention.

Of course, such action would come as a considerable shock to safety specialists who believe they have come quite a way from the red flag, hard hat and perform-safety-or-punish concepts.

The Aviation Safety Record

The question cannot be overlooked as to just why aviation accident prevention practices should be improved, if indeed they need to be improved. One argument states we are well within risks of normal living (whatever that is!). The other argument states we should be continuing to do what we can, where we can to conserve our personal and material resources consistent with a progressive society (whatever that is!).

Implicit in such discussions is a look at the past record and an attempt to project it into the future. Unfortunately, there is no measure that adequately provides a good index of accident prevention potential or even achievement on a short term basis. Accident rates as a function of flight hours may be the least of many evils in after-the-fact assessment. But everyone close to the accident statistics field quickly recognizes that the power of the definition pen far outweighs the power of the plotted data.

Nevertheless, an undeniable improvement has occurred in the last twenty to thirty years in aviation safety; which is really the limit time span in which meaningful records have been kept. However, in our more or less immediate past that includes the jet transport era, the statistical rarity of airline accidents precludes any assessment of trends based on accident rates. General aviation on the other hand has been kind enough to try harder. They are having sufficient accidents that a trend does seem to be detectable, and represents an improvement in the last three to five years compared to a plateau that existed in the previous decade. There has been a rather strong hint from the military accident records that the specialist approach to operational safety has paid good dividends in accident prevention between the early 50's and early 60's. It has also been suggested that this improvement has leveled off, much as a learning curve tends to level off (Miller, 1967). This means that some major breakthrough will be needed to induce additional significant improvement. (The system safety concept represents a possibility in this direction.)

Obviously, rates do not tell the story. They tell little about exposure; they tell little about where the rates are going when the curves are relatively flat; they tell little about the impact of one or more particular kinds of accidents on the public. They tell nothing about the accident the observer may be worried about . . . the one he may be in.

The required perspective for state of the art in safety, however, is aviation in total. The total fatalities in aviation accidents these days (military and civil systems combined) are on the order of 2,100 people annually. This represents less than 2 percent of the total accidental deaths experienced in the U. S. each year; less than 4 percent of motor vehicle fatalities alone.

The total dollar loss in aircraft accidents has never been seriously tabulated to the author's knowledge. Using what data is available, however, this number is believed to be in the region of the 1½ to 2 billion dollars annually. This assumes certain book values for the machines and an estimate of some of the other definable costs. It does not include indirect costs which in the industrial safety field can run 3 to 5 times the direct costs of accidents.

To continue the comparison with the automobile safety field, the aviation accident economic loss is about 15 to 20 percent as large. Hence, it can be argued that in today's market, the cost proportion is significantly larger than that represented by fatalities . . . which only proves once again that statistics is the art of drawing a straight line between unwarranted assumptions and a prejudiced conclusion.

Actually, aviation's concern for safety is not merely based on the past but is far more concerned with the future. This concern could be expressed simply as the threatened single loss of 300 persons and $55,000,000 in an "airbus." It could be the one-a-day brand major catastrophe of a civil airliner forecast by Lundberg for the 1990 period, assuming no major decrease in accident rate combined with increased operations by then (Lundberg, 1965).

Philosophically, it is argued that we cannot morally stand by and permit the number of air fatalities to grow in the manner automobile fatalities have mushroomed. After all, now we have technology to apply toward further aircraft accident prevention; technology that was not even dreamt of at a comparable period of development of surface transportation.

Concluding Remarks

The motivation for the past development of improved aircraft accident prevention methodology has not been personal protection alone. It has resulted from attempts to provide better air transportation or other forms of mission accomplishment at minimal cost in either lives or material resources.

As society becomes increasingly complex in general, identification and solution of problems related thereto become similarly more complex. An evolutionary result which is by no means unique to the safety field, is specialization in tasks . . . specialization in personnel.

Interestingly enough for safety, however, this produces a paradox in view of the broad, interdisciplinary nature of accident prevention. Is the safety professional really a specialist, or is he a generalist? Actually, the safety professional is both. He is a specialist in attitude (accident prevention) and a generalist in knowledge and skills.

This, in turn, produces an interesting comparison with members of the legal profession; for here, too, a lawyer might be described as a specialist in attitude (social justice) and a generalist in knowledge and skills.

Hence, it is not surprising that the same set of facts as exhibited in an accident investigation are interpreted from two different viewpoints; each based on its own contribution to be made to society. Of course the profession of law has been around for quite some time. The profession of accident prevention has just begun.

This paper has hopefully provided the legal profession as well as others, a better understanding of the new arrival.

REFERENCES

Braunstein, M. L., and Coleman, O. F.: An information-processing model of the aircraft accident investigator. *Human Factors*, February, 1967.
Civil Aeronautics Board: Report of the Investigation Involving Aircraft of

U. S. Registry NC 21789 which occurred near Lovettsville, Virginia, on August 31, 1940. Washington, D. C.

Lundberg, Bo K. O.: Aviation safety and the SST. *Astronautics and Aeronautics,* January, 1965.

Miller, C. O.: *Applying Lessons Learned from Accident Investigations Through a Systems Safety Concept.* Chance Vought Aircraft Company, Inc., Dallas, Texas. Presented at the Flight Safety Foundation Seminar, Sante Fe, New Mexico, November, 1954.

Miller, C. O.: *The Role of Flight Safety Engineering in Aircraft Reliability and Effectiveness.* Chance Vought Aircraft Company, Inc., Dallas, Texas. Presented at the first IAS Naval Aviation Meeting, San Diego, California, August, 1957.

Miller, C. O: *Legal Ramifications of Aircraft Accident/Malfunction Data.* Proceedings of the IAS National Aerospace Systems Reliability Symposium, Volume I, New York, AIAA, 1962.

Miller, C. O.: *The Engineer, Lawyer, and Flight Safety.* Flight Safety Foundation, New York, New York. Presented at the SAE-ASNE National Aeronautical Meeting, Washington, D. C., 9 April 1963.

Miller, C. O.: The safety information challenge. *ASSE Journal,* September '66. Originally presented at the Flight Safety Foundation Seminar, New York, 15 October 1964a.

Miller, C. O.: Aviation law-air safety (A Symposium Report). *Alumni Review,* Aerospace Safety Division, University of Southern California, Log Angeles, California, Fall, 1964b.

Miller, C. O.: The influence of systems engineering and management on aviation products liability. *Astronautics and Aeronautics,* September, 1966a.

Miller, C. O.: *The Application of System Safety and Management to the Civil Air Carrier System.* Institute of Aerospace Safety and Management, U.S.C., Los Angeles, California. Presented at the ALPA Air Safety Forum, October, 1966b. (Published in the Proceedings.)

Miller, C. O.: *Hazard Analysis and Identification in System Safety Engineering.* Institute of Aerospace Safety and Management, U.S.C., Los Angeles, California. To be presented at the AIAA/SAE/ASME Reliability and Maintainability Conference, July, 1968.

Miller, C. O.: *The Role of System Safety in Aerospace Management;* A Masters Thesis presented to the Graduate School, U.S.C., January, 1967.

Stewart, C. B.: USAF Director of Aerospace Safety; Address before the Graduating Class, Aerospace Safety Division, University of Southern California, Los Angeles, California, 17 December 1965.

Stieglitz, W. I.: Engineering for safety. *Aeronautical Engineering Review,* February, 1948.

Wood, Amos L.: The Organization and Utilization of an Aircraft Manufacturer's Air Safety Program (Unpublished), The Boeing Company, Presented at the IAS Meeting, New York, New York, January, 1946.

24

SYNDROME OF AGING

Harold R. Willis

This brief item considers age from the viewpoint of human error potential. That sharp focus serves as an introduction to a subject that has often been treated in depth in other sources: the aging process and age as a factor in accident causation. The age of the person is only part of the picture. The other part concerns the tasks the person is expected to perform. The author observes in conclusion that accidents are caused by people young and old.

N o ONE NEEDS to be reminded that with the advance of age— and this commences earlier than we think—the human body has a decreasing capability. The first change many older aviators notice, for example, is not a physical one, but rather an emotional one manifested by signs of increasing caution while flying. You might say that this is one of the four signs representing the "Syndrome of Aging."

The first sign is one of normalcy represented by the carefree attitude with little consideration for the hazards that are present in flight. The second sign is manifested by an increasing degree of caution. The third is an increase of normal caution into distaste or perhaps even a controlled fear of flying. The final phase is a realistic acceptance of both the hazards and pleasures of flight, tempered by proper caution and experience. This final attitude, or syndrome, may not be as much due to the actual physical aging of the individual as it is to his anticipation of decreased capacity which he knows comes with the advance of age. The factor, then, may be more psychological than physical at its outset.

Early evidence of physical aging is found in the increasing degree of difficulty in fighting off and recovering from fatigue. This

This item was publicized by the Flight Safety Foundation, Inc., as Pilots Safety Exchange Bulletin 64–111, December, 1964.

normally appears in the late 20's or early 30's. About this time the individual begins to be sensitive to the extremes of temperature. Whether these are specific or climatic, the individual is prone to be less tolerant of extremes or changes. This is due to decreased body heat production and lessened muscle activity in situations involving low temperatures, and more limited dissipation of body heat through the skin in high temperatures, probably as a result of slowing down of the metabolic process in the body.

It is obvious that aging does not begin all at once for all parts of the body, hence the following qualities versus age are worth noting:

Qualities	Age
Hearing is keenest	10 years
Greatest resistance to infection	15 years
Metabolism starts to slow	20 years
Vision most acute	24 years
Muscles begin to lose strength	25 years

The decrease in visual acuity is probably the most significant factor which nudges the individual into the first recognition of the effects of aging. The lens of the eye has been hardening since late childhood, and at about age 40 the ability to focus on objects has been affected to such a degree that near objects begin to blur. Sometimes, the sharpness of focus for distant objects is handicapped. The slow inroads of decreasing vision capability, and the proneness of many to fight against this admission that they are growing old, often precipitate a situation that may result in an error being committed, with a resultant accident.

The narrowing of the visual field, or peripheral vision, and a decrease in night vision capability are also penalties of aging. Although the older eye will adjust to the dark as quickly as the younger one, it does not achieve the same level of sensitivity. In other words, the older individual requires much more illumination than the younger one to achieve the same results.

Although the older man loses some of his ability to bounce back after sudden or extensive physical stress, his capacity for endurance is greater than that of the younger man for longer and less strenuous efforts. A man in his late 30's would be more suitable for the task of an astronaut than one in the mid 20's, but the latter would be a more suitable fighter pilot operating high-performance aircraft.

One of the factors of aging, which poses potential human error, is the decrease in ability of individuals to accomplish tasks requiring short-time memory retention. Experimental work discloses that in more complex tasks, the older subjects tended to find the "rule of translation"—from one difficult task to another harder one—more difficult to accomplish while actually performing the more complex task. Most of their errors appeared to be due to attempts (probably unconscious) to simplify the task to that of conditions of the less difficult tasks. The most perceptible increase in the time required to respond on tasks of increased complexity occurred after age 54. This appeared not to be the matter of longer time for appearance of a signal to the taking of appropriate action, but of the length of time for which material has to be viewed for accurate identification to be achieved.

Speed of action decreases to a greater degree than muscular strength. Slowing with age produces a number of indirect effects which may be observed. On an industrial job, for example, one of the first signs of slowing is that a man works more continuously, taking fewer short rests for a smoke or conversation. More severe cases may result in items being missed when in a hurry, leading to errors and perhaps to chronic feelings of being harassed. Mitigating factors of the slowing with age is increased experience which can provide ready answers to problems that might otherwise have to be brought out from scratch, and even more important, build up *routines* of action and the ability to recognize sequences in events.

In all fairness to those who are physically and mentally young in spite of chronological age, it must be pointed out that aging is an individual thing. Many people who are sixty years chronologically are physically and mentally the equal of the average fifty-year-old, and in some rare instances equal to the average forty-year-old. People may vary in age bonus six to ten years younger than their chronological age as they advance into the 50's and on. The loss of strength is replaced by an increase in skill that makes a man of fifty superior to one of twenty-five for certain tasks; and people over forty, who are normally fit and healthy, have the capacity to pilot jet aircraft.

A piece of electronic equipment called the Psychomet has been used at the National Institute of Mental Health in Bethesda, Md., to measure true-age. It is a device with push-keys connected to an instrument panel that registers the proficiency of a man performing various tasks. Some tasks take some thinking; others mainly measure reflex speed. An instrument such as this would be invaluable as an aid in measuring true-age of men employed on critical tasks after they have passed the ripe old age of thirty. Such a measurement would certainly be one means of anticipating performance which could make for human error and accidents.

The capacity to learn diminishes very little with age providing it has been used through the years, but learning speed does diminish. Mental power, however, diminishes much less rapidly than physical functions, and the increase of abstract reasoning powers and ability to master difficult concepts up to about age fifty makes the bright mature man more than a match for the bright young man.

Looking at age from the point of view of human error potential, it is true that reflexes, strength, and coordination are at a peak around the mid-20's. But trigger-quick reflexes have been known to get a young man into trouble he can't get out of. Judgment, fortunately, improves with maturity.

In the final analysis it might be said that aging represents one of the many factors that can lead to human error and accidents. But it is also worth noting that age in and of itself does not necessarily cause mishaps. Accidents are still caused by people— young or old—and *people-caused* accidents stem from a lack of proper attention in performing the job.

25

SCIENTIFIC ADVENTURING
AND MISADVENTURES

Thomas L. Shipman and Roy Reider

The authors discuss the need to maintain safety in scientific pursuits without inhibiting the adventuring, and the risk, that are inherent in discovery. They ask, "where do safety professionals fit in this?" The article may be studied by those who seek practical answers to that question. Or, it may be read at another level. It may fascinate with its seldom told tales of scientific adventuring, and misadventures.

Dealing with some of the brightest minds our society produces, the authors at one point arrive at a safety cliche—"understanding is hardly enough"—or as cliche has said it, knowing is not enough. Should that conclusion be a surprise in these unusual circumstances with these unusual people? The industrial safety professional may wish to recast this article into words to fit his own experience, and compare and contrast.

IT IS WELL RECOGNIZED that the problem of accidents occurring in chemical laboratories is not unique to young people, though it is often thought of in connection with that age group. Official responsibility for such mishaps is not limited by age, so any form of scientific adventuring requires our attention and best efforts.

In the younger age group, there is little doubt that it is the A student of high school age who becomes involved in chemical laboratory accidents more often than does the poorer student. It is equally clear that sheer intellect alone does not account for the difference. It appears that girls of equal academic standing do not get into difficulty as frequently as do the boys. The best explanation for this is that experimental science is a form of ad-

From *Journal of the American Society of Safety Engineers*, July, 1968.

venture. Not only are these bright kids, boys primarily, experimenting near the limits of their knowledge, but they also are eager for dramatic things to happen. And, as we will see, the problem is not confined to youths.

Today's students are able to perform more sophisticated experiments. A tragic accident of this kind took place several years ago when a 16-year-old leading chemistry student made private plans for celebrating July 4. Using calcium carbide and water, he generated acetylene, which was passed through a solution of silver nitrate with ammonium hydroxide added to control the pH. The precipitate was silver acetylide, a unique and useless explosive compound of extraordinary sensitivity and whose products of decomposition are entirely solids, elemental silver and carbon.

The precipitate was filtered and moved out of the home laboratory on filter paper in a glass container. In the appropriately isolated location, some elemental potassium was placed on the moist silver acetylide. A sharp explosion pulverized the glass, depositing an infinite number of particles of glass, carbon and silver in the student's face, hands, and eyes. Today, his visual ability is limited to perception of light and dark.

Answers to similar problems have preoccupied man from the beginning of recorded history: Does one impose absolute restraint on such experiments? Does one shake the head and wag the finger?

A grave misadventure in a pseudoscientific inquiry occurred at Los Alamos in 1946, in an experiment to find a suitable location for a reactor exhaust stack. Several engineers and technicians wanted to study wind currents by observing dissipation of smoke. From a formulary reference book they obtained a relative proportion mixture of a variety of ingredients. The list of materials and the quantities used may strain credibility but it is true: Sugar, 2½ lb; potassium chlorate, 3 lb; magnesium metal chips, ¼ lb; barium nitrate, ¼ lb; and red phosphorus, 1 lb.

The phosphorous was being added to the other material when the "explosion" occurred. One man died soon afterward; two were blinded. Three of the men planning the work were university graduates. Later it was affirmed that the men had been notified that fabricated smoke bombs had been available. Accepting this as truth, it must be believed that it was adventure that was being sought rather than an understanding of wind currents.

Valiant experimenters of the late 18th and early 19th century depended almost exclusively on personal observation. They had few instruments with which to work. These natural philosophers insisted on touching, smelling, tasting, and self-experimentation. This letter, written to a scientific journal, is reworded only slightly for brevity:

Dublin, 1814

Carbon monoxide was discovered in 1801; it is combustible, burning with a blue flame, incapable of supporting life.

The experiments of Davy on the respiration of nitrous oxide in 1800 dissipated apprehensions of fatality from the inhalation of compound gases, and demonstrated that many gases, before considered as destructive to vitality, might be breathed with safety.

Desirous of witnessing the effects of carbon monoxide when respired, with a view to analogy to nitrous oxide, I was tempted to inhale it copiously. The consequence was nearly fatal. I made three or four hearty inspirations of the gas, having first exhausted my lungs of common air. The effects were a sudden deprivation of sense and volition. I fell supine on the floor for half an hour, apparently lifeless, pulsation nearly extinct. Several medical gentlemen being present, various means were employed for my restoration, without success. The introduction of oxygen gas by compression into the lungs was suggested, the effects of which were dramatic. A rapid return of animation ensued, though accompanied by convulsive agitations, head-ache, and quick irregular pulsation, and, for some time after mental recovery, total blindness, extreme sickness and vertigo, with alternations of heat and shivering cold, were painfully experienced.

I very much regret the confusion arising from fear of my death so disturbed everyone that no accurate determination was made of the quantity of gas respired. The experiment is rather too hazardous for repetition. Nevertheless, the extraordinary efficacy of oxygen gas in cases of suspended animation produced by suffocating gases is fairly deducible. I hope the results of this experiment may be of practical utility in those cases which are often so awfully fatal. It is the decided opinion of the professional gentlemen present on this occasion, that the free use of the oxygen gas was solely instrumental in restoring me to life.

Mr. Higgins himself had nearly once fallen a victim to a similar experiment with sulphuretted hydrogen, the effect of which, after recovering from a death-like insensibility, were painful and oppressive for many days.

> I am your obedient servant,
> Samuel Witter

Note here Witter's perception on the effectiveness of pressurized oxygen for asphyxia.

Scheele, the Swedish chemist who discovered hydrofluoric acid and started fluorine chemistry, had a bad but typical habit of sniffing and tasting any new substances he found. He died at the age of 44, after many years as an invalid.

It is not certain exactly when Benjamin Franklin flew his kite but he should have had some idea of risk although perhaps not the degree. It is clear that his kite experiment followed the "sentry box experiment." In the latter, a long, grounded rod reached 30 feet above the housetop; the experimenter sat in a sentry box, dry and insulated, and within the house, and stretched out to the long rod a shorter hand-held rod heavily coated with wax at the handle. Electrical sparks were then drawn off the long rod. When Franklin reported his kite experiment about 1752 he said, "When rain has wet the kite and twine so that it can conduct the electric fire freely, you will find it stream out plentifully from the key on the approach of your knuckle."

Shortly after this (1753) an experimenter, Richmann, was electrocuted in St. Petersburg, Russia. He was, however, trying to measure quantitatively the electricity in a lightning discharge through the use of an ungrounded test rod. This was the first accident having fatal consequences to occur during an electrical experiment, and it was discussed throughout the world.

In more recent times, an attempt was made to use the high potentials developed in the atmosphere during electrical storms. Two German investigators in 1932 stretched an insulated cable across a valley between two peaks in the Alps; from it, a conducting cable supporting a terminal was suspended. During thunderstorms high potentials would develop between this terminal and a grounded terminal on the valley floor, and sparks several hundred feet long were obtained. Plans had been made to install a discharge tube for the acceleration of particles, but experiments were abandoned after one man was killed.

The early scientific investigators were motivated toward safety almost exclusively from the standpoint of self-preservation. This self-motivation for preventing accidents depended primarily on understanding what kind of accidents could occur and what their consequences might be. If this knowledge of accidents is speculative or just not known, the risk of course is higher.

But modern investigators are also motivated by direction. Support for scientific programs, which are becoming increasingly large and complex, imposes a directed prudence. Safety standards with almost the force and effect of law have become more numerous.

Yet, adventuring in science is by no means a problem only of past generations.

In the exciting work of the early 1960's, Bartlett of the University of British Columbia and a co-worker were developing compounds of the noble gases. Only 0.39 gram of XeF-4 was dissolved in water and then evaporated under vacuum at room temperature. The remaining white solid exploded, shattering the glass vessel which was being observed closely by the experimenter. Serious eye injuries were inflicted on both investigators.

At an AEC-affiliated laboratory early in 1967, an employee was interested in the optical behavior of liquefied gases as their temperature reached the critical point. Carbon dioxide was liquefied in a heavy-walled glass capillary tube by cold trapping with liquid nitrogen. The filled tube was sealed off. It was then to be transferred into a pipe-fitting safety container while still cold, and allowed to warm up.

This entire assembly was to be cycled several times from 0° to 50° to test the glass for overpressure. This would have been followed by cooling down to—80° C, after which the pressurized capillary would be set behind a safety glass barrier so that a strong light could be projected to allow observation of the interface as the temperature was raised and lowered across the critical point. The critical point for CO_2 is 31.1° C and 73 atmospheres.

This plan was interrupted by the ringing of a telephone just at the point in which the capsule had been sealed, removed from the liquid nitrogen, and placed on a wad of paper in which it was to be wrapped before insertion into the safety container. The ex-

perimenter answered the telephone and an unspecified few minutes later returned and picked up the capsule and wad of paper
to put them in the pipe-fitting. Just then the capsule, which was
about the size of the top of a fountain pen, blew up with a sharp
report, reducing the glass to particles the size of grains of sand.
The man was wearing safety glasses, so no serious or disabling injuries occurred, although he had about 100 cuts about the face
and hands.

It is sometimes difficult to decide when adventure stops and
scientific investigation begins, or vice versa. In March, 1927,
Captain H. D. Gray, a member of what was then the Army Air
Corps, ascended to 28,910 feet in a free balloon for an American
altitude record. Two months later on May 4, Gray reached a world
record height of 42,470 feet but was forced to bail out, so that
record was not official. Six months after that, Gray ascended to an
altitude identical to that of his May flight, 42,470 feet, but did not
survive.

Daring investigations of the sea depths have interested scientists and adventurers alike; again the dividing line is blurred. A
marine biologist, Limbaugh of California, failed to come out of a
long cave penetration in an undersea-underground river in France.
Keller, a young Swiss mathemetician, tried to make progress in
diving techniques by experimenting with light gas and O_2 mixtures. He reached a simulated depth pressure of 810 feet for about
30 seconds, followed by a 49-minute decompression. By 1961 he
had made dives of 700 feet. But at 1,000 feet, an accident resulted
in the death of a co-worker and a rescuer.

A modern, well-supported scientific laboratory, public or private, would not long endure such a haphazard approach to experimentation in which safety cannot be reasonably assured. Yet,
without compromise to the safety of personnel, property, and
program, one can avoid unnecessary restrictions. The significance
of absolute restraint is not difficult to recognize. Conversely, it is
not clear that science requires a free assumption of risk in order
to progress. What is abundantly clear is that modern society will
no longer permit the application of new knowledge without regard to human and esthetic consequences.

Any new employee with academic experience only may need the kind of attention he may not have had from his professors. He will now be faced with multiple safety rules with a requirement for a review of proposed procedures. While professional health and safety people cannot stand at the elbow of every new employee, nor should this be their job, each new employee has a supervisor of some sort who must be made unequivocably responsible for the directions given the new man. He must be made quickly aware of the legal, social, ethical, and contractual responsibilities imposed on his principals from a variety of sources.

Perhaps our greatest challenge in this increasingly complex world is the real understanding of the nature and consequences of misadventures. Understanding is hardly enough. Dissemination by directive, by instruction, by example, by publication, continuously and imaginatively, should be one of our loftiest aims.

Where do we safety professionals fit into this? We certainly have a clear responsibility to keep bodies and souls intact. We are, however, in a difficult spot. Certainly we do not want to be guilty of stifling ingenuity and inventiveness simply by saying "No." There is an unfortunate tendency for those engaged in the broad field of industrial safety to acquire the reputation of being obstructionists.

First of all, we must accept the fact that our mission is to help rather than to hinder. We must so conduct ourselves professionally that we maintain the confidence of every supervisor. He must know that we are friends, possessed of a particular ability, who are anxious to help him get his job done, that we are the proper people to ask for advice in advance of the fact, not after trouble has arisen. It is the supervisor who must impress on his charges the fact that safety engineers, industrial hygienists, health physicists, and physicians are not his natural enemies. They are interested in helping to accomplish whatever needs to be done, assuming that the supervisor is in agreement.

All that we should ask is that these bright young men work in a prudent manner, with all that this implies. More often than not this prudence will involve seeking advice and assistance from someone else. This all adds up to developing good habits of work, habits that will insure greater chances of productivity and success. What better way can we protect the investment which is in part our responsibility?

Make no mistake, this is not an easy assignment. It calls for a high degree of technical competence coupled with a high degree of ability to demonstrate this competence.

26

PRODUCT SAFETY

M. F. BIANCARDI

The author states that his emphasis "will be on ways to organize to prevent—rather than ways to transfer liability or develop defense postures." Insurance and legal defense are a necessary part of a firm's response to the threat of product liability, but the prime contribution of the safety professional must be to prevent the incidents, accidents, and injuries.

In this brief overview (actually a talk delivered to safety professionals), he offers four guides to assess the safety acceptability of a given product. These help to determine the size of the product safety job in any firm. In other publications, Mr. Biancardi has pursued the "how to" techniques in more explicit detail.

M Y COMMENTS on product safety will focus on the responsibilities of executive and middle management, including the safety professional. Yes, I said product safety, not products liability; not that we will ignore products liability—absolutely not! But, we believe that the most successful way—and many lawyers support this viewpoint—to limit products liability claims, suits, and losses is to do what is reasonable and practicable to eliminate incidents and accidents involving products. Once a product accident occurs, new variables that can affect losses are introduced —public pressure, possible adverse publicity, court precedents, a judge or jury and, lest we forget, the plaintiff's attorney. Thus, the manufacturers' ability to control loss exposure diminishes.

Where the Emphasis Will Be

Adequate product safety measures and programming will not only minimize exposure to suit but also strengthen defensive pos-

From *Journal of the American Society of Safety Engineers*, July, 1973.

tures in case the inevitable suit does occur. My emphasis, then, will be on ways to organize to prevent foreseeable accidents and incidents rather than ways to transfer liability and develop defense postures.

First, an observation about our roles as managers and professionals. Depending on how we choose to look at it, each of us is in the happy or unhappy position of being part of that minority that is both manufacturer and consumer. Frequently, our perspective toward product safety will depend on which role we may be filling. Each of us, as we or someone we know comes close to injury using someone else's product may angrily proclaim, "There ought to be a law!" But we may be equally incensed at the slightest suggestion that our own products be controlled by law. A practical and successful approach to product safety and the prevention of products liability losses depends on the skillful blending of these opposing biases.

One more introductory comment: Exposure to accidents and to products liability is not uniform for all products and all businesses. On the one hand, it may be a matter of low priority for some companies but a prime matter of survival for others. Yet, in either instance we need to be aware of the potential existence of a serious problem and the impact it can have on a business. Who knows what design change or new product you may consider tomorrow? And the time to consider accident and liability potential is before the go-ahead decision is made—not after.

A Quick Look at Real-Life Situations

Let's take a quick look at real-life situations in which two of our policyholders are involved.

One acquired a small subsidiary to complement its capital goods lines. The acquired firm makes a relatively inexpensive consumer product which, because of a possible defect, may have to be recalled—at a cost probably exceeding $100,000. Normal products-liability insurance does not cover costs of recall. And the subsidiary has already been acquired!

In contrast, another policyholder is considering producing a new line, but an intensive study of the potential accident and liability exposure is *preceding* that important decision. The point:

Product safety considerations cannot be afterthoughts in industry today.

I always find myself tempted to put some shockers into a talk; shockers not only because of the tragic injuries, but because of the astounding ways that a product accident can cost a company hundreds of thousands of dollars—or millions.

A handyman mechanic lost a leg after being struck by a dumb-waiter counterweight. The counterweight dropped on him while he was in the shaft working on a motor. He had to work under the weights because that's where the access door put him; and there was no buffer, guard, or housing to keep the counterweights from falling onto him. A $200,000 judgment has been affirmed by the U.S. Court of Appeals.

An I-bolt on an electrical control cabinet broke when the cabinet was being hoisted to a truck. The jury said that made the cabinet defective. One of the largest judgments ever made, more than $3 and one-half million, went to a workman left blind, speechless, and paralyzed from having the cabinet come smashing down on him.

A man helping a neighbor build a patio received leg burns from wet concrete. It was held that the ready-mix concrete maker ought to have warned users of the concrete's caustic properties.

No Simple Constructive Answer

I wish I could tell you specifically how far you're going to have to go to protect people against hazards in products. There is no simple constructive answer. Nor is the answer to throw up our hands and say there aren't any reasonable limits; and, therefore, we ought to give up. But, this Australian story almost makes me think so.

Under a caption which went, "Did Swimming Pool Father Baby?" The *Atlanta Constitution* ran this letter to Dear Abby: "Dear Abby: My mother read in the newspaper where a 15-year-old girl got pregnant from swimming in a public pool. Now she won't let me go in the swimming pool. She said the article said that in Sydney, Australia, the courts had decided that the municipal swimming pool is the father of a child.

"It seems that a 15-year-old virgin girl began having pregnancy symptoms after having swum in a public pool. The mother took her to a doctor who examined her and said the girl was still a virgin, and the symptoms were false. The symptoms continued and after nine months the girl gave birth to a healthy baby boy.

"They call this a billion-to-one chance that some male sperm in the water impregnanted the girl. The city agreed to pay the girl a pension."

Now, we may smile at this story, but I'm sure that swimming pool manufacturers and operators see no—absolutely no—humor in it.

I said I could offer no definite answers as to how far we need to go in product safety, but here are four guides in the form of questions that we can share with you. We believe answers to the following questions will generally give a good idea as to the public safety acceptability of a given product:

1. Is it at least as safe as anything produced by competition?

2. If a new model, is it at least as safe as its predecessor? Is the improvement in safety of the new product at least equal to the improvement of any of the other product characteristics such as cost, quality, durability, efficiency, etc.?

3. Are the hazards that remain necessary to the accomplishment of the product's task?

4. Are the remaining hazards and their possible consequences clearly identified for the entire life of the product? Are the instructions for safely living with these hazards reasonable, adequate, and clear?

What Our Own Government Has Done

In the swimming pool story, I talked about something that the Australian government had done. Now, let's look at something our own government has just done.

Congress has passed, and the President has signed, the Product Safety Act. I will give you an overview of the Act as gleaned from summaries prepared by the National Safety Council and William White of the Department of HEW. The stated purposes of the Act are:

1. To protect the public against unreasonable risks of injury associated with consumer products.

2. To assist consumers in evaluating the comparative safety of consumer products.

3. To develop uniform safety standards for consumer products and to minimize conflicting state and local regulations.

4. To promote research and investigation into the causes and prevention of product-related deaths, illnesses, and injuries.

The new act establishes an independent regulatory commission known as the Consumer Product Safety Commission of five members appointed by the President subject to Senate confirmation.

Provisions of the act provide for release of brand-name information to the public, but surround this release with some safeguards:

A. Collect and analyze relevant injury and hazard data.

B. Conduct studies and investigations.

C. Test products and develop test methods.

D. Develop standards governing a variety of product characteristics.

E. Inform consumers of product hazards.

F. Ban products found to be unreasonably hazardous.

G. Define, ban, and seize imminently hazardous products.

H. Require marketing notice and descriptions of new products.

I. Require certification of compliance with the appropriate standard and identification of date and place of manufacture.

J. Require manufacturers, distributors, and retailers to give public notice of defective products.

K. Require manufacturers, distributors, or retailers to:

(1) Bring product into conformance.

(2) Replace with one meeting standards, free of charge, to the consumer.

(3) Refund purchase price, or any combination.

L. Inspect manufacturing plants or warehouses or conveyances at reasonable times—in product safety related areas only.

M. Require recordkeeping of design, production, and/or sales figures. These must be available for commission inspection.

N. Test, seize, and destroy defective imports.

O. Subpoena records, documents, or witnesses.

P. Conduct hearings; file and litigate suits; issue formal notice of noncompliance.

Q. Purchase any consumer product for research, testing, or compliance review.

R. Construct research and test facilities.

S. Establish a Product Safety Advisory Council, five members each from consumer groups, governmental agencies, and industry.

T. Establish federal-state co-operative programs.

Civil penalties for violations of the Act can run as high as $2,000 per violation, up to a maximum of $500,000. Criminal penalties for a person who "knowingly and willfully violates Section 19 of this Act, after having received notice of noncompliance," can be a fine of up to $50,000 and up to a year in prison.

What Options Are Open to a Company

So much for the moral, legal, government, and economic pressures that beset the manufacturer and seller. What options are open to a company? We're going to find that they are the kinds which are best discovered and exploited by the same managerial methods that work whatever the problem may be—identifying it, establishing policy, choosing staff and assigning responsibilities, and determining action priorities. Let's discuss some of these.

You can make progress in identifying the problem and determining its size by reference to your files; communicating with field people; making customer surveys, if that's appropriate; consulting with trade association, legal counsel, and safety professionals. Please avoid unilateral, single-person, or single-function studies simply because biases and narrow-gauge visions can easily produce the wrong conclusion.

In determining the extent to which potential products liability may be a problem for your company, be sure to consider these factors: obligation to the user, image of the company and the product, cost of potential losses, degree of possible harassment (by government or otherwise). Naturally, the size and intensity of any programming should be in proportion to its relative importance to the over-all health of your business.

Once the size and scope of the accident and liability problem have been determined, policy should be considered.

Needs a Basic Policy To Start From

An accident and liability prevention program needs a basic policy to start from. What is needed is a product safety policy which contains not a string of lovely platitudes and generalities, but the foundation and guidelines for full response to the products liability problem and to the prevention of accidents which can cause customers to become disabled or disgusted.

A policy statement should do four things:

1. State safety objectives by tying them to existing safety standards and the current level of safety engineering knowledge and practice so they will continually escalate with these standards and the rising level of knowledge. Broad, sweeping statements like "the ultimate in safety" or "the safest product possible" are well-meaning but dangerous and not much use in guiding everyday activities.

2. Require managers and professional people to include moral, legal, and economic product safety consideration in every managerial and technical decision. Both the costs of safety efforts and the cost of not making them should be counted.

3. Identify the responsibilities of line and staff organizations for product safety, specifying broadly what they are in marketing, service, design, manufacturing and quality control, assigning staff responsibilities for assisting and coordinating the efforts. Product safety is not a one-function job.

4. Clearly make product safety a management accountability factor.

As I visualize him and have actually known him in some companies, the product safety coordinator holds a staff job. He is appointed to help management in the engineering, marketing, and manufacturing functions reduce product accidents, improve customer acceptance, and minimize product liability losses. He and they, with his help, do that by bringing safety knowledge, skills, and techniques to bear on product design, production, use, and application directions.

Staff Coordination Is Necessary

I am not suggesting that it need be a full-time job, although in some organizations it will be. But I am suggesting that if your products liability potential is of any consequence, staff coordination is necessary. The chief engineer, quality control manager, insurance manager, or safety director might be considered. Although chief engineers and quality control managers often get the role, not all of them find it easy to work in a staff capacity in an area where they also have line responsibilities.

A good deal of consideration should be given to a person already holding a staff position, but whoever it is must have direct access to a top operating person who has decision-making responsibilities for the total product.

A short list of the specific responsibilities which might be given to a product safety coordinator will help in making the choice of person to fill the job. For instance, they could include:

1. Identify the product safety responsibilities to be assigned by management to certain operating and staff positions.

2. Assist in communicating product safety responsibilities to those given these assignments.

3. Devise and recommend ways to train and develop people in work affecting product safety.

4. Develop and maintain an incident/accident report analysis system.

5. Consult on safe product design, manufacture, and application.

6. Help in product accident investigations and defense against unwarranted claims.

7. Maintain liaison with business, professional, and governmental organizations and agencies.

The Tip of the Product Liability Iceberg Has Risen

The tip of the product safety iceberg has risen above water. It should long have been readily visible to each of us—executives and safety professionals. By now, however, we should have a full realization of the enormity and complexities represented by the base of this iceberg spawned from consumer interest in safety and health. For us to hope that the problem will go away is wishful thinking. Instead, I hope each of you is saying to yourself, "This product safety thing is taking off. Whether I am a company executive or a safety professional, I'd better get aboard."

PART III
THE CHANGING EMPHASIS

The safety profession, in theory and practice, is changing as never before because society in general is changing as never before. What comes into the scope of safety, what it seeks to accomplish, and what society wants it to accomplish, are being defined and redefined. The selections in this part illustrate some of the facets of this changing emphasis and may convey some sense of why.

27

THE ACCIDENT PROCESS

Alexander H. Hirschfeld M.D. and
Robert C. Behan M.D.

Many safety researchers have been amazed that medical doctors often arrive at findings and conclusions parallel to their own. In compiling the readings in this book, a major source of material to consider has been the speaking and writing activities of medical personnel.

Early in the selection that follows, the authors explain the chain of psychological events leading to sickness and relate it to the chain of events leading to an accident. Perhaps the safety practitioner will be surprised to realize that, medically speaking, the "sequence of events" leading to an accident do not end with the accident. A little reflection will show that from the medical viewpoint, the accident may only be a step on the road to illness and injury.

Common sense tells us that a person would not deliberately hurt himself or cause an accident to happen. Doctors Hirschfeld and Behan throw doubt on such common sense and document many cases where it has happened. So, another safety cliche (a person would not deliberately hurt himself) goes down the tubes. The student has another facet of safety to ponder, and the practitioner has another set of problems and solutions to deal with. The multidisciplinary nature of accident prevention has seldom been better illustrated.

THIS IS A REVIEW of approximately 300 cases of industrial accidents and injuries. All of these patients were referred to the authors during the course of litigation when the workers were seeking to recover damage for their injuries. The cases demonstrated an accident process which resulted from several causes. The multiple etiologies are worthy of comment, because in somatic medicine the germ theory has caused so much concentration on a single causative factor that others are frequently over-

Reprinted from *The Journal of the American Medical Association*, 186:193–199, October 19, 1963. Copyright 1963, by American Medical Association.

looked. Yet, for example, the crucial role of insects in causing yellow fever cannot be neglected. The truth is that this and all other disorders are caused by multiple elements. Following this thesis, it was hypothesized that accidents would be the result of more elaborate causation than, for example, the fact that a man fortuitously slipped on an oil slick which just "happened" to be there, hurting a back which was completely normal beforehand.

In addition to etiological considerations, the clinical pictures are particularly challenging. For instance, in each case legal authorities were attempting to evaluate the extent of both somatic and psychiatric damage. This determination was usually made by asking a question such as: "How much of this patient's pain is due to psychological causes and how much is due to physical ones?" Another frequently asked question was: "Did this man's nervousness develop as a result of his accident, or did the pain and disability of the accident cause his present emotional difficulties?"

Our findings led to the conclusion that these legally important questions actually served to sidetrack the physician from delineating and then treating the real problem. Careful evaluation demonstrated that the emotional difficulties did not arise from the pain and discomfort of the injury. Moreover, they did not pre-exist the accident, only to be "aggravated" by it. Both of these conclusions give the accident and the physical disorder an unjustifiable emphasis. Histories in this series of cases showed that the syndrome develops because of basically emotional, socioeconomic, and sometimes legal reasons. Psychiatric examination also revealed the physical injury to be the result of the psychological process.

This series of psychological events could very properly be called an accident process. Before the accident occurs there is a state of conflict and anxiety within the patient. As a result of this condition the worker finds a self-destructive, injury-producing act which causes his "death" as a worker. From this moment the patient reacts exactly as do other psychiatrically ill people, except for the character of his symptom. Instead of having a presenting complaint of anxiety, depression, or other classical psychiatric symptom, he has the physical disorder which is the result of his accident.

This is more understandable if one recognizes the fact that psychiatric symptoms, like physical ones, serve a purpose. A main segment of this choice of symptom is to hide the real problem. Thus, the neurotic headache may successfully keep the patient from attending a function he doesn't enjoy, but attention is focused on the pain and away from the conflict. Such patients run from doctor to doctor trying to get help they will not accept, because relief of symptoms would refocus attention on the real and too-painful conflict. They also exhibit much hostility toward the physicians with whom they never completely cooperate. How similar to the patient who complains of a low-back pain and becomes involved in an accident in order to occupy attention and to cause distress!

As noted, symptoms do not develop fortuitously. For example, the pneumonic cough grows out of the body's attempt to develop better pulmonary gaseous exchange. This process can be documented and studied. A similar development occurs in industrial injuries, with the accident being an analog of the cough.

As seen in our cases, the accident is therefore only a single event in a continuing dynamic process. Before the injury several events occur, many of them within the mind of the worker. The process is started and carries on to increased anxiety, tension, and often guilt. It explodes in catastrophe and then continues, capturing the pain and incapacity resulting from the accident for its own purpose. Thus, the accident process is a continuum, acting before, during, and after the injuring event.

More complete investigation of accident cases was first directed toward getting more detailed description of the actual injury. In the process of doing this, the patients were able to describe the psychological state (and the conflict which results from it) which precedes the accident.

Behavior Patterns Observed Before Accidents

At the time of their accidents many skilled workers seem suddenly to do things which novices would not make the mistake of doing. For example, a structural steel worker with twenty years of experience at the same job suddenly decided to change the rigging so that the stress of lifting the mechanism and two men was placed on two small screws instead of on a self-tightening joint. He fell to the ground before the rigging had been lifted fifteen feet and was very seriously injured.

At the time of injury, safety rules are often so broken that the worker loses human protection. In two instances tunnelers dug pathways for utility pipes and wires, and were required to work in treacherous clay where large cave-ins sometimes occurred before adequate shoring could be constructed. Because of this, the tunneler always had an "assistant" whose job it was to watch for signs of loosening ground. In both our cases the injured men had (for reasons they could not explain to us) sent their assistants away just before the accidents occurred!

Several infractions of safety rules frequently occur at the same time. This fact of multiple infraction is reminiscent of the experiences of safety engineers, who are usually able to significantly reduce the incidence of accidents. However, they do not eliminate all mishaps. For example, they advise the use of steel helmets for head protection in some situations. When all employees wear the headgear there are no serious accidents, but within a period of a year, a certain number of men begin the practice of leaving their helmets off on some occasions. Even more striking is the fact that some of the helmetless men will also needlessly walk through excessively dangerous areas. This behavior follows such a sharply defined pattern that we suspect statistical predictions will be possible with further study.

At least seven of our patients described this phenomenon clearly. In some factories, but especially in construction work, there are machines which have booms or projections. These appendages create a blind zone behind which the operator cannot see. One such machine is the cement mixer, which has a characteristic large slide for unloading. When this slide is raised the operator cannot see beneath it, and everyone on the job knows this. The danger area may even be marked off with flags. Yet patients have told us that they walked directly through this area (sometimes repeatedly) on the day on which they were not wearing their steel hats. Asked to explain this, their conscious reasons were vague, or even silly, in every case.

A fourth fact which appeared in histories given by these patients was a prediction of impending doom made by the worker himself before the accident. It might well be compared to an aura. Kelman (1945) confirmed this observation.

One man told us that as soon as a particular new assistant had been assigned to him he "knew" there would be an accident. During the history-giving process he went over and over this detail, emphasizing that this fellow could do nothing right. Despite this, our patient did not check the work that his clumsy assistant did. As a result, he exerted considerable pressure on a large steel beam which the assistant had carelessly balanced in such a way that it could not be worked on at all. The patient was nearly crushed to death under the metal when his own machine pushed it upon him.

Our patients frequently reported that, during the period of this aura, they asked for help, sometimes repeatedly. Usually this request was not heeded because of the subtle or even bizarre way in which it was put. Still, union stewards, shop foremen, or sometimes first-aid attendants easily can be taught to report when a man begins bothering them. Such forewarning is not an unknown psychiatric finding. Felix Deutsch (1949) comments on it. In Air Corps Medicine it was also frequently observed, with the result in this branch of service that both flight surgeons and supervisory personnel were uniformly instructed to withdraw flying privileges at such moments. The authors believe that plant medical officers can also deal very effectively with this type of warning, if by no other means than by watching for a sudden increased frequency of sick calls. This is now under study.

One man, who was very dull intellectually, even started to steal finished stock openly from his neighbors when he got into trouble. This behavior forced the patient to the attention of both union and management representatives who came to investigate. A few days after the patient started this behavior and drew this much attention to himself but failed to get any relief, he had an accident which incapacitated him.

Such clinical data do not appear to be isolated phenomena. Rather they form themselves into a meaningful pattern. Something threatening happens inside of a worker and he seeks pain or injury as a solution. Since this foreboding is unacceptable to him he blames the impending danger on his machine or on other parts of his environment. The presence of the unexplained danger is frustrating and frightening enough that the patient soon begins calling for help.

At this time there is often a strong element of depression which is not explained by the observations so far presented. It is an old psychiatric observation, however, that when a man is depressed and has an increasing sense that he cannot take care of himself, he grows both incautious and lackadaisical. He begins to neglect to pay attention. He may not check things out as carefully as usual, or he may forget his steel helmet. He frequently breaks other safety rules at the same time, but, even more important, he unconsciously keeps seeking destruction and will even chase away other workers who would ordinarily protect him.

Careful consideration of these observations will lead to the conclusion that they are antithetical. A man who is supposedly seeking aid is also chasing help away from him. The truth is that many men do both of these things, almost at the same time, because a peculiar prodrome of opposing wishes is being built up—the psychiatrist describes this as a state of conflict. Part of the man is begging people to help and to stop him; another part seems covertly to plan carefully and almost methodically to maim himself. Here is a part of the depressive factor already mentioned. Self-destructive ideas are not easily understood if for no other reason than that they are socially unacceptable. Therefore, they are seldom described consciously and are only rarely thought of in these terms by the patient himself. However, their indicated presence in the accident syndrome is undeniable and depends upon understanding a second group of etiological factors which can be discovered in a description of the meaning of the work process itself.

The Meanings of Work

The first meaning of a job lies in its capacity to make life more purposeful, particularly in middle-class occupations. Nowhere is this more dramatically illustrated than in the instance of the retired worker whose sudden aimlessness almost drives his wife to distraction. Morse and Weiss (1962) made this same point statistically. After they had intensively examined 401 workers, they concluded that 80 percent of the men wanted to keep working, most of them for positive reasons.

In this same study, lower-class workers indicated they would be without "anything to do" if they had no jobs. This is the second meaning of work, i.e. without it many people have nothing to do. In the authors' studies of young criminals (1961) the same point was made repeatedly. The conscious reason for much criminal behavior lies in the fact that it is a relief for the jobless youth who had nothing to do otherwise.

Work is also a social phenomenon. Many well-educated people are surprised to discover that, without their jobs, most unskilled laborers would have practically no social lives at all except with their immediate families. The stop at the bar on payday and the group ride to and from work represent the limits of gregarious behavior for most of these people. In his book, *The Status Seekers,* Vance Packard (1959) cites studies which show that 40 percent of such workers confine their intimate friendships entirely to kinfolk. In addition, unemployed workers often describe to us great feelings of loss of social contact.

Perhaps more importantly, as Deutsch (1949) notes, a job gives a man a particular masculine identification. Both he and others have a picture of him, when he works, as the provider and the rock on which the home is built. This is even more dramatically true in the Negro population in which, historically, the female has been more employable than her mate. The tremendous satisfaction of the established masculine provider has come to this racial group only through the development of union seniority programs. Its vividness, until recent years, was never more clearly shown than in the proud faces of older dining-car waiters, when they told of being able to put their children through college.

In counterpoint to this were some observations about women who were injured. No elaborate consideration of this special problem is possible in the present paper, but we wish to cite the fact that working women who got hurt almost always gave evidence of grave difficulty in accepting the feminine role.

The economic factor of earning a living by holding a job is so well recognized as to preclude elaborate comment.

Consideration of these multiple meanings of work goes far

toward explaining the injured man's conflict. If one pictures such a laborer who is required to lift a 25-lb. weight three times a minute for 8 hours a day, an easy example is established. Usually this work rate, agreed upon by both union and management, assumes the average worker's age to be about twenty-eight. If the worker in our present example is fifty-two, he may come to the doctor saying that his 25-lb. weight is four times as heavy. X-rays show a normal lipping of the vertebrae for the patient's age. In plain language, this means that the man's back is quite different from that of a man whose age is approximately half the patient's. The worker in question is facing loss of his only salable commodity. At least unconsciously, he is losing the purpose and challenge of his life. He is also losing the main thing that he has to do, and most of his opportunity for social life is slipping away. On an inner level, he is losing his strength, his masculine identification. In addition, his economic basis of life is disappearing. This man's status quo heralds bankruptcy, so his depression is hardly a mysterious symptom.

The conflict which this man must endure now become understandable. He wants his position, his masculinity, his social and economic life, but he also yearns to escape pain and the ever-increasing weight of the stock he has to lift every twenty seconds. His position is like that of a soldier on the battlefield, who would run to save his life, but who also wants to stay and be a man. The conflict and the anxiety resulting from it are acute. Both can be relieved with a partial solution—the soldier who is hurt does not have to fight, and the sick laborer does not have to work.

These observations lead to the first clinical conclusion of our study. History-taking in the accident case requires both care and elaboration. If this step is followed, the injury process emerges as the solution to the otherwise insoluble problem of the worker's life.

The identifiable existence of this conflict, its resultant anxiety, and its self-destructive resolution document our belief that the physical injury is part of the psychological process. It is true that such observations are not new, having been made by Heinrich, as cited by Rawson (1944) as early as 1929. However, the glib labeling of this as accident-proneness fails to take into account the real events in an individual's life. The original concept (1955) made the assumption that certain people are always prone to accidents. Our findings do not indicate this at all. They indicate that under special circumstances when certain conflicts exist many individuals tend to cause their own accidents and probably will hold onto the injuries they sustain, because the accidents solve their life problems. Schulzinger (1954) is in agreement with this conclusion.

The data offered in this paper are presented for the purpose of indicating that a psychological accident process produces the injuries which we have observed. However, the material presented is very considerably condensed and does not touch either the variety or the depth of the psychological observations that can be made. For example, depression is not the only mechanism seen. Much hostility, almost always considerably elaborated by the labor-management feud, is usually observed. There is also a problem of character neurosis which acts as a drive to stop work. This can involve factors such as dependency. No discussion of these and other mechanisms has been offered because the point seems to stand on a basis of the material which has been presented. More importantly, all the data mentioned can be elicited in every case by physicians who have no elaborate psychiatric training.

We have tried to avoid technical problems which would have made this paper useful only to psychiatrists. This is based on a conviction against adding another specialist to the already too large team. This can only further the disintegration of the physician-patient relationship, as Balint (1957) has well demonstrated. The unalterable fact is that therapy of industrial injuries must be in the hands of nonpsychiatrists. The significance of the above data must be measured by their usefulness to somaticists.

The Legal Influence

The review of approximately 300 cases of industrial accidents and injuries has been described. We shall now examine a further aspect of the etiological complex, one which operates after the accident and tends to add chronicity to the symptoms. The present phenomenon brings to mind the process of secondary infection, in which the same symptoms may persist, although they result from completely different agents. While the syndrome is grossly unaltered, the reason for its existence has changed materially.

In accident cases, some of the causative elements of chronicity were identified by a series of clinical observations.

It was noted that the patient who repeatedly comes to the physician for chronic symptomatology after an accident may not be approaching the doctor for medical help at all. Dozens of our patients presented themselves saying merely, "My lawyer sent me," or, "The company lawyer sent me." Early in our clinical experience this seemed indeed to be a peculiar type of chief complaint. Pressing the question of why they had been sent by their lawyers, we found most workers reluctant to elaborate. It was finally learned that, "Have you been hurt at work?" is a better question, but even then many patients in this category exhibit difficulty in answering. Although shyness in presenting a chief complaint can be variously interpreted, considerable study has led us to visualize the real problem. Most patients who begin in this manner really do not want to let the doctor know what is wrong, because he might then do something to remove the symptom.

Confirmation of the fact that these patients often do not want the doctor's help is found in noting that the chronically ill patient may indicate complete satisfaction with another doctor who has not been relieving symptoms. A lady seen recently reported that she had been visiting a doctor who was giving her treatments four or five times every week. This had gone on for a period of almost 18 months when she was seen by the present clinicians. She said further that she felt better each morning, but that after visiting the doctor she experienced a good deal of pain. If her real aim had been to get well, the absurdity of this would have caused some reaction. However, to herself she explained that the doctor's office was a long way from her home, and that after her successful treatments the long bus ride made her ill again. Why would a patient who wanted her health continue 18 months with a physician who caused no improvement?

Several patients noted the same fact in a different way; they went to no physician at all despite their claims of serious pain or great disability.

Several chronically symptomatic patients whose difficulties stemmed from the injury process approached the physician for the purpose of securing a useful court witness. One patient referred by his own attorney neglected to say that he had already told his story to another psychiatrist. This doctor had testified for him in Workmen's Compensation hearings. On a basis of this testimony the patient had collected an award because the symptoms were "proved" to have resulted from work. This particular case was of special interest because the basis of the proof lay in dreams which the patient told the first psychiatrist. In his interview with the second, the patient now related all of the same symptoms to an automobile accident, changing the characteristics of the dreams to coincide with things that happened in the automobile accident rather than in the factory. Knowledge of the prior suit remained hidden from the second psychiatrist until the court hearing.

A second case was even more dramatic. A well-educated secretary was interviewed by two sets of physicians, some called by her attorney, and some called by the company. Following court testimony in which the favorably reported examinations won the patient an award, she crossed the courtroom and asked the psychiatrist who had testified against her for treatment. She openly expressed contempt for the doctors who had accepted her story!

The injury patient with chronic symptomatology may express his hostile feelings toward the doctor in disguised but clearly observable ways. One example was a remark made by many different patients. These people told the examiner that they knew how busy the doctor was and really felt guilty for taking a great deal of his time. When such a remark is made by patients who know even before they come to the office that two hours will be set aside for them, it is much more likely that these unhappy people are really expressing their own wishes to get out of the office.

Interpretation of such remarks as isolated phenomena is extremely risky. In fact, psychiatrists are frequently justly criticized for alleging such meanings, when their data are presented as isolated facts. The validity of any guess—and it must be a guess in any one instance—must be established by confirmatory observations, actions, or slips of various types. Experience indicates that repetition in one form or another can establish the true meaning of the patient's utterances.

In our study validity was established by finding repetition both in each patient's own history and in similar material collected from other patients. For instance, injury victims would not infrequently make the kind of remark already noted. Then the same people would indicate how impressed they were with the thoroughness of the examination which was now being conducted, but, they said, they wouldn't have any hope of paying the fees they knew would be charged by this doctor. Such statements do not represent real concern when made before there is any discussion of fee, and at a time when both patient and physician know that financial arrangements have already been completed (either by the patient's own lawyers, or by the company's). A much more likely surmise is that the patient does not want to continue any contact with this doctor.

From these statements it also became apparent that injury patients with chronic problems usually perceived the physician as a type of personality with whom they wouldn't want any contact anyway. It is damning with faint praise to tell a physician that he is so expert that his fees must be too high. This is really saying that the physician does not have enough interest in people to want to help those who can't pay the highest fees. The same sense can be derived from an assortment of other statements these individuals make. Experience has taught us to listen very carefully to the patient who notes that this is the first time he's been in the building where the doctor's office is located, or how well dressed the people in this neighborhood are.

These patients may also regard the physician only as an arm of the company. Their bitterness toward such "antagonists" may be well hidden except for the most minute slips.

A highly-skilled worker whose problem had never gone to litigation, and whose medical and compensation bills had been picked up by the company without demur, gave a surprisingly good account of himself in a two-hour interview. At the end of this time, and upon leaving the consultation room, he became involved in an argument with the receptionist. Investigation showed that he wanted a call made to his plant to order a taxi.

When the receptionist told the patient that there was a near-by public phone, he was enraged. Taking the matter out of the secretary's hands, the doctor found that in fact the patient lived quite close to the office. However, he had driven his car almost twenty miles to the plant, had reported to the medical department there, and had requested a taxi to take him to the consultation. He was now demanding a second twenty-mile taxi ride in order to pick up his own car to return home—only a few blocks from the office! Moreover, his present rage at the receptionist involved the expenditure of a dime.

These data can be synthesized into a very meaningful picture. From their very first productions in the history-giving process these people patently are not coming to the physician because they seek help; they come because they have been sent by someone else. In fact, they often indicate complete satisfaction with other doctors whose treatments obviously have had no favorable effect on their illnesses. Others indicate that though they claim great pain and great disability they do not go to any physician for help. In addition, consciously or unconsciously, they tell only those parts of their stories which will lead the doctor to be a more useful witness in court.

Other points convey very much the same meaning, though perhaps more subtly. These people are attacking the doctor on two bases. In the first place they say they are angry because of things they believe the doctor thinks; since they really do not know the doctor's thoughts, it is hard to believe that this can be the real explanation. In the second place, they attack the doctor with accusations about time or fees which they know are not true. Finally, occasionally one will even play a dirty trick on the company because they are sending him to a physician.

In nonpsychiatric terms, such people are in a blind rage. They view the doctor as a serious threat unless he applies innocuous treatment which will not help the patient to get well. Why?

In addition to the retention of his symptoms because they represent a solution to his life problem, as has been demonstrated before, this pattern of behavior on the part of the patient is related to the principle that an injured man legally has the right of redress. In this country this is elaborated by the philosophical doctrine of "the humanitarian purpose of shifting risk." This is the concept that the expense of an injury is to be borne by the employer, and if possible, passed on to the consumer (Cohen). Workmen's Compensation gives this award or redress not for the sake of the injury, but for the loss of earning capacity. Thus the injured man fights to prove his incapacity. In order to "save" his incapacity he must battle to preserve his symptoms. Every union representative, every lawyer, every workmen's compensation worker who comes into contact with this patient must by inference or direction indicate this necessity to preserve incapacity because, under the law, this is the crucial issue.

Nor is this without effect on therapy. Whether a patient wishes to get well or whether he wants to hold a legally valuable symptom can determine many therapeutic courses. This is particularly true in elective surgery.

In the case of a patient who had injured his back, surgical repair—a laminectomy and two spinal fusions—was performed with good results. After the third one the patient reinjured himself under questionable circumstances, and the surgeon did an exploratory spinal operation. Eight years after the first injury the patient still had back pain. Medical bills amounted to two and one-half times the compensation expenses.

It is small wonder that the physician, who in misdirected kindness tells his patient to "take it easy" because of an injury, may quickly become the most sought-after plaintiff's doctor in town. Conversely, with the legal process in mind, the patient must have a predetermined reaction to any real therapist; any physician who wishes to treat effectively and to remove the legally valuable disorder must be a threat.

Moreover, it is our conclusion that, in most cases in which legal problems contribute to chronicity, the patient's reaction is not unconscious. These people are usually aware of what they are doing.

The conclusion that the patients are aware of their reactions in preserving their symptoms cannot be validated statistically, and probably cannot even be proved legally. However, it is difficult to listen to descriptions of how the patient has come to regard his injury as a means of financing his future without believing that an ordinarily intelligent man knows what he is saying.

In one of our cases a woman described her injury in this way and told that she was planning to win her suit so that she could buy a rooming house which she had already picked out. She explained in detail that she would handle it in certain ways that she had already planned.

In another case, a man told that he had worked in an unpleasant city for a number of years and that he felt that the company owed him an early retirement. He had picked out the home that he wanted in another city, priced it, and knew exactly how much it would take (in winning the suit) to finance this plan.

These are not isolated instances; they are repeated by patient after patient. Review of the tape-recorded examinations revealed so many similar distortions that they could not be ignored. Kamman (1951) noted the same facts and referred to them as "attitudinal pathosis."

Of course these observations do not mean that the authors believe such patients have no unconscious problems. Paranoid projections are clearly suggested in the cases cited, for example. However, the immediate issue of holding onto symptoms in order to get a stated amount of money for a stated purpose does seem conscious. What is behind this?

To begin with, the modern worker does not face his problem alone. His union steward is always at his side and behind the union representative are many organizational facilities, reinforced by batteries of lawyers and by very considerable political pressure. This is an understandable reaction in a world which formerly threw the worker in the scrap heap and forgot him should his physical or mental capacity be seriously impaired for any reason, including injury at work. But such a reaction is not without counteraction, and both the employer and the insurance company feel as set upon and unsupported as the lone worker formerly did.

To perceive such a struggle in moral terms, to think of one side as good and the other side as bad, is to miss the real point. The thing that matters to the doctor is that this is a war. It is sometimes an intensive conflict between two groups of people, and it is almost always a vital individual struggle in the life of any particular worker. When there is such an intense conflict, there are adversaries who fight hard against each other, and not always honestly or fairly. And each time a worker is injured, a segment of this vital skirmish enters the examining room with the patient.

Unfortunately, although this battle is clear enough in the court or from the political rostrum, it may be poisonously invisible in the doctor's office. Yet the informed and perceptive physician will recognize it, because true diagnosis cannot be made otherwise.

With this legal pressure so disturbing the traditional doctor-patient relationship, we thought at first that our facts might be true only in cases which were in litigation, or only in which the patients were adversely reacting to our personalities. To check this supposition, we reviewed 30 additional cases. In these there were no suits, and the companies had agreed to accept their responsibilities for care and support without legal maneuvers at all. None of these patients had seen the authors and so could not be reacting to our personalities. Yet these patients reacted in exactly the same way as those we had examined who were in litigation. Clearly an accident which involves compensation but in which there is no litigation still causes people to act as if the threat of a suit were present. Everyone concerned acts as if the litigation were about to take place even if it is not.

These facts give substance to the original observation that these patients are extremely difficult to treat. Small wonder; the truth is that the physician who attempts to aid this group of patients is facing individuals (1) who are solving their life problems by developing symptoms, and (2) whose symptom formation guarantees them a legal incapacity which will provide for their continued support.

Naturally such patients are hostile to the physicians who try to improve their conditions. In their guilt reactions they do all in their power to produce adverse rather than therapeutic reactions from the doctor of medicine. Consideration of the effects of this attitudinal problem on the physician is the substance of the second article in this series.

REFERENCES

Balint, M.: *Doctor, Patient, and Illness.* New York, International Universities Press, 1957.

Cohen, M.: Psychoneurosis and compensation. *Yale Law Journal.*

Deutsch, F.: Mental health in industry. In *Applied Psychoanalysis.* New York, Grune & Stratton, 1949, pp. 197–216.

Dunbar, F.: Accident habit. In *Mind and Body.* New York, Random House, 1955.

Hirschfeld, A. H.: *Predictability in Criminal Behavior.* Presented to Regional Conference APA, Milwaukee, Wisconsin, 1961.

Kamman, G.: Traumatic neurosis, compensation neurosis, or attitudinal pathosis? *Arch Neurol Psychiat, 65:*593–603, 1951.

Kelman, H.: Character and traumatic syndrome, *J Nerv Ment Dis, 102:*121–152, 1945.

Morse, N., and Weiss, R.: Function and meaning of work and job. In *Man, Work, and Society.* New York, Basic Books, 1962, pp. 29–34.

Packard, V.: *Status Seekers.* New York, David McKay Company, 1959, p. 177.

Rawson, A.: Accident proneness. *Psychosom Med, 6:*88–94, 1944.

Schulzinger, M. S.: Accident syndrome. *Arch Ind Hyg Occ Med, 10:*426–433, 1954.

Workmen's Compensation: Recovery for Mental Disability in Absence of Any Previous Impact or Injury, *Iowa Law Review.*

28

MANHOOD VERSUS SAFETY

Chaytor Mason

This selection may be read as a stirring address to a group of brave men for the purpose of preventing their needless death through misplaced courage. Or, in another view, the reader may perceive a psychologist explaining how our society trains a boy to be a man. We show him, for example, a movie of James Cagney shielding his buddies by embracing a live grenade, with the result that hundreds of boys embraced death in like manner in World War II—something that never happened in World War I.

In hundreds of subtle ways, a boy learns that it is not manlike to be concerned about his own safety, and at the same time he learns that he has to prove his manhood. That conditioning translates to the industrial scene in the failure to define a "man" as one who does his job and does it safely, in the failure to condemn expediency and daring and in the failure to even observe the difference between safe procedure as enunciated and the way employees actually do things.

"Must it continue to be safety versus manhood?" Behind that stirring rhetoric lies the fundamental values of our society, and a hint of methods to be evolved for the practical use of the safety professional.

MAN IN THE PAST 100 years has become more able to control his environment and manipulate NATURE than in any previous 10,000 year period in his history.

There has never been such a period of technological change or materialistic progress, and it gives every indication of increasing in pace rather than slackening. (Maybe this is why the current Fad of Reminiscence—we want to have something, at least a material hold on the past.)

But in spite of all his technological advances, Man knows little

Presented at the Third Orient Airlines Association Flight Safety Seminar, Singapore, May 10–12, 1972.

more about himself as a human being than he did 100 years ago. In fact, his knowledge about himself is in many ways not greatly advanced over his knowledge 1,000 years ago. His lack of knowledge about himself has produced some curious and dangerous predicaments.

Today, because of great potentiality for change of his environment, Man has it in his power to create—or destroy. By one single act, one person can destroy himself, dozens or hundreds of others, or change the destinies of an entire society.

We have arrived at a state of technological and social interdependence so sensitively balanced that the actions of one individual can produce changes and reverberations in society and nature which are beyond prediction or control.

A single failure of attention by an air traffic controller can cause a mid-air collision costing hundreds of lives and millions or maybe hundreds of millions of dollars.

A single rifle bullet by a discontented and disturbed young assassin can change the destiny of a nation and possibly the entire human race in incalculable ways.

We are beginning to see that each decision made by an individual is not made in isolation—but each decision may have infinite effects on others in our world—or even effects on the World itself.

At one time it may have seemed hard to imagine that a single pebble tossed into the ocean near San Francisco would cause changes of some degree even in Japan, but nowadays we have grown to recognize that garbage idly tossed into the ocean will have worldwide effects.

We are also beginning to learn that we may know much about technology and about the manipulation of material things (even garbage) but we know far too little about the behavior of man.

Many of our concepts of man and his behavior no longer serve us in the world we live in today. It has become obvious that mankind cannot survive by teaching its children by untested methods passed from generation to generation. It has become obvious that we must subject man and his behavior to the same microscopic examination and exhaustive testing which advanced the knowledge of man's materials. We have already uncovered some knowledge—but we find more questions. We must do it quickly for the hour is growing very late!

Today, I would like to talk about one of man's behavior patterns—commonly accepted through his history—accepted without question by millions of men—even today—the concept that manhood and safety are not compatible.

Case Study

A group of twelve to thirteen-year-old boys are standing at the base of a high voltage electric power line. They are arguing loudly. They are daring each other to climb to the top (secretly each one is afraid). Finally one twelve-year-old breaks from the group and climbs quickly to the top and waves triumphantly to the group below. As he waves his arm touches the 55,000 volt line. There is a flash. He shudders—and falls—he plunges to the ground dead!

Case Study

A group of teenagers are racing down a Swiss mountainside on skis. One eighteen-year-old youth is falling behind. He takes a short cut that no one else would dare. It is a well known danger area— rocky—very steep—he must get ahead of the other boys. He misjudges a turn and crashes into a jagged boulder at forty miles per hour. He dies!

Case Study

The air is still and calm in this small coastal town. Fog has shrouded the airfield all night. The first flight of the day, Flight 54, a Convair Metropolitan, lets down into the fog—once—twice—and on the third pass finds the runway. Each approach was made below company and published minimums. But a successful landing was made.

Five minutes later, another Convair, Flight 53, drones over the field. Radio contact is made with the Passenger Agent (who also serves as weather observer). Flight 53 is advised that weather is well below minimums but that Flight 54 is on the ground preparing to leave.

Flight 53 overhead makes a VOR approach and pulls up after going 100 feet below the 390 foot minimum. On the second approach 200 feet below minimum ground witnesses can see the vague outline of the airplane as it pulls up again.

On the third approach, there is a sudden orange glow in the fog to the east as Flight 53 explodes through the roofs of three beach cottages at an altitude of 30 feet. Forty-one people die.

Case Study

Due to a fuel system failure, an F-4 flames out at 18,000 feet near a desert air force base. The pilot is told he had too little altitude to make a safe approach but he responds that he is unable to receive. He continues his approach. On touch-down on the runway, his main gear strikes the runway lip as he rolls onto the runway. He makes it.

He receives commendation for his superb handling of the airplane. In the next year, four more pilots try the same thing. Three fail to make it. Six men die.

One of the dead pilots was a Senior Lt. Colonel who although older—was known for trying to keep up with whatever the younger pilots would do.

What is the common problem in all of these accidents? The problem was SAFETY VERSUS MANHOOD.

Many of us act as though looking after ourselves is a sign of cowardice.

The twelve-year-old could not say "It looks dangerous as hell to me—I am not going to climb up there." SAFETY VERSUS MANHOOD.

The eighteen-year-old skier had to prove his skill and daring at any cost. He had to take a chance. SAFETY VERSUS MANHOOD.

The pilot of Flight 54, who landed safely, knew that the pilot of Flight 53 would continue to make lower approaches until he got in—so he took three chances and made it. SAFETY VERSUS MANHOOD.

The copilot on Flight 53 died without a word. He could not express his fear to his Captain as they went below minimums. He would have seemed less of a man. SAFETY VERSUS MANHOOD.

The problem of Safety Versus Manhood can thus, occur at any time—at any age—in any job—in any activity. (Mostly this problem occurs in the teens and early adulthood but it can also show a resurgence in the "Fatal 40's").

SAFETY VERSUS MANHOOD is one of the reasons why younger people have so many accidents in cars, in boats, in airplanes. It is one of the reasons why accidents are the greatest single cause of death in this age group. It is one of the reasons why young people show so little caution. Because there is a more important thing than safety—the proof of manhood. Could this need for proof indicate self-doubt?

Young men must prove themselves through competition. As a result, they have more accidents. More accidents than do young women. Their accidents are also more spectacular than those of the young women who do not have to prove their manhood—but some of them do! (more so nowadays)

How do we become men? What training do we get? How do we know if we are on course? How do we know if we are doing enough?

There is little formal training in life for this very important goal! Do we learn it in school? Do we get any courses on this very important subject? Are there any textbooks? Are there any entrance exams for Manhood? No! Instead, we have very important courses on the dates and places of battles fought long ago, on equations we will seldom use and soon forget. We spend years committing to memory social customs and quotations of yesteryear which have little meaning or importance in our own search for manhood today.

We know now that masculine behavior is not inborn in the human. There are genes which determine what sex we shall be, but no genes determine whether we shall be masculine. No genes determine if we shall be a man!—Only that we shall be a male.

Then where do we learn how to be a man and what is involved in the pursuit? We have various informal ways of learning this very important lesson:

Well, we learn it at Father's knee. Or do we? It is 6:30 P.M., Dear Old Dad droops in the door all tuckered out from a rough client and a hard battle on the freeway. He gropes feebly for the Martini jar.

"Daddy Dear, tell me all about what it is to be a Man."

What kind of an answer do we get?

Well, if we cannot learn it from Dear Old Dad directly, there is always observation and blind emulation. There is plenty of that. In many cases we copy blindly many of the things that Dear Old

Dad wishes he did not do. Anyway, all we can copy is the results which we see and we must imagine the background of how it all started.

Then, there are the radio and TV heroes. Real, down-to-earth types who solve the everyday problems in everyday ways. Real models for the behavior of growing boys. They are the models who always have a definite conclusion to their problems, as the gunsmoke clears away. And the hero never drops a decision either, does he? When you think of it, a lot of kids do model their behavior on these types even if they have to borrow Dad's shotgun to finish the argument.

But, of course there are, and were, the movie heroes. Here is a great place to learn how men behave. You know how accurate and down-to-earth the movies are. There was a movie in the early 1940's called the "Fighting Sixty-Ninth." The hero was a bumbling, scared, battle-shy soldier, played by James Cagney. Although he was not much help to the organization as it fought its way through France in 1918, Cagney removed all doubt as to his manhood when a grenade rolled into his trench. Cagney jumped on the grenade and took the blast full in the stomach. He was a man in the final analysis. There are hundreds of cases on record that boys of the Cagney generation have done the same thing in World War II, in Korea and in Viet Nam. They have learned well. In some cases, there would have been time to throw the grenade out of the trench safely but they jumped on the grenade and died. Did you know that there was never a case of a man jumping on a grenade throughout World War I? It came from a writer's imagined idea of an exciting conclusion to a story. He set the fashion for men to model for generations afterward.

Well, if we cannot trust the movies to give us the straight answer on manhood, there are always books—biography—biographies which are written by commonplace people that most of us will grow up to be like. Biographies written about the everyday ways of handling the problems of manhood. Biographies written by shoe clerks and liquor store owners and computer operators, commonplace people. You cannot recall any? Small wonder. There would be a very small sale for those since they are not *important* figures. They are not the unusual. They are not the standouts. Instead, we read about how the people from the extreme ends of society handle their lives. (If they tell us the whole truth.) Of course, it is just possible that they sometimes varnished their lives a bit with some platitudes and some socially acceptable information. We read what they think they should say, not what they really did think and say.

Then, there was good old Uncle Herman. He could take some time with us—he never had any boys of his own. He had three girls. He gave us the straight scoop. Admittedly, he did tell us about the time he stole the pen knife from the 5 & 10 but then there were the tales of boyhood adventures that were, shall we say, just slightly embellished. The time he looked that rattlesnake straight in the eye. Well, if not Uncle Herman, there was always Mother to give us the word on Manhood. "Always treat girls nicely." "Little gentlemen never talk back to grown-ups." "Don't make so much noise." "If you don't have good manners you could never be a Marine." All good solid information on Manhood and the requirements thereof.

And lastly, there were the other children not much older than we, and with no more solid information than we. In fact, a lot of their "training" came from the same unreal and haphazard sources as our own but we listened and copied and learned.

Is it any wonder many of us were and *are* confused?

Could it be that it is this kind of training which is instrumental in making grown men violate rules which are set up for their own safety?

Could it be that it is this kind of training which is instrumental in making grown men violate even common sense in their pursuit of status?

Could it be this type of training which causes many men pilots to develop a split personality? With the check pilot they fly one way. With their copilot they fly another? Could this type of training make young men and grown men take momentary deadly chances?

Could this type of training make men model their behaviour on the flashy, the careless or the dangerous worker?

Could this be why men refuse to wear protective safety equipment?

Let's take this refusal to wear safety equipment as an example. Let's get a little historical background. Men's games have often been a picture of men's needs just as children's games are a picture of a child's needs.

Baseball was born in the United States in Cooperstown, New York, in 1847. It was a barehand game played with a wooden bat and the same rock hard ball that we know today. It was a game in which there were many injuries. The broken hand was the sign of the baseball player. The broken hand and the broken fingers were testimony that *here* was a baseball player. There was no protection for the hands, or any other part of the body.

At long last in the year 1875, Charlie Waite of the New York Nine, having suffered his third broken hand in a recent game (Blood priority; it takes a severe accident to cause awareness of danger)—came on the field wearing a thin leather protective glove. The audience was astonished and enraged. Pillows flew. (There were no pop bottles in those days.) "Get that 'sister' off the field." "If you are afraid of getting hurt get out!" "Don't muff it, catch the ball." And Charlie, a great first baseman, left the field never to return to baseball. Five years passed before another man attempted to wear a glove onto a playing field.

In 1880, another player, a budding lawyer, endured the ridicule of the crowd and stayed, wearing a glove, and slowly the baseball glove was accepted as part of the equipment for the first baseman. But only the first baseman.

In the year 1885, a well-known catcher named Charlie Bennett, who had many a floating rib sunk by a fast pitch from the pitcher, walked onto the playing field looking a bit more fat than usual. Charlie was wise to the ways of the crowd. Under his coat, he had hidden a thin quilted chest protector—adopted from the fencing sport. By the third inning two of the batters had gotten the idea. As one stepped up to the plate, the other tore open Charlie's coat and he was exposed in his shame. There for all the audience to see was the chest protector. He too was laughed off the field. We would not want to say that at this late and enlightened date that this is the reason why baseball umpires still secrete their chest protector under their oversized blue coat, but then why else?

It was as late as 1883 that Arthur Irwin as a result of a broken hand popularized the glove for the infielders. The pitchers steadfastly refused to have any truck with such cowardly safety appliances until the year 1900. Even then, it was a sign of weakness to wear one. There were many disfigured catchers until the year 1893 when Nig Cuppy finally devised one out of a fencing mask. And you may recall the number of fractured skulls there have been from bean balls until the hard hat was recently developed for batters. Of course, it was developed first for the children's Little Leagues—they were not supposed to be men. They could dare to protect themselves.

Since we are talking about protective equipment in games, let us examine another game. This one is older than baseball by quite a bit—and infinitely more dangerous. Even so, there are still problems in wearing safety equipment. It is the old and honored game we call *War!*

In 1914, there was not the vaguest hint of protective head gear. The Tommies left their pubs and marched to the field of battle wearing their green uniform caps. The Poilus kissed their mademoiselles good-bye at the sidewalk cafes and marched into battle wearing their bright red Kepis. The Fritz's dropped their steins and hastened to the playing field wearing their spiked leather *decorative* helmets. And each of them was an excellent target for any sniper, or piece of shrapnel coming his way.

It was not until 1915 that the steel helmet was developed. When it was, it was laughingly dubbed the "Tin Hat" and refused by many. Frankly, it was not the height of fashion to wear such a piece of head gear. In fact, one British General was so moved by the cowardice of the new breed of troops that he issued an order to his Division; "Any soldier in my command found wearing a "Tin Hat" will be court-martialed for cowardice in the face of the enemy." His order stuck and his division wore cloth hats for the rest of the war.

By the time the United States joined the big game in 1917, steel helmets were mostly worn, the style was established beyond question (although not without an occasional argument) and the American troops returned to Lafayette-land dressed to kill in "Tin Hats."

But there were exceptions. A senior officer, famous even then, refused to wear a steel helmet. In 1917, Colonel Douglas A. MacArthur stated to his aide, "I will not appear as a coward to my men by wearing a steel helmet." He hardly ever did. There was one exception though. In that same year, when he was to receive his dozenth Silver Star from General Black Jack Pershing, Pershing insisted that he wear a steel helmet, not because of the danger of the event, but only because all of the other Colonels were wearing them. That was one of the few times that Mac-Arthur had ever been seen in a helmet. But how about Black Jack himself? There is no record that he *ever* wore one.

It has been the same thing in all of the activities of men. You cannot get them to take precautions for themselves. It has been the same in football, boxing, and hockey. It is the same in light aircraft. Did you ever see a private aircraft operator wearing a hard hat? Or a parachute? In spite of the fact that the territory between Los Angeles and Las Vegas is some of the worst in the world, with desert, mountains and all of the bad things, yet you will seldom if ever see a pilot putting survival gear aboard his airplane.

And how about our old friend and enemy, the family car? Remember the battle we had and are still having in getting people to wear safety belts? Did you ever see a family out for a Sunday drive—all wearing hard hats? (We might remember that two thirds of all deaths in car accidents come from head injuries.)

And then how about the airlines. No one wants to recognize and admit to the chance of accident. After all, if my airline admits the problem, then the passengers might think that "we are going to have an accident." They will think we are scared. So we push safety precautions and planning out of our consciousness. We put all of the passenger survival information on a single little card and hide it away. We back into the "Safety in Flight" briefing with "Government Regulations require that all passengers . . ." and we slide through the rest of it as quickly as possible. And the policy of "Let's not talk about it" filters through all levels of personnel. "Let's not make those exit signs too big." "I do not need ear protectors, I am only going to be out there for a minute." And on and on. . . .

It has been said that politicians are truly representative of people who elect. As the people are, so are their politicians. Let's take a look at safety legislation in the United States in spite of the fact that men were killed by the hundreds and thousands in coal mine and railroad accidents. Factories had no more safety equipment than the owners felt necessary. There was no attempt to legislate even the minimum safety practices or equipment.

But then in 1911 . . . there was a fire in a shirt factory in Newark, New Jersey. In this fire seventy-nine souls lost their lives because there were inadequate fire escapes and these people were unable to escape the flames. The people of the United States arose in compassion and anger. Something had to be done. Finally, the Congress was moved. Legislation was forced through Congress. Legislation was passed which became the basis of all existing safety legislation that we have today. Why were the Nation and Congress so aroused? Because these poor dead souls, trapped in the shirt factory were all women. SAFETY VERSUS MANHOOD.

So there is the problem. Until we accept that it is masculine to consider and even plan for our own safety—to plan for *all* eventualities—to admit the possibility of accident—we men, we leaders of men, we apprentice men will laugh and scorn safety practices.

We may have to revise our ideas on the goals of our masculinity. We will have to decide for ourselves what the goals of manhood mean to us . . . how shall we expend our lives?

Is Manhood really demonstrated by the concept of "Do or Die" or "The show must go on"?

Is Manhood demonstrated by the ability to land the aircraft in less than minimums or is it demonstrated by the wise decision to take the alternate?

We live today in a world where the importance of all human roles and goals is being continuously and agonizingly reappraised. We live today with the knowledge that our individual actions are not performed in a void—that our every action affects the lives and welfare of others. A moment of irresponsible action can destroy; a person, a city, a nation, even the total balance of nature.

Manhood in the past has been shown by daring, selfless devotion to a goal. Men of the present and the future will pursue their goals no less vigorously, but must do so in the recognition that each man is his brother's keeper!

Must it continue to be safety versus manhood? It may not long remain Safety Versus Manhood however—there are signs that the individual is beginning to value his life more highly and as a result is beginning in some cases to consider the value of his neighbor's life.

Safety conferences such as we now have, give safety a status which it has never had before in the History of Man. Such conferences make it seem less reprehensible to place a high valuation on human life.

Industrial safety and flight safety courses and education throughout the world are beginning to demonstrate to individual men that someone, if not they, is interested in their future—is interested in their *having* a future, and that living *for* the future is not wrong.

Since it is obvious that the school systems—always conservative—that is to say "behind the times"—will not be teaching this all important subject to our young men. It is important for those in Management and Training to recognize this problem with young men and with some men at any age. And for them to make sure that this conflict is resolved by coherent safety training. By defining the "Man" as the one who does the job and does it safely. By not commending expediency or daring. By even condemning it. By making sure there is not a difference between the safe operating policy and the ways pilots and employees actually perform.

Since Manhood and Masculinity are by present evidences a learned mode of behavior we should be able—if we play our cards right—to teach men a different and better—and longer use of their lives.

MUST IT REMAIN SAFETY VERSUS MANHOOD?

29

ERGONOMICS

A. H. HANDS

The idea of "fitting the job to the man" makes a poor description of Ergonomics, a term which the author himself takes some pains to define. It includes, says the author, such sciences as anthropometry, physiology, psychology, and engineering, only one of which (safety engineering) has been notably identified with safety. Safety is not the purpose of Ergonomics any more than safety is the purpose of physiology. Yet Ergonomics deals with some of the deepest mysteries and knottiest problems of safety.

In this article, Dr. Hands offers a tiny taste of a great volume of material available on the subject, often under titles other than Ergonomics. Some of the materials available have the quality of a disciplined science, and some are popularizations, even though sound in their own way. Dr. Hands conveys the quality of a disciplined science in this brief article.

THE WORD "ERGONOMICS" means literally "the principles of work." It is a word used in Britain to describe the study of that which fits a machine or process to its operator "a machine being made with man in mind." It aims to enable man to work with optimum physical and mental comfort and to use his special senses with best effect. In the United States the term "human engineering" is used. More recently the term "human factors engineering" has been introduced. This is a natural consequence and is concerned with the relationship of engineering with psychology.

The concept of human engineering began during the First World War but continued in earnest as "ergonomics" by a group of scientists during the Second World War. These men were concerned with matching human skills of operation with the more complex weapon systems which were being developed. This progress has been carried on into civil life and has now become an important aspect of any engineering project. It results in greater efficiency and because of its very nature, it tends to promote safe working. The compound skills of various disciplines are required in order fully to understand and develop the subject. These include:

A. anthropometry, or functional anatomy,
B. physiology,
C. psychology,
D. engineering.

The anthropometrist supplies data of anatomy and human measurements. The physiologist is concerned with the calorific requirements of work and the functioning of the body, including the reception of stimuli, their processing and the effective action taken. The psychologist is concerned with much that appertains to industrial life and safe working. Human factors engineering is possibly the most important part of future development in this field. It is sometimes described as engineering psychology. The engineer must collate the information provided by the above and build accordingly.

The industrial doctor has a part to play since he is professionally trained in the first three of these disciplines and is now employed with the fourth. The safety engineer has to put into practice much of what is provided by the above.

Anthropometry

This is the study of human measurements (shape and size) and should include the range of joint movements. The unit of measurement is known as a percentile. As the term suggests, the table is from 0 to 100. A person who is 80 percentile in height is taller than 80 percent of the measured group and shorter than 20 percent.

As a simple illustration of design procedure, a doorway may be designed so that at least a 95 percentile person may pass through —but a control switch to be reached from a fixed position would be so placed that a 5 percentile person can operate it. The rare or "freak" cases lie at the extremes of the percentile range and cannot normally be catered for. Most design engineers try to meet the requirements of the 5 to 95 percentile range.

Body sizes and anthropometric data are very important in machine design. Much data has been produced in the United States and there are several authorities on the subject. Proper use of anthropometric data eliminates awkward body positions and therefore inaccurate control. No two human beings are identical and the designer must allow for as wide a range of build as is mechanically possible. There are also variations in groups, and in view of this it is wise, if possible, to select the group for which you are intending to manufacture and make your own measurements. If this is not possible, the comprehensive tables in the literature should suffice.

The use of a manikin is now of value. A mechanical figure can be adjusted with a range from 10 percentile to a 90 percentile male, and allows adequate scope for the design engineer with regard to leg room, seat width, and height of viewing. However, it does not include a method of measuring reach. The latter is of increasing importance since a vehicle driver must be able to reach his controls and switches while at the same time remaining strapped by his safety belt. Legislation in certain countries now requires this.

The "average man" constitutes a minority of the population. The term "average" is not, therefore, used in this context since it would constitute only the 50 percentile group omitting 0 to 49 and 51 to 100 percentile.

It is important that sex and race are considered when designing a piece of equipment. For example, the Japanese as a race are shorter than the Negro. The Sikh who is the professional driver in India is obliged, by his religion, to wear a turban. This increases his overall height and must be allowed for.

Comfort angles are concerned with the optimum joint position which is usually neutral, i.e. neither extended, flexed, nor rotated. This allows operation with a minimum of fatigue.

Physiology

This deals with environmental conditions and their effect upon the operator. Man and machine form a system which is tending to become more complex. Man and machine have a relationship which is complementary since each requires the other to fulfill a function satisfactorily. There are certain things which man can do best and others better performed by machine.

Man is flexible and does not require programming. He can cope with the unforeseen occurrence. He has power of recall and, what is probably more important, he can exercise judgment. On the other hand, a machine can store more information, and is faster and more accurate in sorting out information. It can work indefinitely at high speed without fatigue. A machine can control much better than man since the latter is relatively slow, weak, and physically limited; he has a variable performance and is liable to error.

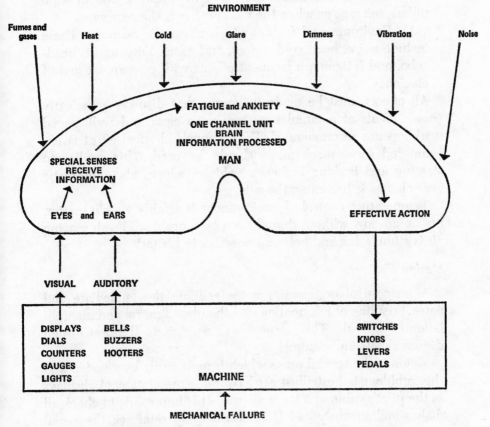

Figure 29–1. Environment.

The five special senses of man are often highly developed over a wide range and are usually more effective than mechanical sensing devices. The aim is to facilitate optimum reception by the operative with efficient processing and appropriate action. Any physical or mental condition which interrupts this flow must be eliminated or reduced.

Factors which interrupt the flow are as follows.

A. Design anomalies which result in a physical inability to reach controls. Often there is failure in standardization of controls which results in an operator becoming confused.

B. Difficulty in manipulation and control when much physical effort is required.

C. Difficulty in seeing clearly due to poor display or obstruction to vision which can occur in a vehicle due to wide pillars, mirrors, or when the load obstructs the rear view.

D. Environmental factors which affect the operator. These include noise, heat, cold, fumes, and gases. Discomfort, headache, and fatigue are frequent effects with consequent loss of efficiency.

All effects must be made to ensure that displays are clearly shown. Dials of a circular pattern with clear and well-spaced markings are recommended. Where much physical effort is encountered servo mechanisms should be used. This applies to steering and braking in heavy vehicles where, also, automatic gear change is becoming the rule.

Temperature control of environment is a fairly simple matter, but an air-flow without draught can be a problem. Fresh moving air is stimulating and helps an operator in his task.

Design Features

A purpose of ergonomics is to facilitate the immediate and correct reading of information and the identification and manipulation of controls. This purpose will necessitate the best design displays dials and controls.

Vision is the special sense which is most easily overloaded and this problem is best illustrated by the presentation of displays in the pilot's cabin of a large aircraft. It is impossible to check all dials simultaneously and it is necessary to reinforce the visual alteration from the normal on a dial by the use of a buzzer which will immediately attract the operator's attention. The arrangement of dials so that the indicators fall into pattern when at normal enables an operator to scan a bank of dials without undue strain. Whenever the abnormal occurs the indicator of the relevant dial will change and so alter the pattern, a fact which is relatively easy to observe.

There are three types of indicator.

A. A check reading indicator which, when demanded, gives information as to the state of equipment. It can also confirm as to functioning of a mechanism when in use. This is demonstrated by the direction flasher indicator in an automobile.

B. A qualitative indicator will demonstrate a normal, satisfactory, or unsatisfactory measurement without exact precision. The ideal example is that of a temperature gauge which measures—cold—normal—hot. The exact temperature is not required.

C. A quantitative indicator will require precision. In this context the speedometer is the best example. A quantitative indicator requires more constant attention than the other two.

A quantitative indicator should never be used if a qualitative one will do. The use of check reading and qualitative indicators presents little problem in design. However, there are several varieties of dial which include the vertical, horizontal, semicircular, round, and open-window types. In the latter the pointer is fixed and the scale moves. In the remainder the pointer moves. Experiment has shown that the open-window dial is the one which produces least errors in reading although the round dial has probably as much merit. It is shown that ½ in. spacing markings on a dial are best suited to accurate reading.

Design of Controls

A similar grouping—of check reading—
    cf. domestic electric light switch.
Position of controls of qualitative indicators—
    cf. set in one of a few positions as with wave band selection
    in radio or T.V. channel selection.
Continuous controls of—quantitative indicators—

cf. steering wheel which requires continuous supervision and manipulation.

The control which is most suited to the operation must be used.

One must consider the "degree of expectancy" which is inherent in most people. By employing a customary movement an operator expects a certain result. For example, if a steering wheel is turned in a clockwise fashion, one expects to turn to the right. With a clockwise turn of a knob one might expect increased output or *vice versa* for an anticlockwise turn. When a switch is pressed down one expects lights to go on and *vice versa*. This is normal expectation. Often, however, this is not so and accidents result. The operator does exactly the opposite to what is required. A big advance in ergonomic design of a commercial vehicle is made when ease of entry and egress are facilitated. Nowadays it is possible to walk right into a commercial vehicle without having to perform the acrobatic feats that were essential until quite recent years.

The instrumentation being centered in a binnacle together with power steering, automatic gear changing, adequate heating and ventilation, insulation against noise and excellent visibility in all weathers has improved the health and productivity and safety of the modern heavy truck operator.

Psychology—Human Factors

It is impossible to design machines which are ergonomically perfect. Mechanical defects nowadays play only a small part in accidents; serious physical disease is the cause of only a small number of road accidents. The human factor remains as the cause of the majority.

An example of this occurs in families with two cars. Unless the cars are identical in make and model, it is certain that the control lay-out will differ. In this event the driver will be confused when presented with an emergency.

There is another case for standardizing controls. This applies principally to the irrational array of lighting and overdrive controls. Habit is also involved in accidents which occur in countries where driving on "the other side" is the rule. A tired driver, will, in emergency, revert to his usual side of the road and probably cause a head-on collision.

The motor vehicle is responsible for more deaths than any other piece of machinery in the world. It is, therefore, very important to study every means whereby the control of this machine can be improved. The equipment may be so badly designed that the operator is unable to take correcting action in time. There may be warning systems but the operator may be in such a state of fatigue that he fails to act. Inattention, distraction and fatigue are basic reasons for human failure when operating equipment. The brain becomes conditioned to "the usual" and, therefore, we must be sure that warning stimuli are acted upon. Thus a combination of flashing light with a warning hooter may be more effective than one alone.

A person has a limited mental capacity which can be overloaded with extraneous worries. The strain of modern living together with a complex operation can produce a state wherein the operator will no longer respond to warning information. The so-called inexplicable failure of a routine operation is often found on further investigation to be due to mental overload. We all experience the "Now look what you have made me do!" syndrome. When a person suffers from mental overload he becomes worried and distracted and in consequence commits actions which he would not normally do. In other words, he becomes what is described as "accident prone." Such a case is usually treated with amusement. However, it is a very real condition and is likely to produce consequences far more serious than dropping china in the kitchen.

It is necessary to have more intelligent operators for the more complicated modern equipment. It follows that a person of low intelligence or one who has been accustomed to a simple machine for many years will not be capable of operating the more complex and costly machines of today. The saying "it is difficult to teach an old dog new tricks" remains a truism. If it is attempted, failure of the operator and damage to the costly machines will often result.

It is no longer simply a question of moving knobs and levers. It is essential for the man to understand the machine and its functions and for him to play his part in the system. There are optimum hours of work and rest and there is legislation in most countries to ensure this. An operator has a limited span of attention which fails after the limit is reached, and it is, therefore, essential that rest is taken before reaching this variable limit. Operating comfort is an ideal which one strives for. Man is adaptable and able to cope with many awkward and uncomfortable situations; he will make his own adaptations to equipment to serve his own particular needs. It is, however, because of his very adaptability that he may become a hindrance to the work of the designer since the latter is frequently not made aware of the difficulties being experienced by the operator.

The work study expert employs those techniques evaluated by the ergonomists. The B.S.I. has defined work study as a "generic term for those techniques particularly Method Study and Work Measurement which are used in the examination of human work in all its contexts and which lead systematically to the investigation of all factors which affect the efficiency and economy of the situation being reviewed in order to effect improvement." It helps to produce the best from both men and material engaged on a working programme and in being concerned with the efficient use of man power and machine, it indirectly promotes safe working.

It is necessary, when engaged in work study, to break down an operation into its component parts and to examine each part carefully. It is a combined study of "how best?" and "how quick?" What is the best way of doing a particular job, and what is the optimum time? With regard to the latter it must be remembered that rest periods are essential, and higher production can often be obtained by ensuring that these rest periods are of the right length. These periods are physiological in requirement and are advised as a result of long experience in these matters by work study experts.

It is important to remember that recovery from fatigue is greatest in the first few minutes of rest. Therefore, frequent short rests are better than fewer longer breaks.

There are two aspects of ergonomics:

A. to design equipment to meet physical standards of the operator; by considering the 5 to 95 percentile group, most problems of a physical nature can be overcome;

B. to understand and plan for the mental capacity and problems of human behavior and reaction which are often unpredictable but, when faced with emergency action, are those of habit; it is this second problem which is a contributory factor to many accidents.

Sometimes a machine design or quality is at fault, but more usually it is human error. The reason for machine design being at fault is that too often there is a failure in standardization but this again leads to human error in manipulation.

This chapter has been mainly concerned with motor vehicles, but it will be easily recognized that the use of ergonomics appertains equally well throughout industry. Few but the largest companies will employ experts in the various disciplines I have described as being necessary for the study and development of ergonomics.

However, there is a comprehensive bibliography available of both British and American origin and the intelligent use of this literature by industrial doctors working together with safety engineers should prove of value. Significant improvements have been attained by many manufacturers of equipment, and as long as this continues there will be a resulting improvement in safe working.

REFERENCES

Edholm, O. G.: *The biology of work.* World University Library (Member of the Weidenfeld Publishers Group), 1967.

Grattan, E., and Jeffcoate, G. O.: Medical factors and road accidents. *Br Med J,* 1: 75–79, 1968.

McCormick, E. J.: *Human factors engineering,* 2nd ed. Maidenhead, McGraw-Hill, 1964.

McGowan, J.: Ergonomics and the driver. *Commercial vehicles—engineering and operation.* Institution of Mechanical Engineers, 1967.

Morgan, Cook, Chapanis, and Lund: *Human Engineering Guide to Equipment Design.* Maidenhead, McGraw-Hill, 1963.

Morgan, C. T.: *Introduction To Psychology,* 2nd ed. Maidenhead, McGraw-Hill, 1961.

Murrell, K. F. H.: *Ergonomics—Man in His Working Environment.* Chapman and Hall, 1965.

30

CONSUMERISM: BURDEN OR BENEFIT

George A. Peters, J.D.

Few persons speak with the authority of Dr. Peters when products liability is discussed. Not only is he a practicing attorney pioneering in products liability and associated fields, he is also a practicing safety professional.

The law has long recognized a user's right to recourse if he suffers injury from the product he uses. As a practical matter, however, and with certain notable exceptions, the legal right has been feeble in the snares of the courtroom. It burst its chains in the complex social change that is labeled "consumerism." Suddenly, business and industry are faced with a whole new exposure to financial loss, often loss of staggering proportions, and a low priority function of safety has become painfully acute.

Dr. Peters elucidates the law, cites examples of huge loss, and shows how the changing legal climate has created exposures that never existed before. The hazards were there, of course. The hazards were recognizable to safety expertise. But the hazards were not "exposures" until legal changes sharply escalated the probability of huge financial loss. Dr. Peters explains those changes and helps the safety professional to recognize new exposures in old hazards, and how to go about reducing them.

BECAUSE OF AN INSPECTION OVERSIGHT, a crack in a bottle went undiscovered and the bottle was filled with dextrose saline solution. Unfortunately, minute bacteria and fungi entered through the crack and multiplied. A twenty-two-year-old woman underwent gall bladder surgery and was given three bottles of dextrose saline solution. The third bottle was the cracked one and

Reprinted by permission of *Quality Progress*, January, 1973.

the toxic contaminated solution led to her death twenty hours later.

A product liability lawsuit followed alleging that the supplier and distributor had been reusing bottles not intended for reuse, and that failure to detect the crack had created a foreseeably unreasonably dangerous condition. (Juries in product liability cases have been instructed by judges to utilize the criterion of whether a defect was "unreasonably dangerous." Recently, this requirement, for a plaintiff's verdict, has been eliminated from jury instructions in California (*Cronin v. J.B.E. Olson Corp.*, California Supreme Court decision, October 17, 1972). Now the jury merely decides whether the defect that caused injury was present in the product when it left the manufacturer's hands.)

The jury awarded the husband and three children $900,000 compensatory damages, including $500,000 for replacement of the housewife's services. The jury also awarded $1 million as punitive or punishment damages. Punitive damages are not coverable by insurance, are high enough to hurt but not bankrupt a company and, because they are an unanticipated cost of doing business, they adversely affect a company's earned reserves or distributable profits. Thus an inspection oversight was worth $1,900,000 and the insurance would not take care of it all.

All too often, the quality and product assurance effort is considered something of a needed luxury. If the company is prosperous or the government procurement office is willing to pay for it, let's have just enough quality-reliability-safety effort to meet the basic need or program appearance requirements. But which organization function is among the first to be affected adversely when we have to cut fat, reduce overhead or trim the organization to meet competitive pressures?

The current threat of product liability lawsuits may be a burden to industrial management, but it is certainly of great benefit to the quality manager in justifying an adequate discrepancy avoidance program even during periods of lean budgets. Specifically, the manager should use as examples those court decisions involving similar companies, products and processes.

New quality program requirements are being defined by the courts in case-by-case decisions in each of the fifty states. The quality manager must be aware of changes in these requirements, and change his concepts, theories, technology and practices to meet the ever higher demands for safe quality products and services. It is not enough to have the appearance of an effective program because the output is tested in the real life marketplace and penalties for harm are determined by a jury composed of citizens representing the community at large. It is their social expectations, and the new legal requirements, by which the effectiveness of a quality, reliability and safety program will be judged.

Just a few years ago, I saw and heard advertisements of a new quality control program at a major consumer product manufacturer. It sounded good and I knew that such a move was long overdue. A short time later, I visited one of the assembly plants. To my surprise, the quality control effort had not been increased. In fact, it had been cut back sharply. The much-advertised new quality control effort was just a public relations cover-up for a cost savings program in which quality control was one of the sacrifices. True enough, immediate production costs went down. All the consequences of diminished quality control were not perceived till months or years later. The product liability implications will continue to be felt as the years progress and claims costs escalate.

Remember that a product manufactured today may cause an injury next year, a lawsuit may be filed nearly a year after the accident and the case may come to trial three years later. In other words, a defective product manufactured in January, 1973, may not result in a product liability cost until January, 1978. The case will be tried under the 1978 law and damages will conform to 1978 economics. For some products, the time lag may be ten, twenty or thirty years.

Only four years ago a product liability lawsuit resulted in a million dollar single injury verdict and one year ago that single injury record jumped to $3.65 million. Earlier this year, the absence of a baffle on an aircraft wing fuel tank resulted in an award of $21.75 million (of which more than $17 million was for punitive damages). That product liability lawsuit was followed immediately by a consumer class action lawsuit for fraud and deceit, asking $800 repair costs for the wing fuel tank on behalf of 15,000 purchasers (plus $100 million punitive damages).

Similarly, when a claims adjuster refused to provide any compensation to those suffering minor injuries from a household product, a class action was filed on behalf of 500,000 purchasers of the product for the sum of $122.5 million. Another class action alleging defective automobile seat assemblies recently was filed in the amount of $120 million. Whereas some people are saying that it is not worth the economic cost to save a few lives (such as $500 per automobile to save 25,000 lives a year), the courts are moving ahead and are increasing the cost of causing harm to others.

Increased Responsibility

The courts, attorneys and general public from which jurors are selected gradually are becoming aware of the quality assurance engineer's responsibility to detect and eliminate manufacturing defects, of the reliability engineer's role in predicting failure modes and their foreseeably hazardous consequences, of the safety engineer's function in identifying unreasonably dangerous conditions, of the design engineer's need to exceed trade standards and customary practices where safety is involved, of the need to test in accordance with foreseeable environmental and human use criteria, of the need to adequately instruct and warn, and of the need to have recall or service control extend until the time of product disposal.

All this means increased job responsibility and further professionalization of those occupational specialties involved in any product liability avoidance and mitigation program. As the experts become more proficient, there will be a higher duty to exercise reasonable care in performing assigned work tasks that could affect product quality, reliability and safety.

The era of criminal sanctions is approaching rapidly for those whose behavior is intentionally harmful and culpable. A few months ago, a Federal court jury convicted the president of a small manufacturing concern of conspiracy to defraud the government and aiding in the illegal falsification of aircraft part serial numbers. It was alleged that attempts were made to con-

ceal poor workmanship by welding over flaws. The company
president faces a maximum fine of $10,000 and a prison sentence
of up to ten years. In the same case, the quality assurance supervisor of the prime contractor was acquitted, the plant manager
and a company officer pleaded no contest and remain to be sen-
tenced, and a vendor quality control representative and two
others remain to be tried.

Not too long ago, a Nader task group issued a report on an arms
manufacturer that has been sent to the Justice Department for
possible action in regard to alleged criminal negligence in regard
to the company's final inspection, test and parts interchange-
ability demonstration activities. While the situations in which
criminal sanctions could be invoked are rare and hopefully will
remain that way, we must remember that such penalties have
been or are being written into legislation dealing with occupational safety, product safety, public health and corporate affairs.

(On October 28, 1972, President Nixon signed into law an act
establishing a new Federal agency dealing specifically with consumer product safety. The actions of that agency may have far-
reaching consequences for future quality management practices.)

The financial implications of product liability and consumerism
demand:

1. That there must be greater organizational responsibility
and *authority* granted to those who maintain surveillance over
the design, test, production and use of the product relative to
its quality, reliability and safety.

2. That there must be greater *professionalization,* creative
technical capability, marketplace relevance and accountability
of the individuals employed in such functions.

3. That increased organizational responsibility and individual professionalism dictate higher status and relative *pay*
scales for this class of industrial workers.

4. That there must be some objective evidence of the minimum *qualification* of key personnel relative to their professional
competence, acceptable to a court of law in a product liability
lawsuit, such as the ASQC quality engineer, ASQC quality
technician, ASQC reliability engineer or certified safety professional designations.

5. That there should be a company *regulatory compliance* activity to stay ahead of state and local codes; Federal legislation; government agency regulations and product evaluations; trade standards and recommended practices; and the hearings conducted by authorized agencies relative to product quality, reliability and safety. In this area, reluctant attempts at literal compliance must give way to technical leadership based on the needs of product liability defense strategems as influenced by a product's service life and safety criticality.

6. That there must be a change in the *marketing game* wherein the amount of safety depends on the price to be paid (for example, safety devices as optional extra-cost items, which suggests that the basic equipment offered for sale without those devices is inherently less safe). Wherever safety is sacrificed for price, there is greater risk of harm to those who only can afford or are assigned to work with a lower cost product (which suggests a discriminatory threat to one class of innocent purchasers or users). All product liability criteria suggests that the motto should be "price consistent with safety," i.e. don't knowingly market cheaper products that are less safe than similar higher cost products or contain latent hazards that would not be anticipated by reasonably prudent persons in the community in which the product will be used.

7. That each company and product division should have a product liability avoidance and mitigation manual and *file*. The manual should contain company policy statements regarding quality and safety; assigned organizational responsibilities and accountability for safety and quality assurance; a what-should-be-done guide to implementation; and a what-to-do guide in case of crisis or emergency. The file should contain briefing materials for defense experts and counsel, pertinent data for consistent and responsive interrogatory answers, test conformance records, final inspection sign-off sheets, design safety analyses, product cross comparison data, key personnel qualification and professional activity summaries, and other information that may be needed five or ten years later in defense of a product liability lawsuit.

8. Management planning and technical decision making that

emphasizes inherent hardware safety and *safe conditions* rather than the seemingly easier, but usually costly and ill-fated, attempts at *post-factum* control of unsafe *acts*.

9. Understanding throughout management that their *affirmative response* to the challenge of product liability is vitally important to the company's future health. For many companies we are discussing survival of the fittest, because the new socio-legal approach to product safety is to penalize, prevent the sale and punish in a way that hurts those who market unreasonably hazardous products. Unfortunately, too many purveyors of unwholesome goods cannot believe that a jury could be so wrong as to point the finger of fault in their direction.

10. That because of the limitations in our technical knowledge, we need to make known or publicize that an investment credit, external funding or independent effort is necessary to perform the extensive *basic and applied* research that can create and infuse our technology with more new concepts, theories, techniques and practices. This certainly involves research on productivity and workmanship as part of the quality-reliability-safety problem, so we are dealing with issues having fundamental and direct relevance to the future health of our economic system.

Bear in mind these maxims: Ignorance of the law and indifference to the rights of others can and should be no excuse. Keep informed and be concerned even though you believe that your product is the best and that you are doing the best job possible under the circumstances. Be prepared to recognize and deal effectively with your responsibilities, obligations and possible rights so that you can react in a timely and legally responsive manner both to the benefits and burdens of consumerism.

31

SAFETY PROFESSIONAL'S ROLE IN PRODUCT SAFETY

Leroy Faulkner

This article stands as one of the early warning signals as the storm of products liability darkened on the horizon. The author placed the problem square in the safety professional's corner. He asserted a pre-eminent role for the safety professional because it is "basically an accident prevention problem."

Much has happened since Mr. Faulkner expressed these views; his outline of safety knowledge applicable to product safety has undergone clarification and expansion, but his basic assertion has become inescapable. Society demands more than a mere shifting of responsibility; it demands prevention of the accident and the injury.

How can the industrial Safety Manager help management on product liability? This is an interesting question but first we should understand what product liability is.

The ASSE Journal and The *National Safety News* have devoted much space to products safety. A recent article highlighted the Safety Engineer's role in product safety. Many articles question the professional competence of the Safety Engineer to cope with this problem, but almost all agree that he can contribute greatly to the control of accidents resulting from use of his company's products. I suggest that you carefully review the reference material for a broad view of the problem as it may affect your industry. From our discussion today we will consider products liability as a catchall phrase used to describe the legal liability imposed upon a supplier of a product or service (manufacturer, assembler, wholesaler, other middle man) for injury or damage to a person or property through the supplier's negligence or breach

From *Journal of American Society of Safety Engineers*, March, 1968.

of warranty. Under the new concept of a "strict-liability" it also is used to describe the legal liability of a supplier for injury caused by some defect of the product regardless of the supplier's negligence or warranty breach.

Since someone has been injured or a property damage claim is the basis of products liability it follows that the Safety Manager should have responsibility to develop loss-control measures. One of the most complete statements of company policy I have ever seen which spells out the basic responsibility of Safety Manager includes 11 items. Item nine says: "Protect the company against public liability claims arising from injuries or damage to the public caused by waste disposal, operation of company owned vehicles, premises hazards to visitors, defective company products or services, etc."

Any effective control program is concerned with reducing hazard in use of the product to a practical minimum and establishing in advance conditions necessary for a successful defense against claims. My experience indicates key elements which can be summed up by three catch phrases: "Guard Against," "Warn Against," "Defend Against." They are equally important and each requires complete cooperation of design, engineering, production, advertising, sales, safety, and other key departments. The Safety Manager should be primarily concerned with the "Guard Against" and "Warn Against" but "Defend Against" is in the area of legal loss prevention and beyond the scope of this discussion.

Guard Against

By "Guard Against" I refer to the importance of reducing the hazard in use of the product to a practical minimum. This is basically an accident prevention problem and involves, in my opinion, five fundamental principles to be assumed by the manufacturer of any product and his safety manager: (1) The manufacturer should provide adequate protective devices and proper containers for his product. (2) He is responsible for designing and formulating his product in accordance with the best engineering techniques and with all pertinent codes and standards. (3) He must be assured that any vendors' components or those made on subcontract adhere to recognized codes and standards. (4) The manufacturer should have a quality control procedure which will assure that in the various stages of manufacturing the product it adheres to any "reliability policy" developed. (5) Sales-engineering and service department personnel must make certain that recommendations for choice of products or special design recommendations adhere to all codes or standards that apply and that all calculations be double checked.

ADEQUATE PROTECTIVE DEVICES. Your customers expect a product that has devices such as power transmission guards, point of operation guards where practical, over-pressure controls, pressure gauges, protective caps, shields, interlocking devices to prevent human element failure in judgment, to name just a few. There are many cases in which the manufacturer failed to provide the recommended device, some involving judgments of $200,000 to $250,000 and I recall one fire loss of over $3 million.

We often see such exaggerated claims of product performance in trade journals, involving many products and even safety devices. I cannot think of anyone more capable of discussing the adequacy of a safety device with design engineers than the Safety professional. No protective device should ever be considered "adequate" unless it adheres to or exceeds the requirements of any and all pertinent codes or standards.

PRODUCT DESIGN IN ACCORDANCE WITH PERTINENT CODES AND STANDARDS. Any indication that the product or component does not adhere to any applicable code, standard or recognized engineering practice becomes immediately a major issue in developing a case against the manufacturer.

Design engineers should be in constant communication with the Safety Department, which can double check the design to see that it is reasonably safe from the product liability point of view and in accordance with code or standards requirements. In all cases where some company policy is not in effect, the Safety Department must take the initiative and contact R & D departments as well as design engineers.

VENDORS' COMPONENTS MUST ADHERE TO CODES AND STANDARDS. The current trend in manufacturing and marketing a complete product is to build only components that can be made locally in a practical way in accordance with manufacturing facilities and technical know-how. Pneumatic, electrical and hydraulic components or any machine are purchased generally from vendors. Another trend is to have a complete product built by others under contract but sold under the seller's trade-mark or manufacturer's name. In either case it is important that the product adhere to the same standards as previously discussed. Specific performance requirements should be prepared by the design engineers and verified by the safety department. Such requirement should be included in purchase agreements as special clauses where necessary. Purchasing agents should not substitute or compromise for a price any products of questionable value in performance.

ESTABLISH AND MONITOR QUALITY CONTROL PROCEDURES. After an accident, the question arises immediately—"Did the part that failed adhere to original design specifications?" "Was substitute material used?" "What procedure is in use to assure that in the manufacturing process there is no break-down in quality control?"

SALES-ENGINEERING AND SERVICE DEPARTMENT POLICY. Many products produced by modern industry are so complex and highly technical in design and application that engineering-oriented personnel are in most constant contact with prospective customers and users. They could be known as sales-engineers, local service managers, factory maintenance representatives, and the like. While they are not usually directly responsible for product design, the nature of their work involves recommendations to customers in the choice of manufactured products, components, replacement parts, and in the case of maintenance contracts the actual physical effort involved in maintenance and repair work. Agreements made between sales-engineering or local service management should be reviewed by product design managers, chief design engineers and Safety Managers to be sure that any performance standards will be right and proper and can be met.

Warn Against

The second key element in any well balanced program is "Warn Against." Many products that reach the market involve a certain inherent hazard which requires accident prevention considerations in installation, use and maintenance. I refer to those for which all the latest technological engineering accident prevention applications have been provided but certain precautions by the users are needed. Many products such as air conditioners, humidifiers, radios, television sets, home workshop equipment, ladders, power mowers, and so on are examples; also chemical compounds, some pharmaceuticals and, yes, even some toys that you and I fondly provide our grandchildren.

The courts have often ruled that a manufacturer must give appropriate warning of known dangers which the user would not ordinarily discover. The likelihood of an accident taking place and the seriousness of the consequences are always to be considered with respect to the duty to provide sufficient warning. It must be adequate, since insufficient warning is, in legal effect, no warning. Whether sufficient warning is given depends on the "language used and the impression which it is calculated to make upon the mind of an average user of the product." Reference should be made to the Federal Hazardous Substances Labeling Act and subsequent regulations published in the *Federal Register*. This must be strictly adhered to. The manufacturer probably would not be held liable when the warning is adequate and the injured's failure to read that warning resulted in injury. Nor is it likely the manufacturer would be liable in cases where the user knew, or in the exercise of reasonable care should have known, that use of the product could cause injury.

Regardless of how warning of hazard is provided, the safety professional is most qualified to evaluate the hazard and prepare whatever safety specifications appear warranted.

32

"ACCIDENT-PRONE" THEORY
CAN AFFECT SAFETY
PERFORMANCE

William W. Allison

This article was not selected to once again reintroduce the confusions and obscurities of accident-prone theory. It was selected because Mr. Allison effectively makes the point of his title: theory can affect safety performance. At a time when ideas, concepts, and theories in safety abound and collide, it's a good point to make.

The "facts" of any situation are illumined by concept. Concept determines what "facts" we are capable of observing, whether we see any "facts" at all, and what the "facts" mean. The author examines the "facts" in a series of accidents involving a certain model of a three-wheel scooter. In the deluded light of accident-prone theory, "facts" were noted which readily pointed to accident-prone people. Meanwhile, investigators could not see any "facts" about the vehicle at all, even though its design made frequent turnover accidents inevitable. Accident-prone theory attaches to people, often blinding us to accident-prone situations created by design engineers, architects, purchasing agents, and others, including the safety director.

OUR OWN IMPRESSIONS can readily lead us to believe that we have observed certain people who are accident-prone. Yet we know that when apparently unintentional little dramas are staged before any group of observers, they inevitably create more false impressions than correct ones. We have also learned rather slowly that the human being is the most complex system known, many magnitudes more complex than the computers, for example. Man changes in his responses even from hour to hour.

From the *Journal of the American Society of Safety Engineers*, July, 1969.

Unfortunately, many early studies which have been published rather profusely claimed to prove the identification of accident-prone individuals. The literature abounds with such concepts as summarized by Viteles (1932). Perhaps the concept lives on because it is something that we in safety engineering and in management would often like to believe about many injury cases. Few seem to have done what the professional safety engineer should be most aggressive about doing. That is, few have both identified the causes back of the symptoms of the injury-repeater and have determined if the real causes remained uncorrected. Frequently, the accident-prone condition or procedure is ignored and is not corrected (Gaudet, 1966; Allison, 1965). It is certainly no surprise to competent statisticians that in almost any group, a few persons will have the majority of injuries based on chance alone (DeReamer, 1958).

The leading authorities in industrial medicine, human engineering, psychology, and safety engineering now all agree that the concept of identifying a person or group of persons as accident-prone is erroneous and misleading. It is not statistically or practically valid (Schulzinger, 1956; Gaudet; Fawcett and Killian, 1965; Simonds and Grimaldi, 1956; DeReamer, 1958; Swain, 1964). Yet we continue to find "new" articles by safety, medical, psychological, and training specialists seriously discussing or even advocating the accident-prone-people concept. I would like to help give this concept a proper and hopefully final burial.

Dr. Thomas H. Rockwell, director of the safety research laboratory at Ohio State University and a former chairman of the American Society of Safety Engineers research committee, said in the January 1963 JOURNAL: "Much of the research on human behavior in safety has been concentrated on the accident-prone theory—a concept which has generally been shown to be invalid (that is without foundation or truth.)"

The first time the accident-prone-people theory fell flat on its face in industry, was in the thirties when a psychologist found that one department of 200 men was having the majority of accidents in a large railroad company. These findings were in the process of being printed when the superintendent of these men was transferred to another department; suddenly the accidents decreased. The following year showed few accidents in this department, but an increasing number in the department to which the superintendent had been transferred. Most of us know from practical experience that we cannot do our best under certain types of supervision. The things that upset a man may vary from day to day; they may include the wife, the family, finances, and so on, but on the job the most important and constant factor is one's relationship with the supervisor.

Others, including the Aluminum Company of America, have since reported similar experiences. For example, "It was found that certain foremen consistently had high accident experience frequencies under their areas of supervision, despite the fact that they supervised several different areas over different shifts during the periods studied" (Viteles, 1932).

Recently, Dr. D. J. Killian (1965) has reported on a careful examination of the "accident-prone" concept. In his study, the records of individuals who had reported the most injuries out of more than 8,000 employes were analyzed, starting with the preconceived idea that they were accident-prone. Their cases were carefully reviewed by a clinical psychologist, a physician, and their supervisor. Their findings showed these individuals to be good workers and conscientious, stable personalities who observed the plant safety rules requiring the reporting of every injury to the letter. There was found little risk of serious injury in the very large number of reported minor injuries.

This confirms the thesis of the High Potential Method (Allison, 1965) that 90 percent of all injuries have no causal relationship to major cases, and that on an overall average, as few as one third of the minor injuries that occur are reported. It is ironical that the worker who conscientiously follows the safety rules of reporting all minor injuries becomes the very one that most safety departments then eye suspiciously (and erroneously) as the accident-prone individual. In some cases, the safety man and supervisor have literally convinced such employes that they were a hazard to themselves and the company, whereupon the individual's self-confidence was shattered and his efficiency was reduced.

To cite but one example of thousands that involve the design and perpetuation of an accident-prone situation, let us consider the three-wheeled scooter, the vehicle used by golfers and by industry from coast to coast. A long series of many incidents at one research site in which frightened and embarassed employes had reported that the scooters turned over while they were driving them around the site, prompted an in-depth investigation. The results showed that, in almost every case, the employe himself had sheepishly but voluntarily admitted to an unsafe act, such as driving into a soft spot or reaching down for a paper that he dropped, or possibly turning too quickly.

Over a period of three years, four people had more than one accident in which the scooter they were driving tipped over. I canvassed nearly twenty different corporate safety directors on their experiences with scooter accidents. All but two assured me that it was not really a problem as they had never had either a fatality or a serious injury and all cases were due to driver carelessness. One reported a fatality due to excess speed and a bad dip in a road. One reported a crippling injury and stated emphatically that he knew such accidents were caused purely by the carelessness of accident-prone drivers; and that such accidents should never make any product suspect.

Apparently, we and many others had a fairly well substantiated history of accident-prone-people. Common sense and observations also gave heavy weight to the idea as did the many popular "horseplay-Harry" and "nut-behind-the-wheel" articles, cartoons, speeches and films.

But then we did what no one else had done. We investigated the design of the scooters themselves. Investigation of the scooter showed that, if the designer had intentionally attempted to design "turnover-ability" into the scooter, he was approaching 80 percent efficiency. (Of course, this was not his intention.)

After a little trial and error, an automobile mechanic and I managed to come up with some slight modifications that eliminated the once-common spills in our existing equipment. New purchasing specifications (Allison) secured safer and more efficient equipment on all of our subsequent procurements. We have not conducted any driver training or produced any films on scooter driving. Nevertheless, we have had only one scooter tipover in the entire five-year period since the accident-prone (design) situation was corrected. In the three preceding years there had been an average of nine accidental tipovers each year by operators who generally blamed themselves.

In the High Potential accident report:

> Safety investigation disclosed that when the single front wheel passed a point about 30 degrees from straight forward, the force of forward motion exerted an extremely high force on the tire, pushing it in the direction of turn, causing the steering tiller to be jerked out of the driver's control; the front tire would then reach a position perpendicular to the scooter and act as a fulcrum to lift and dump the scooter on its side.
>
> All new scooters shall have four wheels, headlights, stop lights, rear lights, heavy-duty service and emergency parking brakes, automotive-type steering, steering wheel, electric horn on wheel or top of steering column, and rear-view mirrors. If cabs are used, turn signals shall be installed. If windshields are used, hand-operated wipers shall be installed. Acceleration shall be by steps that shall produce a slow, smooth change.

There is another example of how successfully safety psychology propaganda has indoctrinated us in the closed-end thinking of accident-people-proneness and the unsafe actions of the victims. A vice-president of research, who drives a car with an automatic transmission during the week, drives a camper truck on weekends. He recently started to back his camper truck out of the garage. The carburetor flooded. He got out, corrected the trouble, reached into the truck and turned on the ignition to check the carburetor. The camper took off out the open door and across the street, dragging the man with it. He nearly lost a leg as it scraped against the garage on the way out. This very intelligent man insisted that a safety memo be circulated in his company, warning of this unsafe act. Yet, with a simple $3 solenoid safety switch, the designer could have prevented this.

If there is any truth to the idea that man's unsafe acts are 85 percent of the safety problem, then it is those long-ignored thousands of such acts made into inescapable accident-prone situations by the design engineers, the architects, the chemical process engineers, the purchasing directors, the plant engineers, and even the plant safety directors. These apparently unassailable members of management literally force their unsafe situations into the daily lives of the worker and of the unsuspecting public. Then when a worker gets trapped by their imposed designs and/ or situations, everyone sees only the unsafe act of the victim.

Let us grant that the victim did commit an unsafe act under the accident-prone situation; isn't it logical to expect more effective and more lasting results by correcting the condition or process than it is to hope that everyone in the future will know or remember how to avoid this particular trap, along with the tens of thousands of designed or built-in traps that we encounter in our lifetime?

I make no appeal for common sense, because common sense never told anyone that a straw could be blown through a board or a tree limb. We had to learn that. Common sense doesn't tell us we can distinguish 80 from 81 decibels of sound better than we can distinguish 10 for 11 db; but it is a fact, nevertheless.

If we could only be completely frank and objective we could, from our own individual experiences, learning, sound judgment and analysis, realize these facts which explain why we really have accident-prone situations which can be corrected once management thoroughly concentrates on high potential situation hazard control.

1. No man, no matter how brilliant, can remain perfectly alert to the task at hand and his changing environment for 60 seconds of every minute, 60 minutes of every hour, all day long. Everyone of us has momentary lapses of consciousness and momentary straying of attention to attractions and/or distractions. Indeed, science has proved that the brain actually "turns off" or goes to sleep for brief moments, one or two times an hour during our best hours, and up to a few seconds or more a minute during our periods of fatigue.

2. Many, if not most design engineers, until very recently, have resisted safety engineering requirements as "do-good," "old-maid," "uneconomical" types of impractical and unnecessary impediments to getting the real job done.

3. From the safe ivory towers of their offices and drafting rooms, both the design engineers and many safety engineers have sneered at the few "impractical" safety engineers who have pursued the goal of all-out safety design. Both have in-

sisted, "You can't make things 'foolproof'" and they have dominated both the thinking and the results.

There are questions to be asked when a person becomes an accident repeater:

1. Is the error rate significantly higher than chance expectancy?

2. Are accident-prone situations presented by the work environment, facilities or tools?

3. Is this a conscientious person who reports almost or even all accidents? (Most people do not.)

4. Is the supervisory situation at fault?

5. Does the repeater need moral support, debt counseling or other assistance?

Certainly we must recognize that problems can overwhelm an individual at times, and he may need all the assistance he can be given. Unfortunately, he too frequently is given warnings about "straightening up or else," instead of an opportunity to unburden himself and a temporary easing of his assignments. At the same time, the very impersonality of our transient and highly mobile life has removed the former real personal concern, services and stabilizing influences of home town, family ties, close friends, family church, and family doctor.

Consequently, the real job facing management, design engineers and safety engineers is to face the fact that everything must be designed to be as compatible as possible with that already superbly designed component of the man-machine-facility-environment system; i.e. man.

We must design equipment, tools, facilities, machinery and work environments so that they are intelligent-proof; i.e. able to withstand the known vagaries of those intelligent, ingenious, ever-variable and most complex components, human beings. In this computer age, we all do need to be reminded that it is these human beings who are to benefit, to use, to service, to install and to maintain the other components designed by mere man. Indeed the new science of human engineering has already demonstrated that this is our most profitable approach to meet today's problems. This is, however, another subject which I have covered in lectures at the University of New Mexico in 1968 and University of Oklahoma in 1969 (Allison, 1965).

The worst part of the "unsafe personal act" mythology is its success in hiding the basic causes that can, if uncovered, be effectively corrected once and forever.

Which approach seems more efficient, less costly, and more reliable in all of the above cases—designed-in safety, or propaganda to convince people to try harder not to be careless?

REFERENCES

Allison, W. W.: High potential accident analysis. *Journal American Society of Safety Engineers,* July 1965; How to foresee tragic accidents by use of HIPO situation method. *Transactions,* National Safety Council National Safety Congress, 1967; The HIPO-Technical and Economical Control of Hazards, University of New Mexico, 1968 and University of Oklahoma, 1969.

Allison, W. W.: *Safety Guides.* SC–M–68–378. Albuquerque, Sandia Laboratories.

DeReamer, R.: *Modern Safety Practices.* New York, John Wiley & Sons, 1958.

Fawcett, Howard and Killian, D. J.: *Safety and Accident Prevention in Chemical Operation.* New York, Interscience Publishers, division of John Wiley & Sons, 1965.

Gaudet, Frederick J.: Safety Design; *Prod Eng.* McGraw-Hill, March 14, 1966.

Gaudet, F. J.: Stevens Inst Laboratory of Psychological Studies.

Killiam, D. J.: *Safety and Accident Prevention in Chmical Operations.* New York, Interscience Publishers, division of John Wiley & Sons, 1965.

Satterwhite, H. G., and LaForge, R. M.: A comparison of three measures of safety performance. *Journal ASSE,* vol. II, No. 3.

Schulzinger, M. S.: *The Accident Syndrome.* Springfield, Thomas, 1956.

Simonds, Rollin H. and Grimaldi, John: *Accident Cost and Control.* Homewood, Richard D. Irwin, Inc., 1956.

Swain, A. D.: Human Factors in Design of Reliable Systems. Proceedings Tenth National Symposium, Reliability and Control, American Society for Quality Control, New York, 1964.

Viteles, M. S.: *Industrial Psychology.* New York, Norton, 1932.

33

SAFETY AND THE NEW AGE
OF PERSONALISM

MICHAEL F. BIANCARDI

In one word, personalism, Mr. Biancardi embraces a host of social forces. "There is also a new tone, something happening to our whole society, an emphasis on the individual, an emphasis on the person, on the potentialities of each person, on each person's well-being, health and happiness. There is a new personalism evident in both our national and private concerns, and those concerns constantly expand into areas which have been encompassed in the word 'safety'."

In the light of the new personalism, the author discusses what's happening in three specific areas of safety. He does so in terms which reveal the vast scope of safety, but the forces of personalism, he feels, are still unfocused, disorganized, and unformed. "A unifying national idea of safety . . . does not yet exist." We are confronted with a unique historical moment in which safety professionals "have an opportunity to shape the course and direction of a new national commitment to human safety."

Mr. Biancardi speaks of his profession as from a mountaintop. Both students and safety professionals may sense a limitless range for individual talent and specialized knowledge in the vista he reveals.

IN JANUARY, 1971, a magazine published in Chicago—*The Critic* —appeared with a cover depicting a stained-glass window entitled "Living Saints." And on the window, along with other figures of public and religious reknown, was a portrait of Ralph Nader.

It struck me then that this homage to Mr. Nader—and the

With modifications from a presentation at the Tenth Annual Florida Industrial Conference, Jacksonville, Florida, February 9, 1971, as published in National Safety News.

widespread interest in his work—should be a definite signal to us that a new age of safety awareness is dawning in this country.

And Nader is not the only signal; there are signs of it every where. *Business,* certainly, is more interested in safety than ever before.

In the field of industrial safety, where until recent times we perhaps had taken progress for granted, there is an obvious urgency to our exploration of the leveling-off in the accident rate; there is deep concern also about whether the rate itself—so long in use—is really the proper measure of our problem; and industry is working harder than ever before on better means of measuring safety and better techniques of safety motivation.

In the fields of automobile and general product safety, corporate expenditure for research and development has never before been on the scale we have today, and concern about safety has begun to permeate every level of corporate activity.

We see a similar corporate concern about air, water, and land pollution, about alcoholism and drug abuse, about highway safety and employee health.

If we look to the public sector we see a similar broadening and amplification of interest in safety.

Mr. Nader and his Raiders are now considered to be one of the most powerful legislative influences in Washington and their influence is also being felt in most of our state legislatures. You can hardly name a field of interest to the safety professional—packaging, labeling, advertising, testing, basic design, and of course dozens more—where they have not had some effect.

In every branch of government—legislative, executive, and judicial—there is daily evidence of new interest in safety and dissatisfaction with things as they have been. New legislation, executive orders, and legal decisions that will profoundly affect our lives and our careers are pouring out in a continual stream, and there's more—plenty more—on the drawing board.

And finally we ourselves—people everywhere—are talking about safety and thinking about safety—what it is and what it means—on a scale I can't recall ever seeing before. But that is not the only change. There is also a new tone, something happening to our whole society, an emphasis on the individual, an emphasis on the person, on the potentialities of each person, on each person's well-being, health and happiness. There is a new "personalism" evident in both our national and private concerns, and those concerns constantly expand into areas which have been encompassed by the word "safety." The new personalism has created a ferment in the safety profession, new challenges and new opportunities.

You can see it in the whole complex of exploration, discussion, and action that we have termed "consumerism"—the people of this country have made a civilization that has won the battle for pure survival and can turn now, as a general rule, to questions about the *quality* of life. People have time today to determine what is *best* for them, to seek what is safe for them to do and to use.

And across the entire national scene—in the press, in popular music, in films, in home decoration and interior design, in education, in our military services—we see a society with the time, the means, and the inclination to place a strong new emphasis upon the dignity and importance of the individual human being.

But all this vast new concern about safety is still rather general, still disorganized, unformed. It has yet to find the means of focusing—and thus releasing effectively—its energy and its power.

The public, for example, is worried about traffic safety—but have any of us really faced the hard decision about whether we are willing to surrender any of our present rights and liberties (or curtail those of our neighbors) in order to achieve it?

And have we decided whether we're willing to pay what safety will cost? Until we do, we are compounding the difficulty faced by business in weighing the costs of consumer protection against the competitive pressures generated by those—consumer and supplier alike—who may shave costs by skimping on safety.

On every level of government, our representatives face the job of reconciling our need for industrial and social progress with the utopian urge to create by legislation a risk-free environment.

The result is an uncertainty on many levels about what should be done. There's a good deal of confusion on the safety scene. On certain problems we have had so much aimless milling about and hollering that it resembles nothing so much as Grand Central

Station on a Friday afternoon just after they've announced that the power has blown and no trains are running. A unifying national *idea of safety*—one that business and government and the private citizen could use as a principle for action, as an ideology —does not yet exist.

But the restless energy, the concern, the huge potentiality are waiting. They could be a means to the most effective safety effort ever seen in this country—if someone, some group, will provide the leadership necessary to concentrate this unfocused energy and then shape both its attitude and its direction.

In my opinion, the group that should attempt this leadership effort is the one comprising the safety professionals of this country.

I believe that the safety professional, at work in business, in labor, in government, or wherever his work takes him—acting both individually and as a group—could become the strongest influence in shaping and directing this new national safety consciousness.

To take the position of leadership will require the ability to marshal and apply the work of many sciences and disciplines in the further exploration of human safety, but such a requirement is an advantage to the safety professional—such inter-disciplinary coordination is *already* part of his mission.

I think we should look upon the times as providing a unique and historic opportunity for our safety discipline—a chance to advance not only the realization of the ideals that underlie this new era of personalism but to advance, also, our safety discipline itself. The underlying ideals are, after all, in both cases the same: a fundamental concern with *persons* and a conviction of the individual person's importance and dignity. If there is "a tide in the affairs of men" which must be taken at the flood, then now is flood tide for the safety profession. The time for action is *now*.

But how shall we seize the opportunity and make it ours?

Certainly one of the primary means to leadership is excellence —and in my opinion it is through his professional excellence, demonstrated day after day through his work and his ideas, that the safety professional can become influential in shaping a national safety effort.

He has to prove that he and his fellows in the safety discipline are able to do the job.

Proving this involves, first, a strengthening of their public and personal commitment to the safety discipline. Professionalism is earned, it is lived; it must permeate everything a man does and says.

Second, the professional must identify and enunciate more clearly both for himself and for the public the basic aims and purposes of the safety discipline. Through broad understanding of those aims, he will ensure that his dedication to them will be a continuous *sign* of his professionalism.

Third, the professional must constantly expand his knowledge of the discipline.

Fourth, the professional must work to *improve* the safety discipline—and must be willing to contribute his time, effort, money, and talent unselfishly to that end.

Another broad goal must be the stimulation of public understanding about the safety discipline and of the promise it offers as a focal point for a unified national safety effort. This might be accomplished if the safety professional would so plan his efforts that they will constantly create and reflect favorable public interest upon his calling.

But personal efforts may be unproductive unless they are supported by an organized, continuous, imaginative public relations program—mounted and financed by the group itself—that will stimulate public understanding of the safety professional's mission and goals. The American Society of Safety Engineers is working in this line, and we should be doing all we can to support their effort.

The final aspect of this drive for professional excellence is to ensure the continued vigor and strength of the safety discipline by recruiting and developing capable new people.

My point in all of this is that we safety professionals must quickly strengthen and expand our *planning*—the charting of our goals and our destination, and what we must do in order to attain them. Certainly we do not lack for challenges. In the pressing safety problems of our time we see a crying need for all our intelligence and skill.

The problems are huge, complex, and extremely demanding. I want to mention just a few of them here to illustrate the nature of the challenge they present for safety professionals.

The Occupational Safety Situation

In our occupational safety situation in this country we have a huge job to do in merely devising the proper definitions for and measure of our problem.

The statistics appear to say that progress in occupational safety has come to an end. The frequency rate has been rising somewhat since 1961 and severity rates, after many decades of annual improvement, have since 1961 remained substantially unchanged.

But do the changes in statistical trends *really* demonstrate a leveling-off in safety progress? *I just don't know.* I don't think *anybody* really knows. Our data are suspect—our measuring and evaluation processes are not well-defined and precise. I'm not certain that our statistical mix has been consistent. Are we getting more reporting from high-hazard industries? Is there now more reporting by smaller plants (which generally show higher frequency rates), or vice versa? To my mind we need a great deal more research—both theoretical and applied—into what we should be measuring, how to measure it, and what the results *mean.*

And even if there *is* a leveling-off, is it the real problem, one that deserves our attention, or is it merely a symptom? I suspect that there are deeper causes, root factors in a national accident syndrome that results from a complex of moral, economic, social, and political factors. It's possible that we may have to isolate, analyze, and study *all* these factors if we are to come up with a means to more progress in occupational safety.

In the meantime, we must *make* progress, *improve* occupational safety—and in that effort some of the new safety management techniques may be of help.

One technique is Systems Safety Analysis. The methods it utilizes, such as fault-free analysis and failure mode and effect analysis, are complex and expensive, but the systems concept itself is extremely important to us. It teaches us to stop looking upon an accident as an isolated phenomenon. Accidents take place and hazards exist within a context, a system, and must be investigated and considered with that system as our reference. I think that systems techniques can be simplified so as to be applicable and effective in occupational safety.

Another technique is one that shows us where safety effort is likely to be most productive. My company has termed it the Concept of the Vital Few and uses it to pinpoint the major loss problems within industries we insure for workmen's compensation. First we break out that small proportion of total injuries which produce by far the greater part of injury cost. We then proceed, industry by industry, to identify the relatively few accident factors (the Vital Few) which produce most of that industry's losses. When safety effort is concentrated upon these defined factors, there generally results a dramatic improvement in loss control.

These are *business* efforts to improve occupational safety. What about action on the governmental level?

At this moment in February, 1971, the big news is the Federal Occupational Safety and Health Act signed by President Nixon on December 29. We are all still assessing how to respond to this new and massive influence on safety and what it will all mean in the end. For the moment, it has given a priority to injury prevention that safety has never had before. It may well stimulate safety action at the state level, and stimulate the development of standards which have lagged behind.

The more important stimulation will come from OSHA's influence on research. Since federal funds will be available for research in occupational health and safety, it should generate more of such research, initially, perhaps, more in the area of occupational health. Safety professionals should be active in aiming this expanded research into areas where we need more information.

One area which I have already mentioned is research on the development of a better system to gather and analyze safety data, a system that will encompass *causes* as well as numbers of accidents and injuries.

The demand for the services and expertise of safety professionals will be increased by OSHA—though there aren't enough of them to go around right now, there'll be an even *bigger* sphere for them not to go around in! It sounds bad—and it probably will be a troublesome situation for a while. But in the long run it should bring new people into our profession, people who will certainly add to its strength and vigor. The increased demand for trained specialists will also cause our educational institutions to modify and expand their curricula in order to meet it—a change that is long overdue.

All these efforts—private, business, governmental—are signs that there's a new day coming for occupational safety. *We'd better gear up for it.*

We have some catching up to do, in my opinion. When you survey the revolutionary changes that have been taking place in management science, engineering technology, and manufacturing processes, you get an uncomfortable feeling that the safety discipline has a lot of homework to do. If we want to be the influential guide, we've got to have a thorough understanding of the terrain.

The Traffic Safety Situation

In the field of traffic safety, there also we face substantial problems of definition and measurement before we can devise practical and effective solutions.

We are turning out stacks of figures on the size and dimensions of what we *hope* are the problems—but whether we are really measuring what we *should* be measuring is still not entirely clear.

There has been some rejoicing on the airwaves and in the press about a turnaround in the traffic death toll during 1970—it is said to be down 1,100 from the 1969 toll of 56,400 killed. I'm pleased to hear of this reduction—but it is too soon to claim that it marks the turning of the tide.

A new spirit of determination to end the slaughter—a spirit that permeates our people, our courts, our law officers, our drivers —only that, I believe, will truly mark the turning of the tide. In that determination, safety will be ranked favorably in *all* our tradeoffs of comfort, cost, and convenience. I cannot see that such a spirit has yet come into being in this country.

Maybe at its essence our problem here has less to do with figures than with a profound collective apathy—and how much research is now underway on the cause and cure of public apathy?

Since apathy—like affluence—is one of those things that no one is willing to concede that he has, perhaps it's not even the proper word to use in setting up our exploration of the traffic safety problem.

We could set this exploration up with a sort of cool, scholarly approach by asking: Why are the American people willing to pay so high a price in the daily loss of human life and health for convenient highway transport?

Why? Who knows. And what are we doing to find out?

Measuring public apathy, tracking and charting the ethical considerations that lie near the heart of this problem—*these* are tasks that require the help of disciplines other than ours. Getting those disciplines involved, getting them interested in work on our problem, is—I submit—a proper and an *urgent* assignment for the traffic safety professional.

In addition to research related to the car and the road, I don't believe there's been nearly enough research on questions such as:

What are the most effective means to stimulate public attention to, and action upon, the traffic safety problem?

And another:

How best can we utilize such means to procure the public action that we see as necessary?

What the American people *do* have, I think, is a profound uneasiness—an uneasiness that is still rather shapeless and unfocused—about all this traffic carnage: a problem for which all the major solutions suggested to date have been complex and difficult, since many of those solutions will require a broad reevaluation of our individual rights and liberties and of how many we are willing to curtail or surrender in order to achieve highway safety.

We safety professionals should realize that we can play a number of roles in this exploration.

As citizens, we should take part in the public dialogue on those aspects of the problem that are governmental in nature.

As specialists on safety, we should raise the level of our activity and strengthen our credibility so that our expertise will be more influential in shaping and directing the dialogue.

And, finally, as an *individual*, every safety professional has to remember the importance of his personal attitudes and behavior in improving traffic safety. We have all heard someone excuse his behavior by saying: "Hell, even half the *safety* people in my company don't use seat belts." We teach—either for good or ill—by our *example*.

The Product Safety Situation

And now, before I wind this up, let's take a quick tour through another national safety issue that's on the front pages every other day: the product safety situation.

Product liability litigation is now considered by most enterprising young attorneys to be the wave of the future. The figures, when I last saw them (they change, like the population clock, hourly) showed that more then 500,000 new product liability lawsuits are being filed annually. The size of damage awards has been soaring, and the premiums charged for product liability insurance have been leaping up right along with them.

Everybody's getting worried about product safety; everybody thinks he'd like to do something about it.

But here again, as with our other problems: Where shall the work begin?

Where are the systems that will enable management to make better decisions about product safety? *How* shall we design such systems? *What* are the factors to be considered in our design? And *if* we devise product safety systems, how are they to be integrated with the entire manufacturing and distribution processes?

If you have concluded from these questions that there is a lot of work yet to be done in this field by the safety professional, you're right, we're just beginning.

Product safety data are primitive, incomplete, frequently inaccurate. The task confronting the safety professional in the products field is huge: he must determine the proper standards to be used; develop the techniques that will produce the information he needs; set criteria for the evaluation of the data; and then ultimately come up with valid, practical conclusions about the *meaning* of the data.

The only consolation is that huge tasks are always accompanied by huge opportunities.

Within business, there's a once-in-a-lifetime opportunity for the safety professional oriented toward management science to take the lead in corporate product safety management. Business needs professional advice on formulating policy that will effectively commit the enterprise to product safety, and then will need men to quarterback the execution and realization of that commitment. Management also needs men who can provide staff coordination to promote product safety responsibility and to assist design, manufacturing, and marketing departments in *meeting* such responsibility.

On the governmental level, there's so much happening that affects product safety that it takes a lot of hustle just to keep aware of what has been proposed, what is being debated, and what is being done. Yet it's essential—if our safety discipline is to assume its proper role—that we keep ourselves well-informed about the issues and the answers.

The National Committee on Product Safety has issued its report; if any safety professional hasn't yet read it, I certainly think he should get the report and do so.

There are a number of bills now before the Congress that relate to product safety. You should learn what they propose, decide which you favor, and why. And then—since safety *is* your business and your career—let your elected representatives know where you stand and what you think.

Each one of us has a choice:

We can help choose the tone and direction of a national policy on product safety—or we can default and let *others* choose (others who may be far less qualified than the safety professional to make such important decisions).

Just those three national problems, those I've mentioned—industrial safety, traffic safety, and product safety—can symbolize for us both the size and the nature of today's safety challenges.

Any *one* of them—and I really mean this—any *one* of them makes landing a man on the moon look relatively uncomplicated. Two of them alone—industrial and traffic accidents—are alleged to be costing the country more than $21 billion a year. All of them are complex, profound, demanding problems. All of them are urgent problems. And I frankly think that solutions for any of them are going to come much more slowly than expected and much more slowly than they might *unless* the safety professional becomes involved at every level of the research and development effort.

I believe we in the safety profession are confronted today with one of those unique historical moments that provide the means for a profession to come of age, to come into its own, to realize—perhaps—our profession's highest aspirations.

I believe that we have an opportunity to shape the course and direction of a new national commitment to human safety.

And I believe that we *could* do it—as long as we remember this: leadership in any great effort never just falls into anyone's lap.

PART IV

THE CHALLENGE

On one hand, the challenge is individual and personal, something each reader accepts for himself. On the other hand, there is a collective challenge, something to be defined by safety as a profession. These selections merely suggest that collective challenge, but surely its ultimate definition will be the result of personal challenges perceived by individuals.

34

ADJUSTIVE BEHAVIOR AND SAFE PERFORMANCE—AN INTRODUCTION

FRANCIS S. McGLADE

This selection is the first chapter in a text which is "based on the thesis that the study of adjustive behavior in relation to safe driving performance will yield information and ideas which can be utilized advantageously in developing accident theory, conducting accident research based on hypotheses derived from theory, and in deriving practical methods and techniques for application in various areas of accident prevention work."

A series of snippets quoted out of context will not do justice to Dr. McGlade's thought, but may suggest the rich flavor of this selection: ". . . new thinking is needed at each stage, from theory, to practice, and to evaluation . . . accident prevention has entered the realm of public policy and procedures . . . good intentions will no longer suffice . . . accident prevention is neither a science nor a discipline . . . many such innovations were intellectually premature, scientifically innocent and lacking . . . sometimes lacked even the most simplistic theoretical foundation . . . a theory must allow verification; it must be able to predict in addition to being a succinct embodiment of hindsight . . . now is the time for long-range multidisciplinary research . . . no one knows precisely what is meant by error, or mishap, or unsafe behavior . . . valid research which is more relevant to the cost/effectiveness practicalities of safety programming."

The editors have sometimes preferred a selection for light and easy reading. Not so in this chapter from McGlade's text. This is material to study, but rare will be the careful reader who does not find something to ponder and pursue beyond these pages.

From *Adjustive Behavior and Safe Performance* (Charles C Thomas, Publisher, Springfield, Illinois, 1970).

THE DRAMATIC CIRCUMSTANCES surrounding the accidental
deaths of three astronauts, referred to in the Preface, cap-
tured the sympathy of the public and resulted in considerable
pressure on politicians and officials associated with the space
program to explain the reasons for the occurrence and to document future plans to prevent a recurrence of such a disaster.

Yet each day equally disastrous events take place, under conditions which the general populace considers mundane, causing
hundreds of deaths and thousands of disabling injuries. But
such events are unheralded and considered routine because they
occur with such day-to-day regularity. This abnormal situation is
exemplified by the countless motor vehicle accidents each day,
many of which involve more than three fatalities. Mass media
publication of these daily events do not include information about
the calculated risks, the human stresses, the unfavorable environmental conditions and the inadjustiveness of human behavior
which permeate and are inextricably interwoven into the fabric
of these accidental occurrences.

British author Colin Wilson (1966) has succinctly described
one syndrome relating to this overwhelming problem in his comments about the "dominant 5 percent" of the human specie; i.e.
the 5 percent who assume leadership, and with whose guidance
the remaining 95 percent become docile followers of instructions.
The facts of Mr. Wilson's comments are that: (1) only a small
fraction of the dominant 5 percent ever reach the top; (2) many
members of the other 95 percent think they belong in the dominant 5 percent; and (3) the unlucky members of groups (1) and
(2) who do not make it to the top become frustrated, hostile, aggressive and risky individuals, and thus become prime candidates
for an accident. Wilson's article continues with a quote from
Norman Mailer: "The juvenile crime problem . . . might be
partly solved by erecting huge ski jumps . . . or tanks in which
teenagers could pit themselves against live sharks."

Such untoward activities might keep the teenage segment of
our society busy and out of trouble, and alleviate the anxieties
and frustrations of some of our adult citizens, but it will not make
even a slight improvement in this Nation's accident problem. At

this point in time, many teenagers are employing motor vehicles to vent their excess energies, rather than ski jumps or sharks.

Mr. Wilson's basic point is well taken and leads to an inescapable conclusion: we must devise ways to channel the impulsivity generated by frustration into creative activities, in which needless risk is avoided. The point assumes greater significance when one looks at the specifics stemming from it: we must develop ways to teach people to perform adjustively so that aggressive, risky behavior is undertaken only when necessary and only under the most appropriate conditions obtainable. This would provide people with emotional releases under reasonable and relatively safe circumstances.

This text is concerned with the function of adjustive behavior in safe human performance.

The Issue

It is somewhat ironic to see the time, effort and money invested in trying to make space flight safe for man when we have had so little success in making man's terrestrial environment sufficiently safe for his efficient and economical performance. This unfortunate state is especially true in relation to the primary mode of transport in this country, the motor vehicle.

It is apparent that so far we have done an inept job of controlling and expediting motor vehicle travel in terms of enhancing efficiency, economy and safety of operations. The basic approach for the past fifty years has been one of constant remonstrations to the driving public highlighting their inevitable human weaknesses and exhorting them to be safe. The inadequacy of this approach has been concisely stated by a colleague: * "Who do we think we are to play God? Why do we expect to *change* people (italics mine)? To make nice, courteous drivers of them? Simply by *telling* them to do so (italics mine)! The history of civilization demonstrates the falseness of this approach. We have had a singular lack of success in changing people through appeals and admonitions."

* This idea was conveyed in personal discussion by Mr. William F. Dalton of the Center for Safety, New York University, in April, 1968.

Obviously an organized safety effort, particularly traffic safety, calls for many approaches. A multipronged attack must be mounted, with a great deal of coordination among the prongs. And the efficacy of each prong must be assessed, and inefficient ones discarded.

To insure comparability of application of each prong, standard operating procedures must be developed. If this is not done, assessment or evaluation is a futile exercise. The development of standard operating procedures depends on criteria. Criteria depend on rationales. Rationales depend on theory. In the field of safety, new thinking is needed at each stage, from theory, to practice, and to evaluation.

This text is based on the thesis that the study of adjustive behavior in relation to safe driving performance will yield information and ideas which can be utilized advantageously in developing accident theory, conducting accident research based on hypotheses derived from theory, and in deriving practical methods and techniques for application in various areas of accident prevention work.

Theory and Research in Accident Prevention

Safety efforts have recently been cast in a new light; the very bright light created by the landmark traffic safety legislation in 1966 and 1967, and the current legislative activities concerning Occupational Health and Safety Standards. There is no doubt that accident prevention has entered the realm of public policy and procedures. This newly acquired status brings with it the obligation to confront major issues and problems, rather than to avoid them.

When a field of activity begins to bear on, and comes under the aegis of public policy, it is forced to reduce its avoidance behavior. Past excesses, embarrassments and controversies can no longer be concealed; they must be laid bare for the policy-makers and the citizenry to see. Accident prevention has reached this point in its evolution. The data on which accident prevention activity is based, and to a large extent the "hunches" which generate much of its endeavors, have entered the arena of public concern and governmental decision. Accident prevention, as a professional enterprise, is now forced to demonstrate its pertinence and its value as an agent affecting the common good.

Many people uphold the concept of an art, science or discipline being an end unto itself. It is difficult to name any field of activity which is more bound to the realities of life, in terms of the obviousness of its end products, than the field of accident prevention. Therefore, more than most fields of scientific work, accident prevention must exhibit a high potential for applicability and usefulness if it is to be supported rather than merely tolerated. Good intentions will no longer suffice.

At this point it should be emphasized that accident prevention is *neither a science nor a discipline*. Accident prevention work per se does not fit either of these descriptions. Rather, the several and varied aspects of accident prevention work constitute a *field* of activity to which must be applied, in a continuing and coordinated effort, the sundry sciences and disciplines, such as engineering, medicine, the physical sciences, the social and behavioral sciences, and a host of others.

The challenge of relevancy has been set before accident prevention, and the challenge cannot be circumvented nor relegated to a collection of well-intended but opinionated commitments. The challenge must be met with results. To accomplish this, accident prevention must reassess its allocation of energy and effort.

Individuals cast in safety leadership roles have ample reason, based on the history of the accident prevention movement, for displaying extreme caution in assuming proponency or sponsorship for any safety innovations which require the support of public policy. There are many vivid institutional memories of events of the past several decades in which safety leaders were conspicuously ready, indeed in many cases they were clamoring, to claim science, or theory, or research as the foundation for safety reforms. In many instances, what was lacking in authoritativeness was compensated for by the certainty of the pronouncements. As a consequence, many of the expounded, accepted and implemented proposals were unsound and unproductive, and in some cases even counterproductive. One cannot argue with the civic motivation which undoubtedly underlay these undertakings;

however, substantial arguments are available which demonstrate that many such innovations were intellectually premature, scientifically innocent and lacking, for the most part, any support in empirical data and research. They sometimes lacked even the most simplistic theoretical foundation and, while they may have had some relevancy in terms of unfounded optimism on the part of the supporters, they were almost entirely lacking in precision and accurate anticipation of the consequences of their application.

Future accident countermeasures and evaluation techniques must demonstrate both immediate and long range potential value, in cost/effectiveness terms, before they are fully accepted. The development of these countermeasures and techniques must be based on scientific research which, in turn, should be based, at least in part, on well-conceived theoretical formulations.

Accident prevention has for too long put the cart before the horse. In the sometimes frenzied attempt to come up with immediately applicable solutions, theoretical development and basic research have been ignored in favor of guesswork as a basis for establishing safety program objectives and procedures. The rationale for this approach has been echoed many times over the years: "We can't sit around and wait!"

Theoretical development is inherently a slow process, but it often has greater payoff in the long run. Further, it frequently has an exponential effect, in that one verified bit of information opens the door to several more and each of these, in turn, leads the way to dozens of other possibilities. So while initial progress may appear slow, the ultimate payoffs may come very fast. It is unfortunate that this approach to accident prevention was not undertaken years ago. If it had been, perhaps by now that exponential point-in-time would have been reached when valid and practical results would be forthcoming in large quantity. This approach was not used years ago; it must be utilized now.

Accident Prevention Theory

The obvious function of accident prevention work is the prevention of accidents. One would be hard put to name another social endeavor whose manifest objective can be so simply and concisely stated. However, one must go beyond the ultimate goal and uncover the latent objectives of a social dictum before complete evaluation is possible. This process reveals the distinction between the policy-oriented individual, such as a time-and-motion analyst or an accident prevention practitioner, and the professional observer or scientist. The latter see beyond the obvious into the latent function of a social phenomenon; they see the gap between the manifest and the latent, in terms of the social consequences which are not apparent and which were not foreseen (see Merton, 1957). And the larger the attainment gap, that is the difference between what has been accomplished and what should have been accomplished, the more this gap can be explained by description of its latent functions. Measuring the gap between desired objectives and the attainment level can guide the quest for information about the hidden significance of the social consequences of an activity. This measurement process is a job for science. One of the tasks within this job is the development and application of theory.

The structure of science involves the explanation of events and behavior by mapping portions of the real world with a linguistic edifice of a determinate structure (Hempel, 1965). Such a linguistic edifice constitutes a theory; a network of integrated propositions from which are derived, by the process of logical deduction, statements concerning observable phenomena. A theory is satisfactory to the extent it *explains* the observable facts; i.e. it is more than a mere summary of known facts. A theory must also contain explicit or implicit statements about events as yet unobserved. Verification of the theory is then obtained by applying the statements to collected empirical data. This is the bulwark of scientific explanation: a theory must allow verification; it must be able to predict, in addition to being a succinct embodiment of hindsight. Prediction, in this context, includes the possibility of bringing about desirable ends as well as preventing the recurrence of the undesirable.

Past efforts (Schulzinger, 1956; Association for the Aid of Crippled Children, 1961; and Haddon, et al. 1964) have attempted the following: (a) to apply theories of behavior to accidents; and (b) develop theories about accidents. In the former instance usually there was little or no attempt to realign the behavioral theory within the perspective of the accident problem. In the latter case, the developed accident theories gave a fairly accurate picture of what had been observed, in terms of circumstances surrounding accidental occurrences, but they were lacking in foresight, either because the implications of the theory did not go beyond what was already known or because the implications were stated in unverifiable form.

One recent theoretical investigation (McGlade and Laws, 1962; McGlade and Abercrombie, 1965) suggested the feasibility of making a fresh start with respect to the very foundation of accident research, through reevaluation of the methods of classifying accident data for research purposes. The evolution of accident reporting and classification has involved primarily identification of factors which assist police and other enforcement officials in the legal aspects of accidents; for example, to fix blame. The theory cited above postulated a conceptualization of accident causation in which classification variables were extracted from accident data based on a matrix of responsibility-situational-social factors. A basic tenet of this research effort was that extant accident classification systems were not grounded in theory and consequently were somewhat inadequate for research purposes. This premise was met with heavy resistance and, in fact, in some circles the authors were labeled as iconoclasts for implying that current schemes for classifying accidents might be invalid for research uses. The point of this discussion requires emphasis: research results can be no better than the data on which they are based; it does not make good sense to begin a research project utilizing secondary data which are inadequate or otherwise suspect. Such an undertaking is merely an exercise in futility. Another equally obvious point is that too often a field of activity succumbs to the temptation to avoid the often slow and sometimes painful procedure of theoretical development, and leaps immediately into the murky waters of panacea promotion, based on unfounded suppositions, in the interest of getting something done quickly.

The inevitable fact is that the frantic scurrying of the past several decades to come up with patent remedies for accident problems has failed miserably. The public and the government now demand to have the facts about the many safety techniques, methods and procedures that have been held sacrosanct for so many years. No doubt many of them will wither in the face of close, scientific scrutiny.

It would appear that now is the time to retrace our steps and start from the beginning, by evolving theoretical formulations which can serve as a solid basis for the implementation of sophisticated safety programs, with sound research as the middle step between theory and practice.

The remainder of this text represents an attempt to identify one construct of human behavior theory, that of adjustiveness, and to relate it through theoretical formulations to safe performance, in such a manner that testable hypotheses can be derived for accident research purposes. Specification and explication of testable hypotheses, however, is not a major goal of the text. The intent is to isolate broad concepts from which hypotheses can be developed by accident researchers, safety educators and other accident prevention practitioners.

Accident Research and Accident Prevention

It has been stated (McGlade, 1962) that "traffic accident research is coming of age as a scientific endeavor . . . there is growing evidence of awareness of the traffic problem by the general public as well as private and governmental agencies . . . but such awareness has also fostered over-eagerness for immediate application of incomplete research results, a propensity for grabbing at research straws without properly assessing their merits."

This same article included the statement that "coming of age (as a scientific endeavor) brings with it all the conflicts and vicissitudes the process of maturation entails." Now, some years later, it appears that conflicts and vicissitudes are the order of the day. The pressure is greater today to acquiesce to the demands of many pressure groups calling for immediate application of panaceas to the accident problem. And these demands are not confined to traffic safety.

These demands make it tempting to take the easy way out. Within this pervading atmosphere, it is easy to consider the dearth of good accident research as a justification for ignoring it completely, and also to consider that the inordinate length of time consumed in research is sufficient reason for circumventing such research and grasping at immediately applicable straws. The suggestion presented previously bears repeating: now is the time for long-range multidisciplinary research, rather than to avoid it.

To be successful, accident research must be grounded in relevant theory, it must utilize comprehensive and accurate data, and it must involve development of appropriate operational definitions of concepts for given research purposes (McGlade and Abercrombie, 1965). At this point, it is meaningful to distinguish between *accident* research and *accident prevention* research. Accident research relates to investigation of casual factors and their interactions. Accident prevention research involves the development of countermeasures and methods and procedures for implementing these countermeasures. Accident prevention research depends heavily, though not entirely, on the quality and quantity of accident research, since knowledge of casual factors, and their interactions and their correlates in other human activities provide a parsimonious approach to designing preventive measures and evaluating their efficiency.

Therefore, thoroughgoing accident research is of primary importance, and effective accident prevention research is a logical concomitant of the former. (Complete expositions of these needs are given in McGlade, 1962; and McGlade and Abercrombie, 1965.)

Whitlock (1963) can be paraphrased at this juncture to emphasize the point: "Since the behavioral scientist is concerned with the study of behavior, for an injury to qualify as an object of inquiry for the behavioral scientist, the injury must be shown to result from human behavior. The object of interest is the 'accident behavior.' . . . The injuries the behavioral scientist can hope to predict are only those which do result from accident behaviors." Whitlock has identified one side of the behavioral coin, but the converse is equally important; i.e. the study and prediction of *safe* behavior. The remainder of this text poses the concept of adjustive behavior as being one approach to the description and prediction of safe performance.

Definition of Terms

Behavioral science research in general, and accident research in particular, seek to identify and measure the conditions which produce the behavior under study through observation of situations in which the behavior occurs frequently. Unfortunately, the selection of situations for observation is too often governed more by convenience and/or tradition than by more rational considerations. One will find among accident research reports a great variety of observed situations and operational definitions. Indeed, in many cases descriptions of the situations and operational definitions are completely lacking.

The problem of operationally defining the terms pertinent to a research project is a difficult one which confronts most disciplines within the behavioral sciences. And it is a problem which must be faced; otherwise, one is trapped in the position of conducting a research project without knowing precisely what is to be researched. At the very least, one should be able to specify in fairly sharp detail some of the behavioral components of the phenomenon under study, such as accident-related behavior, before one can even hope to extract anything of value from the investigation. In this connection, Whitehorn's comments about the study of stress are well taken and are pertinent to accident research (Whitehorn, 1953):

> If we were dealing with inanimate objects, the conceptual and terminological problem would be greatly simplified, because in physics *action and reaction are equal* (italics mine), and stress can be expressed in dynes per square centimeter; but in biology this is not so. Living organisms are specially organized to accumulate and spend energy on their own *discriminately, and not in exact equality to the forces acting upon them* (italics mine). We take this one step further and recognize the psychological factors which further influence this discriminating function and appreciate that our difficulties of description and evaluation have been geometrically expanded.

While the problem of definition may be difficult, it cannot be avoided if meaningful results are to be derived from accident research—results which will lead to effective ways to reduce accidents.

Defining an Accident

It was pointed out in the previous section that the majority of past accident research studies failed to operationally define the phenomenon under study; i.e. accidents. In most cases, researchers have assumed the implied definition inherent in the reasons for collecting the accident data. That is to say, past accident research efforts usually employed secondary data, wherein the data were originally collected for other purposes. For example, enforcement agencies collect accident data to fix legal responsibility for accidents and to identify high-accident street locations. Consequently, when such data are utilized for research purposes, the data and the definitions are biased toward the original enforcement objectives.

This distinctive feature of past accident research becomes apparent when one leafs through dozens of such reports without once coming across statements regarding definitions of terminology. Several studies have made attempts to at least confine the phenomenon of accidents by establishing broad but vague boundaries describing the reasons for including some data and excluding others from the investigation. But such studies are in the minority.

This lack of definitive treatment of the accident phenomenon is the basic reason for lack of comparability among studies which have purported to evaluate the same factors in relation to accidents. How can one reasonably expect study results to agree, when the bases for data selection in the respective investigations are considerably divergent, if not diametrically opposed? The lack of agreement from study to study has caused much consternation, yet, it has only infrequently been suggested that this might be primarily due to incomparability of basic data. Further, and more importantly, the corollary suggestion has not been made: that several studies be undertaken utilizing comparable data and the results checked for agreement.

The term *accident* is used in many contexts and with many nuances of meaning, thus creating considerable confusion about its meaning. It would appear there is little to gain in trying to come up with one definition and trying to coerce all accident researchers to accept it. Such an approach would be begging the issue.

While it is highly improbable that one definition of accident could be developed which would fit all purposes, it is essential that a relatively precise operational definition be evolved for a specific research inquiry. For example, the definition of accident will vary depending on whether one is interested in injuries, fatalities, property damage, or some combination of the three. Another major consideration is the matter of culpability: should one study the personality characteristics of persons *responsible* for accidents or persons injured in accidents? If one is interested in associating personality factors with accidents, in terms of cause-effect relationships, it makes little sense to lump accident-responsible and accident-nonresponsible injured persons together in a research project. Why study the injured passenger in the same light as the vehicle driver who is responsible for the accident? Yet this is the approach that was taken in the majority of past accident research studies.

One can go further in the development of definitive terminology for accident research, by delineating and specifying what does not constitute an accident. In one such approach (McGlade and Abercrombie, 1965) for a given research purpose, accidental events were related to normal persons who were responsible for the accidents. In this project, operational definitions were devised for normality and responsibility, which perforce excluded psychopaths, homicides, suicides, "Acts of God," and "innocent bystanders" from consideration. By identifying what is excluded from the phenomenon under study, one is setting parameters for the investigation and thereby partially carrying out the process of developing operational definitions.

One rather sophisticated accident research study (Guilford, 1965) selected an appropriate definition of "accident," from among existing definitions, before the study began. This represents the parsimonious approach, which is perfectly plausible if the selected definition is suitable to the purposes of the research project. Guilford utilized a definition developed by Arbous and Kerrich (1951): "In any chain of events, each of which is planned or controlled, there occurs an unplanned event, which, being the result of some nonadjustive act on the part of the individual (variously caused), may or may not result in injury. This is an accident."

Guilford was interested in studying the behavioral aspects of accident causation, related behaviors resulting in errors, and "near accidents," as well as injury-producing accidents. Therefore, the selected definition was valid and usable.

Kogan and Wallach (1964), in discussing possible sources of accidentally becoming involved in a war, point up the need to focus attention upon personality dispositions toward rational and irrational behavior and upon the pyschological forms these classes of behavior take: "The very definition of *accidental* implies a situation where essentially irrelevant factors have the potential for becoming dominant and determining" (italics mine). It is obviously of the utmost importance to know something about the irrelevant factors which may impinge on a research project.

Kogan and Wallach's message is significant. Past accident research has too often *presumed* certain factors to be relevant and important to accidents, and the research proceeded from those presumptions. The results of such research, based as it was on vague generalities about the questions to be studied and with no firm definitions of "accident" and other pertinent terms, have not achieved replicable conclusions. If one reversed the procedure and first developed rather precise definitions of relevant terms and then collected data in light of these definitions, it might be possible to identify the relevant from the irrelevant factors surrounding accidents.

The major points of this section are, briefly: (a) operational definitions of relevant terms, particularly of the basic term "accident," are essential to the development and conduct of research; (2) there is no single definition which will suit all research purposes, rather it is a matter of matching definitions to the specific purpose of a given research effort; and (3) the definitions should be developed first in light of the research purpose, and then data collected on the basis of the definitions.

More substantive discussions of these points are provided in excellent articles by Gibson and Suchman (Association for the

Aid of Crippled Children, 1961), and by McGlade (1962) and McGlade and Abercrombie (1965).

Defining Safe Performance

It seems reasonable to assume that if a person engages in an activity and completes it without an accident, however one chooses to define that term, he has performed successfully and safely.

But what about little, inconsequential errors or interruptions to the orderly progress of the activity? The possibility of studying mishaps or errors or unsafe behaviors or near accidents or other forms of interruption to a planned activity, by whatever label they are called, has been suggested in the past (Association for the Aid of Crippled Children, 1961; Brody, 1959). This is a noteworthy suggestion.

At this point in time, however, the suggestion is somewhat rhetorical, since there is no evidence to indicate a correlation between any of the postulated categories of interruptions and actual accidents, and operational definitions have not been developed for the events referred to by these various labels. Therefore no one knows precisely what is meant by *error,* or *mishap,* or *unsafe behavior.* Without operational definitions of these terms, the research atmosphere is no better than it has been for the past fifty years with regard to the study of accidents.

Further, such a suggestion puts one on both horns of another dilemma. Who is to say what constitutes safe or unsafe behavior? Each of us in his lifetime has experienced a situation in which fear of failure has made us reluctant to act; and while fear prevented action, another individual blithely performed the activity successfully, much to our chagrin. Can one say that the performer took unnecessary risks or that he acted unsafely? It would seem that the fear is in the mind of the beholder.

The classic example of the ambiguity of most situations which prevents one from making judgments about safeness, is presented by the remarks of Sterling Moss, a famous British race driver, when he was interviewed after winning a race against extreme odds. His car had stalled several times during the race. Each time

he would make a pit stop and have the mechanics check it. Near
the end of the race, with only a few laps to go, the race com-
mentator concluded that it was impossible for Moss to win. Yet,
he did win. He overtook the leader in those last few laps and
passed him. In an interview with newsmen after the race, Moss
was asked: "Weren't you pushing it to the hairy edge, Sterling?"
To which Mr. Moss replied: "I realized I was a little beyond the
coefficient of adhesion, but then one must consider the fact that I
am a cut above the typical race driver."

Mr. Moss' opinion about the safeness of his racing behavior is
crystal clear. To him the coefficient of adhesion is an *average*
mathematical computation, to which average men should adhere.
But this does not apply to him, since he is above average. Mr.
Moss' conclusion is inescapable, and we are coerced by the facts
to agree with him. He won the race without incident, therefore
he performed in an expeditious and safe manner. One cannot
quibble with this logic.

At any given point in time, successful performance of an activity is contingent on the inherent difficulty of the activity, the general ability level of the performer, and the *immediate* body state
of the performer. The term immediate cannot be overemphasized;
the state of the human organism at any point in time is significantly affected by temporary physical, physiological psychological, emotional and situational factors, and the organism's performance is affected accordingly. Adjustive behavior, consequently, involves awareness on the part of the performer of the
immediate state of his body and the difficulty level of the activity
he is about to perform in relation to his skill or ability to perform it.

The preceding discussion leads to the major point of this section: if a person engages in an activity and completes it successfully without an accident, however the term accident is defined,
the person has performed safely. This idea can be paraphrased by
saying that safe performance is successful completion of an activity in the absence of an accident.

The particular concern of research is to isolate and describe the
patterns of behavior which *consistently* produce safe performance, based on the definition of safeness in performance for a

given research effort. For example, there is considerable difference in the inherent risk of space travel and a game of handball;
therefore, the safety quotients of these two activities differ
markedly.

Adjustiveness is one aspect of behavior patterning. The adjustive aspects of behavior patterns in relation to safe performance
are discussed more fully in later chapters.

Defining Adjustive Behavior

Here again one is confronted with the pervading problem of
operationally defining what is referred to by the term *adjustive
behavior*. There are many terms used interchangeably with *adjustiveness*, leading to considerable ambiguity and imprecision of
meaning. Frequently used terms include adaptability, skill, ability and performance. Previous discussion highlighted some of the
subtle distinctions among these terms and further elaboration is
provided in the next chapter.

Selection of the term *adjustive* was deliberate, in perference to
the much used term *adaptive*. Webster's New World Dictionary
(1964) contains the following comments: "adapt implies a modifying so as to suit new conditions and suggests a flexibility to
adapt oneself to a new environment; . . . *adjust* describes the
bringing of things into proper or harmonious relation through the
use of skill or judgment."

Adjustiveness, therefore, goes beyond the process of simple
change and introduces the concepts of skill and judgment as they
relate to maintaining a state of harmony between the individual
and the environment. The importance of such concepts in relation
to safe performance is obvious in the dynamic, constantly fluc-
tuating driving environment; they are equally important to many
other human activities having high hazard potential. Adaptability, on the other hand, seems to cease with the actual process of
change. For example, when threatened the chameleon changes
the color of its skin; while this is adaptive, in that the skin color-
ing blends with the environment, it may or may not be adjustive.
In some situations it might be far more adjustive for the chameleon to run from the threat; i.e. beyond being adaptive, fleeing
may be a more successful adjustment to the situation.

The term *adjustive,* because of its broader connotations, will be used to describe the process of behavior modification which results in safe performance.

Following the approach of the previous sections, it should be indicated what is not meant by adjustive behavior. Connotations referring to personality adjustment are excluded; i.e. patterns of social behavior and adjustments thereto, or what one might call adjustments to a person's normal social modus operandi.

The emphasis is with adjustive behavior per se, as it relates to safe performance, rather than being concerned with prudential norms of social behavior to which socially adjusted persons rather easily conform. The major concern is with behavior that is not typical or conforming in nature and which, by that very fact, can be extremely adjustive in the avoidance of accidents. Particular interest is focused on behavioral acts immediately antecedent to an imminent accident situation; acts which are successful in avoiding the accident. Attention must also be devoted to identifying *patterns* of adjustive behavior which persons acquire through experience over time, and which they employ in hazardous situations to extricate themselves from accidents. Identification of this parsimonious approach to adjustive behavior, which some persons appear to possess, would be a boon to the teaching of basic adjustive behavior patterns which people could utilize in many situations having similar potential hazards. In this context, the primary intent is to observe and study *consistently* safe behavior, as opposed to accident-disposing or unsafe behavior.

It may well be that observation and study of behavior, within the frame of reference presented above, would yield findings having implications for research in the broader area of personality adjustment; thus generating feedback information of mutual benefit to research in both personality adjustment and adjustiveness in safe performance.

Another concept requiring clarification in relation to adjustiveness in safe performance is that of *risk.* No assumptions are made about the role of risk-taking, nor should any be inferred, in the formulations about adjustive behavior and safe performance. The complementary concepts of risk-acceptance and risk-rejection are still in the formative stages, and to date no research has been conducted on true physical risk; although there have been many studies of simulated physical risk in which, unfortunately, the subjects were aware there was no exposure to real danger and, consequently, the findings cannot be extrapolated to the real world.

Further, the question of how much risk a given person should assume when engaging in an activity is unanswerable at this point in time. What may appear risky to one person may be perfectly plausible, safe behavior to another, particularly if that person has performed the activity successfully many times. This is especially true when the *level* of performance is given primary consideration, as it should. Recall the illustration of Mr. Moss, the professional race driver; his level of performance is high, as evidenced by his many racing victories, and consequently many driving acts which seem mundane to him would be absolutely frightening and risky to the nonprofessional.

Some further comments on the concept of risk, in the form of clarification of the relationship of that concept to adjustiveness in safe performance, are given in chapter eight.

The guidelines discussed in this chapter lead to a definition of adjustive behavior in safe performance: *consistent* successful performance of an activity, in the face of possible unplanned interruptions, is *adjustive* behavior leading to safe performance.

The next several chapters tighten the precision of the definition of adjustiveness in safe performance, through elaboration of the subtle distinctions among various terms and by placing these terms in proper perspective.

Summary

This chapter has documented the undramatic but pervading extent of the Nation's accident problem which so severely wastes our human and economic resources.

The major issue is that of devising new, more productive and efficient research efforts into the accident problem. These new efforts must be based on theoretical formulations, which can serve as a basis for valid research which is more relevant to the cost/effectiveness practicalities of safety programming.

Research effort evolving from new theory must also concern

itself with the problems of developing precise operational definitions and appropriate data collection methods. It appears essential that the multidisciplinary approach be utilized in future research, in order to surmount these many problems.

The thesis of this text is that the construct of adjustiveness in behavior has utility in the study of safe performance, and will lead to research undertakings which will have practical results.

REFERENCES

Arbous, A. G., and Kerrick, J. E.: Accident statistics and the concept of accident proneness. *Biometrics*, 7:340, 1951.

Association for the Aid of Crippled Children: *Behavioral Approaches to Accident Research*, New York, The Association, 1961.

Brody, Leon: Basic Aspects and Application of the Psychology of Safety, New York, NYU, 1959.

Guilford, Joan S.: *Experimental Study of Home Accident Behavior*, Los Angeles, American Institute for Research, 1965.

Haddon, William, Suchman, Edward, and Klein, David: *Accident Research: Methods and Approaches*. New York, Harper, 1964.

Hempel, Carl: *Aspects of Scientific Explanation and Other Essays in the Philosophy of Science*. New York, Free Press, 1965.

Kogan, Nathan, and Wallach, Michael: *Risk Taking: A Study in Cognition and Personality*. New York, Holt, 1964.

McGlade, Francis: Traffic Accident Research; Review and prognosis. *Traffic Quarterly*, October 1962.

McGlade, Francis, and Laws, F. Donald: Classifying accidents: A theoretical viewpoint. *Traffic Safety Review*, 6:1, 1962.

McGlade, Francis, and Abercrombie, S. A.: Accident classification for research purposes. *Traffic Quarterly*, October, 1965.

Merton, Robert: *Social Theory and Social Structure*. New York, Free Press, 1957.

Schulzinger, M. S.: *The Accident Syndrome*. Springfield, Thomas, 1956.

Whitehorn, J. C.: Introduction and survey of the problem of stress. In *Symposium on Stress*. Washington, Army Medical Service Graduate School, 1953.

Whitlock, G. H.: Predicting accident proneness. *Personnel Psychology*, 16:35–44, 1963.

Wilson, Colin: A selection of current events. In the *National Observer*, Dec. 12, 1966.

35

THE LIFE CHANGE UNIT AND ACCIDENT BEHAVIOR

ROBERT A. ALKOV

Dr. Alkov introduces a concept which has been quantified, the "life change unit," and thereby takes some of the fuzz off the idea of accident-proneness. He explains a scheme to measure acute situational factors which may precipitate an accident "rather than attempt to identify a chronic long-term condition which may or may not exist . . ."

These situational factors, or life events (the author lists 43 of them), tax a person's capacity to cope. An accumulation of events, often a quite ordinary combination of events, can occur in the most normal life. At such times, it has been demonstrated that episodes of ill-health are likely to occur. Dr. Alkov suggests that an accident episode may also be likely.

If Dr. Alkov's suggestions were pursued and demonstrated, it should be possible "to construct a life changes factor-weighing score for each individual. This will allow us to predict, within certain probability limits, the likelihood of his being involved in a human error mishap."

HISTORICALLY, human factors analysts have concerned themselves with the determination of personal factors predisposing an individual to "accident-proneness." The accepted definition of accident-proneness referred to a stable lifelong personality trait—a chronic condition. However, investigations into the personality factors which would be correlated with accident-proneness have proven fruitless.

Lifeline, September–October, 1972. This paper was presented at the 43rd Annual Scientific Meeting of the Aerospace Medical Association in May, 1972. The author has edited it to extend its application beyond aviation to the whole naval community.

One of the difficulties was the identification of the accident-prone individual. Although it is well-known that a small percentage of workers have an inordinately large percentage of the accidents, having repeated accidents does not indicate accident-proneness. We must first know something of an individual's exposure to hazard and other factors, which along with accident-proneness, constitute a person's accident liability.

In addition to constructing a hazard exposure index for each man, we need to investigate these other factors which increase a person's accident liability. Rather than attempt to identify a chronic long-term condition which may or may not exist in our population, we might be looking at the acute situational factors which may precipitate an accident. By their nature, they are short-lived and hard to pin down. The confluence of all such factors may never have occurred before and may never occur again, but at the exact moment of the accident they interact and combine to cause a human error.

According to Willard Kerr's adjustment stress theory of accidents, the majority of accident-precipitating behavior of an individual can be explained by personal stresses which cause a man to perform in such a manner as to increase his accident liability. These stresses may be produced internally or originate from the external world and are difficult to predict because of their transitory nature.

A relationship between routine stress and diseases in man has long been sought. The practical use of the stress theory of accident and illness causation has, however, been quite limited. Factors causing stress and ability to handle it vary greatly from individual to individual. This variation makes it virtually impossible to quantify stress and to measure its effects in a statistically valid manner.

About twenty-five years ago, however, a psychiatrist, Dr. Thomas H. Holmes, now at the University of Washington, found that many diseases were caused by life events. In studies, he asked more than 5000 patients to tell about life events that preceded their illnesses. These events covered a wide range—death of a spouse, change of job, divorce, birth of a child, etc. These events were noted on the patient's health records and were referred to in later visits.

Between 1949 and 1964, thousands of tuberculosis patients were studied. These patients had experienced life crises shortly before they became ill—for example, jail terms, financial difficulties, divorces, job changes, and repeated residential moves. The life events that were most frequently cited by these patients as occurring before illness struck them were listed.

Not all of the events were negative or stress-producing—some were ordinary events of the American way of life: family events, economic events, vacations, retirement, etc. The important factor was change—desirable or undesirable—in ongoing life styles: change which would require adaptive or coping behavior.

CRD Richard Rahe, MC, USN, now at the Navy's Medical Neuropsychiatric Research Unit in San Diego, and Dr. Holmes found that illness follows a cluster of events that requires life adjustment. Each of these events which brings about a significant change in the individual's ongoing life pattern requires adaptive or coping behavior on his part.

In order to identify those life events that most frequently preceded illness, they asked 394 persons to rate the amount of social readjustment required for each of the 43 events listed most frequently by patients. By an arbitrary method, the life event given the top ranking by the judges, death of a spouse, was weighted 100 points on the scale. Using the rank order method the other weights were calculated (Table 35–I).

In a pilot study, it was found that of those persons who reported LCUs (Life Change Units) that totaled between 150 and 199 points, 37 percent had associated health changes within a two-year period of such life crises. Of those with between 200–299 LCUs, 51 percent reported health changes, and of those with over 300 LCUs, 79 percent had injuries or illnesses to report. On the average, health changes followed life crises by one year.

Dr. Rahe made a similar study of 2500 officers and enlisted men deployed aboard Navy ships. Life change data were gathered for the 6 months preceding the study. The health change data of these men were examined after they had spent six months at sea. In the first month of the cruise, the high-risk group had nearly 90 percent more first illnesses than the low-risk group. The high-risk group had more new illnesses to report each month than their fellow sailors.

TABLE 35-I

Rank	Life Event	Mean Value
1	Death of spouse	100
2	Divorce	73
3	Marital separation	65
4	Jail term	63
5	Death of close family member	63
6	Personal injury or illness	53
7	Marriage	50
8	Fired at work	47
9	Marital reconciliation	45
10	Retirement	45
11	Changes in family member's health	44
12	Pregnancy	40
13	Sex difficulties	39
14	Gain of new family member	39
15	Business readjustment	39
16	Change in financial state	38
17	Death of close friend	37
18	Change to different line of work	36
19	Change in number arguments with spouse	35
20	Mortgage over $10,000	31
21	Foreclosure of mortgage or loan	30
22	Change in work responsibilities	29
23	Son or daughter leaving home	29
24	Trouble with in-laws	29
25	Outstanding personal achievement	28
26	Wife begins or stops work	26
27	Begin or end school	26
28	Change in living conditions	25
29	Revision of personal habits	24
30	Trouble with boss	23
31	Change in work hours, conditions	20
32	Change in residence	20
33	Change in schools	20
34	Change in recreation	19
35	Change in church activities	19
36	Change in social activities	18
37	Mortgage or loan under $10,000	17
38	Change in sleeping habits	16
39	Change in number family get-togethers	15
40	Change in eating habits	15
41	Vacation	13
42	Christmas	12
43	Minor violations of the law	11

Dr. Holmes says that although reported illnesses have their own special causes, something else helps them along. This something else is what happens when a major life crisis occurs.

No particular event was linked to a particular disease. Undesirable events might bring about severe depression—the death of a spouse, for example. However, a total of life events, each not in itself especially undesirable, frequently leads to infection, allergy, and other disease. The important point was the sum—the total impact of life events which require coping behavior. When the life crisis is severe, the onset of illness is likely.

The application of these findings to accident behavior, however, has never been attempted. The knowledge that the emotionally stressed individual may be more prone to illness and accident is not new. It has long been known, for example, that overstressed individuals often engage in irrelevant activities or rigid stereotyped behavior and experience loss of discriminative skill and mental efficiency. The safe performance of complex tasks (such as those demanded in aviation, for example) is improbable in such a psychological context.

Admittedly, change is a part of the life style of the navyman. Going on military deployments or traveling across the continent, he is constantly on the move, and perhaps he is better adapted

TABLE 35-II

Life Event	Mean Value
Marital separation	65
Change in responsibility at work	29
Change in living conditions	25
Revision of personal habits	24
Change in working hours or conditions	20
Change in residence	20
Change in recreation	19
Change in social activities	18
Change in sleeping habits	16
Change in eating habits	13
TOTAL	249

than most for coping with these changes. After all, part of his reasons for being in the Navy relate to the adventure and stimulation that come from travel and change. The personality of the average career sailor demands this excitement. Certainly, he would not be in the field as a profession if he were content to hold only a nine-to-five desk job.

The life changes involved in a deployment are changes in residence, family separations, changes in working conditions, sleeping and eating habits, social activities, and personal habits in general. These kinds of changes alone can add up to almost 250 points (Table 35-II).

Their total effect may tax the navyman's ability to cope, even though he is adapted to his mobile existence. Additional stresses brought on by life crises in one's personal life may add an intolerable burden to that already imposed by the job.

Of course, each person is an individual with his own unique personality and method of handling stress. Some people are more susceptible to the effects of emotional factors than others. These changes in an individual's daily style of living and personal family matters may have little influence on his performance until they add up to an unbearable psychological burden.

It is incumbent upon those in supervisory positions to monitor and observe how turmoil in the personal lives of their men affects their performance. If this performance is being affected, the individual should be referred to a medical officer.

The knowledge that changes in one's life style, whether positive or negative, can tax a person's coping ability—should enable us to construct a life changes factor-weighting score for each individual. This will allow us to predict, within certain probability limits, the likelihood of his being involved in a human error mishap.

REFERENCES

Belkin, Mark M.: The life change unit as a stress indicator among submariners. *Bioenvironmental Safety Newsletter,* 4–71, pp. 53–55.

Holmes, T. H., and Masada, Minoru: Psychosomatic syndrome. *Psychology Today,* April 1972, pp. 71–72 and 106.

Kerr, Willard: Complementary theories of safety psychology. 45: 3–9, 1957.

Rahe, Richard H.: *Life Crisis and Health Change,* Report Number 67–4, Navy Medical Neuropsychiatric Research Unit, San Diego, California.

36

RELIABILITY AS A QUANTITATIVE SAFETY FACTOR

DAVID V. MACCOLLUM

The author suggests that the safety professional will deal more successfully with his management if he takes an approach based on the physical and mathematical sciences. "Management is interested in costs of accidents, and likelihood of their occurrence. Reliability calculations of risk factors provide a new and meaningful approach to safety."

Mr. MacCollum makes an impressive case for system safety engineering supported by reliability computations, and he asserts that the systems safety engineer must have a flair for mathematics and statistical process ". . . operational reliability is generally computed with exponential expansions; maintainability is computed in the log normal; availability (probability of being ready for use when needed) follows the F distribution; static function of storage, etc., is a binomial factor; and when only a few test samples are available, an applied binomial to exponential results is a common approach."

Whether or not a safety professional has or needs expertise in these statistical procedures, he can perceive their special beauty—a body of safety thought freed of the dominance of common sense, intuition, and semantic manipulation.

The author concedes that the path will be arduous and the mathematical processes involved. Those with limited flair for mathematics need not quail; Mr. MacCollum's message comes through clearly in the absence of mathematical expertise.

SAFETY ENGINEERS are in an age of quantification of risk appraisal, that is, being able to project risk in terms of probability. Reliability prediction provides them with mathematical statistics to evaluate safety prospects of new products, facilities and

From *Journal of American Society of Safety Engineers*, May, 1969.

systems. Application of reliability techniques can place meaningful values on the three major safety concerns—possible machine failure, unsafe man-machine interface, and undesirable human behavior; also, any combinational interaction that may result. The mathematical foundation of the reliability approach gives the safety engineer a more effective tool to predict risk.

The reliability aspect of testing for safety is a particularly complex and demanding job on electronic systems, nervous system of most present day technology. Besides complex defense and space systems, there is not one industry, whether construction, transportation, manufacturing, food processing, or even recreational, that is not dependent on electronic systems to control, direct, or monitor. Integral to this guidance function is the safety of the public.

It is not enough to assume that normal failures will result only in production stoppages. Can we afford the by-product accidents that may result? Impact of such failures are readily recognizable by the chaos that followed the massive power failure in the northeastern section of our country November 9 and 10, 1965. (Massive electric power failure blacked out most of northeastern U. S. and two Canadian provinces. About 80,000 square miles with a population of 30 million were affected. In New York City over 800,000 people were trapped in subways for hours.)

A major problem facing industry, the government, and particularly our space efforts is the high cost of replacing equipment and facilities damaged as a result of accidental causes, not forgetting the human suffering that accompanies these disasters. To combat these losses, a new technical facet of safety known as systems safety engineering, is emerging. It is a professional approach to solving accident-producing problems, and is the application of scientific and engineering principles to control hazards. Its findings are based upon mathematical evaluations so that probabilities of failures (accidents) can be predicted. The advent of the systems and mathematical approach heralds the future of safety as a consultive function to top-level management.

The scientific approach will free the safety professional from reliance on intuitive processes, from the role of the enforcer of petty (unqualified) safety rules, and make him a technical consultant with the same status as a legal advisor or a physician. System safety is, however, still in the rudimentary stage, evolving primarily in the aerospace and electronics community. It presupposes that the overall cost the consumer would have to bear as a result of accidents, can be substantially reduced by allocating funds for a systematic approach to identify all possible hazards during the design and test stages. Then by a process of assigning values to the various failure modes he can project the likelihood of accident-producing incidents. From there, it is a cost analysis for managerial decision-makers to determine where the tradeoff for safety will be made.

In the last decade, experience has shown that by qualifying risk, it has made it easier for management to provide funds for safety. Previously, when dealing with unknowns, management has been reluctant to authorize money for safety modifications. The system technique with reliability factors has shown that hazards can be effectively identified, controlled, and measured without the need of costly accidents to highlight problem areas. System safety supported by reliability computations still requires much positive demonstration by the safety engineers, before it will gain full acceptance and support by top management. Safety still is a term which normally has somewhat unacceptable connotations for most managers.

Professionally, we have been guilty of trying to dress up "safety" with the words, "engineering," "management" and now, "systems." Management groups still have a preconceived categorization that "safety" is something pseudotechnical, in a negative world of "hard hats," "no smoking," and "nit-picking inspectors." This is also supported by lack of safety-design criteria as a measurable requirement. In its place is a maze of "motherhood" statements giving a generalized concept that equipment shall be "intrinsically safe," and codes and specifications having trite statements such as: "suitable safeguards shall be incorporated to provide adequate safety during operation," or "suitable safeguards shall be incorporated to assure adequate freedom from all unacceptable potential hazards." This places safety in a nondefinitive category that precludes positive assessment of compliance.

Management's concept that safety is everybody's business has made it nobody's specific responsibility and has far too often become the road to product-liability lawsuits. Until these handicaps are overcome by sound engineering procedures, safety will never achieve its rightful respect from the other technical professions as a competent protector of man and property. Briefly, system safety engineering must be supported by reliability studies, and include the following concepts: a life-cycle concern unaffected by organizational structure; application of appropriate engineering disciplines; and a technical information-gathering function only for top-management decision-makers.

There are many pitfalls in the use of mathematical techniques to determine probability of accident-producing failures. Some of the most common traps in which we find ourselves when making safety studies are summarized here:

A. Inadequate mathematical foresight can lead to the conclusion that a machine with 100 components in series, each 99 percent reliable, is really only 36 percent reliable; if the machine has 400 components in series, it is only 2 percent reliable; if it ever works at all it is more luck than anything else. In practice, the eventuality of a catastrophic accident is not as inevitably hopeless as the example of a machine with 400 series components. Assumptions applied to this circumstance were: (1) failure of any one component will cause the system to fail; (2) failure of any component is independent of any other components' failure. Yet a machine with many components (parts) is not likely to fail every time any one part fails. Failure of any or many of the parts will cause only reduced level of performance, rather than complete breakdown. So, when applying theory to the impact of individual failure of parts to a machine, it cannot be analyzed by an unknowledgeable safety specialist.

B. Juggling of figures is somewhat commonplace, and knowledge of statistics is needed to avoid hazards in this old wive's tale: A manufacturer does not desire to comply with reliability requirements of his contract for some specialized electronic equipment. He reluctantly sets aside 10 samples of his product for test. The test is run and five samples fail. To avoid trouble with acceptance tests, he hires a statistician to compile results into a favorable report. The statistician uses a table of 50 percent confidence limits for the binomial distribution, showing reliability of the equipment at least 45 percent. His report, minus actual test data, is sent to the buyer's purchasing agent, Mr. Jones. It states only that the item is 45 percent reliable with 50 percent confidence. Mr. Jones has this conversation with his secretary.

Mr. Jones: "Sally, this equipment is apparently 45 percent reliable, but I don't know what they mean by 50 percent confidence."

Sally: "I think it means he is in error 50 percent of the time."

Mr. Jones: "If their statistician doesn't trust his work 50 percent of the time, they should hire someone who doesn't make so many mistakes."

Sally: "Maybe we should send it back and ask for more tests, and maybe they won't make so many mistakes."

Mr. Jones: "Write a letter to that effect."

The manufacturer, when he received the letter, decided not to give up easily, and hired a reliability expert, who had the samples repaired and retested. Two failed, and the other eight, with great stretch of the imagination, passed. Now the expert reasoned he had 20 samples with 13 successes and 7 failures. He also referred to the same table of 50 percent percentage points for binomial distribution, and found his reliability was now at least 48 percent with 50 percent confidence. He reported reliability as 48 percent, not mentioning confidence level or test data.

The false logic is that reliability studies cannot be made without failures, so the more failures the better. If the initial test had 10 successes, reliability could have been stated as 94 percent for this binomial distribution table, with 50 percent confidence. With such mathematical juggling, it is imperative that the safety engineer have a sound knowledge of statistical methods before entering this field.

C. Accuracy of reliability predictions depends on mathematical models and available data, the latter most often a limiting factor. When data inadequacies exist, uncertainties will result in the predictions. When data is unavailable, a Bayesian approach is often taken by applying judgment, beliefs, knowledge, and so on, into the calculations. This should warn that Bayes' doctrine of chance should be applied only to solution of safety problems with extreme caution.

D. Caution should be directed to safety standards as a basis to postulate controls that will prevent accidents by assuming that compliance with the standard will preclude a failure mode. Far too often these industry standards are guides to assure the particular industry the maximum return for the minimum capital outlay, without consideration of all possible accident causes. The National Electrical Safety Code is a classic example. It provides for safety of the utility lineman, but has only "motherhood" statements concerning public safety. Guarding, to preclude access to a transformer bank mounted on an H-frame by a child attempting to retrieve a kite, is nil. Another example is the manufacture and sale of unvented gas heaters of less than 50,000 BTU inferred as safe, while it is known that they will cause asphyxiation in a closed room. The tractor-manufacturing industry (both crawler and wheel) generally avoids standards for roll-over protection for the operator. This range of examples is to illustrate that "safety standards" are invalid bases for total safety concepts. The safety engineer using the reliability technique to support his systems analysis must consider established standards as inadequate when considering an entire systems safety effectiveness.

E. Next is the trap we fall into when making determinations of acceptable risks, which are variable in themselves. For example: A picnic is planned for next Sunday, if it doesn't rain. The weatherman predicts a chance of one in a hundred that it will. The normal planner sees this as an acceptable risk and proceeds with the picnic. But if we are designing nuclear warheads, and physicists tell us a design weakness will cause premature detonation at the rate of one in a thousand, we all view this as an unacceptable risk, because of severe consequences of a nuclear blast. The mathematical and statistical risk-rating function of reliability techniques makes systems safety analysis workable. Reliability is a function of time, conditions of use, and environment. This data is combined with the systems analysis, which considers the worst possible event and makes a comprehensive examination to determine if it can occur under any combination of circumstances. Often this technique is referred to as the fault-tree analysis, which is only a graphic representation of parallel and/or sequential combinations of component states that will result in the worst possible event, or any other undesired events.

F. We also need to examine those events considered to be undesirable. Unfortunately, our initial thoughts are often on the spectacular, such as the death of an astronaut or bridge collapse, or other newsworthy accidents considered to be the result of a gross hazard; while many injuries and deaths of maintenance and operational personnel over a long period are often callously viewed as inconsequential.

G. Because it is man's nature to err, "accidents" can be considered as natural phenomena. "Accidents" will occur if the proper conditions exist, and/or inappropriate behavior is involved. Investigations often reveal gross design omissions as causative factors, which has produced a "blame-placing syndrome" at management level. This management failure has made safety such a disagreeable subject that there has been little incentive for engineers to suggest "logic" and "reliability" studies on new designs to identify accident-producing events. Further, because of this psychological block, there is an inadequate information retrieval system to provide sound basis for avoiding old errors in new designs.

Let us consider the sequence of undesirable events which might surround the loss of a large passenger aircraft as an example of how systems safety is made to work with reliability mathematics. Included in the design of a new aircraft is a horizontal stabilizer taken from the design of an older craft of comparable size. It is operated by an electric switch that controls a reversible electric motor that turns a worm gear that moves a screw jack that forces the stabilizer down or back to level position, depending on the direction in which the worm gear rotates. There is also a manual trim wheel between the pilot's and co-pilot's seat, which accomplishes the trim via the horizontal stabilizer. It is known that the pilots cannot override the electric motor to the worm gear with the manual trim wheel.

Logic analysis showed a critical hazard existed. It was reasoned that if the electric switch to the motor for the horizontal stabilizer were to fail in the depress mode, the craft would be placed in an outside loop, and would crash. This would take only one or two minutes. The pilots would have almost no time to save themselves from catastrophe by finding the circuit breaker and throwing it open. The mechanics of this hazard are simple. The surface of the horizontal stabilizer is very large as compared to elevator surface. The pilots have only a short time to control the aircraft, because the authority of the stabilizer soon exceeds the correction that can be made by the elevator. Therefore, the aircraft is placed quickly in an irreversible outside loop, and then to destruction. The switch is a good example of inadequate safety design.

The designers of the horizontal stabilizer of the earlier aircraft only considered failure of the electric motor, by providing a manual trim as part of the stabilizer. They did not recognize the consequences of the switch failing in a closed position, which would depress the stabilizer, in reality the "worst possible event." Suppose the accident experience of the earlier aircraft included the loss of two planes over the ocean shortly after changing elevation. No investigation would be possible to reveal switch failure because the wreckage could never be recovered. This failure in a closed position could have been the cause.

With an example of a probable accident analysis that could result from an undesired event (such as a switch failing in a closed position,) we can apply some terminology, and develop a fault tree analysis. Logic symbols are used to adapt the analysis to a graphic presentation. The basic symbols include:

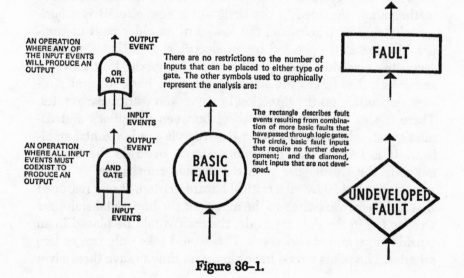

AN OPERATION WHERE ANY OF THE INPUT EVENTS WILL PRODUCE AN OUTPUT

OUTPUT EVENT

OR GATE

INPUT EVENTS

There are no restrictions to the number of inputs that can be placed to either type of gate. The other symbols used to graphically represent the analysis are:

AN OPERATION WHERE ALL INPUT EVENTS MUST COEXIST TO PRODUCE AN OUTPUT

OUTPUT EVENT

AND GATE

INPUT EVENTS

BASIC FAULT

The rectangle describes fault events resulting from combination of more basic faults that have passed through logic gates. The circle, basic fault inputs that require no further development; and the diamond, fault inputs that are not developed.

FAULT

UNDEVELOPED FAULT

Figure 36–1.

A simplified fault tree for the trim system can now be graphically illustrated as shown in Figure 36–2.

The fault tree graphically charts the route that an undesirable event can take to cause catastrophe. It presents clearly a number of choices to the designer where the cycle can be interrupted for the insertion of a safety device that can make the system fail-safe. Caution dictates that a new fault tree should be graphed to show the added safety device to assure that no new hazards are introduced into the system.

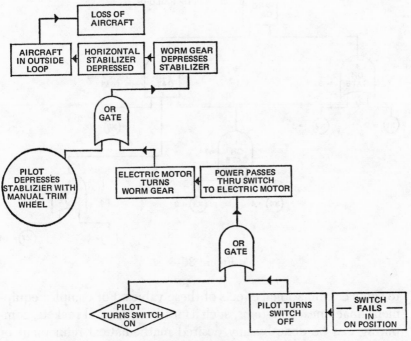

Figure 36–2.

With the sequence of undesirable events shown schematically, risk of accidents can be assessed in meaningful values, i.e. one in a hundred, one in a million, and so on. Likelihood of an accident must be synthesized to determine if management can live with this risk of failure, or can support the cost of design changes to overcome the hazard. With such information available, decisions can be made based on knowledge of the possible mode of the undesired event, likelihood of it occurring, and cost of eliminating this event with which they feel they cannot live.

The safety engineer's ability to assign reliability values of component parts to the fault tree logic format now affords top management an overview of how "safe" the design is, because it includes a basis of determining an acceptable or unacceptable risk.

Boolean algebra is used to express symbolically the fault tree in terms of inputs. These algebraic expressions can be simplified

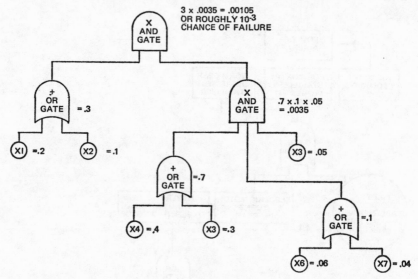

Figure 36–3.

to show combinational effects of these values. For complex equipment, machines or systems, such as intercontinental rockets, computing can be done by any desired mathematical refinement or application, i.e. Monte Carlo, Bayes' formula and the like; these can be mocked up for machine solution by a computer.

A simplified version of determining the chance of accident is shown in Figure 36–3.

The biggest value of this systematized approach is that it affords the safety department a means to identify and quantify hazards during the design period. Corrections on the drawing table are negligible as compared to costly change orders during construction or fabrication. Testing agencies can also make good use of the fault-tree and reliability analysis to assess the existence and probability of all possible undesirable events that can result in a serious accident. Test agencies should develop their own fault-tree graphs as a test of the developers' analysis. A mere review of the developers' fault tree can lead to prejudiced thinking rather than unbiased logic.

Prior to this symbolized approach to safety engineering analysis, our accident prevention methods have been largely dependent on deductive and intuitive processes to identify hazards. As long as we stayed with simple devices, we have been fortunate in recognizing most of the hazards. However, as design becomes involved in more complex mechanisms, the probability of overlooking the latent hazards is steadily increasing, unless the safety profession adopts a scientific approach.

Preliminary system studies can give safety engineers a cut-out of the system, and fault-tree analysis can be applied where detail is required. These technical reviews will smoke out hazards, such as the example of a switch failing in a closed position and over-trimming the aircraft into a crash configuration.

In areas of severe hazards and risks which have horrendous consequences, the Markov processes can be followed to consider all the effects from all interaction of all possible failures within a complex system or subcomponent.

It can now be recognized that with reliability and systems studies, the safety engineer can provide a safety warranty of new products. His aid will also be valued in design review of new facilities for exclusion of all possible hazards in construction and operation cycle. Mathematical reliability approach can provide insight in replacement cycles of critical parts subject to failure. For example, spurious X-ray emission can occur in radio tubes operating with high-plate voltages. This phenomenon often does not become apparent until the tube has been in service several thousand hours. Testing will show which tubes will fail and when, and cause x-radiation. The reliability approach can then predict a safe tube-change cycle to preclude this type of failure. It is easy to see how a change in maintenance instructions to replace the potentially dangerous tube every 1,000 hours rather than its normal 5,000-hour life, can eliminate a hazard and avoid costly redesign of an expensive radar transmitter. Uses of reliability to provide safety insight have almost unlimited possibilities as extension of testing, and for predicting environmental changes, human performance, and even undesirable human behavior.

We now have a methodology to give management a comprehensive safety appraisal of new products, facilities, and systems. The question now is: How can we make this transition? The answer is obvious: We need individuals with a background in systems and knowledge of computer language, so they can develop safety studies of complex systems for machine solution. The system safety engineer must have a flair for mathematics and statistical processes. (In electronics, operational reliability is generally computed with exponential expansions; maintainability is computed in the log normal; availability (probability of being ready for use when needed) follows the F distribution; static function of storage, etc., is a binomial factor; and when only a few test samples are available, an applied binomial to exponential results is a common approach.) The course we must take to fulfill today's requirements for technical safety will be arduous; the mathematical processes are involved and will be different for each discipline of engineering.

The safety manager can no longer exist without technical knowledge. He must be able to conduct his own logic analysis to assure that the design engineer, proficient only in his specialty, is not making a dangerous oversight when it comes to safety. As safety people, we must recognize that today's engineer is normally hired for his specialized knowledge. His talents are directed toward designing a high-performance system. His safety knowledge is limited to his own subsystem and perhaps a safe interface to adjoining parts. Because of his specialization, his safety overview is limited, particularly where many engineering disciplines are involved in the entire system. Therefore, the design engineer needs the help of a special type of professional engineer—one with thorough knowledge of safety, who can participate as a member of the design team and can systematically analyze the system for unsafe conditions.

Management is interested in costs from accidents, and likelihood of their occurrence. Reliability calculations of risk factors provide a new and meaningful approach to safety. The safety profession, as it earns its respect with valid predictions, will become a prestige occupation. This is the service the safety engineer must fulfill in today's technology. Results cannot help but be successful, as we become professional and knowledgeable in our discipline. A better image awaits us, and with it, better salaries as we take a professional approach, based on the physical and mathematical sciences.

37

THE FAMILY APPROACH

WILLIAM G. JOHNSON

Many times it has been said that the family is the major influence in developing safety attitudes. The National Safety Council has long made the family a "safety target" and the author of this selection is a former General Manager of the organization. His contribution is basic to an understanding of the roots of safety influence, the family as "a major center of accident prevention responsibility and activity."

It is not surprising that the chapter was originally intended as a chapter in a book on accident prevention for physicians and public health workers. Few outsiders have more influence on the family.

Mr. Johnson continually emphasizes the do's instead of the don'ts, the right way instead of negative suggestions, and the pleasure of accomplishment instead of the threat of removal. These principles, essential for a safe growth to maturity, are just as vital in developing safety attitudes in business and industry. The relationship is generally well understood. Witness the emphasis on off-the-job safety in industry.

Unfortunately, our good understanding of the family role in safety is not paralleled by any great mass of families marching to a better life through development of safety attitudes. Once again we recognize a problem but cannot vouch for specific solutions.

TO THE ACCIDENT PREVENTION SPECIALIST the family is of primary service in attaining two major accident prevention objectives—dissemination of information and the development of habits and attitudes which will result in the safe behavior of all

Revised and updated, 1973, by Phil Dykstra, National Safety Council. Originally published in *Accident Prevention,* The Role of Physicians and Public Health Workers, Maxwell N. Halsey, Editor. McGraw-Hill, 1961. At the time of writing, the author was General Manager of the National Safety Council.

family members. The family is the origin of constructive motivations and is a continuing educational and developmental experience. *Most important, the family is a major center of accident prevention responsibility and activity.*

There is ample proof of the role of the family as a key group in communicating ideas and effecting measurable changes in attitudes and behavior (Katz and Lazarfeld, 1955). The rich potential of family life for improving safety behavior is clear.

The sentiments associated with family life are a powerful motivation for protection and safety training. However, these motivating forces are frequently in need of guidance if we are to avoid such problems as overprotection, unwarranted fears, and other personal maladjustments.

Many safety specialists are becoming aware of past underemphasis of family approaches to safety. Safety is most often presented as a highly specific topic in terms of particular classes for drivers, pedestrians, or workers. Seldom is specific subject matter presented so that it encourages good safety habits as a normal, logical part of good family life. We may fail to present safety topics in ways which will encourage intrafamily sharing of experience and collective learning.

We need to know a great deal more about accident-producing factors in relation to family situations. Since there is also an acute need for research in all areas having to do with children and family life, the opportunities for meaningful research on accidents in the family situation should be increasingly recognized.

However, health and medical workers who have daily opportunities to influence families must use those opportunities now. What we now know, plus conclusions developed from clinical observation, can undoubtedly point the way toward greater family safety.

The Tennessee Valley Authority expressed its justification of good temporary family housing for construction employees at remote dam sites with the slogan, "Happy workers lower the cost of concrete." TVA and other work studies have also shown: "Safe workers lower the cost of concrete." A happiness—safety relationship on the job and off the job can hardly be escaped.

The Family Has Accidents

Family members are involved in many serious accidents. In a serious accident there may well be questions about the value of the accident in creating a teachable moment, or the teaching may come too late! However, the annual 30 million medically attended accident injuries which are not bed-disabling indicate the opportunities for medical personnel to do effective accident prevention work. The National Health Survey indicates that among these 30 million injuries, almost 13 million are home injuries which could be expected to most readily provide opportunity for family safety work.

Richardson (1945) wrote:

> The individual is a part of the family, in illness as well as in health—the idea of disease as an entity which is limited to one person—fades into the background, and disease becomes an integral part of the continuous process of living. The family is the unit of illness, because it is the unit of living.
>
> Some of the factors which have been recognized by the medical profession in relation to disease also relate to accidents. Socioeconomic, physiologic, psychologic, and other aspects of family life established bases on which to deal with accident prevention.

Dunn and Gilbert (1956) stated:

> It is small wonder that the family drama and crises have a profound effect on the course of health and disease. Fifty years ago the family was the center of medical practice, as suggested in the old revealing term, family practitioner. Before the era of specialization the family doctor had a more intimate knowledge of all the family members, of their incomes and ambitions, of the subtle ways in which the family members reacted to each other. In treating each of his families, he could call on a store of firsthand social, economic, and cultural data, mostly unrecorded on the medical history, and apply this knowledge both to diagnosis and therapy. With the advance of medical science, the family doctor gave way to the specialist who rarely or never saw the patient in the family setting. Public health was devoted to preventing disease in the community at large, particularly through sanitary control of water, milk, and insects.

Today it may be more important for the health worker to suggest oil space-heater maintenance or learn-to-swim classes than to present traditional health advice.

The Family Should Understand Accident Prevention

A better understanding of the philosophy of accident prevention is more important than a barrage of do's and don't's to tax the memory. The creed of the National Safety Council says:

> Safety is positive. It is doing things the right way. It is interest in the welfare of others. It is a contribution to good living, to good government and respect for law and order, to efficient production, and to the well-being of every individual.

The belief that accidents can be prevented is a twentieth century concept, a relative infant in the family of great ideas. Stewart Holbrook's *Let Them Live* (1958) is recommended reading for those who forget how far we have come in a half-century. Holbrook realistically narrates the story of the mine and maritime disasters; accidents caused by unguarded machinery; forest, theater, and even citywide fires; railway disasters; floods; and poisonings, which gave birth to the safety movement. When we contrast the all-encompassing requirements for accident prevention with the short time a cogent philosophy of accident prevention has existed, the need for massive educational efforts is clear.

We must try to educate families that accident analysis or discussion is not for the purpose of fixing "blame," but rather for the purpose of finding out what must be done to prevent the recurrence of a similar accident. Also, the near-accident is a much more frequent (and less painful) symptom of future trouble and provides a rewarding opportunity for analysis and preventive adjustment. The finding that two thirds to three fourths of respondents were surprised by accidents, when coupled with the information that the average family member may have as many as six accidents per year, would point to gross lack of analysis and interpretation of previous experiences (Velz and Hemphill, 1953).

Relatively simple analysis of experiences will lead to preventive steps. When a family accident record was maintained by 114 families in Richland County, Ohio, the rate of injuries dropped 70 percent in 16 weeks! (White House Conference, 1960).

Perhaps most important would be development of the habit of correcting hazards *before* the accident happens. The finding that a majority of respondents were surprised by accidents is one side of a coin, the reverse of which has implications for safety. Respondents who said, "Expected it to happen," "Always happens," and "Expected of Children" were obviously not correcting hazards.

Doctor Karl Menninger stated that the former notion of accident proneness as a constant factor is old-fashioned (Safety in the 60's, 1959). Today, we would rather say that accident proneness is something that all of us may experience. Some people do have more susceptibility than others, and all of us have more at one time than another. Recognition of this can help a mother protect the members of her family as well as give her insight into her own varying accident potential. As a specific example, a housewife should understand the accident prevention values of a pleasant breakfast before her husband and the children leave for their work. Anger or worry are poor preparation for a safe day.

Brody gives a composite portrait of accident repeaters (1959), not in terms of lack of knowledge, skill, or psychophysical ability, but in terms such as distractible, less personal restraint, impulsive, takes risks, asocial or antisocial, aggressive, nonconforming, intolerant, emotionally unstable, lacks insight, needs to feel and act superior, and is insecure. He hypothesizes that "the accident repeater (or potential repeater) is not merely an accident-involved individual but, rather, a class of maladjustment of which one symptom is accident involvement."

Brody goes on to say, "personal problems affect nearly all individuals daily. Under certain conditions such stress may result in temporary accident proneness." Hurry or excitement were noted as factors in almost one fifth of home injuries (Velz and Hemphill, 1953).

If one or more family members have been convinced that *accidents can be prevented* their reactions and adjustments to situations with abnormal accident potentials not only may have important safety results, but also may make a contribution to healthier attitudes for the entire family.

Risk-taking is an inevitable part of living. Insofar as risk-taking is a conscious weighing of risks versus gains the common sense outcome will be enhanced safety consistent with over-all goals. Knowledge of real hazards is a requirement for intelligent risk.

More successful family approaches to accident prevention may be no more difficult than consistent use of the ancient deliberative questions:

What? . . . a new product? a new activity?

How? . . . what was he trying to do?

Who? . . . was he trained? was he angry? was he drunk?

Where? . . . a familiar product or activity in a new place?

When? . . . was he tired? was he alone?

Why? . . . did he plan? did he play the "law of averages?" was his mind preoccupied? did he hurry?

The Family Grows

The accident prevention problems of a family change as the family grows and develops. In 1969, accidents killed 2,425 children under one year of age and 4,548 children one to four years of age. Accidents were the leading cause of death in the one- to four-year group, totaling more than the next two causes combined. While accidental death rates in the one- to four-year group are less than half as high as they were forty to sixty years ago, the incidence of childhood diseases has dropped far more. Accidents in recent years accounted for 37 percent of all deaths in the one- to four-year group (National Center for Health Statistics).

Of the preschool children who suffer nonfatal accidents, two studies indicate that between 30,000 and 40,000 children become permanently crippled or disabled.

More than half of fatal accidents and two thirds of nonfatal accidents to children under 5 occur at home. The boy-girl ratios for fatal accidents are: 1.2:1, under one year; and 1.4:1, from one to four years. The National Health Survey estimated a nonfatal accident ratio of 1.2:1 for children under six; but some special studies have shown even higher ratios for boys.

INFANTS UNDER ONE YEAR OF AGE. Major causes of death are suffocation, motor vehicle, and fire. Leading causes of injury are falls, hot substances, foreign bodies, and motor vehicles.

INFANCY. Poisoning becomes an important problem at this age

since the exploring toddler is beginning to get into trouble. Significant to this phase of safety is the development in major cities of the poison control centers which are equipped to give immediate information to physicians on the chemical composition of a great many proprietary drugs and patented toxic household chemicals and the specific antidote when known. This has been promoted particularly by the American Public Health Association, the National Safety Council, the American Medical Association, the American Academy of Pediatrics, American Pharmaceutical Association, and American Association of Poison Control Centers.

The poison control centers receive their technical information services from the U. S. Public Health Service (White House Conference, 1960).

PRESCHOOL CHILDREN, ONE TO FOUR YEARS OF AGE. Causes of death: motor vehicle, fire, drowning, and poisons. Causes of injury: falls, poisons, cuts, and motor vehicles.

SCHOOL CHILDREN. In 1969 accidents killed 4,050 children five to nine years of age and 4,136 ages ten to fourteen (National Center for Health Statistics).

Accidents accounted for nearly half of all deaths for ages five to fourteen and were by far the leading cause of death (National Center for Health Statistics).

The boy-girl ratios for fatal accidents were: five to nine years, 1.8:1; ten to fourteen years, 2.9:1 (National Center for Health Statistics).

SCHOOL CHILDREN, FIVE TO NINE YEARS OF AGE. Causes of death: motor vehicles, drowning, firearms, fire. Causes of injury: falls, cuts, falling objects, motor vehicles.

SCHOOL CHILDREN, TEN TO FOURTEEN YEARS OF AGE. Causes of death: motor vehicle, drowning, firearms, fire. Causes of injury: falls, cuts, animal or insect, athletics.

YOUTH, FIFTEEN TO TWENTY-FOUR YEARS OF AGE. Fatal accident rates in the fifteen- to twenty-four-year groups are more than triple those of the school child group. This is due essentially to a higher incidence of motor vehicle accidents. Since nonfatal injury rates for youth are substantially lower than those of children, we see a reflection of the severity of the motor vehicle accident in which they are involved.

In 1969 accidental deaths totaled 12,505 for the fifteen- to nineteen-year group and 12,163 for those twenty to twenty-four (National Center for Health Statistics).

The boy-girl ratios are noteworthy:

Fatals 15–19	3.5:1
Fatals 20–24	4.8:1

Again, accidents are the leading cause of death, reflecting gains in control over diseases which formerly exceeded accidents in fatal results. Accidents account for over half the deaths in the fifteen to twenty-four-year group, and more than one third of all motor vehicle injuries occur in these ten years of youth.

Causes of death: motor vehicles (two thirds of all), drowning, firearms, poisons. Causes of injury: falls, cuts, athletics, motor vehicles.

Any discussion of accidents in the fifteen- to twenty-four-year group centers around motor vehicle accidents, largely to boys. Here we draw upon the fine review prepared by McFarland and Moore for the 1960 White House Conference on Children and Youth.

In this presentation an attempt has been made to indicate the role of the automobile in American culture, with particular reference to adolescents and young adults. It was shown that the vast majority of young persons in the United States have become drivers during their late teen years. The influence of the automobile on the behavioral and cultural patterns of youth was reviewed.

Problem areas, in regard to the use of the automobile, included school adjustment, social adjustment and delinquency. The question of safety was shown to be of great significance in youthful drivers. The data on automobile accidents showed a high incidence of injuries and deaths in the younger age ranges. Youthful drivers as a group were also shown to have disproportionately high accident rates. The high accident rates in youth have usually been attributed to inexperience and lack of training, but in recent years there has been growing evidence of the influence of attitude and personal adjustment on one's behavior in driving.

Several studies of adult and youthful accident-repeater drivers were reviewed for their implications regarding the improvement of the safety record and especially the quality of driving by the teenage group. It was also pointed out that there is very little information available on the effectiveness of the various measures employed in an attempt to improve safety. The need for research to supply factual information was stressed throughout. Such factual information is required for the design of effective educative, corrective, and rehabilitative measures in regard to the use of the automobile by youth.

Were it not for the extremely high motor vehicle death total, drownings, and firearm accidents to boys in the fifteen- to nineteen-year group would receive considerable attention. These types of accidents drop in significance in the twenty to twenty-four-year group.

In recent years accidents involving boats and water skiing have been a concern in the fifteen- to twenty-four-year group.

Some child and youth authorities have suggested that the so-called "revolt of youth," which appears in accident studies, may be almost equally described as "abdication of parents."

Do parents understand that they are faced, not with relinquishing their authority, but with a choice of authorities: (1) parental authority; (2) youth authority (responsibility); (3) governmental authority; and (4) natural laws.

In other words, parents may relinquish (1) parental authority. However, if (2) youth responsibility is not well developed, and if (3) governmental authority is undermanned to catch misbehavior, then (4) natural laws will have their inevitable, and sometimes tragic, results.

Parents actually face the relatively simple job of *when* to transfer authority. They should stay ahead of the game. As rapidly as a youth shows responsible handling of one authority, his parents must help and urge him to get ready for the next step in self-control.

Recently, the son of a chemistry teacher was killed in a rocket construction he undertook contrary to parental instruction and after his parents had left the home. Knowledge of hazards is not sufficient for a parent. Knowledge of children and adequate control is important.

When dealing with the motor vehicle category we find it to be a composite of dissimilar types of accidents: pedestrian and bicycle versus others. In the first two, preschool and school children have active roles; in the latter, passive roles. The teen and young-adult group, as drivers (and often as passengers with young drivers), have active roles in nonpedestrian accident situations. Using age groups standard in police summaries we find the following classification within the motor vehicle category (Accident Facts, 1973):

	0 to 4 Years		5 to 14 Years		15 to 24 Years	
	Deaths	Injuries	Deaths	Injuries	Deaths	Injuries
Pedestrian	42%	13%	48%	24%	8%	2%
Bicycle	1	2	13	13	2	1
Other	57	85	39	63	90	97

YOUNG MARRIEDS, BEFORE CHILDREN. Opportunities for safety training will not be numerous as the newly married young adults establish their independence even though safety needs may be great. Perhaps counteraction against the cult of romance, unrealism at its worst, will help foster sounder approaches to accident potentials. Five areas suggest themselves as possible openings for constructive approaches:

1. Different family backgrounds may cause conflicts indirectly related to accident situations. That is, a conflict of ideas on discipline, male role, family discussion, and happiness may be involved in unsafe behavior.

2. Establishing a household with concepts of efficiency and safety in equipment and arrangement.

3. Participation in new types of activity such as skiing, water skiing, and sports in which one or both partners may be a novice and need coaching and practice as a beginner.

4. Preparation for children by beginning of strongly motivated safety mindedness.

5. "Shortly after establishing a family and becoming stable members of the community, young couples may confront the health problems of the aging" (White House Conference, 1960). The extremely high accidental death rates of older persons and the causes thereof may be proper concern of young folks.

MATURE PERSONS. Safety interest of matured couples with married children is naturally centered on their grandchildren. The matter of safety training itself is likely to reveal differences in child-training concepts from one generation to another. Grand-parents may alternately overprotect and spoil, laying groundwork for undue fears and inadequate control by parents. However, the magazine cartoonist may do a lot more to show the results of mother-in-law's best intentions than the health educator.

Mature persons have their own safety concerns. Skills in driving and active sports will wane and require compensating adjustment. Falls begin to rise as a type of fatal accident.

AGED. Accidents result in about 28,000 deaths annually among persons 65 and over. About one quarter of all fatal accidents occur to people in this age group, which includes about 10 percent of the population (National Center for Health Statistics). Falls, motor vehicle accidents, fire, and suffocation by ingested object together cause about 85 percent of these deaths. No other specific cause contributes more than 2 percent of the total.

Almost 75 percent of all fatal falls, about a fourth of the motor vehicle pedestrian deaths, and more than a quarter of all deaths from fire occur among older persons. More than one third of fatal accidents occur at home.

More than 4 million persons sixty-five and over are injured each year according to the National Health Survey. About two thirds of these injuries occur at home.

By age sixty-five, falls outrank motor vehicles as the No. 1 accident killer. Over 75 years of age, 75 percent of all accidental deaths occur from falls.

INJURY RATES IN A LIFE CYCLE. The male rate is high, rises to a peak at school age, and then steadily declines. The female rate is remarkably constant until retirement. Further study of specific activities and age variations within these categories is needed.

The Family and Safety Education

Families with children under 6 years of age were estimated to total 13.9 million in 1970; this represents approximately one-fourth of all families. Because of strong motivations and the new problems they are encountering, this group provides the greatest opportunity for family safety education. For many of these parents this will be the first conscious seeking for safety.

Suchman and Scherzer (1960) have compiled an excellent review of research in childhood accidents. The review discusses physical factors such as age, sex, strength, growth, and development; mental factors, emotional factors; and personality traits. With regard to the latter, they say, "Definite personality characteristics and emotional factors are usually found to be associated with the child who has accidents. Unfortunately, however, the findings of various studies often conflict." The review concludes the background of the child by considering habits and activities and social factors.

The section on the family background summarizes available data on race, religion, socioeconomic status, family composition, child-rearing practices, and living conditions.

Dietrick (1956) stated:

> First, it is necessary to convince parents that accidents are the most important physical threat that confronts their children. This should be done calmly, objectively, and convincingly. Fear and horror should not be used as tools of persuasion . . . Permit parents under intelligent guidance, to develop their rightful role as protectors and providers for their children's safety. Specifically, in the field of teaching parents the importance and the feasibility of accident prevention for their children, we must convey the assurance that this is a project that is their special privilege and responsibility. Most importantly this must be done in such a fashion that each parent will realize that it is an undertaking that is well within the range of his capabilities. It must not be made a frightening or an impossible task. . . .
>
> The education of young children in safe behavior is in no way different in technique from their education in any other remote or allied field. Their instruction must proceed in a graded step by step manner at such a pace as to present the likelihood of success (comprehensive and achievement), and be frequently illuminated by the conquest of minor milestones. To attempt to teach the boy of six the principles of water safety expected of a nine-year-old, would be as defeatingly discouraging to him as trying to teach him algebra before he knew simple arithmetic.
>
> In the education of the child in safe behavior the parent must be aware of the prime role of parental example in influencing juvenile behavior. Parents are smugly proud when the little girl or boy announces that she or he is going to grow up to be just like mother or daddy. But they often overlook the vital responsibility that such juvenile ambitions impose on them, the parents. It means, of course,

that the little girl will attempt to mimic her mother in the performance of household tasks. And it means that the little boy will imitate his father in the handling of firearms and tools. This is perhaps too obvious. But how many parents realize when they take their two-year-old for a casual walk, that they are starting his instruction in pedestrian safety. And how many are aware when they take the same child for an automobile ride that they are starting a 14-year course in driver education?

Educators agree that student or group participation is one of the most effective educational devices. How does this apply to accident prevention in the home? It simply suggests, and validly, that under parental supervision young children should be taught to do all the things they want to and are capable of doing. The boy of six years is going to light matches just as surely as his feminine cousin of the same age is going to turn on the stove. They should both be taught how to do these things safely, and because of evinced parental cooperation they can be convinced that they should only do them when the parents are present. You cannot teach a boy NOT to climb a tree, but an interested parent can teach him how to do it with maximal safety.

It should be pointed out that especially for the toddler, the homely everyday experiences that inevitably result in minor bumps, bruises and burns can be of great educational value. This is only true, however, if the parent capitalizes on the incident by: (1) giving neither emotional nor gastronomic reward; (2) explaining the cause and effect relationship that was operative, i.e. "It was hot, you touched and it burned you." While children learn best by parental example and supervised experience, they can learn much by rote. This is only possible, however, when they have the background of supervised experience, the continuing example of parental safe behavior, and a well-founded confidence in the reasonableness and veracity of the parents.

In another publication Dietrick (1955) summarized: "The critical years, then, are between one and five. It is when they are between one and five that we must be busy not only protecting our children against serious accidents, but even busier teaching them to protect themselves."

Learn and Live! That is the theory of accident prevention.

Kenyon (1958) pointed out:

Unsafe practices are not always the result of carelessness. Often they are due to the lack of cooperation on the part of the family in methods of doing things. Nagging never has been known to bring good results. Instead it should be emphasized that safe practices are a matter of good training and good example.

Every adult has a role to play in identifying the causes of accidents to children and in trying to remove them. Safety education can often be tactfully made a part of regular child care. It is perfectly natural, for example, to point out even to the young child the importance of picking up toys or other obstructions on stairs or floors which might cause a serious fall if they are left lying about. Perhaps you can say to the child, "They will last longer if they are put in a place of their own, and no one knows the right sort of spot for them better than you do. See if you can find a nice place for them."

Some conclusions of Baber, on specific aspects of child rearing seem pertinent in considering how to build sound safety attitudes and how to avoid creating characteristics commonly associated with accident involvement. It is easier to say "don't" than "do," because the latter necessitates understanding, planning, and help. Children subject to undue fears of physical harm as the result of constant warnings of dangers may have anxieties which are not conducive to self-reliant conduct, but rather to indecision, weakness, and avoidance of responsibility. The authority of realism and fact is developed by explaining, not by orders. Overprotection—no toys which might hurt, no pets, no rough games—may deny the child normal development of precautionary habits.

The No Repression school, on the other hand, may underemphasize the first premise of social control; namely, restraint, and thus create a false and unrealistic atmosphere which will lead to accident-producing behavior.

The Only Children as a group have less opportunity for give and take, fair play, and taking turns. In situations where safety depends on these qualities, for example, in driving, accidents can be the result of never having learned them.

Baber reports that firm home discipline was favorable to the later marital happiness of children. Contra, lax, irregular, or overly strict discipline was unfavorable to happiness. Again we can infer that safety and happiness have common roots.

The role of punishment in child training is controversial. However, its proponents often advise that it be "swift and sure." The swift-and-sure philosophy of punishment has a quality that could be most important in developing attitudes of respect for natural laws, since natural forces will not be patient and permissive in an accident-producing sequence. On the other hand, punishment for hazardous activities leads children to resort to lying as a method for coping with an unpleasant situation. As we all know, lying prevents good accident investigation and analysis!

Families Are Different

Families differ widely in socioeconomic, educational, religious, cultural, and environmental situations, as well as in their position in the life cycle. Even though 60 percent of families own their homes, the proportion living in multifamily buildings in a specific city, for example, in New York City, may be very high. Any family-oriented accident prevention effort should take account of the special characteristics of the group to be reached.

There are many indicators of varying needs and interests of different kinds of families. A few examples are:

> 28.5 million families with children
> 13.6 million rural nonfarm families
> 3.8 million farm families
> 24 percent with children under 6
> 2.3 million families whose head is under 25
> 65 percent with children
> 6.2 million families whose head is 65 or over
> 35.8 million families had incomes under $8,000

Up-to-date information on accident rates and causes for different types of families is not available. Several studies done in the past indicate that type and cause analysis is a fruitful area of investigation. Over-all accident rates have generally indicated that all families need safety education.

A study of emergency-room cases in Cleveland showed accident rates on a population basis to be almost twice as high for low rental areas as for middle rental areas. Rates in high rental areas were only two-thirds those of middle rental areas.

For some types of accidents, such as asphyxiations and fires due to family heating equipment, multiple fatalities resulting from single events produce high death rates in lower economic groups. Interpretations of such rates when related to socioeconomic status should consider the number of events as well as the total results.

Studies of incidence of child poisonings, by socioeconomic status, have not shown consistently higher rates for the lower status groups. However, differences in typical kinds of poisonous materials have been noted in different status groups.

Velz and Hemphill found no material differences in home injury rates per person for families of different sizes greater than two (the single person "family" had a high rate). They found substantially higher rates per dwelling unit for crowded homes but said, "injury rates per person may not support this striking relationship between crowded conditions and injuries" (Velz and Hemphill, 1953).

These same investigators found high rates of minor injuries among rural nonfarm persons who own their own homes and major injuries to males in the same category. This finding suggests differences in kinds of activities as compared with urban families and also suggests lesser skills in "do-it-yourself" work as compared with the work of farm families. Velz and Hemphill found little association between income and home injuries.

Death rates of the white and nonwhite populations show distinct patterns of accident type. The pedestrian death rate of nonwhite males is one and one half times that of white males. The drowning rate of nonwhite males is almost two and one half times the white male death rate. Nonwhite death rates from fire and explosion are four times those of the white population. Other types of accidents with a higher incidence for nonwhites are railway accidents, accidents involving mechanical suffocation, poisoning, firearms, and hot or corrosive substances. White death rates were higher for falls, machinery, aircraft, and electrical accidents (National Center for Health Statistics).

In many studies it simply appears that higher income groups tend to get hurt by more expensive agents and activities.

A recently drawn rate map of home accident fatalities in New York City neighborhoods also showed much higher accident rates in nonwhite or foreign born low-economic-level areas. A police lieutenant studying the map said, "That's a map of all our city's troubles."

The Family Plan

Locke (1957), writing of contrasting family patterns in various cultures, described the typical United States family: "The Small Democratic Family is based on . . . making decisions on the basis of agreement of family members with children participating as they advance in age . . . the maximum of individualism consistent with the maintenance of the family."

One can hardly read Lillian M. Gilbreth's *Living With Our Children*, in particular her chapter, "Group Councils—Who Decides," without believing that this fascinating family's unusual emphasis on discussion and system must have produced not only family fun but also family safety.

EVALUATING FAMILY EXPERIENCES. In summarizing research on group techniques as related to safety education in schools, Brody (1959) concludes that democratic methods, good discussion, and group decision are not only of proven effectiveness in changing attitudes and behavior, but also are less likely to produce the personality characteristics associated with accident involvement. The implications for families should be as valid as for the educators he was addressing.

New activities provide the opportunity for family councils and discussions—first day at school, first bike, first trip downtown alone, first spring picnic, first trip to the zoo.

Family recreation, particularly the annual vacation, provides perhaps the finest opportunity for the use of discussion and decision to compensate for new hazards.

Inventions can disorganize the family customs. New products often create a need for family discussion of their characteristics and selection and their use after purchase. Medical views on obtaining safe equipment, conforming to codes, bearing reputable approvals, and with all practical safety extras can be influential (White House Conference, 1960).

The children of the years between now and 1980 must learn very early the art of self-preservation in a world filled with rapidly moving vehicles, high-voltage electric devices, radiation, and a host of other physical phenomena. Though it seems that each generation learns to live with the things present at the time it is born, the problems of education for living safely in a world of speed and tension may be the determinant factor in survival.

TRAINING AND FAMILY PLANS. Recognition of training as a specific entity will do much to improve the safety of family plans. Perhaps our schools do too good a job of smoothly integrating safety training into activities, because the average youngster graduates from elementary school without conscious recognition of training as a distinct step to skill, enjoyment, and safety.

Training as a family affair may be as simple as respect for the written instructions which accompany most products, or the obtaining of expert views from the scout executive, the Coast Guard, the policeman, or the doctor. Training may be in formal courses such as: swimming, driver education, child study, Red Cross first aid, lifesaving, small craft, Power Squadron, Scuba (self-contained underwater breathing apparatus), and firearms. Or the training may be informal, within the family, using only the standard elements of presentation, discussion, demonstration, and practice.

Accidents are simultaneously an index of inefficiencies in training and an index of the realism of training. The trouble is that the indices operate in contrary direction and require the most careful judgment. If a given situation is analyzed with care to determine its potential for minor accidents versus its potential for permanent injury or death, the analysis itself will stimulate planning and training; and the highest desirable level of realism can be maintained.

The family-disorganizing effects of urban blight may be partially offset by family participation in neighborhood renewal and clean-up plans, which are, in themselves, a constructive safety activity.

The trend toward do-it-yourself projects increases the needs for safety information and safe procedures. Dad's carryover of job safety may enrich the family work. Praise for sharing family tasks may create a desire for craftsmanship. Safety as a component of home chores can better equip the youngster for a more productive role in later life.

The Family Shares Experiences

The family is a mechanism for collective learning, which is enriched by sharing the diverse experiences of family members. A few of the common sources of safety experiences are schools and youth groups, father's (and perhaps mother's) job, clubs, and the church.

Organized youth groups often stimulate the sharing of safety experiences either by family participation in programs or by family help in carrying out safety projects. There have been many youth and farm group projects which successfully involved the entire family. It is estimated that more than 9 million boys and girls have participated in the 4-H safety program, in addition to 675,000 in the tractor program. The Boy Scout Safety Good Turn mobilized 100,000 Scout units with the following results:

3,615,073 boys participated.

17,312,000 "boy hours" of Scout activity were devoted to safety.

    98,281 safety projects (28,728 traffic; 20,824 outdoors; 48,225 home) were undertaken.

    30,638 non-Scouters assisted in the program.

      4,449 new Health and Safety committee members were enrolled.

    16,532 radio programs and 6,380 TV programs were broadcast.

Many other youth groups also have splendid programs. Medical and health personnel often act as advisers to such groups and have many opportunities to point out constructive safety projects.

Home hazard hunts, usually with a check list, are a common project for Scouts, for school children, and for other groups. These appear to have a high degree of participation by family members. Where motivation is provided, by a report back to the group, or to an authority or counselor, the amount of safety work accomplished appears to be substantial.

Industry Emphasizes Family Safety

One of the most important safety developments is the growth of emphasis on off-the-job safety by industry.

Employers recognize the economic and humanitarian concern which they share with employees for off-the-job accidents. Employer contributions to the cost of group health and accident insurance, sometimes covering employees' families, provide an economic stimulus to help prevent off-the-job accidents. As a consequence, we can expect business and industry to become increasingly strong forces for public education through the information services they provide for employees.

The startling experience of the DuPont Company is thought-provoking. With an occupational accident rate among the lowest in industry, the company launched an additional off-the-job safety program. In five years, off-the-job accidents were reduced by one-third! The off-the-job accident time loss of DuPont employees is only one-third that of U. S. workers generally. The record for motor vehicle fatalities is even more remarkable—reduced 45 percent while the rate for U. S. workers as a whole declined only 12 percent. Even more encouraging, occupational rates, already very low, dropped 50 percent (Queener, 1960). Did personal and family involvement create greater acceptance of on-the-job precautions? Does DuPont's emphasis on discussion and participation account for its success in off-the-job safety?

It appears that, for reasons having to do with employee relations, companies typically initiate off-the-job safety programs limited to the *employees* themselves. The programs widened in scope to include families in employee participation reflects employees' interests and concerns. This natural broadening has not produced criticism of invasion of privacy or paternalism.

A special questionnaire about off-the-job safety activities is included in the National Safety Council Home Safety Inventory. The most effective off-the-job safety activities, according to companies, are those in which the employee and his *family* participate, and those involving animation, such as a film or safety party. The following activities are listed in the order preferred by most companies:

Red Cross first-aid classes
Family safety meetings
Film showings
Off-the-job safety committee meetings

Letters and bulletins to the home

Cooperation with community agencies (health departments, fire departments, local safety councils)

House organ news items

Booklets and pamphlets passed out to employees

Exhibits and displays

Posters

Advertising

Newspaper, radio, and TV promotion

The company which gives employees vacation safety booklets or child safety booklets may be creating family discussions with important results for safety everywhere.

Some specific illustrations of family approaches in industrial programs are:

1. An employee's guest editorial in the house organ on the employee's interest in family safety.

2. Prizes for wives' correct answers to phone inquiries for the safety slogan or safety tip of the week.

3. Published photos of goggles or safety shoes which prevented an injury on a home do-it-yourself project.

4. Seat-belt promotions for private cars.

5. An off-the-job safety calendar, pamphlets, home inspection check lists, and similar materials.

6. "Safety Everywhere . . . All The Time," a film and materials program developed by Allis-Chalmers Manufacturing Co. in cooperation with the National Safety Council.

7. A safety carnival.

8. The Vehicle Safety-check Program of the Auto Industry Highway Safety Committee.

9. Home Safety essay, poster, and limerick contests for employees' children.

10. Home Safety and Traffic-Safety Days for families with displays and demonstrations.

11. Home fire-extinguisher promotion.

In addition, companies have sponsored a wide variety of public service programs which have provided materials to schools and parks, furnished trained speakers for community group meetings, or organized driver-training courses.

The U. S. National Health Survey showed a ratio of 1.3 accidents off the job to one on the job for persons usually working. However, companies with good records of occupational accident reduction find that off-the-job accidents among their employees outnumber occupational accidents by 5, 10, 20, and even 40:1. For companies with good work safety programs, nonoccupational accidents have come to be a principal concern.

Marvin J. Nicol, Director of the National Safety Council's Civic Leadership Services, points out (unpublished):

> . . . The program approach of the Civic Leadership Services group of the Council is based upon the premise that members of families have experiences as participating members of organizations which impart positive safety attitudes to the individual members. Furthermore, the influence extends to other members of the family, and in many instances to the community. There have been outstanding examples of such influence among youth groups, farm organizations, church societies, women's clubs, and labor organizations. All of the areas of off-the-job safety including home, public and traffic have been successfully attacked as organizational projects among these groups.
>
> Through participation in safety projects, programs and activities of their respective organizations, members become involved and have experience of educational value. As the members of the family become involved in this participation, new and positive attitudes result and the impact influences other members of the family. It does not stop here, but extends to neighbors and other family units in the community, because basically the programs, projects and activities are communitywide. Within the capacity of joint membership efforts to conduct communitywide projects lies the means of reaching the entire community, thereby influencing safety attitudes of families who are not members of organizations.
>
> Much has been said of the threat of expensive and questionable governmental intervention in areas of "off-the-job" safety which should rightfully be reserved for voluntary citizen action. There is no substitute for actual participation, successful achievement and sense of accomplishment as a successful rebuttal to the proponents of "get the government in the safety business."

The family's role in transmitting safety attitudes may be hypothesized in the accident experience of smaller towns where the principal employer has a vigorous occupational safety program.

When the Johns-Manville mine at Asbestos, Quebec, set a world's record for safety, a check of the town's traffic fatality experience showed a very low rate; and this, of course, reflected the experience of the entire population of the town.

In Oak Ridge, Tennessee, a major unit in the atomic bomb development, safety was a major concern in plant and town construction operation. Environmental hazards of all types were more completely controlled than in any other city of comparable size, and this was undoubtedly the basic reason for the town's freedom from accidents. However, many individual instances of transmission or reinforcement of safety messages by family channels were noted. And there can be little doubt that the families were the final source of the "100 percent" attitude toward safety in all activities which prevailed in this community.

The Family Faces Trouble

Trouble both weakens the family approach to safety and fosters conditions conducive to accidents.

Among the broad changes which are confusing and disorganizing to family life (although some of these changes obviously have offsetting advantages) are:

1. The decline of male authority and the new status of women, with consequent uncertainty over roles.

2. Freer choices of children and young folks.

3. The trend away from rural living with changes in housing types, less neighborhood force, increased anonymity, and less family-type fun and work. Three-fourths of our people live in 168 metropolitan areas.

4. Transportation availability, with resulting absences from home and increased exposure to new ideas.

5. The working mother who has less time to give to home and problems (but may work harder at homemaking during available hours and may more readily accept constructive method).

6. Inventions, such as the automobile and TV.

On the level of the individual family, inspection of lists of most frequent and most serious grievances of husbands and wives (quick-tempered; interferes with my discipline; untidy; drinks;

selfish and inconsiderate; spoils the children; lazy) reveals that many, and possibly most, could play a direct part in an accident-producing situation.

Other grievances (feelings too easily hurt; does not talk things over; bored with small talk; no interest in my work; narrow-minded; works outside the home; too interested in clothes, other sex, business; no interest in children) probably play an adverse role in developing satisfactory adjustments to new and newly recognized accident potentials. Still others (nags; harsh with children; tries to improve me; argumentative; criticizes) are barriers to constructive development of safe habits and safety education. Since these grievances were shown to affect happiness in families, we are again drawn to the conclusion that the happy family is the safe family.

Sources of family disorganization or stress create family problems which in turn cause accidents or increase accident potential. We can gain insight into family safety problems by briefly noting basic trends, but we must not range so broadly as to set up extensive social changes as an accident prevention goal. Rather, we should view accident prevention as contributing to solutions of the broader problems.

Accidents and accident potentials offer *tangible* topics for discussion and analysis while other less tangible family problems may be more difficult to view objectively. For example, housekeeping, a reflection of personal habits and traits, appears to have a direct relation to accident experience according to a study of home accidents in Ware County, Georgia. The study bore out the importance of tidiness in prevention of home accidents.

Sound accident prevention activities within the family create and build a family relationship which is pleasant and constructive. And in this way, accident prevention contributes toward solutions of broader social problems through stronger family relationships.

The Family's World

The community, the state, and the nation provide the family with many protective services—police, fire, food, and drug. However, even in family literature we see inadequate recognition that the family is the *unalterable, principal repository of accident responsibility for accident prevention.* Public services can *only* complement and supplement personal efforts.

Since most people think accidents are caused by the "other guy," the stage is set for overreliance on public controls. As a member of a suburban safety committee, the author responded to mothers' claims that speeds were excessive on certain residential streets (which they were not, considering sight distances and practically no parked cars in that area) by predicting that the first child killed in the two new subdivisions would be killed by a mother backing a car on a driveway. The author was, sad to say, right.

There is an acute need for public support and understanding of the work of official agencies. Many specific accident control programs are the legal responsibility of public officials. These officials cannot discharge their obligations without public backing. To ignore for the moment any psychologic trauma, the mother who threatens her child with, "I'll call the policemen," or the father who "watches for cops" as he speeds along, is hardly building a foundation of good personal-community relations.

Examples of lack of understanding of the work of traffic safety agencies are commonly revealed by parents' demands for sign, signal, or police protection at specific places. Well-run traffic engineering and traffic police groups have historically used what the medical profession describes as epidemiologic techniques. That is to say, they maintain spot maps and accident location files to determine accident experience at a particular location. When accident experience or complaints indicate a need, they analyze individual reports seeking relationships to physical and other conditions and design appropriate controls. Lack of public understanding of this work leads to friction between officials and citizens; or, if citizen demands are satisfied, the lack may lead to serious impairment of traffic flow and disrespect for signs, all without safety gains.

Participation in public support for community and state safety services through clubs, groups, and safety councils can have the added advantage of building better family-community relations and partially counteracting one of the disorganizing forces in present society (White House Conference, 1960).

No single profession, organization, program, or family working alone, can be solely responsible for all of the aspects of the health and safety of children. The distribution of medical care and the prevention and protection services are extremely complex phenomena which involve many professions, technical skills, and community organization patterns.

The Family—A Safety Goal

Recognition of the family as the basic unit of society, as the fundamental determiner of motivations, as the most powerful molder of opinions and attitudes, as the means of cultural continuation, and as the most effective forum for the exchange of information and knowledge opens up many possibilities for the propagation of safe behavorial practices. Awareness of the family as a major unit in accident prevention activities can create concepts with coordinating force for those conducting organized safety programs. A synthesis and integration takes place within the family circle of the teachings and influence of many outside forces such as churches and schools as well as informal organizations.

This synthesis is absorbed to different degrees by the various family members and its influence is extended beyond the family circle. If these outside influences are congruent and consistent they reinforce one another.

We may, at least partially, counteract the tendency during the last quarter-century to fracture organized safety efforts into numberless competing and conflicting special interests. The mother, one day concerned about abandoned refrigerators, another day about speeding on a school route, and another day about opportunities for children to learn to swim, is one mother.

Family-centered safety programs can complement one another instead of competing for public attention. They can be parallel in direction rather than tangential. They can all work more directly toward the goal of accident prevention through coordinated action.

REFERENCES

Accident Facts: National Safety Council, Chicago, 1959, p. 61.

Accidental Injury Statistics: Accident Prevention Program, U. S. Public Health Service, Washington, D. C., June, 1958.

Accident Prevention for Public Health Nurses: Publication No. 670, U. S. Public Health Service, Washington, D. C., pp. 27–28.

Baber, R. E.: *Marriage and the Family.* New York, McGraw-Hill, pp. 182–185, based on Terman, L. M.: *Psychological Factors in Marital Happiness.*

Brody, L.: *Accidents and Attitudes.* Center for Safety Education, New York University, 1959, pp. 7–16.

Brown, A. W., Morrison, J. and Couch, G. B.: Influence of affectional family relationships on character development. *J Abnormal Psychol, 62:422,* 1947.

Current Population Report: U. S. Department of Commerce, Bureau of the Census, Washington, D. C., 1961.

Current Population Report: Population Estimate: ser. P-25, No. 187, p. 16, U. S. Department of Commerce, Bureau of the Census, Washington, D. C., 1958.

Dietrick, H. F.: The role of education in accident prevention, *Pediatrics, 17:297,* 1956.

Dietrick, H. F.: Your child's safety. *Nationwide Insurance,* 1955, p. 3.

Accident Facts: 1973 Edition, National Safety Council, Chicago, p. 61.

Dunn, H. L., and Gilbert, M.: Public health begins in the family, *Public Health Repts, 71:*1006, 1956.

Holbrook, S.: *Let Them Live.* New York, The Macmillan Company, 1958.

Katz, E., and Lazarfeld, P. F. *Personal Influence.* Glencoe, The Free Press, 1955, p. 50.

Kenyon, M.: Child safety—whose responsibility. *Home Safety Rev, 15:*24, 1958.

Locke, H. L.: American Corporation. *Encyclopedia Americana,* XI: 3–7, 1957.

National Center for Health Statistics, Washington, D. C.

National Safety News: National Safety Council, Chicago, *81:*6, 1960.

Queener, J. S.: On-the-job training prevents off-the-job accidents. *Supervisory Management,* February, 1960, p. 3.

Richardson, H. B.: *Patients Have Families.* The Commonwealth Fund, 1945, p. 1007.

Safety in the 60's: National Safety Council, 1959, p. 35.

Suchman, E. A., and Scherzer, A. L.: *Current Research on Childhood Accidents, Two Reviews of Accident Research.* Association for the Aid to Crippled Children, New York, 1960, pp. 12, 15.

U. S. National Health Survey: *Persons Injured by Class of Accident,* Health

Statistical ser. B-8, July 1957—June 1958, U. S. Department of Health, Education, and Welfare, Public Health Service, Washington, D. C., 1959.

Velz, C. J., and Hemphill, F. M.: *Home Injuries,* University of Michigan, School of Public Health, 1953, pp. 8, 23, 30, 34.

Wain, H., Samuelson, H. E. and Hemphill, F. M.: An experience in home injury prevention. *Public Health Repts,* 70:560, 1955.

White House Conference on Children and Youth 1960: *Focus on Children and Youth,* pp. 11, 13, 14, 20, 24, 117, 121–122, 124–125, 136, 137, 142, 154.

38

SIMPLIFIED STATISTICS
FOR SAFETY

L. B. BLANK

The contribution that follows has at the same time everything and nothing to do with safety. Safety is mentioned only in the title and in passing. Accident rates receive only a few lines in a highly specialized manner. Why, then, this selection?

Safety managers, and indeed most students of safety, do not seem to be math majors. Even when they are basically engineers, the safety professional seems to run to his bookshelf or company statistician when the subject of statistics is mentioned. A few years ago Dr. Blank published this material in booklet form as a result of student demand.

Since then, hundreds of the booklets have found their way to the libraries of safety managers and military safety officers. Since the booklets are no longer available, the publication of Dr. Blank's contribution in this volume will maintain a unique reference in safety literature, and serve thousands more as it has in the past.

Statistics

Statistics, the collective noun, is defined in the modern sense as the study of decision-making under uncertainty or with incomplete data.

A statistic, the singular noun, is a numerical property of a sample or portion of data; thus, "statistics" in the plural sense are numerical properties of a sample or of samples. The counterpart of a statistic for a population (universe or complete body of data) is called a parameter. However, the latter term is commonly misused to denote a requirement or criterion in an engineering performance sense, but the statistical definition of "parameter" is simply the aforementioned one, i.e. a numerical property of a

Presented to University of Southern California Institute of Aerospace Safety and Management, November, 1969.

population. The chief use of a statistic is to estimate its corresponding parameter.

The principal phases and functions of statistics are descriptive, inferential, and experiment design. Descriptive statistics is that phase which summarizes bodies of data. Inferential statistics involves generalizing from a sample or relatively small collection of facts to the parent population from which it was taken, while the objective of experiment design is the efficient performance of meaningful experiments aimed at either description or inference.

Data, Measurement, and Mathematical Operations

Basically there are two types of data, those that are counted and those that are, in the usual sense, measured. Counted data are called "attribute" or "discrete," and are presented by whole number, e.g. number of persons enrolled in a course, Air Force majors present, tests passed, etc. Synonyms for measured data are "continuous" and "variable." Such data are found along a scale or continuum and, thus, can have an uncountably infinite number of values. Examples of continuous scales include time, distance, pressure, and temperature among other dimensions.

Usually continuous data are rounded off to the nearest unit of measurement. When I say I am 70 inches tall, I mean that I am at least 69.5 but not quite 70.5. There is a notable exception to the standard practice or convention of rounding off variables data. Age, in our society, is usually reported to the last birthday, i.e. a twenty-four-year-old person has turned twenty-four but is not yet twenty-five. Thus, while the average height of 70-inch men is 70.0 inches, the midpoint of their potential range, the average age of twenty-four-year-old men is actually 24.5, since some just turned twenty-four today and some will be twenty-five tomorrow. Also, there is an interesting exception to the age-to-last-birthday exception. Life insurance companies, statistically objective and oriented to both probability and profit, reckon age to nearest birthday, really a sensible practice. Each year, just prior to my "half-birthday," my insurance agency reminds me that I can still take advantage of the premium rate for my current age.

The foregoing discussion has employed some conventions and has at least alluded to the definition thereof: a convention is a standard operating procedure. A related concept and one which, along with "convention" will recur throughout this unit, is that of "assumption." An assumption is a statement accepted as true without proof, e.g. that one's declaration of his own age or height is accurate.

Two more definitions are now in order. The accuracy of a measurement is its nearness to the actual dimension sought, while precision refers to the fineness or coarseness with which it is appraised, e.g. tenths of degrees Centigrade or microinches.

The top level of measurement, the only one usually dignified by the label "measure," is known as "interval," since it is measured along a scale of like intervals (centimeters, pounds per square inch, seconds, etc.). However, beneath interval measurement are two other levels. Lower is "ordered" or ranked measurement. If I did not have a stopwatch to time a race, I could at least rank the participants in their order of finish, though I lose some power in that the dubious assumption is made that neighboring ranks are equal distances apart. Of course, this can be quite misleading since the first runner (or swimmer, horse, boat, or car) may win by the proverbial whisker while the distance between No. 2 and No. 3 may be considerable. Thirdly, descriptive names or class labels are assigned as nominal data, e.g. pass-fail, grades A-B-C-D-F, colors of the spectrum, or girls classified by my former neighbor as good-better-best. The last scheme, I feel, is incomplete.

Sometimes we convert or "transform," i.e. alter data for the purpose of analysis, one level of measurement or type of data to another. For example, a swimming or track and field event, actually a continuous phenomenon to measure, is converted to a rank-order result and then back to a pseudo-measure such as a 5–3–1 scoring basis. Also, we frequently draw a pass-fail line in evaluating test scores for individuals or the performance of aerospace hardware.

A number of symbols commonly used in statistical analysis are described in the following paragraphs.

Equal is signified by =, and ≠ reads "does not equal." Since of two quantities, the first is either less than, equal to, or greater than the second, there are really two basic components or possibilities of inequality. < means less than and > means greater than, each symbol opening toward the larger quantity. x ≤ y indicates that x is less than or equal to (i.e. at most) y, while A ≥ B states that A is greater than or equal to (i.e. at least) B. > > means "much greater than" and < < "much less than." ≃, ≅, ≐ and preferably ≈ stand for approximate equality. Thus we say that π, the ratio of circle circumference to diameter, actually 3.141592 . . . ≈ 3.14 or ≈ 3⅐. The || symbol around a quantity refers to its absolute value, i.e., its size without reference to sign or direction. Therefore $|+8| = |-8|$ and $|-7| > |+5|$.

Upper case Greek letter "sigma,"

$$\sum_{i=1}^{n} x_i$$

is the notational shorthand for a sum of values $x_1, x_2, \ldots x_n$

$$\left(\sum_{i=1}^{n} x_i = x_1 + x_2 + \cdots + x_n \right)$$

and upper case "pi,"

$$\prod_{i=1}^{n} x_i,$$

is the notational shorthand for a product (multiplication) of values $x_1, x_2, \ldots, x_n$

$$\left(\prod_{i=1}^{n} x_i = x_1 \times x_2 \times \ldots x_n \right)$$

Raising a number to a particular power involves writing the number that many times, connected with multiplication signs. Thus 2 to the sixth power or $2^6 = 2 \cdot 2 \cdot 2 \cdot 2 \cdot 2 \cdot 2 = 64$. It is important to note that any non-zero number raised to the zero power $= 1$. The nth root of a number written $\sqrt[n]{\text{the number}}$ is a value that must be raised to the nth power to obtain the given number. Thus $\sqrt[3]{1000} = 10$, since $10^3 = 1000$. When the root is "2," no index is used, second or "square" root being understood. $\sqrt[2]{25}$, then, is commonly written $\sqrt{25}$ and equals 5 or actually ± 5 (read "plus or minus five"), since the product of two negative numbers is positive, just as is the product of two positive numbers. This is equally true for the process of division.

A special concept of great value in dealing, later, with events and their probabilities, is that of the "factorial." The factorial of the number, N, written N!, is the product of the first (lowest) N whole numbers. So $N! = 1 \bullet 2 \bullet 3 \bullet \ldots (N{-}1)(N)$ or, as usually written, $N! = N(N{-}1)(N{-}2) \bullet \ldots (2)(1)$, since order of operation makes no difference in multiplication or, for that matter, in addition. $5! = 5 \bullet 4 \bullet 3 \bullet 2 \bullet 1 = 120$; $2! = 2 \bullet 1 = 2$, and $1! = 1$. $10!$ is a very larger number, somewhat greater than three million. To review, $10! > 3{,}000{,}000$. The pesky and inevitable exception is that, by a convenient definition, $0! = 1$. Keep the faith! (Final punctuation mark is an exclamation point not a factorial sign). Incidentally, the fact that their factorials are equal does not prove that $0 = 1$.

A final bit of mathematical diet appears here in preparation for our later discussion of accident rates. In "scientific notation," large and small numbers are written in terms of appropriate powers of 10. $1{,}000{,}000$ becomes 10^6 or 1×10^6, the latter in the form of $A \times 10^b$ where A is conventionally a number in the range of 1 to 10. From earlier technical notation, then, $1 \leq A < 10$, which is a mathematical sentence stating that A is "at least 1 but is less than 10." We should write the population of Los Angeles ($2{,}900{,}000$) as 2.9×10^6 though the values 29×10^5 and 0.29×10^7 would be, among other alternatives, accurate. A number raised to a negative power equals 1 divided by that number to the corresponding positive power. $10^{-6} = 1/10^6 = 0.000001$ and read "one millionth," and $2^{-3} = 1/2^3 = 1/8$. The model, $A \times 10^b$ holds generally for negative as well as positive powers of 10. However, local technical practice sometimes adopts its own convention, such as stock transactions (in shares) being reported in 100's, i.e. no restriction on the "A" term in the expression $A \times 10^2$. Likewise military practice may and does reckon accident rates in the form of $A \times 10^{-5}$ or A per 10^5 without limiting the range of A.

Tables and Graphs

Tables summarizing data may be arranged progressively with either the highest or lowest values at the top, while in graphic presentation the greater relative values are always, by convention, found by proceeding upward and to the right. We label horizontal distance as being the "X" scale and vertical as being along the "Y" axis (Figure 38–1). Theoretically, there are possible negative as well as positive values along both axes, but overwhelming use in graphs for statistical presentation is made of the first (upper-right or positive-positive) quarter or quadrant of the graphic field.

A further convention in graphing is that the "measurements" are plotted horizontally along the X axis, while vertical or Y distance is used to represent frequency or probability. For our purposes, the scale units will be equally spaced, though there are special graphic scales and paper for unequal (nonrectangular) divisions such as logarithms or powers of numbers.

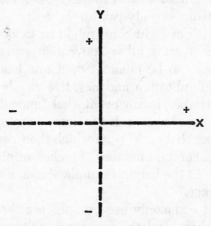

Figure 38–1. Conventional Grid For Graphic Presentation.

Bodies consisting of many pieces of data are commonly grouped, i.e. nearby values collected into a fairly small number of intervals or cells, for reasons of economy of space and effort. It is conventional to use about ten, or at least between five and twenty such intervals. Thus, we may divide the overall range (i.e. differences between the highest and lowest values in a distribution) by 10 to determine the interval size to be used. Recommended interval sizes include 1, 2, 3, 5, 10, 15, 25, higher multiples of 25, and decimal multiples of the foregoing. In other words, use 3 or 5 in preference to 4 and 5 or 10 instead of the integers between so as to yield interval midpoints which are integers. Note that the interval written ("nominal") 10–14 is a 5-point cell, not a 4-point one, whether we count the whole numbers included (i.e. 10, 11, 12, 13, and 14) or realize that, due to rounding off, the possible subrange of values is really 9.5 to (almost) 14.5.

While "transformation" was defined in the proceeding section as changing data to make analysis more *meaningful,* we now define a particular phase of transformation, "coding," as the simplification of data. It is frequently quite economical to transform (1) in location all pieces of a certain group of measurements by adding or subtracting a constant, (2) in change of scale by multiplication or division, or (3) in both of the foregoing ways. The average height of a group of professional basketball guards, all of whom are at least six feet in height, is rendered simpler by subtracting initially seventy-two or seventy inches from each height. Large totals of flight hours might be treated by division of 1000, 1,000,000, or some other convenient power of 10. Thousandths of inches can be eliminated, if one has an aversion to decimals, by multiplication and negative numbers by addition. It is vital to remember, in any event, that "uncoding," the inverse or opposite process of coding, is necessary to return statistical results to the proper "ballpark" from which their components came. For example, the constant number of inches, originally subtracted from each value in the height example above, must be added to the "coded average."

The two most commonly used graphs are the frequency histogram or bar chart, and the frequency polygon or line graph. The former type portrays the frequency of occurrence of each value or group of values as a rectangular bar of a certain height (frequency). It is assumed for the purpose of graphing histograms, that all values within an interval are scattered evenly throughout that interval. A frequency polygon is constructed, as seen in the superimposed pair of graphs (Figure 38–2), by connecting the midpoints (at the appropriate heights or frequencies) to form a broken line. For the purpose of depicting areas, this graph is brought down to the baseline (X axis) at zero frequency at the midpoints of the next (theoretical) interval in each direction from the range of the frequency distribution being graphed. The prevailing assumption for a frequency polygon is that the values are concentrated at the interval midpoints.

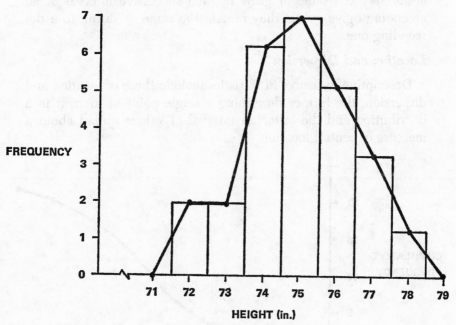

Figure 38–2. Frequency Polygon and Histogram.

A graph should occupy most of the space provided for it and, as shown in Figures 38–2 and 38–3, the zero point in either direction may be so distant from the range of values that, so as to portray relationships realistically while preserving economy of space, the interrupted portion of the scale is indicated.

To indicate a general trend, a polygon is sometimes "smoothed" into a curve, averaging short-term fluctuations into longer term directions.

A polygon showing cumulative frequencies is called an ogive ("oh-jive") and may be of either the ascending (accumulating data less than a given value) or its complement, the descending (accumulating data greater than a given value) type. The assumption is that the values are concentrated at the upper or lower real limits of the intervals respectively for the two types.

The height data plotted previously by pure frequencies are presented in the ascending ogive (Fig. 38–3) by cumulative frequency of occurrence. Cumulative frequencies, unlike pure ones, either stay the same or grow in each successive interval of an ascending ogive, while they remain the same or shrink in a descending one.

Location and Dispersion

Descriptive measures in statistics include those of location and dispersion, the former describing a single point of interest in a distribution and the latter an interval of values spread about a measure of central location.

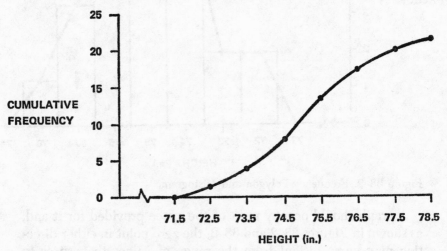

Figure 38–3. Ascending Ogive.

Among measures of location are maximum score, minimum, second highest, and 90th centile or percentile, i.e. the point below which 90 percent of the values are found. The most prominent location measures are those of *central* location, sometimes known as central tendency. The commonly used term, average, is actually a broad nontechnical term encompassing all measures of central or typical value, though it is popularly and erroneously used as synonymous with the arithmetic mean even in some technical statistical literature.

A mode is the value appearing with the highest frequency, seventy-five inches in height for the data represented graphically in the preceding section. A distribution may have more than one mode, as in this set of values: 6, 6, 5, 3, 3,; or it may have no mode, as in 5, 4, 3, 2, 1. It is easily detected in a frequency graph as the high (vertical) point. The mode is most meaningful when it represents a considerable proportion of the values.

The median is a value, $\tilde{x}$, such that one-half of the observations are greater than $\tilde{x}$ and one-half are less than or equal to $\tilde{x}$. It has been said, also, that a median is the middle value or mean of the middle values, about seventy-five inches in the height example, and 5 and 3, respectively, in the two sets of values given in the preceding paragraph. The median, commonly used with distributions of wages and salaries, is interesting in that it divides the distribution into halves of equal frequency.

The arithmetic mean, usually called simply "mean," is the measure of location most familiar to all of us. It is found by adding all of the values and dividing the number of values. You should verify that the arithmetic mean for the heights earlier portrayed is 74.9 or 75, depending upon whether one rounds-off the answer to tenths or whole inches.

The arithmetic means of the distributions 6, 6, 5, 3, 3 and 5, 4, 3, 2, 1 are equal to their medians, 5 and 3. If the latter distribution were instead 105, 4, 3, 2, 1, only the *mean* among the three central measures would be changed to 23 in this case. Since the mean alone gives full weight to each of its components, it is strongly affected by one or more extremely high values.

The arithmetic mean of a population is represented by the Greek letter μ (mu) and is calculated as follows:

$$\mu = \frac{\sum_{i=1}^{n} x_i}{n} \tag{1}$$

where the x_i's are the individual values and n in number of values in the population.

The corresponding statistic (arithmetic mean) is designated by
x̄ (read x-bar) and calculated in the same manner with n being
the number of values in the sample

$$\bar{x} = \frac{\sum\limits_{i=1}^{n} x_i}{n} \tag{2}$$

A concept analogous to the arithmetic mean is that of expectation or mathematical expectation, defined as "long-run average,"
which we shall relate to probability distributions in a succeeding
section. Prevailing symbols are E and μ.

We shall not consider the geometric mean nor the harmonic
mean, both of which are rather obscure, in the unit.

Concluding from the preceding discussion, it can be seen that
each of the three major measures of central location has advantages and disadvantages. To summarize: the mean is valuable in
that it fully credits each of its member measurements but is biased
upward or downward unduly by one or more very large or very
small values. The median serves well to split the upper and lower
halves of a distribution of data arranged in rank order but, sometimes falsely, assigns equal spacing between consecutively ranked
scores. The mode is most useful when it represents a fairly large
fraction of the sample or the population being analyzed but has
little meaning if the *vote* of scores is split into many small frag-
ments or if the range of measurements is very small.

To illustrate the comparative use of mode, median, and mean
with the same set of data, consider a small community of 100
families, 99 of whose annual incomes are $5,000, while the other
family earns $1,000,000. The mode, representing 99 percent of
the subjects is, of course, $5,000 and the median (or 50th centile),
the same or nearly the same. Neither of these is at all affected by
the income of "Mr. Gotrocks." However, the mean is calculated as
follows:

$$99 \times \$5,000 + \$1,000,000 = \$495,000 + \$1,000,000$$
$$= \frac{\$1,495,000}{100} = \$14,950 \approx \$15,000$$

Is this a $5,000 neighborhood or a $15,000 one? The answer really depends on one's goals. For marketing autos, food, or any other consumer product, I'd play to the mode (median, also, in this special case). Gotrocks will shop for his ABC's (artichokes, Bentleys, and caviar) in Palm Springs, San Francisco, or Rome anyway, so it won't pay to cater to his potential purchases. On the other hand, in reckoning potential for support of a local school or mosquito abatement district, it is obvious the Gotrocks pays the bulk of the bill via property and/or income taxes. In this instance, then, the mean or simply the sum of the incomes is paramount.

Dispersion, spread, or scatter is the key concept of the clustering or looseness of a sample or population of values. Though it is used in many text books, avoid using the term "variability," which is similar in structure to the precise technical term, "variance," which will soon be discussed.

The simplest measure of spread, range (R), is found by subtracting the minimum value in a distribution from its maximum one. Symbolically.

$$R = {}^x\text{max} - {}^x\text{min} \qquad (3)$$

The range is somewhat crude, paying no attention to intervening values, but is useful as an overall measure of spread, and in estimating the more precise and valuable numerical property, the standard deviation. Determine now the ranges of the three distributions used in the discussion of tables and graphs.

Variance is defined here as the most commonly used *second* degree (or second power) measure of dispersion, while standard deviation is the most commonly used *first* degree measure of dispersion. While standard deviation is of the same dimension as the original data and the "averages" (e.g. inches, dollars, hours), the variance is of the dimension squared (e.g. square inches). Would you believe "square dollars" or "square hours"? Theoretically this is possible!

The symbols for variance are σ^2 (Greek lower case "sigma" squared) for the population parameter and s^2 for the corresponding sample statistic. Therefore, σ and s are the symbols for standard deviation. The four formulas for calculation follow.

$$\sigma^2 = \frac{\sum\limits_{i=1}^{N}(x_i - \mu)^2}{N} \tag{4}$$

where $x_i - \mu$ is the difference between each value and the population mean

$$\sigma = \sqrt{\frac{\sum\limits_{i=1}^{N}(x_i - \mu)^2}{N}} \tag{5}$$

$$s^2 = \frac{\sum\limits_{i=1}^{n}(x_i - \bar{x})^2}{n-1} \tag{6}$$

where $x_i - \bar{x}$ is the difference between each value and the sample mean

$$s = \sqrt{\frac{\sum\limits_{i=1}^{n}(x_i - \bar{x})^2}{n-1}} \tag{7}$$

For large samples, i.e., when n is at least 25, n may be used as an approximation for $n - 1$ in the denominators for formulas (6) and (7).

For the population consisting of 5, 4, 3, 2, 1, variance and standard deviation are calculated as follows:

x_i	$x_i - \mu$	$(x_i - \mu)^2$	
5	+2	4	$\sigma^2 = \dfrac{10}{5} = 2$
4	+1	1	
3	0	0	$\sigma = \sqrt{2} \approx 1.41 \approx 1.4$
2	−1	1	
1	−2	4	
		$\Sigma = 10$	

But if these data were a sample, $s^2 = 10/4 = 2.5$, and $s = \sqrt{2.5} \approx 1.58 \approx 1.6$.

Verify that the variance and standard deviation of the heights of the twenty-six basketball players, repeated from above, equal about 2.25 and 1.5, respectively.

Invariably, the question arises as to when one should use variance and when standard deviation in analyzing spread. Basically, the answer is: use standard deviation to describe, along with the appropriate measure of central location, each distribution individually; use variances to compare the dispersions of two or more distributions. Commonly, we say "the mean height is seventy-five inches and the standard deviation 1.5 inches" or "the variance of one group of measurements is 3.2 times as great as the variance of another."

Accident Rates

The "accident rate," as we know it, is really a special form of average. It is the arithmetic mean number of accidents per (divided by) some base number of flight hours, usually 100,000 or 10^5 for U. S. Air Force purposes and 10,000 or 10^4 for U. S. Navy. These, too, are conventions, since different "ballparks" for the range of accident rates might dictate the use of 1,000,000 or 10^6 or some other convenient base total. A reported rate of "4.7" really means, in the Air Force, 4.7×10^{-5} or $4.7 \div 10^5$, i.e. an average of 4.7 accidents for each 100,000 flight hours. This rate could have been achieved from an infinite variety of pairs of accident count and exposure hours, two of which might be 47 accidents in 1,000,000 hours or 940 accidents in 20,000,000 hours. The foregoing discussion and nearly all of our work on accident rates is limited to flight hours as a reference, excluding other interesting exposure considerations such as takeoffs and landings and their relative severity.

It is important to note that two or more accident rates can not be averaged directly to provide an overall or grand rate but must be weighted appropriately, since their individual numbers of exposure hours may be vastly different. This discrepancy is illustrated as follows: In January, our organization experienced 20 accidents in 500,000 hours, while in February we had 2 accidents in 100,000 hours. Averaging the individual rates, 4.0 and 2.0, we would obtain a two-month rate of exactly 3.0, which is both deceiving and incorrect. The proper treatment is to divide total accidents, 22, by total hours, 600,000, both obtained over the two-month period. The correct rate, thus, is 3.67 accidents per 10^5 hours.

While a frequency ogive, as stated earlier, can not both rise and fall, this is not true of a cumulative accident rate graph. Cumulative means can grow or shrink, of course, with the addition of the latest data.

Care must be taken not to be unduly influenced by *small* numbers, which can often be misleading. The basis of comparison must be recognized and considered, so that one is not stampeded by actually-moderate changes in accident rates, either upward or downward, any more than by a savings and loan firm which boasts that its interest rate of 5 percent is "25 percent more than the banks' rate" (of 4 percent). In similar vein, a critical eye should be turned toward the so called research claim that a 160-pound person who has consumed three cocktails is 16 times as likely to have an auto accident as a similar individual with no drinks under his belt. *Perhaps* the basic probability is so infinitesimally small that multiplication by sixteen leaves it still insignificant.

Events and Probabilities

An event or set is a collection of points, elements, or "things" of any kind, e.g. course attendees, aircraft engines, or odd one-digit numbers.

The probability an event occurs or does not occur is certainty, i.e. the probability of an event and of its "complement" (lack of or "not") must add up to 1. Symbolically, $P(A) + P(\bar{A}) = 1$, read "probability of A plus probability of not A always equals one."

The simultaneous occurrence of two events is called their "intersection," and the occurrence of at least one of the two is known as their "union." Intersect is read "and" and appears as $A \cap B$ as in $P(A \cap B)$, while union is read "or" and appears as $A \cup B$ as in $P(A \cup B)$. This is a special mathematical "or" and really means "and/or." The concepts of intersect and union are extended to three or more events.

Product or system *reliability*, the probability a piece of hardware works for the required duration when called upon, will now be used to illustrate the intersection and union concepts. The multiplication rule states that the probability of occurrence of a *series* of *independent* events, i.e. those which do not affect each other, equals the product of their individual probabilities. The addition rule states that the probability of occurrence of at least one of a group of *mutually exclusive* events, i.e. those that can not occur at the same time, equals the sum of their individual probabilities.

The success probability of a series of two independent components, A and B, each 0.9 likely to work, is $0.9 \times 0.9 = 0.81.$, while the corresponding reliability for a parallel or redundantly designed element consisting of the same components is $1-(1-0.9)(1-0.9) = 1-(0.1)^2 = 0.99$, easily calculated if we understand first that a product 0.9 likely to work is 0.1 likely to fail and second, that system success in the latter case is *anything except* the failure of both components. The addition rule could be applied to the parallel case in that the system success probability equals the sum of the three mutually exclusive events: A works and B fails, A fails and B works, and both A and B work. Arithmetically, this is $0.9(1-0.9) + (1-0.9)(0.9) + 0.9(0.9) = 0.09 + 0.09 + 0.81 = 0.99$. These two cases appear in the logic or block diagrams shown here.

SERIES COMPONENTS

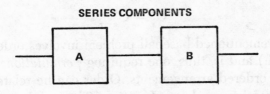

PARALLEL COMPONENTS

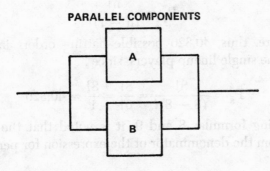

Frequently, we are interested in the possible "arrangements" of events, e.g. the number of ways that exactly two aircraft engines out of four can fail or the batting orders a manager can try with eight players excluding the pitcher.

The former case is an example of unordered arrangements called *combinations* and designated C_r^n in general, where n is the number of objects possible from which r objects are to be selected ("combined"). In this instance, the order of failure of engines is not important. The formula for determining the number of possible combinations of "r out of n" things is

$$C_r^n = \frac{n!}{r!\,(n-r)!} \qquad (8)$$

There are, thus, 6 ways that exactly 2 engines out of 4 can fail, since

$$C_2^4 = \frac{4!}{2!\,(4-2)!} = \frac{4!}{2!2!} = \frac{4 \cdot 3 \cdot 2 \cdot 1}{2 \cdot 1 \cdot 2 \cdot 1} = 6.$$

How many ways can one engine of four fail? Three engines? No engines? All four engines? Are any of these results equal to each other? Logically, there are as many unordered ways of selecting r elements from n as there are leaving r elements unselected, i.e. selecting (n-r) elements. Verify that

$$C_r^n = C_{n-r}^n$$

The aforementioned baseball problem involves order (of time in this case) and is, thus, one requiring *permutations* which are defined as ordered arrangements. Order can be related to time, physical location, rank, or function. The number of possible permutations of "r out of n" objects is found by the formula

$$P_r^n = \frac{n!}{(n-r)!} \qquad (9)$$

There are, thus, 40,320 possible batting orders in which to permute the single lineup players, since

$$P_8^8 = \frac{8!}{(8-8)!} = \frac{8!}{0!} = \frac{8!}{1} = 40,320$$

Comparing formulas 8 and 9, it is noted that the r! term is missing from the denominator of the expression for permutations.

Thus, there are always at least as many permutations as combinations of n things taken r at a time and usually more of the former; greater, in fact, by a factor of r! Verify that

$$C_r^n = P_r^n$$

only when r = 0 or 1. How many outfields of three players can be selected from seven if positions are disregarded? If positions are considered?

The concept of combinations will be used to a much greater extent than that of permutations in the next section.

Conditional probability is defined as the probability an event will occur *given* that another event has already occurred. Consider this phenomenon, as well as that of independence, in the problem that follows.

Late evening television talk shows have recently publicized a time-honored example from the study of probability, to wit: What is the probability of having one or more common (duplicated) birth dates (month and day, not necessarily year) among a group of n individuals? Stated another way, what is the minimum number, n, of such persons that will make the probability of at least one shared birth day at least 50 percent of 0.5? Eliminating the possibility of a Leap Year (February 29) birth and that of twins or other multiple siblings in the audience for simplification, the probability that the first person's birth date *does not* duplicate a previously reported one is unity, 1 or 365/365. Given the first report, there is a probability of 364/365 that the second individual *does not* share the first one's birthday. Given no prior duplication, the chance of a third separate date is 363/365. Thus the series of probabilities for these independent births may be multiplied to determine the overall probability of "no repeats" and then subtracted from 1 to determine its complement, the probability of "one or more repeats." The expression for ten events (persons) appears as follows:

$$P \text{ (some repeats)} = 1 - \left(\frac{365}{365} \cdot \frac{364}{365} \cdot \frac{363}{365} \cdot \frac{362}{365} \cdot \frac{361}{365} \cdot \frac{360}{365} \cdot \frac{359}{365} \cdot \frac{358}{365} \right.$$
$$\left. \cdot \frac{357}{365} \cdot \frac{356}{365} \right),$$

a series of factors all decreasing slightly from 1 and fairly economical to solve by the use of logarithms. P (no repeats) $\approx$ P
(some repeats) $\approx$ 0.5 or "even money" for a group of twenty-three
or twenty-four persons as the series is thus extended.

Probability Distributions

We shall define and discuss briefly five kinds of probability
distributions, two of the discrete (counted events) type and three
of the continuous (measured quantities) variety. The former are
the binomial and Poisson, while the latter include the normal,
lognormal, and exponential types.

Binomial literally means "two names," i.e. occurrence and nonoccurrence, the possible outcomes of an individual trial. Sometimes we label these results "success" and "failure," but that implies a value judgment that is frequently contradicted in that we
wish to count failures rather than successes when the former are
less numerous. The binomial probability distribution is generated
by, or composed of, repeated independent trials, each having two
possible results and a constant probability of occurrence. Coin-
flipping produces a binomial distribution, since its trials lead to
either "head" or "tail," do not influence each other, and each outcome has a fixed chance, ½ or 0.5 for a true (balanced) coin, but
an unbalanced one would also form a binomial. The occurrence of
a "1" on the one dice six-sided or otherwise, or a "7" on two dice,
also fall into the binomial family.

A binomial distribution is symmetrical, i.e. balanced from left
to right when graphed, when and only when its occurrence probability, p, equals ½. We designate the probability of nonoccurrence
as q, and only in this special case does p = q. When a distribution
is *not* symmetrical, we say it is skewed, that is pointed, away from
its large number of values and *toward* the few values. Thus, are

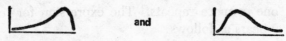

said to be skewed left (negatively) and skewed right (positively),
respectively. You will soon be able to verify that when p > ½,
the resulting binomial distribution is negatively skewed, and when
p < ½, it is positively skewed.

The probability of obtaining *exactly* r occurrences in n binomial trials is given by the formula

$$P(r) = C_r^n \ p^r \ q^{n-r} \tag{10}$$

In other words there are C_r^n ways in which a particular collection of events can take place. Each collection of r occurrences and n-r ("all but r") nonoccurrences has the probability $p^r q^{n-r}$ of happening. If one fourth (0.25) of the baseballs in a lot are defective, what is the probability that an umpire will find exactly two bad ones out of six in his pocket?

$$P(r = 2) = C_2^6 \ (1/4)^2 \ (3/4)^4 = (15) \ 3^4/4^6 = \frac{15(81)}{4096} = \frac{1215}{4096}$$
$$\approx 0.30$$

The probability of *at least* two defective balls out of six would be the sum of the probabalities of finding exactly 2, 3, 4, 5, and 6 (events mutually exclusive of each other) or, simpler, the complement of the sum of the probabilities of no defectives and 1 defective. Symbolically,

$$P(r \geq 2) = P(r = 2) + P(r = 3) + P(r = 4) + P(r = 5)$$
$$+ P(r = 6) = 1 - \{P(r = 0) + P(r = 1)\}$$

The expectation (μ) of a binomial probability distribution, its variance (σ^2), and its standard deviation (σ) are evaluated by the formulas below when n is the number of trials.

$$\mu = np \tag{11}$$
$$\sigma^2 = npq \tag{12}$$
$$\sigma = \sqrt{npq} \tag{13}$$

So the expected number of occurrences of two dice showing a total of "7" ($p = 6/36 - 1/6$) in ten rolls of the dice is $10(1/6) = 5/3 = 1.67$. Expected and most likely values are not necessarily identical. In the preceding example, the most likely number of "sevens" is 2, a plausible result, while the expectation, $1-2/3$, a good "hedge," can not actually occur. Verify that σ^2 and σ, the preceding example, are approximately 1.39 and 1.18.

The definition of the Poisson distribution (for Simeon Poisson, whose name means "fish" in French) is similar to that given above for the binomial with two notable added requirements (1) the independent trials must be "many" (say, at least 20 or 25); and (2) the constant probability of occurrence must be "small" (i.e. at most 0.1). With $p \leq 0.1$ therefore $<< 0.5$, it is seen that the Poisson is always at least somewhat skewed to the right.

Like the binomial, the Poisson's expectation or mean

$$\mu = np \text{ but its variance} \tag{14}$$
$$\sigma^2 = np \text{ as well, and, thus its standard deviation} \tag{15}$$
$$\sigma = \sqrt{np} \tag{16}$$

The probability of exactly r occurrences in a Poisson probability distribution is fairly easily calculated when μ or its factors n and p are known

$$P(r) = \frac{e^{-\mu} \mu^r}{r!} \text{ where e} \approx 2.72, \text{ the base of natural} \tag{17}$$
$$\text{logarithms}$$

A component lot is known to contain 5 percent defectives. What is the probability of finding fewer than three defectives in a sample of 40 parts? $\mu = 40(0.05) = 2$. (Incidentally, σ^2 also $= 2$, though that is irrelevant here).

$$P(r < 3) = P(r = 0) + P(r = 1) + P(r = 2) = \frac{e^{-2}2^0}{0!} + \frac{e^{-2}2^1}{1!}$$
$$+ \frac{e^{-2}2^2}{2!}$$

$$= e^{-2} + 2e^{-2} + 2e^{-2} = 5e^{-2} \approx 0.677 \approx 0.68$$

Operations involving "e" are not nearly as frightening as one may at first think. In fact, with meager tables, Poisson problems are rather easily solved. Also, quite usefully, the following approximation may be used in Poisson and, later, exponential probability expression:

$$e^{-x} \approx 1 - x \text{ when } x \leq 0.1 \tag{18}$$

When, for example, $x = 0.1$, equation 18 yields $1 - 0.1 = 0.9$, while actually $e^{-0.1} = 0.905$, which is quite close!

We are fortunate in being able to substitute the Poisson as an approximation to the binomial when n is large and p is small, since the Poisson is simpler mathematically and requires only brief tables compared with thick ones needed for binomial calculations (how would you like to evaluate for example, C_7^{100} $(0.05)^7$ $(0.95)^{93}$?). Classically, Poisson distributions have been said to arise from such rare events as fatal horse kicks, suicides, and goals scored in soccer or hockey. Modern examples of Poisson processes might include the number of aircraft accidents, chocolate chips in chocolate chip cookies, and a host of items in-between.

The first and most popularly used and misused continuous type of probability distribution we shall consider is the normal, sometimes known as Gaussian, which arises very frequently but not always in measurement, in nature, machine dimensional tolerances, and mechanical and electromechanical life distributions.

The beauty and utility of the normal lies not in its bell shape, which can easily be distorted by a cunning graphic con man, but in its mathematical properties. Not only is it one-humped and symmetrical (mean = median = mode), but its heights and areas at, beyond, or within any certain values are completely determined by knowledge of the mean and standard deviation. You may be aware that the subrange of one standard deviation above and below the mean of a normal distribution includes the middle 68 percent of its value and $\pm 2\sigma$ includes 95 percent. Given the population I.Q. mean of 100 and standard deviation of 15, we can readily determine that 95 percent of I.Q.'s fall between 70 and 130 (i.e. 100 $\pm 2 \times 15$) and only 2½ percent above 130. It is mathematically though perhaps not practically as important to know that the height of the normal curve at $\mu + 1\sigma$ and at $\mu - 1\sigma$ is about 60 percent of its ultimate height at the mode.

The normal frequently provides an accurate and very economical approximation to the binomial distribution and, under certain conditions, to the Poisson.

The lognormal probability distribution is defined simply as a distribution of measurements whose logarithms (to any base selected) are normally distributed. This distribution, said to be representative of many distributions of repair times, is always skewed positively, and its most interesting measures of location in maintainability analysis are its median (half of all repairs take less time) and a near-maximum point, usually the 90th and 95th centile (a sort of worst case).

The exponential probability distribution is used and sometimes misused as a model for numerous classes of life distributions of electronic and human elements. The exponential is skewed right, thus, it can be seen in Figure 38–4, its mean life is likely to be survived or surpassed by somewhat less than one half of all such components.

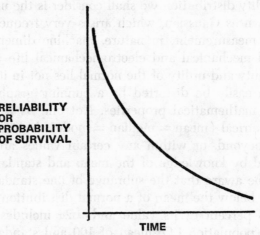

RELIABILITY OR PROBABILITY OF SURVIVAL

TIME

Figure 38–4. Exponential Reliability Curve.

Formally, the probability a component whose expected lifetime is μ will survive at least t hours of operation is given by

$$P(\geq t) = e^{\frac{-t}{\mu}} \tag{19}$$

during the so called "useful life" period, i.e. subsequent to burn-in (infant mortality) and prior to wearout (age degradation). The single symbol, μ replaces the common reliability four-letter words, MTBF and MTTF (respectively, mean-time-between-failures and mean-time-to-failure). Sometimes the expression in equation 19 is written as $e^{-\lambda t}$ where λ (Greek "lambda") is the failure rate, expected failures per hour, and equals $1/\mu$.

The probability a part type having $\mu = 1,000$ hours will last at least 1,000 hours equals

$$e^{-\frac{1000}{1000}} = e^{-1} \approx 0.37.$$

Its chance of surviving 2,000 hours, twice its mean, is only

$$e^{-\frac{2000}{1000}} = e^{-2} \approx 0.135.$$

Without pushing the component's state-of-the-art and paying a premium for more durable hardware if available, we consider such possible improvements as design with redundant or spare parts or cycling the component so as to reduce its operating time. If the time required were only 100 hours, the resulting success/survival probability would be

$$e^{-\frac{100}{1000}} = e^{-0.1} \approx 0.9.$$

From this point, as the negative exponent t/μ shrinks below 0.1, we can profitably use the approximation recommended in the Poisson discussion above. Thus the probability of operating an exponentially-failing, 1,000-hour component for at least 20 hours is

$$e^{-\frac{20}{1000}} = e^{-0.02} \approx 1 - 0.02 \approx 0.98 \text{ and so on.}$$

Confidence and Risk

Confidence is the degree of assurance associated with any statement, statistical or otherwise, while risk is its complement or lack of assurance. A confidence statement never stands alone but is always paired with something. It is a probability statement, expressed either in percent or decimal proportion, about a statement of an attribute, an average, a limit or pair of limits, or even another probability statement. It conveys one's willingness to bet on or back a claim or prediction.

For example the weather man, who until recent years, boldly said "it will rain" or "it will not rain," now couches his prediction of the attribute called measureable rainfall (presumably at least 0.005 inches rounded off upward to 0.01) in confidence terms such as "there's a 70 percent chance of rain."

Complementarily, risk is the "short-end odds;" the chance you're wrong in making a statement. Risk limits in statistically-based research are conventionally kept below 10 percent, most commonly either 5 percent or 1 percent. Somewhat in contrast, however, confidence levels on aerospace hardware reliability, itself usually of the realm of 0.9, 0.99, 0.999 or even higher, may be anywhere from 50 percent upward to, perhaps, 99 percent. Sixty percent confidence is typically associated with the success probability of current electronic equipment.

Sampling

The basic purpose of sampling, i.e. analyzing small or partial bodies of data, is that of inference or generalization to larger, parent bodies or populations. In other words, the goal of sampling is economy.

The primary characteristic or property of a useful sample is its representativeness. A representative sample is very much like the population from which it is drawn. If the sample contains all levels of the population in roughly their true proportions, we call it, by characteristic, stratified. Levels or strata may occur by geography, rank, education, ethnic group, occupation, age, height, or almost any other criterion. A stratified sample of USAF safety officers would include, in reasonable proportions, all commissioned ranks.

By method or technique, samples are also classified. A random sample is one chosen such that each member of the population has an equal chance of being selected. Let us emphasize that there is no such thing as a random sample by characteristic, merely samples selected by random methods. A balanced device (spinner, die, etc.) or a published table of long-run random digits should be used in random selection. The layman's approach to randomization (numbers in a hat, straws, etc.) could well lack randomness due to variation in size or consistency. The *Literary Digest's* classic *faux pas* in sampling, supposedly at random, voter preference in 1936, arose due to using lists of telephone subscribers, automobile owners, or some similarly biased group in those days of economic depression.

Deliberate or purposeful action in selecting a sample is called structuring. There arc many subtechniques used in structured sampling including the previously introduced term, "stratified," this time in the active sense. A stratified sample, by method, consists of deliberately choosing members such that all levels of the population are included and in their approximate parent proportions. For example, if the four geographic sections of a city contain respectively 15, 20, 25, and 40 percent of the population, we might require of our sample (and assure) that these percentages be retained, at least within some reasonable tolerance such as ± 5 percent for each section.

Randomness and stratification are frequently combined in sampling. One can randomize within a stratified framework, selecting randomly after first constraining the individual segments or strata. On the other hand, the sampler can refine a random sample by stratification.

Sampling many members from a few points of a population, called cluster sampling, is quite economical as compared with choosing single sample pieces from many "locations" within a population.

Two additional structuring methods of fairly recent origin are "sequential" and "peripheral." Sequential sampling or testing can be quite economical and flexible in that after each member of the sample is taken and evaluated, one of three decisions is made: either (1) the lot or hypothesis (theory) being tested is accepted, or (2) it is rejected, or (3) sampling is continued until

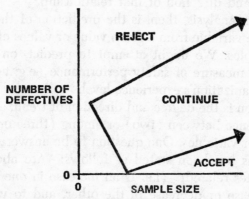

Figure 38–5. Sequential Sampling Plan.

the choice of one of the first two avenues becomes reasonably clear-cut. A graphic example of a sequential sampling plan appears in Figure 38–5.

Peripheral sampling or testing consists of sampling or analyzing first one or a few cases, best and/or worst (maximum and/or minimum values). Chewing away at the periphery, thus, frequently makes unnecessary the analysis of intermediate values.

Significance

There are two kinds of significance to be considered in this unit of subject matter, "practical" and "statistical." The former refers to such mundane criteria as cost, time, manpower, administrative feasibility, and other realistic factors. Statistical significance refers to the probability that a particular result could have arisen by chance of sampling alone. If, given that the hypothesis is true, such a result is quite unlikely to have occurred by sampling accident, let's say 5 percent or less, we deem it statistically significant. The essence of statistical significance is the twin concept of confidence-and-risk.

Regression and Correlation

Regression and correlation analysis both fall into the category of comparing two or more variables. Their principal difference lies in that regression analysis seeks to describe the form of a relationship, while correlation analysis seeks to determine merely the degree and direction of that relationship.

Regression analysis, then, is the prediction of the most likely value of one variable from a given value or values of one or more other variables. We might attempt to predict, on the basis of sampling, a measure of safety performance (e.g. accident rate) from an organization's experience level.

Correlation is the degree and direction of trend, association, or correspondence between (two) or among (three or more) characteristics or variables. One question to be answered by correlation analysis has been stated as follows: "Are abort rates and accident rates related?" (i.e. Is an increase in one accompanied by an increase or decrease in the other, and to what extent?) However, beware of concluding that a strong positive or negative numerical correlation implies cause-and-effect. There are *causal* relationships and, on the other hand *casual* ones, i.e. accidental, such as human birth rates and the size of the local stork population. Correlation numbers or coefficients r or the Greek letter ρ ("rho") are limited by -1 and $+1$. Mathematically, that is $-1 \leq r \leq +1$ or $-1 \leq \rho \leq +1$.

In the absence of *measured* data or as a quick-and-dirty approximation to pure correlation, simple special methods using *ranks* are available.

39

THE CHRONICLE
OF RELIABILITY

Vernon L. Grose

Of the many misused terms allied with safety, "reliability" has been one of the most misunderstood. It has been seen by some in unlimited light; it has been at the heart of countless controversies.

Dr. Grose clears up much of the misunderstanding by presenting a history of reliability from its inception in functional management to its proliferation in manned spaceflight and to its present maturity as a way of doing business.

Reliability, generally thought to be an adjunct of management, is also a natural adjunct of safety. The sometimes synonymous use of safety and reliability makes this article an essential bit of reading to set the matter straight. Reliability emerged a few years ago as a glamourous rising star with magic answers for all, but it finally assumed a mature stability. Those numerous parties who hitched their wagon to the star have either jumped off or assumed a rightful (and reliable) position.

T HE HISTORY of the discipline of Reliability as a management/ technical adjunct can be considered to consist of seven periods of time or ages. These ages are not necessarily sequent or mutually exclusive, but in general, the ages have existed in the order discussed.

The Age of Antiquity

The roots of Reliability lie far below the surface. They can be traced to the growth of business organization away from the venerated family-owned small business up through the diversifi-

Prepared under the auspices of the American Institute of Aeronautics and Astronautics System Effectiveness Technical Committee, June, 1968.

cation and decentralization of business fostered by the creation of railroad networks. Decentralization led to specialization or the functional approach to management.

Functional management divided the "big picture" into many small but manageable pieces. The ideal of craftsmanship gave way to less-than-total end products. The rise of science and technology produced machines which were complex beyond the total comprehension of any single individual.

Subtly throughout this evolution, the need for separate and overt Reliability activity was seeded.

The Age of Awakening

The magnitude of World War II, in terms of geographic distribution, logistics, weapon technology, and number of personnel involved, triggered an awakening to two aspects of technology. First, the capability of the machines resulting from technology impressed and even awed those who utilized them. Secondly, the awe concerning machine capability was tempered by dismay at the unpredictable and sporadic operation of these wonderful machines. Particularly in the electronic field, wartime experience during World War II and the Korean War caused many to doubt that machines would ever become consistently dependable.

Commercial airlines, in their rapid expansion after the Second World War, were plagued with unreliable VHF communications equipment. This problem encouraged the establishment of Aeronautical Radio, Incorporated (ARINC), one of the pioneer organizations in this country devoted to Reliability activity.

Likewise, the military picture was clouded by unreliable equipment. The Strategic Air Command, under General Curtis LeMay, was also experiencing great difficulty in maintaining a deterrent, twenty-four-hour airborne alert because of reliability problems. During this time period, the complexity (and unreliability) of equipment was growing at an exponential rate.

Perhaps the single individual who is best remembered for sounding a clarion call for Reliability is Robert Lusser, who had worked on the German V-1 missile testing program at Peenemunde, Germany, during World War II. He joined Dr. Werner Von Braun at Redstone Arsenal following service with the U. S.

Navy at Point Mugu, California. Almost immediately after his arrival in this country in the late 1940's, he began to agitate, provoke, and stimulate interest in Reliability.

The foundation for a Reliability awakening was laid when, a decade or more earlier, the need for other management adjuncts such as statistical quality control was recognized. In other words, management had already acknowledged the need for occasional and special assistance in the development of complex equipment. A slumbering discipline had stirred and would seek a place among the management adjuncts.

The Age of Propaganda

In retrospect, it was perhaps inevitable that a term with such widespread and common understanding as "reliability" should provide a ready tool for propaganda. Almost overnight, aerospace advertising fell in love with Reliability. Millions of magic metaphors mesmerized the multitudes.

Although there was growing public pressure for better missile reliability due to spectacular Cape Canaveral failures in the early 1950's, there were not yet contractual commitments beyond platitudes. Therefore, no specific funding was available for Reliability.

The opportunist, the dedicated, the incompetent, and even the "couldn't-care-less-what-the-company-wants-me-to-do" all jumped into the fray. Cultism sprang up, often with defensive but esoteric semantics. The call went forth for national Reliability conferences and symposia. The committee structure of the professional and trade societies began to list Reliability assignments and tasks.

The word was now being spread.

The Age of Statistics

The statistician, whose employment had declined since the end of World War II, was not long insensitive to the propaganda of Reliability. In fact, he immediately detected this phenomenon as a rising star, a new vista, and an unlimited horizon.

Obviously, Reliability possessed a probabilistic aspect. Responsible men such as Dr. R. R. Carhart of Rand Corporation noted this legitimate statistical interest in 1953. He, perhaps, is the first individual to issue a meaningful call for data which would enable a quantitative approach to Reliability.

During this period, the Department of Defense established the Advisory Group on Reliability of Electronic Equipment known as AGREE. The influence of the AGREE report of 1957 is still felt throughout the Reliability community.

Reminiscent of this age also is the familiar "bathtub curve" which was an attempt by statisticians to relate equipment life with human mortality (a major field of endeavor for statisticians prior to the rise of Reliability). Its applicability has been debated from its first proposal, and its remains controversial to this day.

Statisticians were not remiss in displaying the human tendency for cloistering themselves in a cloak of mystique, generating and expounding semantics known only to themselves. Almost in self-defense, the Reliability community became engaged in widespread (but often ignorant) chatter concerning the exponential, Weibull, and log normal distributions as well as Monte Carlo techniques and the Bayesian school of statistics.

For a certainty, statistics had made an eternal imprint on Reliability.

The Age of Specification

The Government, in the role of a monolithic customer for all aerospace products, soon reached the limit of the frustration index. The use of the word "goal" or "objective" in describing Reliability attributes proved to be only a heat generator. In the late 1950's, cynicism on both the Government and industry sides of the negotiation table was on the increase. The definition of failure, long the subject or private interpretation, had to be resolved.

Even though the definition of Reliability was still in a state of flux (and continues in irresolution to this day), the Government boldly began to issue requirements. Admittedly, these requirements did not yet contain demonstration criteria. However, such specification was considered a step forward.

The Government even took additional steps beyond a numerical requirement to detail certain basic activities which each contractor was expected to utilize in achieving the requirement.

Typical of these activities was design review, failure mode and effect analysis, and failure prediction during early design phases. This age was likewise characterized by a rise in testing activities under increasingly realistic environmental conditions.

Reliability had arrived as at least a topic for "small talk" during contract negotiations.

The Age of Showdown

The American free enterprise system produces, among other things, ingenuity in the face of contractual obstacles. This industrial ingenuity rapidly accommodated to penalty-free Government specification of Reliability. Since there was no demonstration necessary for the Reliability requirement, essentially no penalty could result if the equipment was less reliable than the requirement. In fact, under the CPFF climate, greater profits could be realized with unreliable equipment than with reliable equipment because more spares were needed.

Faced with this economic reality, Reliability was at the crossroads. The future of Reliability was threatened, on the one hand, by a deliberate choice of top management to ignore Reliability requirements in favor of cost and schedule. Without top management support and recognition, Reliability would waste away to nothing. On the other hand, without contractual "teeth," Reliability found itself in the unenviable position of espousing self-evident, moralistic precepts which only alienated its colleagues and aided its demise.

Two major factors produced a showdown for Reliability in the early 1960's. First, the concept of incentive contracting rapidly displaced the previously predominant CPFF contract. Secondly, America's manned spaceflight program emerged.

While incentive contracting (even with a separate profit determinant for Reliability) did not solve the economic dilemma of Reliability, it did refocus some objectives and goals of aerospace equipment which had long been either dormant or defamed through excessive emphasis on cost and schedule. More importantly for Reliability, incentive contracting challenged Reliability to prove that it could convert platitudes into economic tradeoff indices.

Manned spaceflight likewise provided Reliability with the challenge to convert its idealistic methodology into successful performance in an unknown environment which could not be simulated realistically here on earth. This conversion had to be made in the face of the small-sample insensitivity of classical statistics and the lack of representative data. The stakes in this adventure exceeded profit dollars—they included the lives of men and the Nation's prestige. Reliability technology proved its mettle when the chips were down—every Mercury and Gemini astronaut returned safely.

The age of showdown, though ostensibly desired by Reliability from its birth, demanded more than a tranquil response from Reliability when it arrived.

The Age of Maturation

Reliability is in the process of responding to the age of showdown. Indications to date abound that the response is progressively mature. This age may last longer than the first six combined. It will be characterized by less emotion and by more interdisciplinary empathy than existed in the first six ages.

Early signs of maturation appeared when Reliability exponents rose above their parochial interests to acknowledge a larger viewpoint represented by the supra-discipline of System Effectiveness. The work of the Weapon System Effectiveness Industry Advisory Committee (WSEIAC) in 1965 is a prime example of this viewpoint.

The maturing process for Reliability will continue to resound with economic overtones. The longer the Reliability problem is studied, the greater the evidence that economics is the common denominator for Reliability just as it is for all other aspects of management. Reliability personnel in this age must continue to develop their yet embryonic interest, sensitivity and knowledge concerning top management's three-legged stool of cost, schedule, and performance. Rather than trying to add a fourth leg to the stool (we all know that a four-legged stool is inherently unstable), Reliability will reach maturity much earlier if it is able to think, act, and express its activities in the constraints of the three classical areas.

The adoption of Reliability technology by the commercial world hinges on the ability to relate the formalized disciplines of Reliability to the profit-and-loss sheet. Already, the automotive industry and commercial airlines have incorporated much of the technology of Reliability assurance.

Some of the problems of Reliability achievement not yet totally solved include the proper utilization of human motivational resources (getting everyone in the system development process to "care"), the ability to assess Reliability under conditions of insufficient data, and the relationship between cost of Reliability activities and product yield in terms of profit and/or competitive market posture. However, these problems are receiving increasing attention and effort, and solutions are emerging.

The joys and sorrows of childhood are past for Reliability— the responsibilities of adulthood dare not be evaded.

40

HOW ARE YOU
COMING THROUGH?

Virgil R. Carlson

*When Virgil Carlson, a research scientist, was first appointed chair-
man of the safety committee, he thought his main task would be to
provide opposition to unnecessary rules and regulations originating
in the safety office. His gradual realization of the importance and
place of safety in organizations composed largely of scientists has led
to this article.*

*Quite possibly, his article should be titled "The Care and Feeding
of Scientists in Safety Matters." Anyone who has a group of highly
educated and highly specialized persons in his care will welcome
Carlson's observations. The practical application of his writing is
found not by pointing out how scientists are different from other
people, but how they are so very similar. His thought should make it
easier for the safety person to deal with the scientific community.*

M Y PRIMARY JOB is that of a research scientist in an organization conducting basic research. My own research has nothing directly to do with safety, but I am also the chairman of our
safety committee and I have developed more than a passing
interest in the topic for that reason. I don't have to be convinced
of the necessity and importance of an effective safety program.

We have about a dozen members on our safety committee, representing various kinds of research activity from chemistry and
biology to psychiatry and sociology. The members of the safety
committee don't have to be persuaded of the need for a safety
program, either. We would probably agree with most any reason-

Taken from the *1969 Transactions of the National Safety Congress,* Research
and Development Sessions, published by the National Safety Council, 525 North
Michigan Avenue, Chicago, Illinois.

able safety regulation, or principle regarding safety, that you might seriously propose. But we're only thirteen among an immediate working force of several hundred scientists, working within a larger community of several thousand scientists.

What I am going to try to do is to represent to you the attitudes one finds in such a group of research scientists toward safety and toward professional safety personnel—not the attitudes of all research scientists, nor perhaps even of a majority, but possibly of a plurality.

I'm not going to report what scientists *say* their attitudes are. They know very well that it is not officially acceptable to oppose virtue, motherhood, free enterprise, or safety, and they will not voice such opposition—not for the record, anyway. I shall try, rather, to infer their attitudes from my experience of their reactions to safety measures we have tried to implement or encourage.

Scientists are not different from all other groups of people, but it may not be so obvious which other groups they are similar to. For example, you may wonder whether they would be analogous to piecework factory employees or to employees getting paid by the hour or other time period rather than by actual production. You might wonder about this, because the problem of getting workers to conform to safe working practices can be quite different for these two bases of compensation. If employees are getting paid on a piecework basis, many will cut corners and engage in unsafe practices if they think they can increase their output by doing so.

I have a friend who at one time operated a machine which punched a hole in a small metal item. He was paid partly by the number of items he processed, but the machine was supposedly constructed so that the operator could not get his fingers in the way of the punching die no matter how fast he worked. He positioned the piece to be punched with his left hand and had to press two buttons, one with each hand, in order to operate the punching mechanism. The buttons were located so that his fingers had to be clearly out of the way when the punching operation occurred. My friend discovered, though, that he could go through the operation in less time if he held one button in with his knee, so that he didn't have to remove his left hand so far from the item being punched. He increased his production quite a bit, until one day his right hand wasn't paying close enough attention to what his left hand was doing, and the left hand lost a finger.

Well, our scientists get paid every two weeks whether they have completed an experiment or have had a creative idea or not during the pay period, so one might think that problems associated with piecework occupations would be irrelevant. But I don't know any scientist conducting original research who feels that he does his work simply because he gets paid for it. First, he is genuinely interested in the subject matter for its own sake. Once he has invested a lot of thought and background research in an experiment, he is highly motivated to do the experiment in order to find out what the results are, even if he had to go ahead and do the experiment without getting paid for it. But this work attitude does not stem altogether from altruism or from pure intellectual curiosity. The scientist gains in stature and respect in the scientific community at large in proportion to the amount of competent research he is able to accomplish. In terms of the longer range rewards open to him, he functions much more like the piecework employee than the employee who works by the hour or the week.

One general consequence is that the scientist takes a very dim view of anything that interferes with the accomplishment of his research in the way that he thinks it should be accomplished. Unfortunately, it is in the nature of most safety requirements that they do require more care, more effort, and more time than doing something without regard for considerations of safety; and the need for such requirements has to be pretty definite and compelling before the scientist will take them very seriously.

Let me repeat that it is not only anything that interferes with the accomplishment of his research that the scientist abhors, it is anything that interferes with doing the research in the way that he thinks it must be done in relation to the scientific requirements of the problem. If a safety engineer should presume to tell a scientist that his experiment must be done some other way because it might be safer that way, he is likely to run into some pretty fierce opposition. I would, as a matter of fact, join the opposition myself on that issue.

The analogy to piecework employment—some kinds, anyway —can actually be carried quite a bit farther but there are also important differences, and I won't pursue the comparison any further. Instead it might be worthwhile to point out a respect in which you might think scientists would be different from other groups but are not, as far as I can tell. Scientists are excellent logicians, many are accomplished mathematicians, and most at least understand the basic principles of probability very well. You would think, therefore, that they would more easily appreciate the logic and tenets of probability theory behind any sound safety regulation, but such is not necessarily the case.

One of our safety engineers told me of an unsuccessful attempt he once made to get a scientist to attend a training session on how to use the fire extinguishers in his laboratory. The scientist's argument was that when a fire broke out in his laboratory he would then set about learning how to use the fire extinguishers but he wasn't going to waste time on this matter as long as there was no fire to be concerned about.

Now the basic problem here is not as absurd as it sounds. We're all guilty of illogicality in this respect at times. Consider the motorist driving down a residential street where a child might run out from behind a parked car. No motorist in his right mind will exceed the speed limit when he thinks there is a significant probability of a child running in front of his car. But if the motorist is in a hurry—and his mission may be quite urgent—he is more likely to exceed the speed limit. He is in effect assuming that the probability of a child running out into the street is less because he, the driver, happens to be in a hurry. But the reason he is in a hurry has no logical connection with the reason a child might decide to run into the street. It doesn't matter what the cause of the motorist's urgency is, it cannot reduce the probability that the child might choose that particular moment to get in the way.

In the laboratory, one can see this same illogic operating time and again. If it does not cost the scientist any great time, effort, or inconvenience, he will agree that adherence to a given safety regulation is worthwhile, even that it is important to do so. If, however, it would cause appreciable difficulty to adhere to the regulation, then he acts as though the probability of an accident arising from that source is sufficiently remote that he can safely ignore the regulation. Usually the reasons for the inconvenience or difficulty to the scientist have no logical connection with the probability of an accident occurring in the particular instance, any more than there is a causal connection between the motorist's reason for being in a hurry and the child's reason for running out into the street; but the scientist is not automatically aware of this lack of connection.

One of our laboratory chiefs located a drying oven out in the public corridor in front of his laboratory. This was illegal for several reasons; one being that this kind of oven can overheat, and if a passerby happened to lean against it he could get badly burned. Fortunately this did not happen, but the oven did overheat, igniting some plastic and wooden materials which someone had left on top of it. The fire department put the fire out before any great damage was done, and the safety office insisted that the drying oven be taken out of the corridor.

The laboratory chief then relocated the oven in an equally unacceptable spot—in a public area next to a freight elevator. He agreed that if he had the space in his laboratory, that's where the oven should be; but he argued that there was no room in his laboratory for it and the oven was so important to his research that he had to operate it either in the corridor or in that space next to the elevator. He simply overlooked the fact that the probability of the oven overheating and of someone coming into contact with it accidentally was completely independent of why he needed to operate the oven in the corridor or the elevator space.

So, with this characterization of the scientist as being no less irrational than anybody else when it comes to matters affecting his own personal interests, I had better get on with listing the attitudes scientists have toward safety, acknowledging that for each attitude one can find one or more other groups who manifest a similar attitude. Perhaps the particular set of attitudes I shall mention are unique to scientists, although I wouldn't be at all sure of that.

I have said that the scientist generally considers safety matters as being of secondary importance. That is at least true for pretty obviously necessary safety regulations, where the consequences of unsafe practice are not completely certain but are nevertheless reasonably definite—although of secondary importance, he at least thinks of such regulations as important. The situation is far worse with respect to conditions which favor an uncertain probability of accident occurrence. A shelf can be overloaded with equipment and hang on the wall for years without actually falling down on anyone. What is the scientist's attitude toward procedures directed merely at lessening the probability of accidents rather than clearly preventing injury or damage?

To the scientist, the safety program and its personnel are part and parcel of the administrative system—he puts requirements for budget justifications, accounting for travel expenses, requirements for eight copies of every form, and the safety rules and regulations all in the same bag, labels it "bureaucratic red tape," and thinks of it generally as something that ought to be kept to an absolute minimum, if not abolished altogether. He thinks that anyone whose full-time job is concerned with safety can and probably will think up many rules and requirements which are actually unnecessary and primarily serve the purpose of giving the safety people something to do. Anybody, he feels, can come up with a comprehensive set of restrictions which would prevent accidents but would also prevent getting any productive work done.

When I first became chairman of our safety committee some years ago, I remember I fully expected that my main task would be to provide opposition to unnecessary rules and regulations promulgated by the safety office.

We have an excellent safety office and excellent safety engineers, however, who try hard to make sure that the rules and procedures they develop have purpose, are defensible, and are reasonably enforceable. I learned that by working with them. I have tried to convince our scientists of it, but I'm not optimistic that many really believe it. One problem is that we do have some —not many, but a few—rather arbitrary and unwieldy regulations, which have evolved in spite of the best efforts of the safety office rather than because of the safety office, but that evolution is rather complicated and easily misunderstood and the safety office is the culprit in the eyes of many.

There is another way in which the attitude that the safety regulations are simply part of the general set of administrative rules and procedures leads to an unfortunate result. The scientist feels that he should himself be the judge of the extent to which he will conform to administrative requirements. In part, this attitude is due to the fact that scientists are probably generally more or less non-conforming by nature and as a matter of principle are not likely to conform to any rule simply for the sake of conforming. There are, certainly, instances where this viewpoint is legitimate and valuable.

For example, the working day for most employees at our place is from 8:30 A.M. to 5:00 P.M. The scientists, however, see no sense in sticking to these hours if they can get their work done better on some other schedule or according to an irregular schedule; they do pretty much determine their own work schedules, and, I am sure, get far more worthwhile work done than if they were forced to stick to the 8:30 to 5:30 routine.

There are other instances, however, where conformance to rules is not better left to the individual's own determination. We could evolve a system in which each motorist determined whether or not he would stop at a red traffic light. We might allow him to go through the light if he judged that he was on an important enough mission and if he judged that he could get across the intersection safely. While this system might be defensible on rational grounds, as a practical matter it would be worthless. Accidents would probably increase; but even if they didn't, can you imagine the legal entanglements we would get into in trying to determine which motorist was on the more important mission and whether or not he had sufficient grounds for thinking he could get across the intersection without mishap?

If the safety rules and regulations are reasonable ones, the scientist is not really better off in the long run if he has the prerogative of determining whether he will conform or not in each specific instance. One of our rules is that storage cabinets can be located in the corridors according to certain criteria, one of which is that nothing is to be put on top of the cabinets.

One day I noticed a colleague putting a cardboard box on top of a cabinet; I pointed out that it was illegal for him to do that, and he should put the box somewhere else. He argued that this box was not likely to fall down on anyone, and even if it did it was not heavy enough to hurt anybody. I told him that that particular box might not constitute a direct safety hazard in and of itself but that it did nevertheless constitute a safety hazard in the following sense: If he were allowed to violate the rule, then another person down the hall would argue that he should have the right to place his glassware on top of his cabinet. With the box and the glassware in plain sight, someone else would put a heavy microscope stand up there, and so it would go.

When all of the first-order space was taken up, people would start piling items on top of the box, on top of the glassware, and on top of the microscope stand, and we would end up with a situation in which it would be worth your life to bump against one of those cabinets. We would have to set up a committee to consider and pass judgment on every individual application for placing an item on top of a cabinet, and the scientist himself would object to this procedure as an example of bureaucratic red tape of the worst kind.

The principle, however, that it is advantageous to the individual to conform to a rule even when the rule seems unnecessary in the particular instance, is one that goes especially hard with scientists, and although I won the argument with that individual over the cardboard box, I wouldn't be in the least surprised to see that same individual leave a gas cylinder standing in the corridor on the argument that it didn't constitute a hazard because it was empty.

The scientist sees the need for a professional safety office most clearly in terms of making available a needed service when he wants it. Everyone appreciates the value of having a fire department one can call in case of fire. The chemist appreciates the value of an expert source which he can contact to find out the hazards associated with a new compound with which he has not worked before. But scientists want this service on a "Don't call me, I'll call you" basis.

How much effort do they exert to see that the personnel in their laboratories are observing acceptable safety practices on a routine day-to-day basis? Paradoxically, they feel that this, too, is the responsibility of the safety office, not realizing that in order to be able to accomplish this task effectively the safety office would have to set up a superstructure of monitoring procedures which would be quite unacceptable to the scientists themselves.

While on the subject of paradoxes, scientists are likely to see the problem of safety as consisting essentially of analyzing the accidents that occur and determining what measures should be taken to prevent those accidents from recurring in the future. But usually, once an accident has occurred, the means of preventing that particular accident seem so absurdly obvious and simple that no one learns anything generally useful from it. We recently had an instance where technicians were storing dry ice in an inadequately ventilated room. They began to wonder why they became drowsy when they were working in that room. Any scientist would know immediately why they became drowsy and would say that the dry ice ought to be taken out of there. It presented no problem, of course, to take the dry ice out of the room. The problem was, and still is, to create a system for detecting and correcting any hazard before an unfortunate incident occurs. We would not now know, any better than we do, how to solve that problem if someone had actually suffocated in that room instead of merely becoming drowsy.

I rather think that the occurrence of an accident, even though it may lessen the probability of another occurrence of exactly the same kind, may actually increase the probability of other accidents, because attention is focused on the particular details of the accident itself and drawn away from the real problem.

I think this paradoxical effect of the actual occurrence of accidents may be true for an additional reason. Consider a chemist or a physiologist who is told about that dry ice incident. He is likely to think that dry ice and people should not be located in a nonventilated room at the same time, that it doesn't take any great ability to figure that out, and safety in general is a pretty dull topic. If I were to identify any one attitude the scientist has which creates the greatest obstacle to the establishment of a successful general safety program, I would say it is just that— the scientist simply finds the subject intellectually uninteresting.

If he would think the problem out carefully, he would find that it does involve intellectually challenging issues, and he would probably develop an attitude of safety consciousness and willing cooperation with those whose responsibility it is to try to construct an effective safety program. But how do you get someone to think carefully about a topic that he presumes is uninteresting and mundane? If you send him an essay in the mail, it is likely to go directly into the wastebasket. If you schedule a meeting on safety, you won't need a very large room to accommodate scientists who have no special reason to be there. If you sponsor a movie on safety, you may attract those employees who see it as a welcome break in their regular routine, but you are not likely to pull the scientist away from his work.

I don't think the problem is necessarily insoluble, but I am pretty well convinced that the answer does not lie in protesting to the scientist that "Safety is, too, interesting." He is likely to think, "Well, fine, if you think so, then you go ahead and be concerned about it," or, "You're probably right—I'll have to give it some thought some day." What should be done in order to deal effectively with this and the other attitudes I have brought up is not a simple matter.

41

MEN SHOULD FIT MACHINES

DAVID MEISTER

Several selections in this volume deal with ergonomics, human factors engineering, the design of machines in expectation of the interface with the human operator. There is a special reason for another: Why is this body of knowledge so often ignored, even rejected, by the design engineer? Mr. Meister directs himself to that question in this selection.

The author feels strongly about the almost traditional conflict between the human factors engineer and the design engineer. He gives three reasons why "they" won't listen. Writing as a human factors specialist, one of his reasons is, "The design engineer couldn't care less." He does, however, try to see both sides and discusses his three reasons in some depth.

In this article, Dr. Meister addresses himself to the design engineer and makes a good case that the design engineer should change his ways. It would be interesting to speculate on how the human factors specialist should change his own ways to get on the same wave length as the design engineer. Their failure to communicate is often glaringly evident and poses a fundamental challenge.

> Engineers are often loath
> to disturb the beautiful
> symmetry of machines by
> providing for the people
> who have to operate them.

N OVICE SPECIALISTS in human-engineering factors learn quickly that their views are little considered when new systems are being developed, even when the human-factors engineer is part of the design team.

Dr. David Meister is Technical Director of Bunker-Ramo Corp.'s Human Factors Programs. His article is based on work for the government by his staff, and is reprinted from Engineer, November–December, 1967.

Theoretically, the human-factors engineer is just as important to systems design as any other engineer. In practice, he is seldom listened to.

The problem lies in the relationship between the design engineer, who is oriented by training and experience toward the functional, concrete and physical dimensions of design, and the human-factors engineer, who is concerned with the behavioral implications of that design. How to translate these behavioral concepts into physical engineering terms is the primary difficulty facing both types of engineer.

It Should Be Obvious

To the human-factors specialist, it is obvious that personnel requirements affect system design. The number of men who will operate and maintain the equipment, their skill level, the jobs they will be asked to perform, and their limitations and capacities as anthropomorphic humans cannot be ignored. The problem is to demonstrate these factors in concrete terms.

To take a somewhat fanciful example, if a customer specifies that the operator of one device shall never be shorter than 6 ft. 4 in., but for another the maximum operator height shall be 3 ft. 6 in., then the scale of the two devices must be greatly different, even though their functions are identical.

Fortunately, personnel requirements are rarely so extreme. Designers generally work within a "normal" (5 to 95 percentile) range of personnel characteristics, so that human factors do not completely control equipment configuration. But this means that the human-factors engineer finds it much harder to demonstrate, and the system developer to realize, the importance of human factors to design.

The problem is complicated by the difference between what human-factors specialists call "hard" and "soft" inputs. "Hard" inputs, such as the operator's reach distance, or the amount of force he can exert, influence or deal directly with hardware design, such as the nature of controls and displays. Design engineers readily understand and incorporate "hard" inputs.

"Soft" inputs describe the characteristics of equipment operators, such as the amount of work they can handle and their skill level. It is much more difficult to translate "soft" information into hardware design, and the human-factors engineer who provides this data has a much harder time convincing the design engineer of its relevance.

What use the design engineer makes of the human-factors information he receives depends very much on: the form in which he receives it; its timing relative to the design problems that sent him to seek the information in the first place; the quantity of other engineering information with which the human-factors data must compete; and its comprehensibility.

The effectiveness of the information depends on the engineer's willingness to accept it as *relevant* to his problem, as well as on its actual usefulness toward solution of the problem.

Why They Won't Listen

There are three major reasons why human-factors information may lack significant impact when presented to the engineer:

The timing may be wrong.

It is not relevant to the design.

The design engineer couldn't care less.

The third reason, which we can express as engineering attitudes, is frequently the most significant.

Let Us Discuss These Obstacles In Detail

TIMING. Much information on personnel tends to lag design decisions rather than anticipate them. Indeed, even to be concurrent may be too late.

The average human-factors engineer, whose engineering background may be minimal, is heavily dependent upon engineering information from others on which to base his own contributions. But though military specifications imply that the human-factors engineer is to be an integral part of a project team, too often he is more or less isolated, especially if he does not understand the engineering implications of what is going on.

Thus the human-factors engineer is often frozen out of the early design work at precisely the time when fundamental decisions are made—decisions that he will later find extremely difficult to reverse if he doesn't agree with them.

(This negative atmosphere causes human-engineers to comment wryly that their specialty is the first to feel and the hardest to be hit by the impact of any economies required during system development. Their gloomy claim to priority when the cuts come might be disputed by the public relations department, whose motto is: "Last to know; first to go.")

RELEVANCY. This means "What is the effect of the information on design?" Even if we assume that every human-factors input has some implication for the design configuration, that implication is not always obvious.

If, for example, the human-factors specialist tells the engineer that the people who will operate his system will have relatively little training, then the engineer needs to know what he should do to compensate for those training deficiencies.

Should he increase the information flow by adding displays? Should he reduce the operator's need for understanding by eliminating displays? Should he use pushbuttons rather than toggle switches? Does it really matter? We believe it does.

Since the engineer is not a behavioral scientist, he cannot realistically be expected to extrapolate from human factors data to hardware unless the data are provided to him as concrete restraints on design.

ATTITUDES. Aside from whatever inadequacies human-factors information itself possesses, the fact that design engineers give such information a rather low priority complicates the problems.

Sure We Hear You

When questioned directly, engineers say they automatically consider the personnel aspects of their designs. However, actual observation of engineers at work reveals that their consideration of human factors is usually after the design fact, if at all. Like reliability, maintainability and value engineering, which the engineer has been forced increasingly to accommodate in his pure design-responsibility, human factors has had to contend with the ignorance or indifference of some engineers and the active hostility of others.

The problems we have described are not merely anecdotal. Several experimental studies were performed at Bunker-Ramo

Corp. to investigate how design engineers actually made use of human-factors information illustrated all of these difficulties.

But You Don't Listen

Our studies are as interesting for what they did not reveal as for what they did. Most of the engineer-subjects had little or no interest in human factors, no matter what they said, and they had a similar lack of interest in human-factors information, or in the application of human-factors to design. Almost all of them failed to recognize a human-engineering design problem when it arose. Most of the subjects failed to make any use of the human-engineering guides that they had available during the tests, nor did they pay any attention to the human-engineering specifications called out in the design statement of work.

When the drawings the engineers developed during the tests were reviewed after the sessions, the subjects failed to mention any human factors that had directed their designs—this despite the fact that the problems had been created precisely to make use of such information.

Rather than use available data, the engineer typically solved human-factors problems by placing himself in the role of the equipment operator (commendable, in some walks of life, but not here). For instance, to determine the appropriate height of the console-desk required by the test specification, the engineer measured the height of the desk at which he sat. Yet the requirements for such desks are spelled out in every human-engineering handbook.

It is informative about their way of doing things that in the subjects' collective past experience, which in some cases covered as many as twenty years of design work, not a single engineer had ever consulted a human-factors specialist on any design problem.

One might infer that the need for human-factors information is exaggerated since design engineers so often ignore it. However, our analysis of the drawings done by the thirty engineer-subjects turned up many inadequacies that could be traced directly to ignorance of human-engineering requirements.

There are several reasons why some engineers ignore human factors.

But It Worked Before

Engineers often design on an experiential basis, meaning that they tend to develop a pattern of design, which they then apply to all their later work. For example, one of the design problems in our experiment required a decision between a single-man or a multi-man console, the choice to be based on the amount of operating work involved. All subjects chose the single-man concept because this was the type they had designed previously.

Absence of any human-engineering indoctrination in the academic training of engineers reinforces this tendency.

Another and more serious reason why engineers fail to use the available data is because, as provided, it too often lacks design-relevancy. The principles presented in human-engineering guides and specifications are overly general, and frequently do not express clearly their implications for design.

In addition, our tests indicated that engineers prefer to have their data presented in graphic or pictorial rather than verbal form. But unfortunately, most human-factors data are verbal—even verbose.

Revise the Books

The engineering psychologist has attempted to communicate his findings on developing special handbooks, checklists and guides on human engineering for the equipment engineer. How effective these materials are in communicating data to the engineer is another question, which is particularly cogent in view of the on-going revision of a Joint Services (Army, Navy, Air Force) Guide.

This Guide was first developed in 1954 as a series of Air Force reports. It was eventually published, in 1963, as "Human Engineering Guide to Equipment Design," Morgan, et al., McGraw-Hill.

The continuing revision of Morgan, et al. is under the general supervision of the Engineering Psychology Branch of the Office of Naval Research. The Branch has sponsored a series of studies to determine what could be done to improve the applicability of human-engineering handbook material to the engineer. Our experiment was part of one of these studies.

None of the engineers that we tested owned a human-engineering handbook, nor had they ever even read one. Indeed, a later effort to provide the Bunker-Ramo design group with a free copy of the Morgan et al text was rejected by the group supervisor. He felt that the handbook would never be used by his people.

Persuading design engineers to make greater use of human-factors engineering is not an easy task. But we do have some suggestions:

Human-engineering handbooks designed for general use can be substantially modified by excising all irrelevant material. The remaining material should then be presented in palatable form, avoiding the quasi-scientific style of writing that human-factors specialists seem to favor.

A major revision in human-engineering texts and standards is long overdue. But before any new material is written, there must be an investigation of design problems and of the kind of human-engineering information that engineers need. We at Bunker-Ramo Corporation have started such a study, having as its aim the development of a new human-engineering guide.

When the human-engineer presents an input to his designing colleague, he must ensure that the system equipment implications of that input are expressed explicitly. If he cannot state these implications clearly, then he should reject the input as inappropriate for the design engineer, however meaningful it may be to the human-engineer.

It is much more difficult to suggest a way to motivate the engineer so that he will pay greater attention to human factors.

Catch Them Young

It may be necessary to include courses in human engineering in the engineers' academic curricula, catching him during his most impressionable years, and there infusing him with respect for the importance of human factors in his future designs.

A more immediate solution could be the brute force approach, where procurement specifications would demand the incorporation of human engineering in design. However, this course would probably work only if the customer efficiently monitors the design process.

Another solution, on government work, might be to bypass the engineer and have the government perform the required human-engineering analyses and include them in the design specifications as fixed design criteria. We are dubious about this approach, knowing well how engineers resist any restrictions on their freedom to design.

The ultimate solution seems to lie with the human-engineer himself, and on his ability to provide information that the design engineer recognizes as design-relevant. Though not an engineer myself, I incline to this approach, in the belief that engineers are reasonable men who will recognize the utility of inputs when these inputs are actually useful.

It is unlikely that the human-engineering discipline will go away just because some engineers refuse to acknowledge its existence. The government particularly, which has a vested interest in the development of satisfactory systems, will continue to demand the integration of human factors and engineering efforts, if only because too many systems developed in the past without enough thought to human factors have turned out to be less than adequate.

Engineers have a responsibility, therefore, to be open-minded about human engineering and to make the dialogue between themselves and human-factors specialists truly a two-way conversation.

42

COST/BENEFIT OF SAFETY
INVESTMENTS USING FAULT
TREE ANALYSIS

David B. Brown

The author mates a new methodology, fault tree analysis, to an older concept of cost/benefit. "The purpose here in quantifying fault tree analysis is effective allocation of the safety budget."

Dr. Brown explains the methodology of fault tree analysis, defines the terms used, and illustrates the symbols and Boolean techniques. All this has been done before, and the author acknowledges the work of others in discussing the qualitative uses of fault trees. He then proceeds "to examine one quantitative application," for Dr. Brown asserts, "the full potential of the technique cannot be realized without quantification."

His special contribution lies in the one quantitative application he offers. By this method, a measure of negative utility can be obtained for any head event. Quantitative tools are badly needed in the safety profession, and Dr. Brown presents this one in sufficient detail to serve as "a working guide to the use of fault tree analysis for such cost/benefit analyses."

FAULT TREE ANALYSIS is a technique frequently discussed in safety literature (Kolodner, 1971; Recht, 1966). It is a logical approach to identify the areas in a system that are most critical to safe operation. According to Recht (1966), fault tree analysis was developed in 1962 by H. A. Watson of Bell Telephone Laboratories. Although it has been used extensively in the design of spacecraft by NASA (Noland, Cannizo, & Johnston, 1972), its

Reprinted with permission from the *Journal of Safety Research*, a National Safety Council publication, Volume 5, Number 3.

application to occupational safety and health has been limited.

In the past, many inexpensive efforts, such as safety campaigns, slogans, goals, etc., have been used to attack the problem of industrial safety. When measured in terms of cost/effectiveness, the low cost of these activities probably renders them a favorable investment. The same is true of inexpensive equipment such as hard hats and fire extinguishers. The effectiveness of these items has been clearly demonstrated.

But we are now at a point where Congress, through the Williams-Steiger Occupational Safety and Health Act of 1970, has stated that these primary investments are not enough. More rigid safety requirements have become mandatory, generally requiring additional financial outlay by industry for safety and health. There is, of course, a limited amount of money that can be practically spent in this area without unfavorably altering the competitive position of American products. Although there are still some recognizable expenditures that must come first, most of the obvious measures have already been taken. A large problem has developed in determining those expenditures that will prevent the most accidents and save the most lives. Since this is a problem of cost/effectiveness, its solution is the direct responsibility of the Industrial Engineer.

This paper presents a working guide to the use of fault tree analysis for such cost/benefit analyses. It is recognized that the mere construction of a fault tree for a system brings about a benefit in understanding the system with respect to safety. However, quantitative aspects of fault tree analysis greatly multiply its power. The methodology and techniques of fault tree analysis presented are based primarily upon the terminology used by NASA (Noland, et al., 1972). Some quantitative techniques are suggested for obtaining additional benefits by determining the most cost/effective areas for system improvement.

METHODOLOGY

In order to discuss the methodology of fault tree analysis, some basic definitions must be understood. These are presented below.

1. *Event.* A previously defined and specified occurrence within the system. It may be defined at the system or compon-

ent level. Examples: (1) Switch A fails to perform properly, (2) Switch A fails due to extreme temperature, and (3) System mode change by operation of Switch A. An event does not have to cause failure; it can be a normal happening within the system.

2. *Fault event.* An abnormal occurrence resulting in some type of failure, an undesirable event.

3. *Normal event.* An expected and desirable occurrence. A normal event could possibly become a fault event due to timing and therefore it is important that the timing of a normal event be specified if necessary. (Note: Fault and normal events are mutually exclusive and all encompassing.)

4. *Basic event.* An event (fault or normal) that occurs at the element level, where element refers to the smallest subdivision of the analysis of the system. For example, if failure rates are available for certain system components, these components would form the elements, inasmuch as any further subdivision of the components would be unnecessary. Thus, a basic event would be the failure of one of these components.

5. *Primary event.* An event caused by some characteristic inherent in the component, such as the failure of a lightbulb due to a worn filament.

6. *Secondary event.* An event caused by an external source, such as the failure of a lightbulb due to excessive voltage.

7. *Head event.* The event at the top of the fault tree that is analyzed by the remainder of the tree. This is generally a resultant failure that removes the system (man or machine) from normal operation.

The symbology of fault tree analysis will be presented in the next section. To obtain an understanding of the procedure, it is first helpful to get an overview of the general fault tree approach. Construction of a fault tree originates by a process of synthesis and analysis, as illustrated in the following outline:

A. Synthesis

    1. Determine at the most general level *all* events that are considered undesirable for the normal operation of the system under study.

    2. Separate these events into mutually exclusive groups ac-

cording to some common relationships (such as similar causes).

3. Utilizing the common relationship, establish one event that encompasses all events in a selected group. This event is the *head event* and will be considered by a separate fault tree.

B. Analysis: Top Down Approach

1. Select one head event, the event that is to be prevented or whose probability is to be reduced. (One system might have many head events as indicated in step 3 above.)

2. Determine all events that could cause the head event.

3. Determine the relationship between the causal event and the head event in terms of the AND and OR Boolean operators.

4. Determine the value of further analysis of each event determined in steps 2 and 3. For each causal event that is to be further developed, repeat steps 2 and 3 with the term "head event" replaced by the particular causal event to be analyzed.

5. Continue to repeat steps 2, 3, and 4 until all events are basic events, or until it is not desirable to develop the event further because of insignificance, lack of data, etc.

6. Diagram the events using the symbols presented in the next section.

7. Perform qualitative and quantitative analyses as discussed below.

It should be clear that more than one fault tree may be developed for each system. Each class of undesirable events will probably require a separate tree. Although the trees may later be linked together, it is beneficial to keep them separate at the development stage. Further, if a system operates in more than one mode, it may be necessary to develop a different set of fault trees for each mode of the system.

Consider the following example as an illustration of the synthesis process. Suppose the system under consideration is a grinding operation and, according to Synthesis step 1, the following fault events must be prevented:

1. Hand or fingers touch wheel.
2. Arm contacts wheel.

3. Clothing gets caught in machine.
4. Speck of metal contacts eye.
5. Improper grounding causes electrical shock.
6. Motor overheating produces fire.

Of course, this is a partial list of possible undesirable events, but it is sufficient to illustrate the procedure. A more complete list could be obtained from past accident reports.

The second step is to separate these events into mutually exclusive groups according to some classification scheme. This is, in a sense, an art rather than a science and depends highly upon the ability of the analyst. Certain relationships should be immediately apparent, however. Events 1 and 2 are very closely related and could be analyzed concurrently; the same is true of events 5 and 6. Event 4 is unique and should be analyzed separately. Event 3 might be included with 1 and 2; however, since it refers to clothing rather than direct contact, we prefer to analyze it separately.

With these four groups, the following four head events can now be created:

Events	Head Event
1 and 2	Wheel contact with person
3	Clothing caught in machine
4	Chip in eye
5 and 6	Motor-related accident

Each of these head events should be used to begin a top down approach to constructing a fault tree as indicated under Analysis above. Prior to continuing this example, however, the symbols and Boolean techniques of fault tree analysis must be understood.

SYMBOLS AND BOOLEAN TECHNIQUES

The fault tree diagram is especially useful in qualitative analyses of a system for safety. In order to use the diagrams to their greatest advantage, it is helpful if the standard symbols are used. The following symbols are recommended:

1. *Rectangle*. The rectangle is used to identify events that will generally be developed further in the analysis.

2. *Circle*. The circle is used to identify basic events, that is, events that are in no further need of development because of the sufficiency of empirical data.

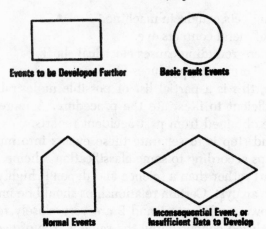

Figure 42–1. Event Symbols For Fault Tree Analysis.

3. *House.* This identifies events that are expected to occur in the normal operation of the system.

4. *Diamond.* This is used for an event that will not be developed further in the logic diagram because of insufficient data or because the event itself is inconsequential. (Fig. 42–1 illustrates the first four symbols.)

5. *AND Gate.* The symbol in Figure 42–2 is used for an AND gate. Two or more inputs (lines from symbols below) and one output characterize this symbol. In order for the event immediately above the symbol to occur, all of the input events must occur.

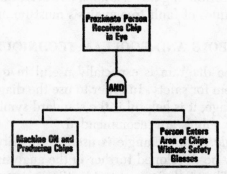

Figure 42–2. "And" Gate Both Input Events Must Occur For Output Event To Occur.

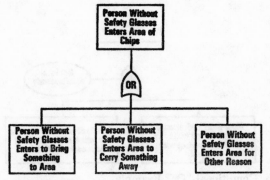

Figure 42–3. "Or" Gate At Least One Of Output Events Must Occur For Output Event To Occur.

6. *OR Gate.* The symbol in Figure 42–3 is used for the OR gate. As with the AND gate, multiple inputs and one output are required. In order for the output event to occur, at least one of the input events must occur.

7. *Conditional AND and OR gates.* In many situations strict Boolean AND and OR functions are not appropriate. For example, in some AND situations the sequence of events is important. Also, there may be an EXCLUSIVE OR situation where one or the other input events would cause the output event, but if both occurred simultaneously the input event would not occur. In situations like these, the AND and OR gates are modified as in Figures 42–4 and 42–5. Generally, an oval is used to qualify the AND or OR gate; however, a rec-

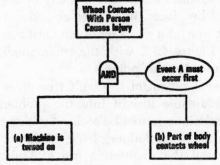

Figure 42–4. Conditional "And" Example.

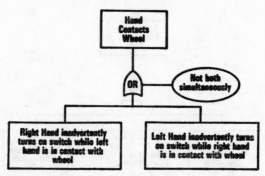

Figure 42–5. Conditional "Or" Example.

tangle has also been used in aerospace applications where the particular time relationships between input and output events are important.

8. *Matrix notation.* When the same or similar events must be repeated often in the same diagram, it is helpful to use some type of abbreviation. There is a variety of useful matrix notation styles. As long as the notation is well defined and adequately documented, the analyst may use the style that best fits his purposes. Generally the triangle is used in conjunction with matrix notation.

9. *Transfer symbol.* The triangle is also used to transfer to another diagram or to another part of the same diagram. In a sense the triangle symbol is always used for transfer, since matrix notation is a type of transfer to an abbreviated notation. Figure 42–6 incorporates some of the symbols given above into a fault tree. It should be noted that many of the events now in diamonds could be placed in rectangles and developed further. Further, a fault tree for a given set of circumstances is not unique; comparison of Figure 42–3 with the corresponding branches in Figure 42–6 illustrates this point.

While the development of the fault tree gives the analyst an otherwise unobtainable insight into the problem, the full potential of the technique cannot be realized without quantification. Since other authors (Kolodner, 1971; Recht, 1966) have adequately discussed the qualitative use of fault trees, we will proceed to examine one quantitative application.

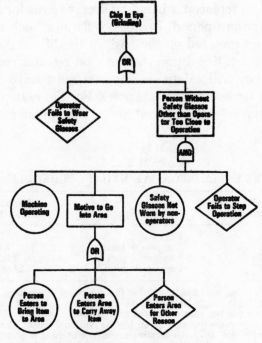

Figure 42–6. Example Fault Tree.

QUANTITATIVE ANALYSIS

The purpose here in quantifying fault tree analysis is effective allocation of the safety budget. The various alternative safety investments are considered in light of their effect upon the fault tree and the resulting head event. A measure of cost/effectiveness is then determined for use in decision-making.

For this discussion, the term "cost/effectiveness" is defined as the dollars spent per negative utility reduction. This can be better understood if we separate, for the time being, the measure of cost from the measure of effectiveness. Cost will be defined as the dollar outlay for the incorporation of a device, method, procedure, etc. (henceforth called a safety investment) into the industrial system for a period of one million man-hours of exposure. (Any unit of time or production could be substituted for the million man-hour unit, which is used throughout this presentation for consistency.) The cost of devices that must be periodically recharged and/or replaced is based on average costs for a 1,000,000 man-hour exposure period. Permanent fixtures, such as machine guards, can be prorated on the basis of the life of the machine. The cost of educational programs can be prorated according to their frequency. All safety investments must have a common denominator for comparison purposes. For the example here, all costs were conveniently reduced to cost per million man-hours of exposure.

TABLE 42–I

EXAMPLE NEGATIVE UTILITY SCHEDULE

Severity Classification	Severity	Negative Utility (U_i) [a]
1	First Aid	20
2	Temporary total	345
3	Permanent partial	2,500
4	Permanent total [b]	21,000

[a] This value need not be a dollar figure if other intangibles, such as social costs, are to be considered. For this example, first aid was a dollar value per case estimated by the author. All other figures are average costs per case given by the National Safety Council, *Accident Facts*, 1971. Generally, management judgment will be required to formulate the negative utility values consistently with company policy.

[b] Including fatalities.

The measure of effectiveness, negative utility reduction, requires a thorough explanation. There is a negative utility (or cost in terms of dollars and personal well-being) associated with every accident. This negative utility depends directly upon the severity of the accident. Each head event chosen to be analyzed by a fault tree will consist of or result in an accident, the severity of which may not be constant. Historical records can be used to determine the relative frequency of the head event causing a first aid case, temporary total, permanent partial, or permanent total (including fatalities). For each of these classifications, a negative utility can be established as in Table 42–I.

The expected negative utility of the head event if it occurs can now be calculated by the following:

$$1. \quad E = \sum_{i=1}^{n} p_i u_i$$

where p_i is the probability of occurrence of the ith severity class given that the head event occurs, n is the number of severity classes, and u_i is the negative utility associated with the ith severity class. Note that this gives the expected negative utility *if the head event occurs,* so it is not an absolute measure of criticality. The head event occurs with some probability, P, so an absolute measure of criticality of the head event is:

$$2. \quad C = P \cdot E$$

In order to determine P, the fault tree can be used. A probability must be determined for each of the "end branches," that is, those that have no further development. These probabilities can generally be obtained from reliability tests or safety records. In the OR situation, any of the events will cause the subsequent event to occur and therefore, assuming independence, the probability of occurrence of the subsequent event is given by:

$$3. \quad P_o = 1 - \prod_{i=1}^{n} (1 - q_i)$$

where q_i is the probability of the ith causal event and n is the number of parallel branches.

In the AND situation, all of the events must occur for the subsequent event to occur and therefore, assuming independence, the probability of occurrence of the subsequent event is given by:

$$4. \quad P_A = \prod_{i=1}^{n} q_i$$

Through a reiteration of this process, the probability of the head event can be determined from the probabilities of the branch events. This is the value of P that is used in equation 2 to obtain the absolute expected negative utility associated with the head event. A system modification will produce a change in this value of negative utility, thus providing the measure of effectiveness. For example, consider the fault tree developed in Figure 42–6. In Figure 42–7 the probabilities of occurrence are given for the end branch events for any million man-hour period. Suppose that records show that in the past there have been ten accidents of this type of which seven were first aid cases, two were temporary total (man had to leave job), and one resulted in a permanent partial (caused permanent eye damage). Using Table 42–1 and equation 1, the following expected negative utility is obtained, given that such an accident occurs:

$$E = .7(20) + .2(345) + .1(2500) = 333$$

To determine the probability of occurrence for the head event, Figure 42–7 is used along with equations three and four. Those

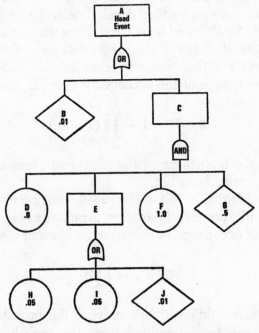

Figure 42–7. Example Fault Tree With Probabilities Assigned.

end branches whose parallel branches are also end branches should be considered first. For example, in Figure 42–7 the three bottom events have no further development and can thus be combined to determine the probability of the subsequent event. Since they are related by an OR function, equation three will be used as follows:

$$P_0 = 1 - (1 - .05)(1 - .05)(1 - .01)$$
$$= 1 - .8935 = .1065$$

Thus, probabilistically speaking, Figure 42–7 reduces to Figure 42–8.

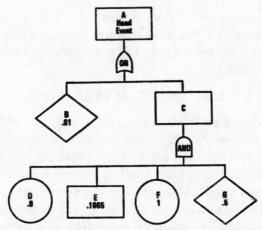

Figure 42–8. Reduction Using Equation 5 Determination Of Probability Of Event E.

Similarly, by using equation 4:

$$P_A = (.8)(.1065)(1)(.5) = .0426$$

Figure 42–8 reduces to Figure 42–9. Finally, the probability of the head event can be determined again, using equation 3:

$$P = 1 - (1 - .01)(1 - .0426)$$
$$= 1 - (.99)(.9574) = .0522$$

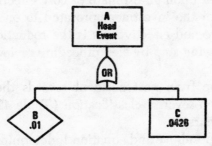

Figure 42–9. Reduction Using Equation 6 Determination Of Probability Of Event C.

This is the probability of occurrence of the head event in any million man-hours of exposure. To obtain a measure of the criticality associated with the head event, equation 2 is used:

$$C = P \cdot E = (.0522)(333) = 17.38$$

If Table I were in units of dollars, this value would represent the expected cost per million man-hours of exposure from this particular hazard. Generally Table I is not restricted to dollar costs, however. (Table 42–I)

EVALUATION OF ALTERNATIVES

Using the above methods, a measure of negative utility can be obtained for any head event. If the same negative utility-severity table (Table 42–I) is used for all head events, a consistent measure of the criticality of each head event will be produced. The primary advantage in this analytic approach, however, is in evaluating alternatives for the solution of safety problems.

If money is spent to improve the safety of a system, one or more of the basic event probabilities in the fault tree will be reduced. This in turn will reduce the probability of the head event and the expected negative utility. The amount by which the negative utility is reduced will provide a measure of effectiveness for the change that was made. Hence, a measure of effectiveness for any safety investment can be estimated. Negative utility can include all costs, machine repair, production interruption, etc., tangible and intangible, associated with the head event.

The decision to proceed with a particular safety expenditure can now be based upon an estimate of cost/effectiveness, where cost is the cost of the investment prorated to one million man-hours of exposure and effectiveness is the reduction in negative utility. The following step-by-step procedure reviews the method given above.

1. Determine from past accident records the relative frequency for each severity classification (Table 42–I) when the head event occurs.

2. From step 1 above and equation 1, determine the expected negative utility if the head event occurs.

3. Using fault tree analysis and equations 3 and 4, determine the probability that the head event occurs.

4. From steps 2 and 3 above, and equation 2, determine the expected negative utility associated with the head event.

5. Repeat steps 3 and 4 above, substituting another alternative into the fault tree. Determine the expected reduction in negative utility, given the new probability or probabilities of this alternative.

6. Determine the cost per expected reduction in negative utility for the alternative.

7. Repeat steps 3 to 6 for all alternatives for all head events.

8. To aid decision-making, set up a table such as Table III. Some form of decision algorithm, such as dynamic programming, might be applied to determine an optimal combination of alternatives for the allocation of the safety budget.

TABLE 42–II

PROPOSED ALTERNATIVES, COSTS,
AND ESTIMATED EFFECTS

Alternative	Description	Prorated Cost/mmh.	Effect
1	Insure that operator stops operation whenever anyone enters area	$25	Reduce probability of event G to .05
2	Move storage area away from grinding area	$15	Reduce probability of events H and I to zero
3	Both 1 and 2	$30	Same effects of both 1 and 2

This procedure will now be illustrated by a continuation of the example. Consider three proposed alternatives to reduce the probability of the head event "grinding chip in eye." These three alternatives are given in Table 42–II in terms of their costs prorated to a million man-hours (mmh.) of operation and the estimated or measured effect on the fault tree (see Figure 42–7). There are many other obvious alternatives; these three are given for simplicity. The first alternative is to have the operator shut down the grinding operation whenever someone comes around.

It has been noted in the past that he has done this about 50 percent of the time without instruction. Therefore, if allowed to continue, .5 provides an estimate of the relative frequency with which he will shut the machine down. It is estimated that, even if he is instructed to stop the operation when someone approaches, he will not in 5 percent of the cases either because the operation is at a critical point or because he does not see the approaching person. The cost incurred results from delays caused by stopping the process.

TABLE 42–III
SUMMARY OF ALTERNATIVES

Head Event	Alternative	$ Cost	Original Negative Utility	New Negative Utility	Cost/Effectiveness
1	1	25	17.38	4.73	25/12.65 = 1.98
1	2	15	17.38	4.65	15/12.73 = 1.18
1	3	30	17.38	3.46	30/13.92 = 2.16
2	1	50	5.75	3.00	50/2.75 = 18.18
2	2	100	5.75	2.00	100/3.75 = 26.66
2	3	75	5.75	1.00	75/4.75 = 15.79
3	1	5	80.20	60.00	5/20.20 = .25
3	2	90	80.20	40.00	90/40.20 = 2.24

The second alternative is to eliminate as much as possible the need for other persons to be in the area by removing a tool storage shelf from the area. Since these tools are used primarily for grinding, a cost will be incurred for the inconvenience of storing them outside the area as well as for the initial relocation cost.

Alternative 3 is a combination of alternatives 1 and 2. The cost is not the sum of costs, however, since if fewer people enter the area, there will be fewer shutdowns. Other alternatives, such as the use of safety glasses by all persons or the purchase of a duplicate set of tools, could also be evaluated.

The new probabilities are substituted into the fault tree analysis to determine the new negative utility associated with the investment. Each of the three alternatives evaluated is listed in Table 42–III on the rows corresponding to head event I. In addition, let us assume that identical analyses have been performed for two other head events, two and three. Table 42–III gives a review of the alternatives for the decision-maker.

The original negative utility for each head event will generally be different since both the probability of occurrence and the expected negative utility as given in equation 1 will vary. The new negative utility is obtained by repeating the calculations and substituting the new probabilities for the old. Effectiveness is the difference between the new and the original negative utilities.

Generally, the best investments are those with the lowest cost/benefit figures, and these should be made first. This is especially true with comparisons between head events. For example, Alternative 1 under head event 3 is obviously superior to the others since a cost of five dollars buys a reduction of 20.20 negative utility units. Under head event 1, which was discussed in detail above, alternative 2 is superior to alternative 1 in terms of cost/benefit. Alternative 1 only provides .08 additional reduction over alternative 2, but costs ten dollars more. Clearly, there are other ways to spend this ten dollars which are superior.

Conclusion

The procedure given above quantifies the decision process by providing the facts required to choose among alternatives. The actual decisions depend most heavily upon the outside budget appropriated for safety. Work is continuing to determine methods for allocating a specific budget in an optimal manner. Research should also continue for the purpose of determining end-branch probabilities. Accurate and complete safety records are essential for this task.

Quantitative tools of this nature can provide safety professionals with improved ability to make proper decisions. This technique is not without limitations, however. One is the necessity that the analyst anticipate head events. If he does not anticipate a particular failure, obviously it cannot be evaluated. Similarly, the method itself forces a modelling of reality that will yield only an approximation of the true answer. This is not a reason for rejecting the system, however. Rather, continued use of the method should be regarded as a means of refining and perfecting it.

In conclusion, it should be stressed that great care and judgment must be used if this technique is to be applied effectively.

A thorough understanding of both the results and the techniques applied is essential. No hard and fast rules should be made for choosing the lowest cost/effective alternative first. Rather, it should be understood that this method is designed to improve the ability of the decision-maker and not to relieve him of his prerogative. When viewed in this perspective, it becomes a powerful tool for improving the quality of safety investments.

REFERENCES

Kolodner, H. H. The fault tree technique of system safety analysis as applied to the occupational safety situation. American Society of Safety Engineers Monograph, June, 1971, No. 1.

Noland, C. A., Cannizo, W. M., and Johnston, J. T.: NASA Technical Memorandum, NASA TM-X-0000, February 23, 1972.

Recht, J. L.: Systems safety analysis: The fault tree. *National Safety News,* 93 (4):37–40, 1966.

43

TOWARDS AN ACADEMIC DISCIPLINE OF INJURY PREVENTION

E. C. WIGGLESWORTH

The author directs himself to a question that has obsessed and baffled some of the best minds in safety education. Safety draws its knowledge from all the physical sciences, and from all the behavioral sciences, from all knowledge of things and people; all academic disciplines and branches of knowledge contribute to it. In a subject content potentially all-embracing, what knowledge must be acquired (and offered in an academic discipline) to enter the safety profession?

Mr. Wigglesworth, from an extraordinary experience in safety education and safety practice, displays good reason for optimism that this bottomless-topless question has an answer. Along the way, he outlines obstacles to the creation of a safety discipline; defines and explicates six criteria of a profession; contrasts professional knowledge with the technical detail usually acquired in practical experience; and offers four objectives of safety education with comments thereon.

This is neither the first contribution, nor will it be the last, on this subject. It has, however, a special lucidity that makes it appropriate in this volume, this volume which offers a smorgasbord display of some (only some) of the facets, problems, skills, and knowledge which go into the practice of the safety profession.

S AFETY IS AN ACTIVITY that has many paradoxes and dichotomies. Some of these only become apparent after many years of involvement; others are abundantly clear to the most casual observer. In the latter category comes the dichotomy that exists between the prevention of accidental trauma on the one hand and the medical management of accidental trauma on the other.

From *The Journal of American Society of Safety Engineers*, March, 1973.

Two aspects of this situation are worthy of special comment for they are indicative of the current deficiencies in injury prevention work and in the development of the injury prevention discipline.

First, medical and surgical management of trauma is not related to the patient's activity at the time of injury; whether the patient was injured at home, on the roads, or at work is rightly regarded as an item of minor importance. The contrast with injury prevention could hardly be greater. Road safety, home safety, and occupational safety activities tend to be carried out in a series of uncorrelated, disparate, and almost watertight compartments. Practitioners in any of these areas rarely examine related aspects of injury control in other fields, and the specialist whose expertise is derived from more than one of these sources is still very much the exception and not the rule.

Educational Requirement Is Lengthy

Secondly, the educational requirement of the injury management specialist is lengthy, firmly based on a complete understanding of the basic theoretical concepts, formulated into a set of academic principles, supplemented by carefully supervised practical experience, and reinforced by constant and continuing research into new developments, the whole operation being carried out at a tertiary level. The successful graduate from this course can legitimately be described as "professional."

The injury prevention specialist is usually less well endowed. Some practitioners hold a first degree in engineering, mathematics, or the behavioural sciences and are attracted to the prevention field. These men and women are able to make significant contributions to the injury prevention field by adaptation of their expertise within their own discipline. Consequently, few see the need to widen the basis of their knowledge to include behavioural and engineering aspects. Hence, they fail to see the need for the establishment of a comprehensive injury prevention discipline.

If their university work included a formal segment on safety, it is likely to have been long on technical detail and practical procedures, short on concepts and philosophies. This, as will be shown, is not a desirable state of affairs. Usually, however, the injury prevention specialist either gains his formal training from some lower course or, in some cases, gains his expertise exclusively from practical experience. This is an even less desirable situation. No profession gains status—or even exists—if many of its practitioners learn their trade exclusively from practical experience. Every profession gains its status from the existence of an extensive body of knowledge, structured into a coherent, disciplined syllabus. Hence, if the injury prevention specialty is to develop professional status—and this is the ultimate goal—it requires a coherent discipline. In the opinion of this author, the primary obstacles to the creation of this discipline are the two problems of (a) compartmentalisation and (b) the continuing presence of inadequate, unprofessional safety education.

Compartmentalisation

Compartmentalisation of preventive activities into such mutually exclusive eyries as road safety and job safety has probably already received its death blow in the work of Haddon (1969). He defined injury as "a unit of bodily damage caused by the delivery of energy that exceeds the body's threshold tolerance." This definition has a universality of application that transcends the conventional compartments. It matters not whether the terminal phalanx of the thumb was amputated by energy from a lathe, a car smash, or a do-it-yourself home carpenter; the relevant fact is that the thumb has been decapitated.

This definition was first included in the book by Haddon, Suchmann, and Klein in 1964. Eight years later, Klein delivered a colloquium in the Department of Psychology, Monash University, Melbourne. The room was packed to capacity with road safety and occupational safety men and women. Of particular interest to this author was the way in which his stimulating comments provoked questions in roughly equal proportions from both groups of practitioners, displaying a communality of interest that, in some cases at least, had been previously unsuspected.

Hopefully, this process of boundary demolition will continue so that gradually there will emerge a greater realisation of the underlying unity of purpose. There seems to be a marked comparison here with the medical specialties of infectious disease, neurosurgery, cardiac failure, and so forth. These specialities flourish within the comprehensive framework of the medical profession. Similarly, this author believes that road safety, work safety, sporting, recreational, and domestic safety should all be regarded as specialities within the comprehensive framework of the profession of injury prevention. If this concept is accepted, the clear need is for a rapid solution of the second of the two earlier problems, i.e., the provision of adequate, effective, professional education. Fundamental to any consideration of this problem are answers to the questions, "What is a profession?" and "What are the hallmarks of effective professional education?"

Professional Education

A profession is an occupation that has a monopoly of some extensive and difficult body of knowledge, the understanding of which is necessary for the continued functioning of the community. The members of this profession are of fundamental importance to the community, for nobody else can understand or effectively apply this specialist knowledge. Flexner (1915) defined the requirements rather more closely by defining professional activity as:

A. basically intellectual, carrying great personal responsibility.
B. learned, being based on knowledge.
C. practical, rather than academic or theoretical.
D. teachable in that its techniques can be taught in professional courses.
E. organized internally with strict control of entry exercised by the profession itself.
F. motivated by altruism, the professionals seeing themselves as working for the good of the community rather than for personal reward.

Using these criteria, it is easy to see that professional education should be a dynamic process with emphasis on general principles and a theoretical treatment of the specialized subject matter. This expands as knowledge increases.

The requirement is therefore not for manual skills and the acquisition of a great weight of technical detail derived from practical experience, but rather from a synthesis of the general principles of the subject, derived from research and logical analysis. Not to do this merely emphasizes the rote learning of masses of technical details, facts, regulations, and routine procedures.

This data carries a high risk of rapid technological obsolescence due to the accelerating swiftness of advances in knowledge. There are two further and more serious objections to rote teaching of technical material. First, if students believe that one textbook or one course of study fits them for permanent employment in a professional field, they are unlikely to develop the lasting habits of self-education, critical analysis, and intellectual self-enlargement that are essential for continued professional development. Secondly, such emphasis is also likely to result in the course being described as "vocational" and not as "professional," and hence as being unworthy of university status.

It is one of the hallmarks of the existing professions that, over the years, their curricula have developed from early, narrow, and often almost exclusive emphasis on technical knowledge and skills to a more theoretical treatment of the specialized subject matter.

There is one exception to this general rule. Basic to the effective performance of any professional functional specialist is the ability to communicate. Hence skill in written as well as oral communication is essential. Clarity, simplicity, logic, and even the humble skills of correct grammatical construction and accurate spelling are implicit, professional prerequisites.

Application to Safety Education

If safety (or, more precisely, injury-and-loss control) as a separate, disciplined activity is ever to achieve professional status, it should first demonstrate its conformity with Flexner's six criteria. For the purposes of this discussion, it is convenient to consider them in three groups of two items each.

INTELLECTUAL AND LEARNED. First, the activity should be basically intellectual and learned. Historically, this has generally not been the case. Much safety teaching in the past has been in the hands of interested but educationally unqualified groups simply because they wished to be involved.

Courses developed in this way were rarely successful, because they were usually ad hoc in nature, unstructured, unstratified, and with no clear objectives in the minds of the organizers. Many of these "courses" adopted a mechanistic approach by emphasizing procedural aspects of the daily task and were either structured around some gimmick (the three E's of safety) or couched in single-syllable kindergarten terminology (what was the unsafe act?).

Against this background, it is hardly surprising that formal courses for safety professionals have taken so long to develop. What is more surprising is that they have managed to emerge from the morass at all. However, this historical legacy remains. So, unfortunately, does the terminology which is simplistic, emotive, and notoriously imprecise. This has prompted the observation that, as kindergarten terminology is most appropriately applied to kindergarten concepts in kindergarten teaching, safety as a topic is academically dull and intellectually unrewarding.

This view is still fairly widely held and constitutes a handicap to progress. However, it has been less frequently heard since the work of Haddon and McFarland was published. The contribution of human factors specialists, stemming from the work of McFarland (1964) has been thoroughly professional since its inception. To say that it has led to significant developments in safety education is a gross understatement; it has triggered a revolution in safety education that now permits the development of carefully structured courses at any desired level, on a par with other older disciplines. Taken in conjunction with the work of Haddon, the new approach to safety education is outstandingly capable of development as an academic discipline. There is a theoretical frame of reference (Wigglesworth, 1972) that draws together the interdisciplinary contributions into a basic methodology; this methodology can then be applied to the solution of the principal safety problems in both the road and the occupational fields. These applications are challenging, stimulating tasks requiring a high degree of analytical capability, whilst the results of these analyses reveal all too clearly the paucity and limitations of existing knowledge.

Taught in this manner, the subject becomes intellectual and learned with wide educational applications. It is suitable for incorporation into courses for engineers, psychologists, physicians, and designers of all kinds as well as in the professional training of safety specialists themselves.

PRACTICAL AND TEACHABLE. Secondly, the activity should be practical and teachable. In this regard, the problem of advanced education in safety has something in common with similar problems in such established professions as medicine and law. The successful practitioner draws on scientific and analytical concepts, but also makes decisions on the basis of experience and precedent. The former can be taught at university and tertiary establishments, the latter cannot. No university can give on-the-job experience, just as no amount of practical experience can compensate for the lack of higher education. Consequently, safety education consists of two parts. The first is the university task of instilling analytical capability and appropriate technology into the student in a way that will develop qualities of mind and judgment: the second is the practical application of these skills to the solution of the daily problems of injury-and-loss control. Both are continuing processes, for the true professional is continuously updating and extending his repertoire of skills for the full period of his professional life.

CONTROL AND MOTIVATION. Finally, the activity should be organized internally with entry requirements delineated and controlled by the profession itself; motivated by altruism and not by pecuniary reward. In the occupational area, steps are being taken in all countries to meet the first of these criteria. OSHA has given a strong impetus to the creation of a minimum standard for occupational safety specialists in the U.S.A., and the Certified Safety Professional is now a meaningful description of a person who has specified minimum operating skills. Similarly, as from January 1, 1973, the Safety Engineering Society of Australasia will admit to the grade of Member only those persons who hold a Society-approved Certificate from one of the State Education Departments. In both countries, the levels are capable of upgrading, but the principle is now clearly established.

The spirit of altruism is less well established. That the profession should be motivated by a desire to serve the community in preference to the customary motives of status and personal reward is a concept that is not frequently discussed.

It should be discussed, for the opportunity to benefit the community by reducing the frequency and severity of personal injury is a wholly professional and thoroughly desirable goal. Wider advocacy of this basic concept would serve not only to raise the status of injury prevention specialists in the community but would also help the cross-transfer of expertise from the various operational areas of road, work, and recreational activities in a way that seems wholly beneficial.

In this regard, the newly-developing concepts of damage and loss control, with their heavy emphasis on cost benefits seem at first glance to be antagonistic to the required concept of community service. To this author, however, there seems to be no conflict. In his view, the true professional has at the forefront of his thinking the primary requirement of injury prevention. This is his first priority. In order to obtain the data necessary for accurate analysis of injury-causing problems, he has to rely not only on information about damage to people but also about damage to plant and equipment. Since all damage is caused by excess energy delivery, it seems perfectly legitimate and proper to use all damage information that is available and to apply this to the task of preventing injury. If, additionally, it is capable of reducing loss or damage to plant, equipment, and other items of hardware, this is a bonus of considerable value in a cost-conscious environment. Used in this way, the damage control techniques can add to the repertoire of the professional skills that are available for the task of injury prevention.

In summary then, safety education has in the past not been able to meet all the criteria necessary for the development of an academic professional discipline. However, with the advent of medical, human factors and other interdisciplinary contributions, and reinforced by the determination of the practitioner bodies to upgrade their entry requirements to a professional level, there seems to be no fundamental impediment to the ultimate progression of safety education into a wholly professional academic discipline.

Objectives of Safety Education

If this development does take place, it is pertinent and relevant to identify the objectives of safety education.

Four aims are listed here:
 i) to qualify men and women for injury-and-loss control work.
 ii) to instill a scientific and professional attitude.
 iii) to encourage contributions of new knowledge.
 iv) to initiate and develop research into safety problems.

i) To Qualify Men and Women for the Practice of Injury Prevention

This seems to be so self-evident as hardly to need explicit listing. In fact, it depends on at least three assumptions. These are:

A. that there is a specific body of knowledge that is applicable to the practice of injury prevention.

B. that it can be taught.

C. that those who have been taught have understanding and knowledge that differs significantly from those who have not been taught.

As has been shown, these assumptions have not always been met in the past, but there seems no reason at all why they should not be met in the future. The greatest impetus to this development will probably come from the practitioner bodies themselves in their requirement for prescribed minimum standards for admission to one or more levels of membership.

ii) To Instill a Scientific and Professional Attitude

Perhaps in no other field of human activity has there been so much instant expertise. The beliefs that safety is simply a matter of common sense and that empirical solutions to safety problems are readily deducible from superficial assessments of particular situations are at once simplistic and fallacious. That they have persisted for so long is itself indicative of the need for better safety education and of the need for that education to be firmly based on a scientific, analytical, and professional approach to the accident problem.

iii) To Contribute Knowledge to the Scientific and Professional Literature

In the course of their careers, most safety professionals tackle specialized problems that arise from their particular interests or as a consequence of the technology of their professional environment.

Most find solutions to these problems, but few bother to write up their solutions in the open literature. Consequently, what is essentially the same problem has to be solved many times over by different persons in different places. Not only is this a time-consuming and wasteful misallocation of limited resources, it also means that the body of knowledge that should underpin the professional task is deprived of a major source of continuing expansion.

Today's education should teach the student how to solve new problems by application of basic principles, how to test the adequacy of that solution objectively, and then how to describe it adequately, accurately, and precisely in the literature so that others may read it, learn from it and, where appropriate, apply it.

iv) To Initiate and Support Pure and Applied Research Into Accident Prevention Problems and Into the Development of Effective Countermeasures

Safety professionals tend to be long on opinion, short on information. As examples of this somewhat sweeping statement, some rudimentary questions to which factual answers are currently not available are posed below.

1. What is a reasonable, sensitive, and accurate measure of progress?

2. Using this measure, will a company employing a safety professional attain a lower rate than an identical company without one? If so, by how much?

3. If the answer to question 2 is dependent on the type of work, size, and management structure of the company, what are the relevant parameters? How can they be measured?

4. If the answer is dependent on the personal qualities, basic education, and experience of the incumbent, what are the relevant weights and how can these be measured?

5. If the answer to question 2(a) is affirmative, would it be in the community interest to appoint similarly-qualified road safety specialists with parallel responsibilities and duties?

6. In what way, and from what bases, can predictive techniques be developed to replace today's largely retrospective analyses? Have there, for example, been any follow-up studies

to the Tarrants (1963) work on the application of the critical incident technique?

The list can be extended almost at will according to the personal interests of the questioner. It therefore seems reasonable to repeat the view that safety practitioners tend to be long on opinion and short on information, even in areas that are of crucial importance to the development of their professional task.

Summary

By comparing the requirements for professions and for professional education with the current state of safety and safety education, it is suggested that there is no fundamental impediment to the development of safety education as a new professional discipline in its own right. Some changes of emphasis are however required.

REFERENCES

Flexner, A.: Is Social Work a Profession? Proceedings of the National Conference of Charities and Correction. Chicago, Hildmann Printing Co., 1915.

Haddon, Wm. Jr.: *Accident Research, Methods and Approaches.* New York, Harper and Row, 1964.

Haddon, Wm. Jr.: The prevention of accidents. In Clark, D. W., and McMahon, B., (Eds): *Textbook of Preventive Medicine.* Boston, Little, Brown & Co., 1969.

McFarland, R. A.: Human factors engineering. *J Amer Soc Saf Engrs,* 9, 2, 9–20, 1964.

Tarrants, W. E.: *An Evaluation of the Critical Incident Technique as a Method for Identifying Industrial Accident Causal Factors.* Ph.D. dissertation. New York University. 1963.

Wigglesworth, E. C.: A teaching model of injury causal mechanism and a derived theory of countermeasure selection. *Journal of American Society of Safety Engineers,* 17, 8, 27–32. 1972.

NAME INDEX

485

SUBJECT INDEX

A

Accident,
  cause undetermined, 197
  defined, 41, 346
  high potential defined, 32
  not the same as injury, 33, 112
  to solve life problems, 269
Accident Analysis, High Potential, 31
Accident Behavior, Life Change Unit, 355
Accident Causation,
  88–10–2 theory, 38
  causal factors other than hazards, 40
  countermeasures, 41
  definition of accident research, 344
  differentiated from loss reduction strategy, 91
  dynamics of, 58
  human errors, 197
  lengthy sequences, 59
  man prevents accidents, 69
  multifactorial background, 57
  multiple etiologies, 261
  no new causes, 215
  nonroutine operating modes, 59
  presence of a hazard, 40
  probable cause, 234
  psychological factors, 262
  separation of culpability, 38
  sequences, 56
  sequence diagram, 60
  300–29–1 ratio, 112
Accident Classification System, 342

Accident Investigation, 187
  adversary system, 234
  feedback, 71
  human factors viewpoint, 233
  investigation by MORT, 61
  legal fault versus prevention, 233
  proximate cause, 233
Accident Prediction,
  depression, 266
  frequency of sick calls, 265
  by traffic offenses, 82
Accident Prevention,
  definition of accident prevention research, 344
  multidisciplinary, 261
  not injury prevention, 71
  not science nor discipline, 339
Accident Problem, epidemiological approach, 35
Accident Process,
  described, 262
  solution to a problem, 268
  (see Accident Causation)
Accident Prone, 5, 268
  dual thinking, 10
  highway safety, 82
  random occurrences, 7
  research theory versus practical officials, 15
  statistical base, 13
  statistical evidence, 10
  statistical viewpoint, 313
  terminological confusion, 17
  theory, 312

488

228476

HV   Ferry, Ted S. comp.
675
.F47   Directions in safety

© THE BAKER & TAYLOR CO.